Praise for Leslie Jamison's

THE
RECOVERING

"An astounding triumph…A recovery memoir like no other… The book knows no bounds, building in depth and vitality with each passing concern…There's something profound at work here, a truth about how we grow into ourselves that rings achingly wise and burrows painfully deep." —David Canfield, *Entertainment Weekly*

"A sprawling, compelling, fiercely ambitious book…Its publication represents the most significant addition to the canon in more than a decade…Jamison's writing throughout is spectacularly evocative and sensuous…She thinks with elegant precision, cutting through the whiskey-soaked myths…Jamison is interested in something else: the possibility that sobriety can form its own kind of legend, no less electric, and more generative in the end." —Sophie Gilbert, *The Atlantic*

"Masterful…beautifully honest…Essential reading…The most comprehensive study of the relationship between writing and alcohol that I have read, or know about…The prose is clean and clear and a pleasure to read, utterly without pretension. Although the subject is dark, Jamison has managed to write an often very funny page-turner…In short, *The Recovering* is terrific, and if you're interested in the relationship between artists and addiction, you must read it." —Clancy Martin, *Bookforum*

"Magnificent and genuinely moving. This is that rare addiction memoir that gets better after sobriety takes hold." —Dwight Garner, *New York Times*

"Such is Jamison's command of metaphor and assonance that she could rivet a reader with a treatise on toast. We perhaps have no writer better on the subject of psychic suffering and its consolations."
— Gary Greenberg, *The New Yorker*

"Jamison provides unexpected perceptions and expertly distilled research... *The Recovering* bursts with insight on how we scramble together our identities, told in a voice that manages by some literary legerdemain to be both winsomely idiosyncratic and resoundingly collective... Along the way, it mutates from one gifted and successful young woman's tale into a larger inquiry into how we seek to heal ourselves...Part confession, part literary criticism, part cultural analysis, part musing, and part hard-edged reporting, *The Recovering* creates its own grainy context, defying all the usual tropes of addiction memoirs....Jamison has written an extraordinary document of self-reckoning that will make you think and rethink the trajectory of your own life in its 'mundane realities' as well as its 'cinematic epic mode.' This is a book about one of us, all of us, and the yearnings that take us to dark-as well as light-filled places."
— Daphne Merkin, *New Republic*

"Stunning...Jamison's language manages somehow to be simultaneously lush and piercing... *The Recovering* is nothing if not classically beautiful: implausibly so, almost ludicrously consistent in its fierce freshness and poetry from page to page to page."
— Ellen Wayland-Smith, *Los Angeles Review of Books*

"Jamison writes about personal experiences in a way that feels universal...Her vulnerability and determination are present on every page."
— Maris Kreizman, *Esquire*

"A remarkable feat...Jamison is a bracingly smart writer; her sentences wind and snake, at turns breathless and tense...Instead of solving the mystery of why she drank, she does something worthier, digging underneath the big emptiness that lives inside every addict to find something profound."
— Sam Lansky, *Time*

"Riveting…Jamison orchestrates a multivoiced, universal song of lack, shame, surrender, uncertain and unsentimental redemption…Quite on its own terms, *The Recovering* is a beautifully told example of the considered and self-aware becoming art." —Priscilla Gilman, *Boston Globe*

"*The Recovering* changed my life. It's an anti-memoir: Generous with details of her own experience of addiction and recovery, Jamison insists on the existence, or primacy, of other stories as well…She writes beautifully, with furious clarity." —Chris Kraus, *Paris Review*

"Brilliant…We are aware, most fundamentally, of Jamison's urgency. This, of course, is as it should be, for she is writing to survive… *The Recovering* leaves us with the sense of a writer intent on holding nothing back." —David L. Ulin, *Los Angeles Times*

"Leslie Jamison has written an honest and important book…The most important thematic thread may be its insistence that the talented artist who needs booze or drugs to support his work and withstand his own vision does not, in fact, exist…Vivid writing and required reading." —Stephen King

"Leslie Jamison demonstrates great wit, penetrating intellect, and an enormous heart. This strangely exhilarating book is about recovery, but it is more resonantly a book about desire, consciousness, kindness, self-control, and love—and hence a Tolstoyan study of the human condition." —Andrew Solomon, National Book Award–winning author of *Far from the Tree* and *The Noonday Demon*

"Thoughtful, fiercely honest, and intimate, *The Recovering* is a must-read that is Jamison at her best." —Jarry Lee, *BuzzFeed*

"Gritty…Raw…Fascinating in ways you might not expect… *The Recovering* ventures beyond the cliché and the ordinary to remind us once again of both the fallibility and resiliency of the human condition." —Alexis Burling, *San Francisco Chronicle*

"Precise and heartfelt...*The Recovering* is a magnificent achievement."
—Scott F. Parker, *Minneapolis Star Tribune*

"Jamison is a writer of exacting grace...Like Mary Karr's *Lit* or Caroline Knapp's *Drinking: A Love Story*, Jamison's perceptive and generous-hearted new book is uncompromising on the ugliness of addiction, yet tenderly hopeful that people can heal."
—Nora Caplan-Bricker, *Washington Post*

"As engaging as it is thoughtful. Jamison proves both an insightful guide to decades of literature by and about addicts, and a self-aware chronicler of her own struggle with alcoholism...In *The Recovering*, she has written a movingly humble book, filled to the brim with lessons learned the hard way." — *The Economist*

"As a reader of this most consuming book, I celebrate Jamison's deep openheartedness, deliberate unselfishness, immaculate, inculcating vision, and her language—oh, her language...For her intelligence, her compassion, her capaciousness, her search, her deep reading, her precise language, Jamison must be honored here."
—Beth Kephart, *Chicago Tribune*

"A latter-day Susan Sontag...the author of the genre-changing collection *The Empathy Exams* takes her blend of the personal, reportorial, and scholarly to expansive new lengths and depths...The uniqueness of her case studies, as well as the power of addiction as metaphor, really make it stand out." —Boris Kachka, *New York*

"The breadth of Jamison's knowledge on this subject is impressive...The writing is beautiful. There are descriptive phrases that are simply breathtaking...I couldn't put the book down...More than that, I was genuinely moved by how accurately Jamison captures the experience of addiction, the hollows we all try to fill with one thing or another."
—Roxane Gay, author of *Bad Feminist*

THE
RECOVERING

INTOXICATION
AND ITS AFTERMATH

LESLIE JAMISON

BACK BAY BOOKS
LITTLE, BROWN AND COMPANY
New York   Boston   London

For anyone addiction has touched

———————

Back Bay Books / Little, Brown and Company
Hachette Book Group
1290 Avenue of the Americas, New York, NY 10104
littlebrown.com

Originally published by Little, Brown and Company, April 2018
First Back Bay paperback edition, January 2019

Back Bay Books is an imprint of Little, Brown and Company, a division of Hachette Book Group, Inc. The Back Bay Books name and logo are trademarks of Hachette Book Group, Inc.

The publisher is not responsible for websites (or their content) that are not owned by the publisher.

The Hachette Speakers Bureau provides a wide range of authors for speaking events. To find out more, go to hachettespeakersbureau.com or call (866) 376-6591.

ISBN 978-0-316-25961-3 (hc) / 978-0-316-25958-3 (pb)
LCCN 2017946582

10 9 8 7 6 5 4 3 2

LSC-C

Printed in the United States of America

CONTENTS

THE
RECOVERING

— I —

WONDER

The first time I ever felt it—the buzz—I was almost thirteen. I didn't vomit or black out or even embarrass myself. I just loved it. I loved the crackle of champagne, its hot pine needles down my throat. We were celebrating my brother's college graduation, and I wore a long muslin dress that made me feel like a child, until I felt something else: initiated, aglow. The whole world stood accused: *You never told me it felt this good.*

The first time I ever drank in secret, I was fifteen. My mom was out of town. My friends and I spread a blanket across living room hardwood and drank whatever we could find in the fridge, Chardonnay wedged between the orange juice and the mayonnaise. We were giddy from a sense of trespass.

The first time I ever got high, I was smoking pot on a stranger's couch, my fingers dripping pool water as I dampened the joint with my grip. A friend-of-a-friend had invited me to a swimming party. My hair smelled like chlorine and my body quivered against my damp bikini. Strange little animals blossomed through my elbows and shoulders, where the parts of me bent and connected. I thought: What is this? And how can it keep being this? With a good feeling, it was always: *More. Again. Forever.*

The first time I ever drank with a boy, I let him put his hands under my shirt on the wooden balcony of a lifeguard station. Dark waves shushed the sand below our dangling feet. My first boyfriend: He liked to get high. He liked to get his cat high. We used to make out in his mother's minivan. He came to a family meal at my house fully wired on speed. "So talkative!" said my grandma, deeply smitten. At Disneyland, he broke open a baggie of withered mushroom caps and started breathing fast and shallow in line for Big Thunder Mountain

Railroad, sweating through his shirt, pawing at the orange rocks of the fake frontier.

If I had to say where my drinking began, which *first time* began it, I might say it started with my first blackout, or maybe the first time I sought blackout, the first time I wanted nothing more than to be absent from my own life. Maybe it started the first time I threw up from drinking, the first time I dreamed about drinking, the first time I lied about drinking, the first time I dreamed about lying about drinking, when the craving had gotten so deep there wasn't much of me that wasn't committed to either serving or fighting it.

Maybe my drinking began with patterns rather than moments, once I started drinking every day. Which happened in Iowa City, where the drinking didn't seem dramatic and pronounced so much as encompassing and inevitable. There were so many ways and places to get drunk: the fiction bar in a smoky double-wide trailer, with a stuffed fox head and a bunch of broken clocks; or the poetry bar down the street, with its anemic cheeseburgers and glowing Schlitz ad, a scrolling electric landscape: the gurgling stream, the neon grassy banks, the flickering waterfall. I mashed the lime in my vodka tonic and glimpsed—in the sweet spot between two drinks and three, then three and four, then four and five—my life as something illuminated from the inside.

There were parties at a place called the Farm House, out in the cornfields, past Friday fish fries at the American Legion. These were parties where poets wrestled in a kiddie pool full of Jell-O, and everyone's profile looked beautiful in the crackling light of a mattress bonfire. Winters were cold enough to kill you. There were endless potlucks where older writers brought braised meats and younger writers brought plastic tubs of hummus, and everyone brought whiskey, and everyone brought wine. Winter kept going; we kept drinking. Then it was spring. We kept drinking then, too.

Sitting on a folding chair in a church basement, you always face the question of how to begin. "It has always been a hazard for me to speak at an AA meeting," a man named Charlie told a Cleveland AA meeting in 1959, "because I knew that I could do better than other people. I really had a story to tell. I was more articulate. I could dramatize it. And I would really knock them dead." He explained the hazard like this: He'd gotten praised. He'd gotten proud. He'd gotten drunk. Now he was talking to a big crowd about how dangerous it was for him to talk to a big crowd. He was describing the perils of an Alcoholics Anonymous meeting to a meeting of Alcoholics Anonymous. He was being articulate about being articulate. He was dramatizing what the art of dramatizing had done to him. He said: "I think I got tired of being my own hero." Fifteen years earlier, he'd published a best-selling novel about alcoholism while sober. But he relapsed a few years after it became a bestseller. "I've written a book that's been called the definitive portrait of the alcoholic," he told the group, "and it did me no good."

It was only after five minutes of talking that Charlie finally thought to begin the way others began. "My name is Charles Jackson," he said, "and I'm an alcoholic." By coming back to the common refrain, he was reminding himself that commonality could be its own saving grace. "My story isn't much different from anyone's," he said. "It's the story of a man who was made a fool of by alcohol, over and over and over, year after year after year, until finally the day came when I learned that I could not handle this alone."

The first time I ever told the story of my drinking, I sat among other drinkers who no longer drank. Ours was a familiar scene: plastic folding chairs, Styrofoam cups of coffee gone lukewarm, phone numbers exchanged. Before the meeting, I had imagined what might happen after it was done: People would compliment my story or the way I'd told it, and I'd demur, *Well, I'm a writer*, shrugging, trying not to make too big a deal out of it. I'd have the Charlie Jackson problem, my humility imperiled by my storytelling prowess. I practiced with note cards beforehand, though I didn't use them when I spoke — because I didn't want to make it seem like I'd been practicing.

It was after I'd gone through the part about my abortion, and how much I'd been drinking pregnant; after the part about the night I don't call *date rape*, and the etiquette of reconstructing blackouts; after I'd gone through the talking points of my pain, which seemed like nothing compared to what the other people in that room had lived — it was somewhere in the muddled territory of sobriety, getting to the repetitions of apology, or the physical mechanics of prayer, that an old man in a wheelchair, sitting in the front row, started shouting: "This is boring!"

We all knew him, this old man. He'd been instrumental in setting up a gay recovery community in our town, back in the seventies, and now he was in the care of his much younger partner, a soft-spoken book lover who changed the man's diapers and wheeled him faithfully to meetings where he shouted obscenities. "You dumb cunt!" he'd called out once. Another time he'd held my hand for our closing prayer and said, "Kiss me, wench!"

He was ill, losing the parts of his mind that filtered and restrained his speech. But he often sounded like our collective id, saying all the things that never got said aloud in meetings: *I don't care; this is tedious; I've heard this before.* He was nasty and sour and he'd also saved a lot of people's lives. Now he was bored.

Other people at the meeting shifted uncomfortably in their seats. The woman sitting beside me touched my arm, a way of saying *Don't stop.* So I didn't. I kept going — stuttering, eyes hot, throat swollen — but this man had managed to tap veins of primal insecurity: that my story wasn't good enough, or that I'd failed to tell it right, that I'd somehow failed at my dysfunction, failed to make it bad or bold or interesting enough; that recovery had flatlined my story past narrative repair.

When I decided to write a book about recovery, I worried about all of these possible failures. I was wary of trotting out the tired tropes of the addictive spiral, and wary of the tedious architecture and tawdry self-congratulation of a redemption story: It hurt. It got worse. I got better. Who would care? *This is boring!* When I told people I was writing a book about addiction and recovery, I often saw their eyes glaze. *Oh, that book,* they seemed to say, *I've already read that book.*

I wanted to tell them that I was writing a book *about* that glazed look in their eyes, about the way an addiction story can make you think, *I've heard that story before,* before you've even heard it. I wanted to tell them I was trying to write a book about the ways addiction is a hard story to tell, because addiction is always a story that has already been told, because it inevitably repeats itself, because it grinds down—ultimately, for everyone—to the same demolished and reductive and recycled core: *Desire. Use. Repeat.*

In recovery, I found a community that resisted what I'd always been told about stories—that they had to be unique—suggesting instead that a story was most useful when it wasn't unique at all, when it understood itself as something that had been lived before and would be lived again. Our stories were valuable because of this redundancy, not despite it. Originality wasn't the ideal, and beauty wasn't the point.

When I decided to write a book about recovery, I didn't want to make it singular. Nothing about recovery had been singular. I needed the first-person plural, because recovery had been about immersion in the lives of others. Finding the first-person plural meant spending time in archives and interviews, so I could write a book that might work like a meeting—that would place my story alongside the stories of others. *I could not handle this alone.* That had already been said. I wanted to say it again. I wanted to write a book that was honest about the grit and bliss and tedium of learning to live in this way—in chorus, without the numbing privacy of getting drunk. I wanted to find an articulation of freedom that didn't need scare quotes or lacquer, that didn't insist on distinction as the only mark of a story worth telling, that wondered why we took that truth to be self-evident, or why I'd always taken it that way.

If addiction stories run on the fuel of darkness—the hypnotic spiral of an ongoing, deepening crisis—then recovery is often seen as the narrative slack, the dull terrain of wellness, a tedious addendum to the riveting blaze. I wasn't immune; I'd always been enthralled by stories of wreckage. But I wanted to know if stories about getting better could ever be as compelling as stories about falling apart. I needed to believe they could.

I moved to Iowa City just after my twenty-first birthday, in a little black Toyota with a television riding shotgun and a winter coat that wasn't even thick enough to keep me warm through autumn. I lived in a white clapboard house on Dodge Street, just below Burlington, and hit the circuit right away: backyard parties under branches strung with tiny white Christmas lights, mason jars full of red wine, local bratwurst on the grill. The grass shimmered with mosquitoes, and fireflies blinked on and off like the eyes of some coy, elusive god. Maybe that sounds ridiculous. It was magic.

Writers ten years older than I was—twenty years older, thirty years older—talked about their drumming careers and prior bylines, their prior marriages, while I found myself without much life to talk about. I'd come to live. I was going to do things at parties here that I might talk about at parties later, elsewhere. I was thrumming with that promise, and nervous. I drank quietly, quickly, staining my teeth with Shiraz.

I'd come to get my master's degree at the Iowa Writers' Workshop, an institution barnacled with history. It seemed to me the program was always asking you to prove why you deserved to be there, and I wasn't sure I did. I'd been rejected from every other program I'd applied to.

One night I showed up at a potluck—brick building, basement unit, carpeted floors—and found everyone sitting in a circle. It was a game: You had to tell your best story, your absolute *best*. I can't remember anyone else's. I'm not sure I even listened to anyone else, I was so afraid no one would like what I said. When it was finally my turn, I pulled out the only story of mine that reliably made people laugh. It was about the community-service trip I'd taken to a Costa Rican village when I was fifteen. I'd run into a wild horse on a dirt road, on my walk home one day, and then later confused the words for *caballo* and *caballero* while I was trying to tell my host family about the encounter. When I saw the concern on their faces, I tried to reassure them that I actually loved horses and ended up telling them how much I enjoyed riding gentlemen. At this point, in the carpeted basement, I got onto my feet and mimed riding a horse, as I'd mimed it for my host family years earlier. People laughed, a little bit. In my horse-riding position, I felt like an overzealous charades player. I quietly arranged myself cross-legged again.

The structure of that basement game was nearly identical to the structure of the program itself: Every Tuesday afternoon we gathered in workshops to critique each other's stories. These discussions happened in an old wooden building by the river, beige with dark green trim. When we clustered on the porch before class, under the red-leafed October trees, I smoked cloves and listened to their sweet crackle. Someone had once told me cloves had little bits of glass in them, and I always pictured shards glittering through the smoky chambers of my lungs.

Whenever it was your week to get critiqued, copies of your story were stacked on a wooden shelf—always more than enough copies for everyone in your class. If other people in the program were interested in your work, all the copies of your story would disappear. You'd sell out. Or else you wouldn't. Either way, you'd sit at a round table for an hour and listen to twelve other people dissect the virtues and failures of what you'd written. Then you were expected to go out afterward, with those same people, and drink.

If most days in Iowa were like a test, some version of that first night swapping stories in a basement, then sometimes I passed, and sometimes I failed. Sometimes I got high and worried about sounding stupid, even though the whole point of getting high was that you weren't supposed to worry if you sounded stupid. Sometimes I went home at the end of the night and cut myself.

Cutting was a habit I'd picked up in high school. It was something my first boyfriend had done, the same one who took enough mushrooms at Disneyland to get scared of the frontier. He'd had his reasons, traumas in his past. At first, I told myself I was doing it because I wanted to get closer to him. But eventually I had to admit I was drawn to cutting for reasons of my own. It let me carve onto my skin a sense of inadequacy I'd never managed to find words for; a sense of hurt whose vagueness—shadowed, always, by the belief it was unjustified—granted appeal to the concrete clarity of a blade drawing blood. It was a pain I could claim, because it was physical and irrefutable, even if I was always ashamed of it for being voluntary.

I'd been shy for most of my childhood, afraid to speak because I was afraid of saying the wrong thing: afraid of popular Felicity, a girl in eighth grade who'd cornered me by the lockers to ask why I didn't shave my legs; afraid of the girls in the locker room who laughed in a huddle and finally asked me why I never wore deodorant; afraid even of the kinder girls on my cross-country team, the ones who asked why I never spoke; afraid of dinners with my father, which happened maybe once a month, when I wasn't sure what to say, and often ended up saying something sullen or bratty, something that might compel his attention. Cutting was a way to do something. When my high school boyfriend told me he thought we should break up, I felt so powerless—so spurned—that I threw a stack of plastic cups against my bedroom wall so hard they shattered into shards. I drew these shards across my left ankle until it was a messy ladder of red hatch marks.

It makes me cringe, looking back at my own theatrical production of angst, but I also feel a certain tenderness toward that girl, who wanted to pronounce the size of how she felt, and used what she could: disposable plastic picnic cups, the mode of harm she'd borrowed from the one who was leaving her. It had been a kind of camaraderie between me and him—wearing long sleeves during Southern California summers so our parents couldn't see the cuts on our arms, explaining the Band-Aids on my ankles as shaving nicks.

Cutting and writing were the ways I'd found around my chronic shyness, which felt like constant failure. At Iowa, my short stories were the kind that got called character-driven, because they never had plots. But I was suspicious of my characters. They were always passive. They suffered from diseases; they suffered assaults; their dogs got heartworms. They were either fake, or else they were me. They were cruel and cruelly treated. I sent them into suffering because I was sure that suffering was gravity, and gravity was all I wanted. My work followed pain like a heat-seeking missile. Even as a young girl, my princess characters had died by dragon breath more often than they'd gotten married. In tenth grade, I'd been assigned to write a response to another student's painting, an abstract swirl of red and purple, and I wrote a story about a girl in a wheelchair dying in a house fire.

That first year at Iowa, I lived with a journalist in her thirties who had spent years writing newspaper articles about the New York City art scene. She knew how to roast a chicken stuffed with whole lemons, hot and pulpy and sour. The fact of cooked lemons seemed undeniably *adult* to me, a sign of having crossed some sort of threshold. On Wednesday nights we drove out to the farmers' auction in a big barn just west of town—tractors and livestock and estate sales, old LPs and old swords and old Coke cans, trash and treasure—where you could buy funnel cakes and watch the auctioneers ride their giant high chairs through the aisles, speaking their incomprehensible staccato language: *nowfourfifty-canigettafivenow-fivefromtheback*. Back home, we sweated in our kitchen, melting goat cheese and torn-up basil into couscous and then spooning it into the little purses of fried squash blossoms. The smell of oil-blistered vegetable skin was everywhere. Those days were like that: humid, insistent. I had this thought that sautéing things would make me an adult.

Some nights when I got restless and had trouble sleeping, I would drive out to the biggest truck stop in the world, forty miles east on I-80. It had a fifty-foot buffet and showers for the truckers. It even had a dentist and a chapel. I scribbled character-driven dialogue in my notebooks and drank mugs of black coffee filmed with broken lily pads of grease. At three in the morning, I ordered apple dumplings and vanilla ice cream and cleaned the bowl with my tongue, miles of darkened cornfields all around me.

It seemed like everyone drank in Iowa City. Even if no one drank all the time, there was always someone drinking at any particular time. When I wasn't pretending to ride a cowboy, trying to earn my seat on the shag, I spent my nights balancing on leather stools at the writers' bars on Market Street: George's and the Foxhead. "Writers' bar" was a nonexclusive term. Really any bar where writers drank could be a writers' bar: the Deadwood, the Dublin Underground, the Mill, the Hilltop, the Vine, Mickey's, the Airliner, that place with a patio on the Ped Mall, that other place with a patio on the Ped Mall, that place with a patio just a block from the Ped Mall.

But the Foxhead was the most writerly bar of all, and also the smokiest. The ventilation system was just a hole someone had shoved a fan into. The girls' bathroom was covered with marker scrawl about men in the workshop: So-and-so would fuck anyone, so-and-so would fuck you over. Some of the guys called me *barely legal*, because I was so young, and I wondered if that phrase lived above a urinal in the guys' room. I hoped. It seemed like living, to be someone who inspired gossip in black marker.

Even as Iowa got colder, I always wore my cheapest jacket to the Foxhead because I didn't want to get my other jackets smoky. My cheapest jacket was thin knee-length black velour with a faux-fur trim so large I felt comfortably recessed within it—shivering, arms crossed tight across my chest. Years later, I read about an undergrad in Ames who had gotten drunk and died in the snow, his body found at the bottom of the stairs in some old agricultural warehouse. But back then I wasn't thinking about dying in the snow. I drank until I couldn't feel the cold. After the bars closed, I kept drinking in the chilly apartments of boys who were trying to save money on their heating bills.

One night I ended up in the chilly apartment of a boy I liked, or who I thought might like me—the two possibilities were nearly indistinguishable, or else the first barely mattered. There were a few of us at his place, and someone brought out a baggie of coke. It was my first time ever seeing coke, and it was like stepping into a movie. During high school, it seemed like all the other girls had been doing coke since they were toddlers. Popular Felicity, with her smooth-shaven legs; I was sure she'd done it all the time, while I'd been drinking Diet Cokes at PG-13 movies, spending weeks choosing an ankle-length blue lace semiformal dress.

Truth be told, I wasn't sure exactly how to do coke. I knew you snorted it, but I didn't know what that looked like. I tried to summon every movie I'd ever seen. How close did you get? How close had that girl gotten in *Cruel Intentions*, snorting from a secret stash in her silver crucifix? I didn't want to tell this guy it was my first time doing coke. I wanted to have done coke so many times I couldn't even *count* how many times I'd done coke. Instead I was someone who needed to be reminded, gently, to use the cut straw.

"I feel like I'm corrupting you," this guy said. He was twenty-four but acted like those three years were a canyon between us. They were. I wanted to say: *Corrupt me!* I was wearing bright white pants with a big silver buckle attached, kneeling in front of this guy's coffee table, doing a line straightened by a credit card that was honestly probably a debit card, sniffing loudly.

There was nothing feigned about how much I loved that icy swell, that sense of *so much to say*. We had all night. The woman who'd brought the coke was gone. Everyone was gone. We could talk till dawn. I imagined him saying: *I've always wondered what you were thinking.* Other people were always the ones who got noticed, the Felicitys of the world, but now this guy was putting on a record, *Blood on the Tracks*, and Dylan's scratchy voice filled the cold room, and the coke charged my pitter-pattering heart and it was finally my turn. The icy swell believed in me, and it believed in what this night could become. I'd only ever kissed three guys. With every one of them, I'd imagined an entire future unfolding between us. Now I was imagining it with this one. I hadn't told him about it yet, but maybe I would. Maybe I'd tell him while dawn broke over the park beyond his bay windows.

"Who actually wears white pants?" he asked me. "You see them, but you don't think of anyone actually wearing them."

I kept sitting on his couch, for hours and hours, waiting for him to kiss me. I finally asked him, "Are you going to kiss me?"—meaning, *Are you going to try to sleep with me?*—because there was enough coke and vodka inside me to ask out loud, to peel away whatever feeble skin remained between the world and my need to be affirmed by it.

The answer was no. He wasn't going to try to sleep with me. The closest he got to trying to sleep with me was saying, just before I left, "Hey, not everybody can pull off white pants," as a kind of consolation prize.

As I was leaving, he kissed me in his doorway. "Is that what you wanted?" he said, and a sob rose in my throat, salty and swollen. I was drunk but not drunk enough. It was the worst humiliation: to be *seen* like this, not desired but desiring. I couldn't let myself cry in front of him. So I did it on the way home, walking through the cold, at four in the morning, my white pants gleaming like stretched headlights in the dark.

When I got home that night, I stumbled upstairs, tripped, and fell face-first onto the steps, hard enough that the next day a huge bruise ripened on my shin. That night, freshly spurned, I wanted to see what he'd seen when he turned me away. In the mirror, I was someone red-eyed—someone who had been crying, or maybe had allergies. She had some white dust under her nose. She took it on her fingertip and rubbed it on her gums. She'd seen them do that in the movies, too. She was sure of it.

We weren't the first people who'd gotten drunk in Iowa. We knew that. The myths of Iowa City drinking ran like subterranean rivers beneath the drinking we were doing. They surged with dreamlike tales of dysfunction: Raymond Carver and John Cheever tire-squealing through early-morning grocery-store parking lots to restock their liquor stash; John Berryman opening bar tabs on Dubuque Street and ranting about Whitman till dawn, playing chess and leaving his bishops vulnerable; Denis Johnson getting drunk at the Vine and writing short stories about getting drunk at the Vine. We got drunk at the Vine too, though it was in a different building now, on a different block. We knew this too: how imprecisely we squatted in the old tales, how we only got them in glimpses and imperfect replicas.

I often thought about Iowa with that *we:* We drank here. We drank there. We drank somehow with those who would drink after us, just as we drank with those who had come before. One of Johnson's poems described being "just a poor mortal human" who had "stumbled onto / the glen where the failed gods are drinking."

When Cheever showed up to teach in Iowa, he was grateful for the glen. It was a place where he could drink without his family asking why he was killing himself. Back home, he'd been hiding bottles under car seats and lacing his iced tea with gin. But in Iowa, there was no need to pretend. Carver drove him to the liquor store first thing in the morning—it opened at nine, so they left at eight forty-five—and Cheever would be opening the car door before the car was fully stopped. Of their friendship, Carver said: "He and I did nothing *but* drink."

These were the legends I inherited. The air was thick with them. Richard Yates spent his hungover mornings at a booth in the Airliner, eating hard-boiled eggs and listening to Barbra Streisand on the jukebox. One of his students, Andre Dubus, offered to lend him his wife during a rough patch. Yates took Dubus drinking after his first novel didn't sell, and I took my best friend drinking when her first novel didn't sell—at the Deadwood, during the part of the afternoon called Angry Hour, which came just before Happy Hour and had even steeper discounts. I tried and failed to think of what to say, and wondered if I'd ever finish a novel, and how much it would sell for.

In *John Barleycorn*, a novel published in 1913, Jack London conjured two kinds of drunks: the ones who stumbled through the gutters hallucinating "blue mice and pink elephants," and the ones to whom the "white light of alcohol" had granted access to bleak truths: "the pitiless, spectral syllogisms of the white logic."

The first type of drunk had his mind ravaged by booze, "bitten numbly by numb maggots," but the second type had his mind sharpened instead. He could see more clearly than ordinary men: "[He] sees through all illusions.... God is bad, truth is a cheat, and life is a joke.... Wife, children, friends—in the clear white light of his logic they are exposed as frauds and shams...he sees their frailty, their meagerness, their sordidness, their pitifulness." The "imaginative" drunk bore this vision as gift and curse at once. Booze granted sight and charged for it, with "a sudden spill or a gradual oozing away."

London called the sadness of drinking a "cosmic sadness," not a small sorrow but a grand one. In the old British folk song in which he'd first appeared, John Barleycorn was the personification of grain alcohol itself—a spirit attacked by drunkards laid low by booze, men seeking revenge for what he had done to them. In London's novel, he was more like a sadistic fairy godmother, granting the harsh gift of bleak wisdom. He'd certainly visited the writer legends of Iowa, the ones who cast their long, staggering shadows over our carved-up bar booths.

Carver's shadow was the drunkest of them all. His stories were painful and precise, like carefully bitten fingernails, full of silence and whiskey, *just-one-more* rounds and *next-one's-on-me* rounds. His characters cheated and got cheated on. They got each other drunk and dragged each other's passed-out bodies onto porches. People got roughed up, no big shucks. A vitamin saleswoman got drunk and broke her finger, then woke up with a hangover "so bad it was like somebody was sticking wires in her brain."

The stories I'd heard about Carver's life suggested a rogue running on booze and fumes: leaving meals unfinished because he was getting all his sugar from liquor, walking out of restaurants before he'd paid the bills, moving the class he taught from the English department to the back room of the Mill, one of his favorite bars. "You can't tell a bunch of writers not to smoke," he insisted, as his department had tried to do. One time he ended up with a stranger he'd let crash in his hotel room after a hard night of drinking: The young man stripped to leopard-print briefs and pulled out a jar of Vaseline. Another time Carver showed up uninvited at the home of a colleague, holding a bottle of Wild Turkey, and said: "Now we are going to tell each other our life stories."

I pictured Carver in terms of hijinks and love triangles, petty theft and seductions, ash falling unnoticed from the tip of his cigarette as he sat engrossed at his typewriter, riding the comet's tail of a bender into its ruthless wisdom. Whatever psychic ledges his long drunks had taken him to, whatever voids he had glimpsed from those perches,

I pictured him deftly smuggling that desperation into the quiet betrayals and pregnant pauses of his fiction. One of Carver's friends put it like this: "Ray was our designated Dylan Thomas, I think — our contact with the courage to face all possible darkness and survive."

That was my default sense of *all possible darkness*, back then: Carver, Thomas, London, Cheever, these white scribes and their epic troubles. When I thought of addiction, I certainly wasn't thinking about Billie Holiday incarcerated for a year in West Virginia, or handcuffed to her deathbed at a midtown Manhattan hospital. I wasn't thinking of the elderly white drunks gathering every morning at the nonwriters' bars at the edges of our cornfields, veterans and farmers — the ones for whom intoxication wasn't mythic fuel but daily, numbing relief, the ones who didn't narrate their drunken binges as brushes against existential wisdom. Back then, I was too busy imagining Carver falling asleep past dawn with polka-dot burns on his hands and a stack of heartbroken pages in his lap, a diplomat from the bleakest reaches of his own wrecked life. I kept expecting to see notes for one of his stories carved into a wooden booth at the Foxhead. I could only imagine the bathroom-marker gossip he'd inspired.

"It was really difficult even to look at him," one acquaintance said, "the booze and the cigarettes were so much there that they seemed like another person with us in the room." During the worst of his drinking, Carver claimed he was spending twelve hundred dollars a month on liquor, a handsome monthly salary he paid the other person in the room. "Of course there's a mythology that goes along with the drinking," Carver once said. "But I was never into that. I was into the drinking itself."

I was into the drinking, too, but I was also into the mythology of the guy who wasn't into its myth. I was pretty sure we all were.

Carver loved London's *John Barleycorn*. He recommended it to an editor over noon drinks, told him — emphatically — that it dealt with "*invisible* forces," then left the table and walked out of the restaurant.

Early the next morning, that same editor got a call from county jail, where Carver was sleeping on a cement floor behind bars.

D aniel was a poet who lived above a falafel shop and drove a garbage truck. I met him at the Deadwood, a downtown bar full of pinball machines. We were drunk, of course, blinking against the sudden lights of closing time. Daniel had dark hair and blue eyes and when someone said he looked like Morrissey I had to look up who Morrissey was. I let him take me home and lay me down across his lumpy futon mattress. We ate chocolate ice cream from the carton, under his scratchy wool blanket, and watched porn. I'd never seen porn. I wanted to know if the delivery guy was going to fall in love with the nurse. "There's not really a plot," he said. But he was a plot. Daniel had a history of misadventures that I always wanted to hear more about, as if I were a pickpocket rummaging for anecdotes: that time he'd dressed up as a pirate and woken up in his apartment stairwell covered in vomit, that time his ex had contacted spirits using a Ouija board on a picnic bench outside a doughnut shop in Wyoming.

Life with Daniel was weird and ragged and unexpected. It tingled. He was a messy eater. There were bits of cabbage in his beard, patches of ice cream melted on his sheets, crusted pots and pans in his sink, tiny beard hairs all over his bathroom counter. He left scraps of possible poetry scribbled on the covers of old *New Yorkers* piled around my bedroom: "Reality is survival...equipped with drawers of underwear, a few bathroom candles, and maybe a scepter...hidden up somewhere in the attic." When we went to a party where everyone was drinking single-malt scotch and writing tasting notes, other people wrote, *Mossy, smoky, earthy*, while Daniel wrote, *Tastes like the dust thrown up by the wheels of a chariot in ancient Rome.* When we did coke together, it wasn't the first time I was doing it. We had sex one night in a graveyard at the edge of town. We drove to New Orleans because we had a car. I canceled the classes I was supposed to teach—or got friends to cover—so we could watch the History Channel under mustard-yellow scratchy motel blankets in the middle of Wherever, Mississippi. We got shots of well whiskey in the early afternoon and ran through the back alleys of the French Quarter.

Daniel and his friends, a crew of older poets, spent evenings shooting air rifles at empty PBR cans. I watched his profile flicker in the glow of bonfires. I was self-conscious about being so young, only twenty-one, so I lied and told Daniel I was twenty-two. That math felt right at the time. Daniel's friends intimidated me. He told me his friend Jack had slept with 125 women. I wondered if Jack wanted to sleep with me. One night I told Jack that I sometimes drove out to the truck stop in the middle of the night and worked in the vinyl booths by the supply shop, overlooking all those chrome hubcaps in the aisles. "You just got a *hundred* times more interesting," he said, and I tried to divide myself by a hundred, right there in front of him, to figure out what I'd been before.

If there was one book that everyone worshipped at Iowa, poet oracles and prose architects alike, it was Denis Johnson's *Jesus' Son*. This collection of stories was our Bible of beauty and damage, a hallucinated vision of how and where we lived, full of farmhouse parties and hungover mornings, blue skies bright enough to make your eyeballs ache. Half the book took place in Iowa City bars. Crazy things happened at the corner of Burlington and Gilbert, where we now had a Kum & Go gas station. The story "Emergency" took its title from the big sign on Mercy Hospital: glowing red letters against brick that I associated with walking home drunk on winter nights, numb to the chill. In the world of Johnson's stories, you leaned close to sip your liquor "like a hummingbird over a blossom." There was a farmhouse where people smoked pharmaceutical opium and said things like, "McInnes isn't feeling too good today. I just shot him."

In *Jesus' Son*, even the cornfields mattered. They surrounded our town like an ocean, green and bristling in summer, high enough for mazes in September, then ravaged into dry husks for the remainder of autumn—dreary ranks of desiccated, skeletal brown stalks. It was like Johnson was drunk-dialing us from the end of time to tell us what they meant, these sweeping fields whose edges were beyond our sight. One of his characters looks at the giant screen of a drive-in cinema and mistakes it for a sacred vision: "The sky was torn away and the angels were descending out of a brilliant blue summer, their huge faces streaked with light and full of pity." Johnson had mistaken the ordinary Iowa around us for something sacred, and drugs and booze had helped him do it.

When Johnson arrived in Iowa City as a college freshman in the fall of 1967, he wrote his parents to say he'd accidentally purchased baby blankets he'd mistaken for towels at the Goodwill—but he was glad to find a collection of "personality-ridden ties." He complained about a guy who played the banjo loudly outside his dorm-room door. By November, he'd done his first stint at the county jail. While he was locked up, his friends sent him a drugstore greeting card covered with cartoon people whose droopy faces were distraught: *"PLEASE COME BACK!!! We all miss you very much and besides..."* The interior added: *"The coast is clear!"* His friend Peg wrote: "Boy, I tried all day to get you out of jail, but they wouldn't do it. Your court costs are paid so you can leave Thursday night." Peg was getting by okay—"Right now I'm at a truck stop on I-80 having a coke"—but she wanted him to know: "We're all anxiously awaiting your triumphant return."

By the time Johnson was nineteen, he'd published his first book of poetry, and by the time he was twenty-one, he'd been put in a psych ward for alcohol-related psychosis. I'd heard that *Jesus' Son* was just a bunch of memories he'd stuffed into a drawer and then sold to a publisher, years later, to pay off the IRS.

I liked to read one of his closing paragraphs aloud in my Iowa bedroom: "I kissed her fully, my mouth on her open mouth, and we met inside. It was there. It was. The long walk down the hall. The door opening. The beautiful stranger. The torn moon mended. Our fingers touching away the tears. It was there." He was insisting that a single stupid kiss could matter, that one swooning-drunk moment could matter, that even the most ordinary things could matter—the walk down the hall, the opened door, even the stranger without a name. They all added up to something. What that something *was*, who knew? But we could sense its ragged edges.

There was something beautiful and necessary about the role of pain in Johnson's stories. Truth lurked past the edges of destruction and sorrow. Something got *made*, like a jewel or a hatched bird, when people hurt. When a woman was told that her husband had died, behind a hospital door that let out a single bar of bright light, as if "diamonds were being incinerated in there," she "shrieked" as the narrator "imagined an eagle would shriek," and he wasn't horrified but entranced. "It felt wonderful to be alive to hear it!" he said. "I've gone looking for that feeling everywhere." My undergraduate students thought it was cruel, the narrator's hunt for pain, but I thought, *I get it.* I would have clawed under the hospital door looking for those diamonds, too, for the great heat and shriek of their destruction.

At the end of that story, the narrator addressed us directly from the page: "And you, you ridiculous people, you expect me to help you." But I wasn't seeking his help so much as his glorious vision of what it meant to be broken. His characters played the part of prophet drunks, our Virgils to their hell. "Because we all believed we were tragic, and we drank," his narrator tells us. "We had that helpless, destined feeling." His stories insisted that everything around us mattered: the dream and clove-smoke and sharp cold of this place. *It was there*, he wrote. *It was.*

I wanted to think of my early months with Daniel in terms of their magic, but in truth they were also saturated with anxiety. For me, so many of our carefree adventures—the sudden trip to New Orleans, the graveyard sex—were striated by doubt, hardly free at all. They were more like attempts to prove, to him and to myself, that whatever was happening between us was happening on a grand scale. Our stumbling drunken run through the French Quarter played in my mind like an art-house film: wrought-iron balconies, pastel shotgun apartments.

I didn't just need Daniel to want me; I needed him to want *everything* with me. Anything less seemed like rejection. For him, I imagine this was somewhat exhausting. I had no stomach for that murky state that came between being strangers and being passionately committed for the rest of our lives—in other words, dating. I needed it all, right away: *More. Again. Forever.* I can remember Daniel telling me once: "I like you, but I'm not sure I'd want to marry you," though I've conveniently repressed whatever I said to make him say that, probably something like: "Don't you want to marry me?!" If he didn't, after a month, I was ready to read it as my own failure. Drinking with Daniel wasn't just about delivering myself into the wild hands of his recklessness, it was about surviving his uncertainty. I read this uncertainty as a metaphysical conundrum, a referendum on the possibilities of intimacy, when in fact it was just honesty. It was the honesty of a twenty-six-year-old poet living above a falafel shop.

As we were stumbling home from a barbecue one night, silly in the darkness, he stopped me in the middle of the sidewalk. When he told me, "Back there, I was in love with every fucking word coming out of your mouth," it came as the confirmation of a hunch. I'd always suspected love came as a reward for saying the right things.

Daniel had an ex-girlfriend who'd had cervical cancer. He'd given her HPV and felt responsible for her illness. Even though she was healthy again, and they weren't together anymore, he was still preoccupied by the specter of their relationship, and by his culpability in her sickness. I didn't worry about her coming out of remission, and didn't even worry about getting HPV myself; I only worried I would never mean as much to him as she had.

One weekend we all went camping out at Lake Macbride, me and Daniel and his crew of older poet friends. It was early spring. The air smelled like wet dirt. Everything was raw from just-melted snow. I was scared of saying the wrong thing but also scared of saying nothing at all. How much more could I say about the truck stop? What else did I have? I sucked down beer after beer and hardly touched my hamburger. I remember being nervous and then I remember nothing. I woke up in a tent the next morning and Daniel told me they'd gotten worried. The night before, I'd wandered off into the woods and hadn't come back. He'd thought I was peeing but then I *still* hadn't come back. He went looking and eventually found me hunched at the base of a tree. What was I doing there? he wondered. We wondered together.

I was starting to learn the social etiquette of the postblackout processing session, letting someone tell me what I'd done and then helping him figure out why I might have done it. *I did WHAT?* I'd ask. *Why would I do THAT?* I pictured myself stumbling through the trees, a weird survival impulse at work, my body fleeing my own tyrannical desire to impress. My drunk self was like an embarrassing cousin I was responsible for—a houseguest in the woods who was undeniably my fault, though I couldn't remember inviting her.

In 1967, *Life* magazine published an eight-page profile of John Berryman titled "Whisky and Ink, Whisky and Ink." It featured photos of the bearded genius-poet befriending entire Dublin pubs, holding forth over a flock of foam-lipped empty pints, carrying the burden of his wisdom and the antidote of his whiskey. "Whisky and ink," it began. "These are the fluids John Berryman needs. He needs them to survive and describe the thing that sets him apart from other men and even from other poets: his uncommonly, almost maddeningly penetrating awareness of the fact of human mortality."

It wasn't quite the white logic, but it was close. Whiskey didn't grant Berryman his vision, but it helped him endure it. The profile still sketched that shimmering link between drinking and darkness, between drinking and *knowing*. It also included a full-page Heineken ad.

Berryman's most famous poems, *The Dream Songs*, conjure a landscape full of booze and tortured knowledge. "I am, outside," his speaker announces. "Incredible panic rules....Drinks are boiling. Iced / drinks are boiling." Even the iced drinks are boiling. It has come to that. Berryman's persona, Henry, often speaks with a drunk voice sweating heavy on the page, asking himself some questions: "Are you radioactive, pal?—Pal, radioactive.—Has you got the night sweats & the day sweats, pal?—Pal, I do." *The Dream Songs* breathe a weird new form of oxygen. "Hey, out there!—assistant professors, full, / associates,—instructors—others—any," Henry announces, "I have a sing to shay." *I have a sing to shay.* His drunk voice performs its intoxication to the point of absurdity, suggesting that creation has to happen beyond the borderlines of comfort. One of Berryman's friends once told him that he lived like he'd spent his "whole fucking life out in the weather without any protection...eyes ragged from what they have seen & try to look away from."

Berryman arrived for his own stint in Iowa City at the age of forty, with plenty of baggage back in New York: a recent separation from his first wife, a girlfriend getting an abortion, an overdue bill to his analyst. "At present, the figure is mountainous, which discourages you from starting," this analyst wrote to him. "But please start."

The day Berryman showed up in Iowa, he fell down a flight of stairs and broke his wrist. He developed a reputation for praising Whitman's long lines in bar booths, and drunk-dialing his students in the middle of the night. "Mr. Berryman often called me," Bette Schissel recalled, "usually in a deeply agitated state...often incoherent and rambling...seeking reassurance that he had been 'outstanding' or 'brilliant' at his morning lecture." He was a fragile oracle. Of Henry, he wrote:

Hunger was constitutional with him,
wine, cigarettes, liquor, need need need
Until he went to pieces.
The pieces sat up & wrote.

Hunger ran in the family. Berryman's mother wrote to him about craving her own mother's affection: "I, who longed for her love and have love-groped my way through life for the need of it." Berryman's own need broke him into pieces, but the pieces got the writing done. "I have the authority of suffering; extraordinary suffering, I think," Berryman insisted, and he identified with the drunk tormented geniuses who had come before him: Hart Crane, Edgar Allan Poe, Dylan Thomas. He compared himself to Baudelaire: "in violent temper & razor sensibility to disgrace," in his "savage self-contempt which is brother to mine." The dead were always breathing down his neck. His father committed suicide when he was eleven.

Part of Berryman was attached to his own trauma and its residue. He even wrote to his unpaid analyst confessing anxiety about the risk of impeding his creativity by resolving his emotional problems. He compared his case to Rilke's. "I would not worry," his analyst replied, "about an analogy to Rilke, and a possible damage to your creative skills. These are not in your case so intertwined with your emotional problems that the solution of one must lead to the destruction of the other."

For many years, this was Berryman's operative logic: Pain promised inspiration, and booze promised relief, a way to endure the authority of suffering. Berryman's friend Saul Bellow echoed the notion that Berryman's drinking allowed him to withstand his own dark wisdom: "Inspiration contained a death threat [and] Drink was a stabilizer. It somewhat reduced the fatal intensity." But if Berryman believed this—that drink helped him survive the fatal intensity of his own poetic vision—he couldn't deny that it left other intensities in its wake. He got fired from his teaching job at Iowa after going to jail on charges of public intoxication and disturbing the peace.

When I encountered the legend of Berryman, I found an appealing air of *complicatedness* in his affairs, the sweet boozy whiff of tangle and rupture. "With your work," a friend wrote to him, "I often have the feeling that yr poems are the light we see now from a star that is already ashes."

What role could sobriety possibly play in that glorious arc of blaze and rot?

In *The Dream Songs*, I saw proof of a tormented consciousness, and proof that you could write from torment. I saw what Berryman's pieces sat up and wrote: "Something can (has) been said for sobriety / but very little."

In Iowa, I spent my days reading dead drunk poets and my nights trying to sleep with live ones. I love-groped my way through the future canon. I was drawn to the same unhinged sparks of luminous chaos that had animated the old legends. I idolized the iconic drunk writers because I understood their drinking as proof of extreme interior weather: volatile and authentic. If you needed to drink that much, you had to *hurt*, and drinking and writing were two different responses to that same molten pain. You could numb it, or else grant it a voice.

My ability to find drunken dysfunction appealing—to fetishize its relationship to genius—was a privilege of having never really suffered. My fascination owed a debt to what Susan Sontag calls the "nihilistic and sentimental idea of 'the interesting.'" In *Illness as Metaphor*, Sontag describes the nineteenth-century idea that if you were ill, you were also "more conscious, more complex psychologically." Illness became an "interior décor of the body," while health was considered "banal, even vulgar." Sontag was writing about tuberculosis, but there was a durable logic connecting suffering with sensitivity, with rarefied perspective, with being *interesting*. In the early days of my drinking—in the shadows of all those legendary Iowa drinkers, and in the longer shadows of Faulkner, Fitzgerald, and Hemingway, Poe and Baudelaire, Burroughs and his junkies, De Quincey and his opium, a canon whose boundaries I hadn't yet come to see as deeply limited—addiction seemed generative. It seemed very much like interior décor, an accessory that spoke to inner depths.

When my drinking passed a certain threshold—a threshold I imagined as an existential tunnel, hidden under the fifth or sixth drink—it plunged me into darkness that seemed like honesty. It was as if the bright surfaces of the world were all false, and the desperate drunk space underground was where the truth lived. Novelist Patricia Highsmith's argument that drinking helped the artist "see the truth, the simplicity, and the primitive emotions once more" reimagined Jack London's white logic as a visible core, something vital that remained once booze had stripped away the trivial distractions of everything else. It was another layer in the complicated, circular relationship I was constructing between drinking and making: Booze helped you see, and then it helped you survive the sight. The appeal wasn't just about intoxication—as a portal, or a bandage—but about the alluring relationship between creativity and addiction itself: its state of thrall, its signature extremity. The person who found himself in that state of thrall was someone who felt things more acutely than ordinary men, who shared his living quarters with darkness, and then eventually the drama of enthrallment became—itself—something worth writing about.

But why was it always *him*? The Old Drunk Legends were all men. It was like they'd built their own tombs from one another's myths, in a testosterone-steeped lineage of inflated egos and glorified dysfunction: Carver loved London's white logic; Cheever imagined himself dying like Berryman; Berryman imagined himself following in the lurching footsteps of Poe, Crane, Baudelaire. Denis Johnson said he read only one book the whole time he was a student at Iowa, and it was Malcolm Lowry's *Under the Volcano*. It was Lowry's hero, the Consul, who put it bluntly: "A woman could not know the perils, the complications, yes, the *importance* of a drunkard's life."

Maybe Elizabeth Bishop learned something about the perils and complications of a drunkard's life during her three-day binges, or her decades of Antabuse. Maybe she knew something about them by the time she died of a cerebral aneurysm, in 1979, when the alcohol-thinned blood vessels of her brain finally burst. "I will *not* drink," she wrote to her doctor in 1950. "I'll go insane if I keep it up." And then, two decades later: "*Please* just don't…scold me for any past lapses, *please*…I feel I can't bear to be made to feel guilty *one more time* about the drinking."

Maybe Jane Bowles understood something about the complications of a drunkard's life when she stripped naked at Guitta's, her favorite bar in Tangier, or when she kept drinking in the aftermath of her giant cerebral hemorrhage at forty. Maybe Marguerite Duras understood something about these complications after liters of cheap Bordeaux, or after the brutal disintoxication treatments that left her almost dead. Maybe she understood something about the shame of being a woman who understood something about drinking. "When a woman drinks," she wrote, "it's as if an animal were drinking, or a child."

Female drunks rarely got to strike the same rogue silhouettes as male ones. When they were drunk, they were like animals or children: dumbstruck, helpless, ashamed. Their drinking was less like the necessary antidote to their own staggering wisdom—catalyst or salve for these Virgils to the fallen world—and more like self-indulgence or melodrama, hysteria, a gratuitous affliction. Women might know something about the complications of a drunkard's life, but their drinking would never be *important*, as Lowry put it, not like a man's. If they weren't drinking like children, they were drinking instead of caring for their children. A woman escaping into drink was usually a woman failing to fulfill her duties to home and family. Describing the "traditional beliefs" that inflect how male and female drinking have been understood differently, one clinical textbook puts it like this: "Intoxication in a woman was thought to signal a failure of control over her family relationships."

No one knew this better than Jean Rhys. Rhys was drinking hard in Paris when her infant son was hospitalized with pneumonia. She'd arrived in early autumn of 1919, six months pregnant, and spent her first afternoon drinking wine and eating ravioli at a sidewalk café. "I've escaped," she wrote of that first day. "A door has opened and let me out into the sun."

Even though they were young and poor, Rhys and her husband — Jean Lenglet, a Belgian expatriate who worked as a journalist and spy — lived happily in a cheap hotel room near the Gare du Nord, where he made them cups of chocolate over their *flamme bleue* each morning, and they drank wine on the wrought-iron balcony each night. "Paris tells you to forget, forget, let yourself go," Rhys wrote; but years later, she worried she had let herself go too fully: "I was never a good mother." She let her baby, William Owen, sleep in a little basket near the balcony door, and at three weeks old, he fell ill. "This damned baby, poor thing, has gone a strange colour," she remembered thinking, "and I don't know what to do, I'm no good at this."

William was taken to the Hospice des Enfants Assistés, and a few nights later, when the hospital said he had a severe case of pneumonia, Rhys grew anxious because he had not been christened. Her husband brought her the only thing he knew could calm her down: two bottles of champagne. "By the time the first bottle was finished," she remembered, "we were all laughing." The next morning, the hospital called to say her son had died at seven-thirty the previous evening. "He was dying," she wrote later, "or was already dead, while we were drinking."

Jean Rhys wrote about drinking with the futile precision of someone who had never escaped its thrall. She wrote four novels dissecting the emotional dynamics of her own drinking, but kept drinking
herself into oblivion anyway—a lifelong kamikaze dive. All the self-
awareness in the world couldn't keep her sober. "I know about myself,"
one of her heroines says to a lover. "You've told me so often."

The recurring heroine of Rhys's novels is a drunk woman making
a spectacle of her weeping, and her work confronts this woman not
just as a mess but as an *unappealing* mess, an eyesore, always clutching
at the pity of others—also their love, and their wallets—and
degraded by her constant clutching.

Rhys's heroines shuttle between dingy hotel rooms and disappointing love affairs. They drink at Parisian street cafés and in train-
station hotel rooms choked with smoke. When they think about love,
they imagine a wound, bleeding slowly. They look at flowers on the
wallpaper of their cheap flats and see crawling spiders. They "struggle with life," one critic observed, "the way a sleeper struggles with a
tangled blanket." Their lives look a lot like Rhys's: itinerant, moving
between various European capitals, often in love, often drunk, often
broke. Her heroines' drinking is never done. It's always another
brandy, another Pernod, another scotch and soda, another bottle of
wine. Their public sadness is part of their crime, and booze is their
accomplice. Other characters ask them, *Do you want a coffee? Do you
want a hot chocolate?* And it's like a recurring joke, always with the
same punch line: *No, I'd like a drink.*

Across the course of Rhys's first three novels, drinking is a shape-
shifter. It sheds its various costumes of pleasure and exposes itself as
an attempt to flee the same sadness it always ends up deepening
instead. For one of Rhys's heroines, early in her drinking, wine suf-
fuses an ordinary city view with meaning: "It was astonishing how
significant, coherent, and understandable it all became after a glass of
wine on an empty stomach." Wine turns the "sullen" Seine outside

shuttered windows into an expansive ocean. "When you were drunk," she thinks, "you could imagine that it was the sea." But drinking eventually becomes something more desperate. "I must get drunk tonight," another one of Rhys's heroines decides, after her lover sends her away. "I must get so drunk that I can't walk, so drunk that I can't see."

By *Good Morning, Midnight*, Rhys's fourth novel, her heroine, Sasha, has arrived at "the bright idea of drinking myself to death." Even the prose signals her erosion, dissolving into ellipses and drifting into the white spaces of unremembered blackout. Sasha has come to Paris after trying—and failing—to kill herself in London. She gets a cheap hotel room on a dead-end street and spends her days sleeping, taking pills to sleep more, and wandering a city that reminds her, in every café, at every corner, of a youth that didn't keep its promises: the marriage that ended, the baby boy who died. The novel is honest about the price of drinking—how small it makes the world, how much it saps the spirit—as well as its logistics: the ease of getting drunk on an empty stomach, the nostalgia for early days of lower tolerance.

"Sometimes I'm just as unhappy as you are," another woman tells Sasha. "But that's not to say that I let everybody see it." A bartender stops serving her. "You said that if you drink too much you cry," her lover tells her. "And I have a horror of people who cry when they're drunk." Sasha deforms the icon of the Drunk Genius: the poet with his ink and whiskey, turning intoxication to lyric. Sasha's pieces can't sit up and write. When she gets expressive, her expression is shameful, something others ask her to hide: the embarrassment of drunken tears, not the brilliance of song. If the mythic male drunk manages a thrilling abandon—the reckless, self-destructive pursuit of truth—his female counterpart is more often understood as guilty of abandonment, the crime of failing at care. Her drinking has violated the central commandment of her gender, *Thou shalt care for others*, and revealed itself as an intrinsically selfish abnegation of that duty. Her self-pity compounds the crime by directing her concern away from an implicit other—real or imagined, child or spouse—and funneling that concern back toward herself.

Rhys once wrote that she learned early that "it was bad policy to say that you were lonely or unhappy," and Sasha is an explosion of bad policy. Her consciousness runs on an engine of wearisome hydraulics, bringing in the booze and pumping it out as tears. Sasha is a grotesque version of what Rhys always feared she would become: a pariah who drove everyone away by showing the intensity of her unhappiness. "I could deny myself," she once wrote in her diary. "Then I could make them love me and be kind to me...That has been the struggle."

For Sasha, that struggle—to dissemble, to pretend—is done. She cries wherever she pleases. She cries at cafés, at bars, at home. She cries at work. She cries in a fitting room. She cries on the street. She cries near the river, drinks until the river becomes an ocean, and then cries some more. "Now I have had enough to drink," she thinks each night, "now the moment of tears is very near."

— II —

ABANDON

I learned about the efficiency of drinking on an empty stomach by starting to drink when I wasn't eating enough. This was during my freshman year of college. I had made one good friend—Abby from Indiana, who had grown up evangelical and would become one of the great friends of my life—but if we weren't together, I was alone. My roommate had an unnervingly attractive boyfriend she had met on a pre-orientation camping trip. It seemed like everyone had met her boyfriend on a pre-orientation camping trip. When I looked in the mirror, I saw someone tall and ungainly, with a large nose and pleading eyes, a frizzy triangle of thick brown hair. Most evenings I walked into Harvard's version of a freshman dining hall—the cavernous interior of an old Gothic church, its long tables surveyed by callous stone gargoyles—petrified by the prospect of finding someone to sit with. It wasn't that I assumed no one else felt this way; it was that I didn't even bother to think about it. My loneliness was a full-time job.

I called my mom from pay phones so my roommate wouldn't see me crying. Scheduling phone dates with my high school friends grew embarrassing because of the asymmetry in our lives, their busy schedules and my constant availability: *That time would ALSO work for me!* I was told my ex-boyfriend had hooked up with his college's mascot, a giant tree.

I wasn't at ease—at school, in the dorms, among others—and starving myself was a way of acting as if I weren't fully there, as if my life were on pause and I would hit the Play button again once I was happy. I looked up at lit windows and was convinced that other people were happy behind the buttery glow of their glass. I lost five pounds, then ten, then fifteen. I kept a calorie notebook in my desk drawer where I tallied everything I ate, and a scale in my closet with bright red numbers on its screen. I lived by those red numbers, whatever they told me. If I had a setback, the same weight too many days in a row, then the next day began grimly, with a trek through the cold to the law school gym, where the One-Ls pounded their feet across their treadmill belts with a robotic fortitude I knew I could only impersonate. Another girl on my hall, who also had an eating disorder, always drank cups of hot water at meals. I started doing that, too. I looked unwell.

One night I took a jar of peanut butter down to the dumpsters in the basement of my dorm because I was afraid I might eat the whole thing in one sitting, and I knew that if I threw it away in my room I could just fish it out of the garbage can. Down in the basement, before I tossed it, I scooped out some peanut butter with my fingers and ate it in gobs. Then I threw the jar away. Then I went back to the elevator. Then I returned to the dumpster, found the jar, twisted it open, and stuck my fingers in again. *That* was the truth of me: not the skinny girl who never ate but that girl with dirty fingers, leaning into the trash.

I started going to meetings at the college literary magazine, the *Advocate*, which had its own wooden clubhouse on South Street, and even its own motto — *Dulce est periculum*, "Danger is sweet" — as well as its own crest: a Pegasus flying toward God knows what kind of trouble. Flying toward it since 1866, we were told. The magazine threw legendary parties and held notorious initiations. I heard that one girl had been forced to suck tampons soaked in Bloody Marys. But it wasn't easy to join. I had to spend several months *comping*, which was the Harvard way of saying "wanting something." In this case, it meant a tryout process that involved writing two essays, giving one presentation, and showing up to twice-weekly meetings of the fiction board, where we discussed stories that had been submitted to our wooden mailbox in the library. About twenty-five people were comping the fiction board, and we were told maybe five would be selected. We sat in the Sanctum, otherwise known as the second floor, which had perpetually sticky hardwood and a cluster of ratty velvet couches with stuffing and springs thrusting up through rips in their fabric. There was a bar in one corner stocked with lukewarm gin. Before I spoke, I ran every possible comment through a wash cycle in my mind—scrubbing its fabric and wringing it dry, getting rid of its dirt—trying to make it good enough to say aloud.

The other compers must have been terrified too, but I couldn't see it—not back then. I could only see them as silhouettes through lit windows, anonymous bodies onto which I projected happiness and social ease, all the things I lacked. It was selfishness disguised as self-deprecation, claiming all the loneliness in the world for myself, a stingy refusal to share the state of insecurity with others.

When I got onto the *Advocate* fiction board in October, I was thrilled. After initiation, I imagined, I would be able to stride under the dining hall gargoyles without fear, toward friends: tray held aloft, bearing something besides cups of hot water. The theme of my initiation was World Wrestling Federation. I dutifully showed up in Spandex, and got taken immediately to the basement—where one of my wrists was handcuffed to another initiate's, who was also handcuffed to a clanging metal pipe. I was handed a screwdriver, my first.

The next thing I knew, I was waking up in my dorm room, twelve hours later, with a note from one of the editors on the whiteboard—*Hope you're okay*—and my roommate telling me that her photogenic boyfriend had stayed up the whole night checking my pulse to make sure I wasn't dead.

All this was news to me. It was also news to me that you could lose a night entirely. The last thing I could remember was the first screwdriver: the tang of cheap vodka and citrus. I had shards of memory from that night, a man's body next to mine on a couch, but couldn't fit these shards together. I thought I'd been roofied. I spent months telling people I'd been roofied. Then someone told me about blackouts.

A year later, I was telling a friend all about how I hadn't vomited since I was nine years old, and she told me I'd vomited all over the inside of her car the night I'd been initiated. I made a joke, uneasily, and apologized, profusely. I would make the same jokes with Daniel years later, with the same uneasy laughter, about my night in the woods with his poet friends, peeing on a tree, disappearing into the night: *I did what? Why would I do that?* I pictured my body during blackouts like the body of a stranger — clad in Spandex, eager to belong — chugging her vodka, sucking it down, throwing it up again.

I lost twenty-five pounds that first semester. I started getting light-headed. It was proof of something — of what, I wasn't sure. I worked for an immigration lawyer in Boston, doing research to help her clients' asylum cases. Had they suffered enough human rights abuses to meet the criteria necessary for political asylum? I took a second job, transcribing interviews with HIV-positive mothers. My own pain seemed embarrassingly trivial, self-constructed and sought.

To get to the lawyer's office each afternoon, I walked across a broad concrete plaza in downtown Boston, near North Station, and I remember those walks during the numb heart of January: my frozen fingers and the chill inside, my body — at that point — skeletal. One day I got so dizzy in the hard winter sun that I sat down on the chilled concrete, in the middle of everyone, so that I wouldn't faint. Business-men walked around me in their striped suits. My tailbone ached. I was already five minutes late to work on our Eritrea case. It was an indulgence, this weakness. I knew that.

It seemed shameful that my sadness had no extraordinary source — just the common loneliness of leaving home. So I found a more extreme costume for it: the not-eating. *This* was the thing that was wrong. But at heart, I sensed I was more like a binge eater than an anorexic — that my restrictive eating was just an elaborate front. In addition to my calorie-counting notebook, I kept another journal, full of fantasy meals I copied from restaurant menus: *pumpkin-ricotta ravioli; vanilla-bean cheesecake with raspberry-mango coulis; goat cheese and*

Swiss chard tartlets. This journal was the truth of me: I wanted to spend every single moment of my life eating everything. The journal that recorded what I actually ate was just a mask—the impossible person I wanted to be, someone who didn't need anything at all.

I had two longings and one was fighting the other," Rhys once wrote in her journal. "I wanted to be loved and I wanted to be always alone." She believed that she was destined for sadness, and destined to spend her life being told to make her sadness less visible. She called her unfinished memoir *Smile, Please,* a command she'd been given as a child, posing for a photographer. It was the constant pressure she'd felt from the world: *Hide your unseemly angst.* As a little girl, she once smashed a doll's face with a stone because her younger sister had gotten the doll she wanted: "I searched for a big stone, brought it down with all my force on her face and heard the smashing sound with delight." Then she wept for the doll, buried her, and put flowers on her grave.

Rhys grew up on Dominica, in the West Indies, with wreaths of frangipani in her hair. "I wanted to identify myself with it," she wrote of her native island, "to lose myself in it.... But it turned its head away, indifferent, and that broke my heart." As an old woman, she could still remember "the sound of cocktail-making, the swizzle-stick and the clinking of crushed ice against the glass," like a regular pulse in the twilight. The frangipani branches bled white, not red. Everything was hot. At their family home, a ramshackle old estate, Rhys's grandmother sat with a green parrot on her shoulder while her mother stirred guava jam in a coal pot and read *The Sorrows of Satan.* The story was simple, its ending predestined: Satan wanted grace, but it was never meant for him. Rhys grew up dogged by a sense of doom. Hanging above the family silver, there was a picture of Mary, Queen of Scots, being led to her execution. Rhys's writing could never fully reckon with the suffering closer at hand, and larger than herself: the long shadow of slavery, and her family's participation in that legacy. Her own pain was too cloistering.

When she was twelve, a friend of the family reached his hand up Rhys's skirt. His name was Mr. Howard. "Would you like to belong to me?" he asked. She said she didn't know. He said: "I'd seldom allow you to wear clothes at all."

Years later, she wrote: "It was then that it began."

What was *it*? On one level, *it* was the story he began to tell her: "The serial story to which I listened for was it weeks or months — One day he would abduct me and I'd belong to him." In these stories, Mr. Howard described the house where they would live, how they would stand on their veranda and watch the bats fly at sunset while the moon rose over the water. On another level, *it* was the sense of being cursed, of being written into a story Rhys couldn't control.

In later years, whenever she looked back, Rhys could find relief from this story only by getting drunk or by writing stories of her own, stories that tried to make some sense of the sadness that consumed her. "I've made a complete wreck of myself," she wrote after one binge. "Or rather I've certainly put the finishing touch to the wreck — And do you know where I was sure I'd find myself? In Mr. Howard's house."

In Rhys, I recognized a woman trying to write an origin myth for her own despair, trying to build a house in which it might live, a logic or a narrative by which it might be justified. But I also sensed her pain was older than Mr. Howard's house, or that his house was just one way of pronouncing something less explicable — a sense of taint or doom.

"I wish I could get it clearer this pain that has gone through all my life," Rhys wrote. "Whenever I've tried to escape it has reached out and brought me back. Now I don't try any longer." It wasn't easy, just living in it. "You've no idea darling," she jotted in her diary, as if rehearsing for a letter, "how I've been drinking."

❖

Rhys drank for a long time. She never forgave herself for drinking while her infant son was dying, and she kept the receipt from his burial for the rest of her life: 130 francs and 60 centimes for a carriage, tiny coffin, and temporary cross. She and Lenglet had another child, who survived—a daughter named Maryvonne—but Rhys couldn't take care of her. Maryvonne lived in a convent and then mainly with her father, who spent time in prison but managed to parent more consistently than Rhys anyway. One time when Maryvonne came to stay with her, Rhys exploded at the woman who'd been taking care of the girl all day—angry that the two of them had come home at four in the afternoon. "You're much too early!" Rhys yelled. Rhys wanted to be alone, to drink and to write.

Rhys never understood herself as a rogue genius, like the drunk male writers of her generation. She was always forced to understand herself as a failed mother instead. The "traditional beliefs" that deemed her intoxication a badge of shame, a failure of control, might tell the story like this: When Rhys drank, she was taking. She was greedy for relief or escape. When she wrote or mothered, she was giving. She was creating art, or sustaining life. But the sadness that fueled her work often made her pull her care away. She wanted to be loved. She wanted to be alone.

One problem with living as if your sadness takes up the whole world is that it never does—and the people who live beyond its borders often have needs of their own. At six years old, Maryvonne told a friend: "My mother tries to be an artist and she is always crying."

I got sick of starving myself. It was tedious and cold, no matter how many cups of hot water I drank. I started seeing a psychologist, who leaned forward when I told her about my mother's job. "Your mother's a nutritionist?" she said, perking up. "Do you think you did this to get her attention?"

My mother wasn't *that* type of nutritionist, I explained. She'd written her doctoral dissertation on infant malnutrition in rural Brazil. She'd spent months weighing underweight babies in a village near Fortaleza. Her career in nutrition didn't have anything to do with the self-indulgent angst of her anorexic daughter. Plus, I added, I already had my mother's attention. My mother wasn't the problem. In fact, I said, my eating disorder had been more like a pathetic betrayal of everything wonderful about my mother, especially her largely untroubled relationship to food and to her body; her selfless devotion to problems that actually merited it. I was so irritated by how obviously *irrelevant* my therapist's question had been.

That summer I was supposed to get jaw surgery to correct an injury I'd sustained several years before, which meant my mouth would be wired shut for two months. But I wouldn't be able to have the operation if I didn't weigh more than I weighed, so I allowed myself to gain weight temporarily, with the surgery as an insurance policy on the other side: I knew that I'd lose it again.

For the first two months after the surgery, I squirted various flavors of Ensure through the small gap between my molars and the back of my mouth—with a dumbstruck, horrified awe at letting such concentrated calories into my body again. It was a relief that I couldn't get anything more inside me. But I was afraid that once they unwired my mouth and I let myself start eating again, I wouldn't know how to stop. The other self, the one I'd kept banished to my notebook of imagined meals, would keep eating forever. I came back for sophomore year ostensibly done with my eating disorder, but that other self—the one who always wanted *more*, the one I'd tried to starve away—wasn't gone. She was ready to drink.

During the next few years, college shimmered into myth: I got initiated into a social club with a secret panel that unlocked the front door, like a magician's lair. For my initiation, I had to bring cognac, wrangled with great courage and a terrible fake ID (V.S.O.P., which seemed like it should stand for something more glamorous than Very Superior Old Pale), and the upperclassmen drank it while I drank Beefeater gin in the dirt-floored basement, which had chicken-coop wiring everywhere. I had to smoke eight cigarettes at once—with skill, without coughing—and climb on top of a four-foot pillar while club members shone a spotlight in my face and heckled me when my answers to their questions weren't witty enough. When I was asked to close-read a piece of erotic fiction in front of everyone, we all learned that my close-reading skills stuck around deep into intoxication, much longer than my hand-eye coordination or my common sense. I got home at five in the morning, smelling like half-curdled whipped cream from a food fight, and tried to finish a paper about Virginia Woolf that was due at noon. This was living.

Drinking felt like the opposite of restriction. It was freedom. It was giving in to *wanting*, rather than refusing it. It was abandon. *Abandon* as in recklessness, but also sudden departure: leaving behind the starving self, its cold skeletal shell. Drinking let me live behind those lit windows I'd seen on my way to the law school gym.

Late one night I danced with a boy I liked in the middle of the Advocate Sanctum, when I was so drunk I could barely stand. I was wearing a strapless dress that fell down to show my bra, in front of everyone, and he pulled it up, and then we kissed, and I woke up the next day giddy and nervous. What would happen next? Nothing happened next. All I had was the piecemeal memory of my dress falling down to the middle of my stomach, and him gently picking it up again.

At the Advocate, I initiated other people just like I'd been initiated—made them hand-roll cigarettes for me using the college hazing codes as rolling papers. I was supposed to be terrible to them, but I was terrible at being terrible. "Get on your fucking knees and *beg!*" I'd yell. And then, softer: "If that makes you feel weird, or uncomfortable, you totally don't have to." I inherited the expired driver's license of a woman named Theresa—who wore glasses, and looked nothing like me—and loved the minor thrill of wearing glasses out, just to make my false identity more convincing.

Halloween of junior year, a friend of mine was dressing up as a hamburger and asked if I wanted to use his matching french fry costume. I said yes. He was a good friend; we'd been doing early-morning poster runs together for a year, taping up flyers for the magazine—*Submit!*—with our freezing hands. There's a photograph of us, the hamburger and the french fry carton, sitting side by side on one of the Sanctum's ratty couches, velvet splitting at the seams. In the photo, I'm determinedly smoking my cigarette through the armhole in my fry costume, plastic Solo cup at my side. I'm trying to look nonchalant, but you can tell I'm happy. He was my boyfriend for a year. He lived in a tall concrete tower overlooking the river. The whole building swayed when the wind got heavy. I loved coming back from a party and crawling into his bed drunk and breathing my gin breath into his shoulder. Getting drunk and spooning meant my body's presence had been requested, another way to quiet the same stubborn unease I'd always felt in my own skin—the one that made me count calories, count my ribs, seek a way out.

When I stepped into drinking, its buzz and glint, I felt like Wu Tao-tzu, the Chinese artist someone had once mentioned in the Sanctum. As legend had it, he'd painted the mouth of a cave onto a wall in the emperor's palace, then stepped inside and disappeared for good.

At a certain point in my drinking, passing out was no longer the price but the point. This was after a breakup during my second year in Iowa. Not Daniel. I'd already ended my relationship with Daniel—once it became more ordinary, more stable, more secure, the things I'd told myself I wanted, but couldn't actually stomach—and I'd found the same giddy headlong plunge with someone else, another poet. The relationship itself had been embroidered with drinking memories that were easy to get nostalgic about, especially when I was drunk. We'd driven to a covered bridge outside of town and drunk cold foamy PBRs, eaten a basket of fried cauliflower and dangled our feet over the water. We'd taken a bottle of wine into the cemetery one night and read poems to each other by the meager light of our flip phones. I started showing up in his poems, or wanted to believe I had: "I drink less since I met you," he wrote in one, as if trumping booze was the ultimate compliment. We still drank. He loved when I was drunk, he told me once, because I got as stupid as everyone else. He liked when I said simple things.

I had moved out of the clapboard house on Dodge—because I wanted a place of my own, and in Iowa could afford one. For just under four hundred dollars a month, I was renting a stuffy third-floor studio in an old wooden house: Apartment 7. It was dusty with layers of accumulated heart-swell and epiphany from the other writers who had lived there. It was also dusty because I never cleaned it. I sensed it was the type of place a very old person might die in. The windows were perfectly positioned to admit no cross-breeze during the summer. My oven dial had no numbers, which meant that every baking project was also an exercise in circular geometry and estimation: *325 is...right about there!* I became an expert in banana cream pies, which required no baking at all. I watched movies alone on my black pleather futon, drinking plastic cups of wine. I wasn't accountable to anyone. I loved that I could see a creek from my windows—one of them, anyway, though you had to press yourself against the wall to see it. But still. I loved that the creek had ducks in it. I wrote everyone I knew: *I have ducks*, as if they were mine.

After a few weeks of seeing each other, the poet had started spending every night at my apartment. He put my extra key on his keychain, which I took as prelude to a proposal, telling myself I was a hopeless romantic, sleeping in a vintage Chevy Camaro T-shirt that said BUILT FOR SPEED. But he eventually started to stay out later drinking. The night he told me that he needed space, I excused myself from our conversation and went into my bathroom to pull out a razor and cut myself, three strokes swelling with the old familiar beads of red. He sat in my kitchen on the other side of the wall. Then I put a Band-Aid on my ankle and came back out and said "Fine." He needed space. I was okay with that.

One night I got so restless, waiting for him to come back to my apartment, that I drove to the truck stop at three in the morning. I left him a terse note like a country song: *Couldn't sleep, drove to truck stop.* I was dead sober and nearly insane with anxiety that he was leaving and I couldn't stop him. I wanted to drive for long enough to molt my urgent need. I drank my oil-spotted coffee above the hubcap store, but the drive didn't feel like the old days, the old freedom, because it was so fully contoured by his refusal.

When he finally broke up with me, it was on the stairs of my apartment building, a degraded mise-en-scène: He tried to leave as I buried my face in my arms and begged him to stay. I came up to my apartment and curled up on the floor and cried. The carpet was still filthy. In the middle of my weeping, I actually sneezed.

My problem was simple but insoluble: I didn't want to feel what I was feeling. Then I saw the bottles on my fridge, clustered together like a little village — triple sec and Bacardi and Hawkeye Vodka and Midori. It wasn't exactly God in the clouds, but it was something. It was pragmatic. I wondered: How much till I pass out?

That winter I woke early most mornings and smoked on my fire escape, in the bitter cold. Sometimes I put my boom box in the kitchen window and blasted Tom Petty's froggy voice singing "Don't Come Around Here No More," a song of banishing. I wanted to carve up my ex like cake, like Petty did in his video, slicing Alice in Wonderland into neatly frosted wedges. It was less that I wanted to hurt my ex, and more that I wanted to bring him into me again. We had our first snow and the creek froze solid. I wondered about my ducks: Where would they go?

Each day I woke up and immediately started calculating when I'd start to feel better, knowing it wouldn't be until five, or—maybe, actually—four-thirty, when I let myself open a bottle of wine. It helped that it was winter, and getting dark earlier. That felt like permission. I also liked giving myself a head start at home before I started drinking around other people. If I got a buzz on before I left, it helped me stay more serene at the bar, waiting patiently for everyone else to finish their first or second round, because I was already on my fourth or fifth.

In the meantime I taught two sections of an introductory litera-ture course. When we tried to discuss *Jesus' Son*, I realized Johnson's main character had no name. Because his friends called him Fuck-head, we called him Fuckhead too: *Fuckhead's character arc. Fuckhead's crisis of conscience.* My students loved how strange his world became when he was high. "What is he trying to escape from?" I asked them, then headed home for my evening ritual. I knew that drinking as much as I'd started to drink meant I was taking in hundreds of extra calories, often more than a thousand. So it made sense to compensate by restricting my calories. Eating less also made it easier to get drunk. Two birds, one stone. I wasn't sure why anyone ate before drinking, honestly. It seemed like a waste of the empty-stomach buzz.

If I was eating alone, dinner was always the same. Using one of my four plates, I took two circles of lunch meat (each one thirty calo-ries) and eight Saltines (each one twelve calories) and sliced the circles into four quarters each. Then I placed each of the eight quarters onto one of the eight crackers: open-faced sandwiches. Ever since I'd gone into therapy for my eating disorder, and gained back most of the weight, I'd hovered right around what I thought of as my blood line, the weight that meant I'd get my period. Sometimes I dipped back under it, just to prove to myself that I could. It was like a secret con-versation I was having with my own life. Drinking gave me another way to pronounce how bad I felt, to organize the emotion into a set of actions.

One night I sat in the passenger seat of a friend's car, asking him to tell me I was better-looking than my ex. It was 6 p.m., and I was already drunk. He told me exactly what I wanted to hear, and who can blame him, because how else was he going to get me out of his car? I went upstairs and passed out around sunset.

I told myself the drinking was about my ex, but his absence was just the reason I gave myself. I demanded intensity from everything in my life, even the ducks beyond my window. Their survival carried the weight of epic. By spring, they were back in the creek below, same as ever—no different or better for having survived the winter.

After her first lover left, Rhys said, "I'm finding out what a useful thing drink is." This seemed right to me. Heartbreak wasn't the reason you drank, but it could be an occasion to discover what drinking might do for you.

Rhys's first lover, a man named Lancelot, had called her his kitten. "Kitten," he'd written, "you make my heart ache sometimes." When Rhys got pregnant—by another man, after Lancelot had broken her heart—Lancelot didn't take her back, but he paid for her abortion. He gave her a rose plant and a long-haired Persian cat. Rhys went to the seaside for a week. She put the Persian in a home on Euston Road, and when she came back they told her it was dead. She wept on the top deck of a London bus. She started sleeping fifteen hours a day. "And then it became part of me, so I would have missed it if it had gone," she wrote. "I am talking about sadness." Things had been lost—a man, a kitten, the possibility of a child—but something else was granted: a new vision of her oldest tenant, sadness, something she would have missed *if it had gone*. The conditional tense was full of weary prophecy. It never had; it never would.

"The whole earth had become inhospitable to her," her friend

Francis Wyndham wrote, "after the shock of that humdrum betrayal." Rhys was always getting accused—by other people, by critics, by readers—of making too much of her humdrum hardships. She knew the charge of self-pity, and alternately loathed herself for it and proudly owned it. She once wrote to a friend: "You see I like emotion. I approve of it—in fact am capable of *wallowing* in it." She was the Scheherazade of wallowing. She spun her stories from its excess. She barely survived it. Her novels got so much right about alcoholic drinking: the shut-in quality, the bait and switch, how booze promised freedom but eventually just left her on her knees, retching.

After Lancelot left, Rhys toured with a musical variety show making a circuit through the dreary towns of the Midlands and the north: Wigan, Derby, Wolverhampton, Grimsby. Even their names were predatory, apt. One of the boys in the company drew a sketch of tour life—the gloomy alleys, the lamp-lit rooms—captioned simply "Why We Drink."

But Rhys never needed a *why*, or else she had too many. Lancelot was only the first of many pretexts. "On an extended canvas," said one review of her work, "one becomes more than ever conscious of the unsatisfactoriness of getting drunk as a remedy for every trial and trouble."

Rhys ended up turning her heartbreak into a career. She took the shame of getting dumped by Lancelot—and the ways she wrecked herself in the aftermath—and made these things the subject of her first manuscript, *Voyage in the Dark*. Her heroine, Anna, is mistress to a man named Walter until he doesn't want her anymore. Even then, Anna can't bring herself to hate him. "I'm not miserable," she says. "Only I'd like a drink." The landlady scolds her for leaving her silk eiderdown comforter covered in wine stains.

Anna's life after Walter is full of stained comforters and withered curls of uneaten bacon. It's full of men slipping five quid, ten quid, perhaps a little more into her purse in the middle of the night, after they fuck her, then writing her so they can fuck again, or not writing—it always comes to that, eventually, the not-writing.

When I first read *Voyage in the Dark*, Anna's abjection made me physically ill. Not because I was disgusted by it, but because I recognized it. I watched her stillborn letters fan across the bed: *Dear Walter, Dear Walter, I love you you must love me I love you you must love me.* Drinking and missing men, drinking and missing money, drinking and missing home—all these got tangled together. When she's bleeding out from her illegal abortion, Anna says: "I'd like a drink. There's some gin in the sideboard."

On Christmas Day, 1913—after Lancelot had a tree delivered to her boardinghouse room, months after ending things between them—Rhys decided to drink a whole bottle of gin and then jump out her bedroom window. A friend came over and saw the bottle and asked if she was throwing a party. "Oh no," Rhys said, "not a party exactly." When she shared her plans, her friend said she wouldn't die from jumping; she'd only cripple herself—"and then you'd have to live smashed up."

Rhys didn't jump out the window, but she did drink the gin. And then she bought a notebook and started writing in it. Or at least, that's how she liked to tell the story: that she almost died, but was reborn to write. In truth, she'd kept notebooks before. But perhaps she managed better prose in this one. Perhaps it appealed to her to imagine the writing as her resurrection.

During my winter of Saltine sandwiches, I started sleeping with more men. This was easier when I was drunk. There was the stand-up comic, the tow-truck driver, the man building his own house. Drunk sex became a way of purging feeling, siphoning it off and putting it somewhere else, like collecting the rendered fat off cooked meat and pouring it in a jar, storing it away so it wouldn't clog the drains.

My workshop instructor that last semester found something seriously wrong with almost every student story we discussed, and he could spend an hour dissecting why the language wasn't working. One week he flipped through a whole story trying to find a single phrase he liked. It took me a while to accept that he wasn't an asshole; that he was hard on us because he believed in what our writing could do. He didn't think my first submission did much. But his intelligence had an integrity and precision that made me hungry for his praise. Not getting it only sharpened the hunger.

Outside the classroom, I'd met an older man who lived outside of town. I'd show up at his big house, with its oven dial full of actual numbers, and cook him chicken stir-fry, the only dish I knew how to make. We'd get drunk — or I'd get drunk. I actually have no idea if he got drunk. We'd have sex and afterward I'd put on one of his basketball jerseys and go cry in the bathroom. At the time, I felt sorry for myself. Now I look back and feel sorry for him, with this girl showing up at his place to cook her rubbery chicken and demanding his compliments in return, then sobbing in his bathroom, clearly wanting *something* from him, but what? Neither one of us knew.

After a few weeks, he told me over dinner one night that he couldn't taste any of the food I was cooking. He wasn't being figurative. He had no taste buds. It was a condition he'd had since birth. Somehow this seemed sad to me — not just that he couldn't taste anything, but that I'd been making these meals without knowing he couldn't taste them. Whatever we were doing, we weren't doing it together. My desire to be wanted was like something physically gushing out of me — *need need need* — and it disgusted me, this broken spigot I'd become. A man telling me he wanted to fuck me, whispering it into my ear, it was like taking the first sip of whiskey, that hit of warmth, straight to my gut. The beginning was usually better than what followed: the cotton-mouthed morning, the strange bed, sweat on the sheets.

I tried to live better. I tried yoga. I got a little houseplant, and by coincidence my friend got me another little houseplant, and so I decided to throw a little party about it. Maybe we would drink. One of my plants, a weeping ficus, hung in my kitchen above the other one, a little fern. I named them both after an Andrew Marvell poem: "Annihilating all that's made / to a green thought, in a green shade." The big plant was Marvell, the little one the Annihilator. I decided my party would be green. Everything would be a green thought in a green shade. This meant lime Jell-O shots, pistachio cookies with food coloring, celery, spinach hummus, and someone else's pot. I made my Jell-O shots in the morning and couldn't open my liter of vodka because I'd gotten the cheapest kind and the cap was messed up. I had to run to the corner store as fast as I could—my Jell-O was cooling by the minute!—and demand vodka at eight in the morning.

I got my Jell-O shots made, but they were too strong. It was too hot in my kitchen, with too many bodies packed together. Nobody was as amused by the name "the Annihilator" as I'd thought they would be. One friend had just spent the previous night in jail for a drunk-driving arrest. She was teary in the corner. Another friend smoked too much pot and ended up fainting on my kitchen floor. My home seemed toxic, like you could catch something—a state of frailty, or an absurd despair—just from spending time in it.

Several months after the breakup, my friends started to ask me— gently, kindly—why I was still talking about it so much. Why was I taking it so hard? Honestly, I wasn't sure. Rejection was a worm that kept burrowing into me, my own humdrum betrayal, and I kept trying to dig it out by getting to the bottom of why I hadn't been good enough for him. I started seeing a therapist at student services, as an experiment. He had an accent that made it hard to understand some of his similes. "Love is like a toaster," he told me. "It comes and destroys everything."

I thought, *No, love is Tom Petty on a boom box.* I imagined the burnt bread heels of my toasted heart. It turned out the therapist meant *twister,* not *toaster,* and that spring there actually was one. An actual tornado flipped the whole roof off a sorority house. It tore off leafy branches and flipped cars into tree trunks. It tossed the shed from my backyard into the creek. I kept my fingers crossed for the ducks. *My* ducks. This was Iowa, a pathetic fallacy writ large: You spoke of love and its metaphors came alive; they spun the air all around you.

I decided to write a story about the breakup, because it was all I could think about. But a breakup story seemed like artistic suicide, and I could already picture my workshop instructor flipping through it in class, pointing out my trite articulations of heartbreak. I wrote the story anyway, but I took care to make my heartbreak more dramatic. My main character smashed a glass of wine against her fridge, and then licked all the red trails of Shiraz running down its beige door. I'd only ever drunk my wine from water glasses and plastic cups, but the shattered glass and licked trails of crimson seemed like more artful articulations of ache than my own redundant glugging.

The day of my workshop, our instructor said: "The only thing wrong with this story is that it doesn't have any page numbers." It was the only thing I wrote at Iowa that anyone really liked, and it confirmed my hunch: Things got dark, and you wrote from that darkness. Heartbreak could become the beginning of a career.

I wasn't good at taking care of myself then, myself or my weeping ficus, which withered to a crisp in the heat of July. I put it out on the fire escape so I wouldn't have to look at it dying. I wanted to believe that this new type of drinking I'd been doing, drinking intentionally and explicitly and self-consciously toward passing out, was introducing me to a part of myself I'd never known before—that I was fumbling to learn its shape, like an object under murky water. *In vino veritas* was one of the most appealing promises of drinking: that it wasn't degradation but illumination, that it wasn't obscuring truth but unveiling it. If that was true, then my truth was passing out partway through the romantic comedies I watched alone at night, before the booze took me under.

—III—

BLAME

E very addiction story wants a villain. But America has never been able to decide whether addicts are victims or criminals, whether addiction is an illness or a crime. So we relieve the pressure of cognitive dissonance with various divisions of psychic labor — some addicts get pitied, others get blamed — that keep overlapping and evolving to suit our purposes: Alcoholics are tortured geniuses. Drug addicts are deviant zombies. Male drunks are thrilling. Female drunks are bad moms. White addicts get their suffering witnessed. Addicts of color get punished. Celebrity addicts get posh rehab with equine therapy. Poor addicts get hard time. Someone carrying crack gets five years in prison, while someone driving drunk gets a night in jail, even though drunk driving kills more people every year than cocaine. In her seminal account of mass incarceration, *The New Jim Crow*, legal scholar Michelle Alexander points out that many of these biases tell a much larger story about "who is viewed as disposable — someone to be purged from the body politic — and who is not." They aren't incidental discrepancies — between black and white addicts, drinkers and drug users — but casualties of our need to vilify some people under the guise of protecting others.

"What do we hold against the drug addict?" asks theorist Avital Ronell, and answers with a quote from Jacques Derrida: "That he cuts himself off from the world, in exile from reality, far from objective reality and the real life of the city and the community; that he escapes into a world of simulacrum and fiction....We cannot abide the fact that his is a pleasure taken in an experience without truth." This vision of the addict, as an agent of betrayal, undermining the shared social project, has been an enduring character in what criminologist Drew Humphries calls the drug-scare narrative. It's a classic

American genre that singles out a particular substance as cause for alarm—often arbitrarily, without an increase in use—to scapegoat a marginal community. It happened with Chinese immigrants and opium in nineteenth-century California; with black cocaine use in the early-twentieth-century South; with Mexicans and marijuana in the 1930s; with black heroin use in the 1950s; with the inner-city crack epidemic of the 1980s; with the rise of meth in poor white communities at the turn of the twenty-first century. Meth was called "the most malignant, addictive drug known to mankind." Barns across America showed graffiti as prophecy scrawled across their peeling paint, METH IS DEATH. Posters and commercials showed ghouls who were strung out, rake-thin, yellow-fanged, picking at their facial sores and neglecting their babies. But by the time a 2005 *Newsweek* cover story called meth "America's New Drug Crisis," meth use had been declining for years.

Calling the drug-scare narrative a toxic genre isn't a denial of the damage drugs can cause, or the devastation addiction leaves in its wake, only an acknowledgment of the ways that "addiction" has always been two things at once: a set of disrupted neurotransmitters and a series of stories we've told about disruption. Addiction becomes a contagious epidemic, a willful abnegation of civic duty, a valiant rebellion against the social order, or the noble outcry of a tortured soul. It depends on who is doing the telling, and the using. Columbia University neuroscientist Carl Hart writes about the drug story that *hasn't* gotten much airtime, the "not particularly exciting nonaddiction story that never gets told," which—as Hart reminds us—is the experience of most drug users. Yet addiction has been presented as both inevitable and unilaterally devastating in order to serve various social agendas—most notably, the War on Drugs.

The twentieth-century American crusade against drugs was effectively launched by a man named Harry Anslinger, who took over the Federal Bureau of Narcotics in 1930, just as Prohibition was starting to fall apart. Anslinger effectively channeled the punitive impulse that had fueled Prohibition—the impulse to see addiction in terms of weakness, selfishness, failure, and danger—and redirected it toward narcotics. It wasn't just a metaphoric connection or a psychic sublimation: Anslinger's Bureau of Narcotics physically took over the same grim offices that the Prohibition Agency itself had occupied.

But during the decades that followed, the American legal system would polarize alcohol and drug addictions into separate categories in the public imagination: the former a disease, the latter a crime. It can be tempting to equate "hard" drugs with addiction, or booze with recreational use, but in truth the distinction between them is mainly grounded in social norms and legal practice; and it hasn't always been this way.

Before the Harrison Narcotics Tax Act of 1914, which regulated and taxed the distribution of opiates and cocaine, you could easily order drug works from the Sears, Roebuck catalog, a syringe and cocaine package deal for $1.50, or buy Mrs. Winslow's Soothing Syrup, made with morphine, from your local pharmacy. By the 1950s, however, Anslinger was describing the majority of heroin addicts as "psychopaths" who were "created by infectious contact with persons already drug-conditioned." *What do we hold against the drug addict?* Anslinger's language of contagion synthesized competing notions of disease and vice, imagining the addict as a morally culpable patient zero. It resurrected rhetoric he'd used when he'd worked in the Bahamas during Prohibition, urging the Navy to round up bootleggers and smugglers by claiming they carried "loathsome and contagious diseases" that would infect the people who drank their booze. Anslinger understood himself as a moral crusader but dressed like a mafia tough guy, the same guys his policies kept in business, wearing shiny suits and ties printed with Chinese pagodas. He struggled in the early years of his crusade to keep his agency afloat, and after his funding was nearly cut in half in the mid-thirties, he was hospitalized for a nervous breakdown in 1935.

This was the same year he oversaw the introduction of a radical new step in American drug legislation: the Narcotic Farm, a federal facility for addicts that opened outside Lexington, Kentucky, in May of that year. Part prison, part hospital, jointly administered by the Bureau of Prisons and the Public Health Service, the Narco Farm was the institutional embodiment of America's ambivalent relationship to addiction. (It was also a working dairy farm, the source of its nickname; although more than one administrator worried that it would be mistaken for a facility that actually grew opium.) At any given time, roughly two-thirds of the fifteen hundred "patients" at Lexington were prisoners who had been convicted of violating federal drug laws, and the other third were volunteers seeking treatment—though often these "volunteers" had been in trouble with the law themselves, and were seeking an alternative to legal punishment. If addiction was both vice and disease, then residents at the Narco Farm were both prisoners and patients: "vols" and "cons." They were being simultaneously punished and rehabilitated.

By the time the Narco Farm opened, in 1935, America didn't know what story to believe about addiction—whether to punish it or heal it—and everything about the Narco Farm reflected this confusion: the names it was called, the press coverage it got, how it was run, even how it was built. It had towering walls and barred windows like a prison, but it was also full of day rooms with huge windows overlooking the rolling green hills of Kentucky, and its vaulted ceilings and soaring arches suggested something more religious, like a monastery—the architecture of possible salvation.

Harry Anslinger wasn't just a policy maker, he was a storyteller. But most of his addiction stories didn't get to the part about redemption; they were just stories about deviance—meant to inspire fear and to justify punishment. In his case for "making war on the narcotic addict," Anslinger was fond of quoting a Los Angeles police officer: "I feel that these people are in the same category as lepers, and that the only defense society has against them is segregation and isolation whenever possible."

After Anslinger's budget was slashed, his fearmongering became more urgent. He spent the rest of the thirties creating a reason for his agency to matter by drumming up public anxiety about drugs, and he ruthlessly exploited racial fears in his campaigns. Arguing that marijuana unleashed black male lust for white women, he gave the House Committee on Appropriations a speech about "colored students" partying with white coeds "and getting their sympathy with stories of racial persecution. Result: pregnancy."

Racial paranoia has been part of American drug-scare narratives as long as they've been told, even though the majority of drug users have always been white. Even before Anslinger, this paranoia fueled public support for the Harrison Act. NEGRO COCAINE "FIENDS" NEW SOUTHERN MENACE ran a *New York Times* headline in 1914, and similar articles spread the myth of the black "fiend" as an almost supernatural enemy. In 1914, a *Literary Digest* article claimed that "most of the attacks upon white women of the South are the direct result of a cocaine-crazed Negro brain."

In 1953, Anslinger published a book called *The Traffic in Narcotics*, a manifesto defending the drug war he'd spent the last two decades waging. It was also meant to pave the way for legislation he supported: the Narcotic Control Act of 1956 mandated minimum sentences for distribution—five years for a first offense, ten years for a second one—and expanded the provisions of the Boggs Act of 1951, which allowed the death penalty for selling heroin.

Later that decade, James Baldwin published "Sonny's Blues," a short story that dramatizes the fact that every addiction lives at the intersection between public and private experience. It's a story about trying to understand addiction from the outside, and it focuses on the relationship between two brothers, both black men raised in Harlem: a schoolteacher trying to parse his jazz-musician brother's inscrutable dependence. In Baldwin's account, addiction is both social and interior. Though heroin is part of the reality of being black—in Harlem, in the middle of the twentieth century—it's also part of a deeply individual inner conflict. Sonny struggles with the junk that brings him bliss—that feels like a woman singing in his veins—but also traps him alone "at the bottom of something" that is often unbearable.

Anslinger's *Traffic in Narcotics*, published just four years earlier, advertised itself as "the first book to treat with authority the horrifying national problem of drug addiction," but its posture was precisely the opposite of Baldwin's: Instead of respecting the contradictions and depth of any addict's consciousness, it created cartoon villains who would be easy to justify locking away. The book's flap copy insisted that it had been written "not to satisfy a desire for morbid sensationalism but as a basic description of the current situation." Its mission was simply to "guide and implement the national desire to strike at the roots of a disturbing menace, a source of crime and wrecker of young lives."

No "sensationalism" here, only the wreckage of young lives. Anslinger was just going to tell you about the marijuana fiend who raped a nine-year-old, and the one who killed a widow, the one who "brutally attacked" sixteen women to steal the money "to buy wine and reefers which he consumed at the same time." You can almost hear the hysteria: *At the same time!* Anslinger was not going to "satisfy a desire for morbid sensationalism," but he did want you to know that when judges dished out discretionary "vacations" instead of doling out real hard time, bad things happened. Case in point: the marijuana dealer who was fined only twenty-five dollars for possession of "17,000 grains of marihuana," and the next year raped a ten-year-old girl "while under marihuana intoxication."

Anslinger described his book as a "long-awaited reliable survey," suggesting that he was refusing to pander to the rising tide of drug panic, but the syntax was a sleight of hand. He'd spent much of the last two decades stoking the flames of this panic in order to generate support for his floundering federal agency. The most toxic agendas often disguise themselves as pure transcription.

In his manifesto, Anslinger insists he doesn't like to generalize. He just observes that addicts want to be shielded from the world. While "normal people" feel no need to rise above their "usual emotional plane," addicts are invariably greedy for more and more pleasure. Anslinger's accusations summon Derrida's argument that we resent the addict for taking pleasure "in an experience without truth."

Six years after *The Traffic in Narcotics*, William Burroughs would write that "the face of 'evil' is always the face of total need," but Anslinger was busy reconfiguring the face of total need as evil. His concept of illness was selective and self-serving: He called addicts infectious, but dismissed anyone who called them sick.

Blueschild Baby—an autobiographical novel about a heroin addict named George Cain, by an author (and heroin addict) named George Cain—was published in 1970, nearly two decades after Anslinger's manifesto, but still bears the residue of Anslinger's punitive campaigns. The novel turns on a powerful scene of shaming—when George goes to see a doctor for help in kicking his habit, and gets treated like a criminal—that asks the same question: Are addicts sick?

It's not incidental that George is a black man. He's also fresh from prison, where he was serving time for possession, but by the end of the novel he's deep in the throes of withdrawal. Even his vomit shows signs of struggle: "Live things, frogs and insects kick in the liquid coming out." When George's girlfriend, Nandy, suggests that he see a doctor, George knows better. He tells her, "A doctor won't help." And sure enough, as soon as George tells the doctor he's a drug addict, the doctor immediately proves him right. He backs up from his desk and draws a pistol.

The scene doesn't unfold as a conflict between men so much as a conflict between narratives of addiction that don't agree. George and Nandy insist on addiction as a disease—"He's a sick man. You're a doctor," says Nandy, and George insists, "I'm sick, in pain like anybody else that comes to you"—but the doctor and his gun won't surrender the narrative of addiction as vice: "Get out of my office before I call the police."

I am precisely the kind of nice upper-middle-class white girl whose relationship to substances has been treated as benign or pitiable—a cause for concern, or a shrug, rather than punishment. No one has ever called me a leper or a psychopath. No doctor has ever pointed a gun at me. No cop has ever shot me at an intersection while I was reaching for my wallet, for that matter, or even pulled me over for drunk driving, something I've done more times than I could count. My skin is the right color to permit my intoxication. When it comes to addiction, the abstraction of privilege is ultimately a question of what type of story gets told about your body: Do you need to be shielded from harm, or prevented from causing it? My body has been understood as something to be protected, rather than something to be protected from.

In her memoir, *Negroland*, Margo Jefferson describes the ways black women in America have been "denied the privilege of freely yielding to depression, of flaunting neurosis as a mark of social and psychic complexity." That is a luxury available to white women. It's been "glorified in the literature of white female suffering."

It took me years to understand that my interior had never been interior—that my relationship to my own pain, a relationship that felt essentially private, was not private at all. It owed its existence to narratives that made it very possible for a white girl to hurt: stories that suggested her pain was interesting; that it was proof of vulnerability rather than guilt, worthy of sympathy rather than punishment.

When I started to drink, to *really* drink, to become conscious of my drinking not just in terms of pleasure but escape, I was ashamed, but also proud. My urgent attempts to disappear from myself suggested there was something dark and important—depression, neurosis, psychic complexity—that required disappearing *from*. It wasn't that I slipped on pain as a garment. It was more that I tried to understand the pain as psychic compost, something with an aesthetic purpose. I wanted it to complicate and deepen me.

I did most of my unpunished drunk driving in California, during the winter after I graduated from the Writers' Workshop, when I lived with my grandmother—Dell, my father's mother—in her sun-struck home at the top of a hill, the house my family and I had lived in for much of my childhood. I was trying to write a novel. She was dying.

During those months, I stayed in a bare room without much furniture to speak of. I lived for the relief of drinking alone on my futon mattress, after night shifts as an innkeeper at a bed-and-breakfast by the ocean, a ten-minute drive away, and often drank at work, in secret, then drove home tipsy—always anxious—to drink more, back in my room, where I didn't have to worry about anything.

Each day, I woke as early as I could and smoked on a little wooden balcony. The days were perfect blue skies and sun, eerily identical, and every day I grimed the salt air with puffs of smoke; left tiny gray piles of crumbled ash on the slats of wind-scoured wood. My fingers yellowed. I made Dell oatmeal and sat with her while she ate it, resenting this time because I wanted to be writing, and feeling guilty about my resentment because I wanted to be someone who didn't feel it.

Dell had been a constant presence through my childhood, had lived with my family for years—a generous, resourceful, steely-nerved, and intensely loyal woman who loved us fiercely, me and my brothers, who'd raised two manic-depressive daughters and survived her marriage to an alcoholic husband, who'd left the Daughters of the American Revolution because she didn't agree with their politics. My favorite memories of Dell, though, were of little things: our weekly bridge lessons, with every trick carefully observed by the porcelain mice on her bookshelves. She always warned against the dangers of bidding too high, but bid aggressively in practice. We played for nickels and dimes in the pot. I loved Dell, respected her stoicism and her selflessness and remembered all the ways she'd cared for me— wanted to return that care, but felt overwhelmed by what she needed, and hated to see her need so much.

My brother and sister-in-law were also living with Dell, and I kept my empty bottles away from our communal recycling, in a separate plastic bag in my closet, so they wouldn't see how many I'd accumulated. Dell was falling more frequently, sometimes falling asleep on the couch beside a cooling patch of spilled coffee. She was mixing up her pills, and I didn't even know what pills she was on. I was terrified for her, and for myself. How was I supposed to take care of her? There was a photo of us I loved in her bedroom, her holding me in her arms when I was a baby. She looked so happy, so utterly capable. In those winter months, she almost never complained about pain, or her decreasing mobility. By contrast, with little to complain about, I was animated by self-pity like toxic electricity.

We eventually installed something called a Lifeline medical alert system, a direct phone line Dell could activate—if she fell—using a button that hung around her neck. Sometimes I would come home to find she had fallen in her bathroom, or that she was bleeding on the carpet with spilled chicken soup hardening beside her. One morning I found the machine beeping in the corner, a voice on the other end of the line asking, "Are you okay?" And then I tried to talk to it: "I'm here," I said, and the voice asked: "Are you the caregiver?" And I honestly didn't know what to say. I was, and I wasn't. I was trying to help Dell change out of her bathrobe, because it was soaked in coffee, and I was crying, and Dell was asking me why I was crying, and I was trying to pretend I wasn't crying, and I was picturing that photograph, me as a baby in her arms, and now the voice was asking: "Is this the caregiving situation?" It was like some distant, useless god was living in that machine and judging us.

Is this the caregiving situation? My brother and sister-in-law and I were doing what we could. It clearly wasn't enough. My father and my aunt, both passionately devoted to their mother, were calling every day, but they both lived on the other side of the country. Intellectually, I knew it wasn't my job to keep her from dying, but it still felt like what I was supposed to do.

Sometimes my sister-in-law and I went to the grocery store and loaded our shopping cart with sweet things—boxed coffee cake, mint chocolate chip ice cream, pink champagne—and binged on it all, just for the relief and escape of total indulgence, putting things into our bodies to remind ourselves we weren't anywhere near dying. My life with food was a boom-bust cycle, composed of succumbing to fits of indulgence and then compensating by eating very little for days. It was still easier to eat when I was drunk. One night when I was sick we rented *Legends of the Fall* and I took a shot of liquid Benadryl and passed out after three paper cups of cheap pink champagne, curled into the couch. Staying awake meant unimaginable exhaustion. I fell asleep with Brad Pitt's long hair swinging like a curtain between one state of consciousness and the next.

In those days, I tutored students who went to the same high school I'd attended. Their parents were impressed by my credentials, and slightly dismayed by the life these credentials had secured for me—full of days spent tutoring their children. After tutoring, I drove to the bed-and-breakfast and showed guests to their rooms: suites with tasseled curtains and floral patterns and Jacuzzis. When they made their reservations over the phone, married women often said, "We need a king bed," and you knew they meant it. I also imagined *being* all the guests that I checked in, with longing or schadenfreude, as I carried their luggage and wormed my way into the inner lives I had constructed for them, cheating on their spouses, or else—miraculously—still loving them, with a full or partial ocean view as backdrop to their love.

Every evening I put out wine and cheese for the guests, and after it got quiet enough, I put out wine and cheese for myself. I never thought of this as *drinking on the job*, although strictly speaking—or really any way of speaking—it was. I drank carefully, usually, enough to get a good buzz but not so much that I'd show it, or mess up the nightly credit card batch; not so much that I'd lose my specially cultivated innkeeper serenity when guests came into the kitchen to make small talk. I imagined myself blurting out, *At home my grandma fell down again*, saying, *Pull up a chair.* I ate little cheese cubes on crackers to soak up the excess booze inside me, or dug a spoon into the bowl of cookie dough in the fridge and ate it like yogurt. I usually left with an extra bottle or two from the pantry, tucked into my purse, walking out gingerly so they wouldn't clank together. Sometimes I tucked a sweater between them. The great secret of evening wine and cheese was that the guests could drink half a bottle of Chardonnay or three, who would know? I had a margin.

Driving home every night in my red Dodge Neon, a thousand-dollar buy with a ragged stick shift, I was especially anxious about the stop sign on the steep hill just behind the inn. I always revved the engine when I pulled off the clutch, perpetually scared that my revving would draw the cops from secret perches in the darkness. Even on the flat stretches, I drove slowly—no doubt suspiciously so—jerking and wrenching as I toggled between gears.

Once I got home, I would go up to my little bedroom and drink one of the bottles I'd stolen from work. I didn't care that the wine wasn't chilled. When you're drinking cheap Chardonnay called Two-Buck Chuck—and drinking it alone, on a futon mattress, Googling people from high school and scanning the real estate firms they work for—it turns out temperature isn't the point. On that futon mattress, drinking tepid wine, it was impossible to deny that getting drunk was the point, just like it had always been the point.

During those California days, I still nursed a certain romantic notion of myself as a lonely writer, drinking heavily but waking every morning to write my novel—not *but*, actually, something more like *and*, something more like *because*. My nights of lonely drinking were part of the same psychic descent that was producing the grim novel I was starting to imagine, about a lonely young woman taking care of her dying grandmother. It didn't have a plot beyond that.

This wasn't exactly the romance of the white logic, Jack London's myth of the drunk prophet and his truth serum of booze. I was living with my grandmother and my brother and my sister-in-law, barely supporting myself with two jobs, ducking like a coward out of my meager responsibilities; passing out on pink champagne and cold medicine, a long-haired Brad Pitt haunting my strange dreams. This life wasn't backyard parties with bratwurst on the grill and lights in the trees; it wasn't drinking with other drunk writers at bar tables carved up with the initials of more famous drunk writers. This was just a futon and a bottle of room-temperature Chardonnay. Sometimes I poured the wine and sometimes I didn't. The glass had started to seem like little more than a contrivance.

In 1944, a novel came along that rejected the white logic entirely. Charles Jackson's *The Lost Weekend* refused the idea of drinking as metaphysical portal. In the novel, alcoholism isn't particularly meaningful, it just *is*. The plot moves roughly like this: A guy named Don Birnam gets drunk. He's gotten drunk before and he'll get drunk again. He drinks, passes out, wakes up. He keeps drinking till he runs out of money, then he finds some more money and picks up where he left off. At one point he tries to pawn his typewriter for cash, and walks almost a hundred blocks before realizing all the pawnshops are closed for Yom Kippur. Another time he steals a woman's purse to see if he can get away with it. He doesn't.

That's pretty much the whole story: drinking, and then more of it. As critic John Crowley has observed, the novel was revolutionary in its unrelenting simplicity and redundancy—its rejection of an abiding mythos. Don Birnam wasn't a new type of protagonist because he was a drunk. He was a new type of protagonist because his drunkenness marked him as a man with a disease rather than an existential albatross around his neck. Don isn't broken by the fallen world, or the horrors of war, or the cruelties of love, like Ernest Hemingway's drunken specimens of masculinity, or William Faulkner's wasted southern patriarchs, or F. Scott Fitzgerald's prodigal patrician husbands. Don is just dependent on a particular physical substance. His drinking is pathetic and repetitive. It doesn't deliver him into the subtle clutches of metaphysical angst, it simply means he makes a fool of himself all over midtown Manhattan.

Published when Jackson was forty-one years old, eight years after he got sober (for the first time) in 1936, *The Lost Weekend* was an immediate bestseller. It ended up selling almost a million copies over the course of Jackson's lifetime. The *New York Times* called it "the most compelling gift to the literature of addiction since De Quincey," and argued that it could be a "textbook for such organizations as Alcoholics Anonymous," an organization that—at that point—Jackson despised.

When he was drafting the novel in 1942, Jackson wrote to a psychiatrist at New York's Bellevue Hospital, Dr. Stephen Sherman, to request permission to visit his alcoholic ward for research purposes. Jackson had been there himself as a patient, but—not surprisingly—couldn't remember much. He also sent Dr. Sherman his first few chapters, looking for feedback, or probably just affirmation. Dr. Sherman thought the novel "should have definite clinical value," and said it had taught him "more about what the alcoholic is really thinking" than most of his patients, especially in its evocation of loneliness and an "identification with forlorn genius."

In the novel, Don has big plans to write the story of his life. "If he were able to write fast enough," he thinks—and, presumably, keep his typewriter out of pawn—then "he could set it down in all its final perfection." But the titles Don imagines for his book suggest his insecurities: "Don Birnam: A Hero Without a Novel" or "I Don't Know Why I'm Telling You All This." He wonders why anyone would be interested in the story of his life: "Who would ever want to read a novel about a punk and a drunk!" The joke is clearly on us, his readers, who are doing exactly what Don can't imagine anyone wanting to do: reading a novel about a punk and a drunk, a would-be writer who can't summon enough sobriety to tell the story of his own intoxication.

Don helpfully catalogs all the aesthetic failures of his own story: It has no climax or closure. It holds no emotional suspense. He already knows how he will feel after the first drink and after the tenth, how he will feel after he wakes up hungover the next morning, because he has already felt all these ways before. During a particularly embarrassing "climactic moment" near the end of the book, Don finds himself facing off against a maid, trying to get her to unlock the liquor cabinet, and is overwhelmed by a distinctly literary moment of self-loathing: "Melodrama! In all his life he had never been in any situation so corny, so ham. He felt like an idiot. His taste was offended, his sense of the fitness of things, his deepest intelligence."

I Don't Know Why I'm Telling You All This: Jackson was ashamed of his own story as he wrote it, and he outsourced that shame to his protagonist. Don is ashamed not simply of his actions but of his *genre*, the fact that his own drinking doesn't amount to anything compelling: "It wasn't even decently dramatic or sad or tragic or a shame or comic or ironic or anything else—it was nothing."

One afternoon when I was nine, and my father was forty-nine, I asked him about drinking. Why did people drink? Why did some people do it so much? We were standing in my parents' bedroom. The huge glass windows were hot with sunlight, the sky blue and shameless beyond.

I can still remember where my father was standing, as he closed the rolling cedar door of his closet, wheels squeaking in their tracks;

and I can remember his creased khaki slacks, the cloud of intensity and distraction he moved through like a private weather system. I remember these details as if they were seared into me, saying, *Pay attention*, saying, *Listen up.* Listen to what?

A single moment: That day, my father told me drinking wasn't wrong, but it was dangerous. It wasn't dangerous for everyone, but it was dangerous for us.

It was thrilling to share any type of *us* with my father, who was a magical figure to me. There was always some part of him that was elsewhere. Every few weeks my family had "calendar sessions," nights of curt tones, explanations, bargaining, when my father drew his work trips as color-coded blue and purple lines across the grid of days on a dry-erase whiteboard calendar. Sometimes he joked that he wanted a color to mark the trips he *hadn't* taken. He had grown up moving constantly, as an Air Force brat—to Japan, California, Maryland—son of an alcoholic pilot. As an adult, my father was part of all the frequent-flier clubs named after precious stones and metals. He was the mileage king.

He was an economist working on health policy in the developing world, and his work took him to Thailand, Switzerland, Rwanda, India, Kenya, Burma, Mexico, distant places where he met with other influential people—always men, I imagined—to figure out how to spend money most efficiently to *alleviate global disease burden*, a phrase I learned young. The things he was interested in talking about always seemed to involve things I didn't know. What did I know about? Hopi kachinas, and Mark Twain's real name. Whenever my father praised my intelligence, it was like a bread crumb in the forest. If I could just keep doing that, he'd keep paying attention.

I listened hard, to show him that I was a good student, absorbing everything he was telling me. He told me about the Concorde, which went faster than the speed of sound; how your pee went backward if you went to the bathroom while it was decelerating. He had seen places I couldn't imagine. He once told me about an acid trip he'd taken that was the first time he'd ever believed it might be okay to die. He loved amaretto cookies and good Burgundy. He played tennis in striped sweatbands. His laugh was everything. He brought me miniature shampoos from all the hotels—an apology paid against the ledger tally of his absence, all those lines on the whiteboard calendar. Years later, I would learn about his affairs. He was often cheating, even on his mistresses—driven not by malice, never that, only a certain restlessness.

When I was young, six or seven, my dad gave me a stuffed tiger named Winifred. He chose her name, which was much better than if I'd named her myself. It was like he'd embedded a piece of himself right in her plush stripes. When he went away on trips, Winifred stayed. When he returned, he told me stories about the adventures she'd had, wherever he'd been: If he'd been to Bangkok, she'd had adventures in the jungle. If he'd been to China, she'd had adventures in the Gobi Desert. I don't remember how I squared the logic of these tales—how Winifred's body stayed behind, while another version of her lived a gossamer life beyond my reach—but I imagine it was comforting to consider the possibilities of a split self: how a person's heart or mind might stay at home, while the body traveled elsewhere.

My father loved to tell a story about seeing me as a newborn, in the hospital hallway, and I loved to hear him tell it: how he'd looked into my eyes, under my pink beanie, and seen something piercing in my gaze—a curiosity he'd loved from the start. It signified some primal bond that lay between us. The few times I stayed alone with him, when my mother went out of town for work, all we ate was ramen and popcorn and milk shakes. It was divine. It was our secret, another bond sealed—like when he said drinking was dangerous for *us*, including me in the same danger.

When I was nine, he moved across the country for eighteen months, for work, and when he moved back to Los Angeles, my parents separated officially. This was the same window of years when my brothers—nine and ten years older—moved to college. In only a few years, we went from a family of five to a family of two: just my mom and me. The men were gone. After my second brother left for college, I drew a picture of myself crying in his bedroom, because I missed him so much. I even gave it a title: *Jealous Sorrow*. Certain truths had turned transparent as glass, because they were so ingrained: People would probably leave, it was just a question of when. Attention was something I had to earn, not something I could take for granted. I had to seduce at all moments.

My brothers were witty and kind but also a tough crowd, smart and reserved—not willing to give up their laughter or praise for just anything. (My oldest brother, Julian, taught me how to solve an equation for x when I was seven. "Great," he said, "but can you solve when x is on *both* sides?") I loved my brothers wildly, extravagantly. Loving them was like flinging myself against something—as I often flung myself at their tall bodies to hug them, demanding their love with the sheer force of my hurtling forty-pound body. I was always loved, but I always wondered, also, what that love depended on. It did not seem unconditional. I wondered what I had to do to keep deserving it. I can't remember a time when I wasn't trying to figure out what to say at the dinner table, especially on French nights—when everyone was practicing a language I didn't speak.

After my parents divorced, when I was eleven, my father got an apartment overlooking a grove of eucalyptus trees. Maybe once a year I spent the night, scouring the fridge for things to pack in my school lunches: a half-drunk bottle of mineral water, leftover sushi with a torn packet of soy sauce jammed underneath. In those days, I didn't know how to talk to my dad, so I stared blank-faced at a TV while he asked me why I was getting a B minus in World Cultures on my midterm progress report. I craved his approval like I craved perfect grades, perfect test scores, or I craved these things like I craved his approval. Getting good grades was the natural extension of being a little girl trying to figure out the next right thing to say at the dinner table. I was alternately stone-faced and sarcastic in those days of early adolescence—shy at school, convinced I smelled bad, that I loomed like a giraffe—and quiet with my father. I couldn't ask for what I wanted then because I didn't know I wanted it. Loving him was always like reaching for something luminous. Reaching was what love felt like.

My father's love was always there—in a tiger, in milk shakes, in his gaze, in his laugh—but I was most sharply aware of his care when my own body was in danger. When he visited me during the year of my eating disorder, in college, he left me with hundreds of pages of photocopied academic-journal articles about anorexia. He fixed me in the full glare of his concern.

I remember a particular moment between us as strangely sublime: It was just before my jaw surgery, after freshman year of college, when I was headed into six hours in the OR, lying under a heated hospital blanket, giddy from the pre-anesthesia laughing gas, Valium making me feel tucked in like a soft quilt. My dad watched as they wheeled me away on the gurney, his eyes glistening with tears, and I wanted to tell him—from the comfort of my laughing gas, my Valium perch—that everything would be okay.

If drinking was dangerous for us, I came to learn that drinking had been particularly dangerous for one of us: my aunt Phyllis. Phyllis was my father's middle sister, a woman I had never met. The history of her estrangement from our family had been explained to me vaguely, a blurry story, but as I grew older, her distance from the family was always described in terms of drinking and mental illness, like twin knobs bringing the microscope slide into focus. Phyllis had started fights. She'd slapped my grandmother. She'd once chased someone with a knife.

As a girl, I was obsessed with Phyllis—with the fact of her distance and the mystery of its cause, with questions about what she had been like before and what she was like now. My father wasn't even sure where she lived. I begged for the most recent address we had, and sent her hopeful letters—*Hi, I'm your niece!*—that never got a reply. As I grew older, I began to identify with Phyllis, or with the ghostly shape of her absence, for no logical reason I could name, except that she'd clearly been someone who had trouble living in the world as she was supposed to live in it. I always lived in the world as I was supposed to live in it, but I sensed there was an animal in me— beneath all that obedient living—some part of me that wanted to do what she had done: start fights, make scenes, fall apart.

When I was young, I turned Phyllis into a romantic hero— blaming her estrangement on my family, imagining her all alone somewhere out there, in exile—but as I got older I realized it had been more complicated, that you can commit yourself to a troubled person, over and over again, and it might never be enough.

Back in my childhood home, watching my grandmother die, I kept imagining Phyllis: Where was she? Did she miss her mother, wherever she was? How could she not? My drinking didn't look like her drinking had, but I wondered if there were blueprints inside both of us that weren't so different. When I went outside to smoke each morning, I passed the closet door where I could still picture my father standing, saying: *Drinking isn't dangerous for everyone, but it's dangerous for us.*

Addiction has always been more dangerous for some people than for others. When Nixon launched the original War on Drugs in June 1971, he called drugs "public enemy number one." But it was actual human beings who were imprisoned.

Blueschild Baby—George Cain's novel, published just a year earlier—had effectively predicted Nixon's war before it officially began: "They say you're arrested for crime, narcotics, prostitution, robbery, murder," George thinks in the novel, "but these are not the reasons for locking you away." In an interview decades later, Nixon's domestic policy chief, John Ehrlichman, confessed precisely this: "Did we know we were lying about the drugs? Of course we did." He said the Nixon administration couldn't make it illegal to be black, but they could link the black community to heroin: "We could arrest their leaders, raid their homes, break up their meetings, and vilify them night after night on the evening news."

Cain understood the ravages of heroin as well as anyone, and his novel summons that devastation without mercy or reserve: a pusher shoving ice up a woman's vagina to bring her back from an overdose, or a "haunted huddle" of junkies "nodding, stinking, burning, high," lit by the glow of a TV playing cartoons. When George visits the projects where he was born, he gets a junkie named Fix to cop for him, a guy so sick he's desperate for a cut: "gaunt and hollow...skin strapped tight around the skull...there's not enough junk in the world to quench his need." But Cain also understood that criminalizing addicts only compounded the damages that addiction itself had wrought, and *Blueschild Baby* is a difficult, prickly book in part because it's trying to tell two stories that sit together uneasily: the damage of drugs and the ways this damage is deployed as moralizing rhetoric.

The War on Drugs was officially launched twice. Nixon announced his war in 1971, but it wasn't until Ronald Reagan's call to arms—a decade later, in 1982—that the war truly took off. Drug use was actually declining in 1982, and only 2 percent of Americans thought drugs constituted the most important issue facing the nation. But by launching its war, the Reagan administration effectively created an enemy—another version of the figure Anslinger had called "the addict violator." As sociologists Craig Reinarman and Harry Levine put it, it was easier to place the "ideological fig leaf" of a crack epidemic over the devastating impact of trickle-down economics than face this impact directly.

Reagan's War on Drugs picked up where Anslinger's crusade against addicts left off, placing a new set of addict archetypes—crack mothers, tweakers, base heads—inside familiar narrative dioramas about moral deviance, reality avoidance, and epidemic irresponsibility.

A 1986 feature in *Time* magazine called "The House Is on Fire," one of the first major media accounts of crack, presented its addicts as villains in a doomed morality play:

> The argument began, police say, when Beverli Black accused her boyfriend of spending their last $15 on crack. She stormed out of their one-room apartment in Freeport, L.I., late one night last week to try to borrow some food stamps. Daren Jenkins, 23, an unemployed cabinetmaker, stalked over to the bed where Black's son Batik was sleeping. High on crack, an extremely potent and addictive form of cocaine, Jenkins allegedly beat the little boy to death. Batik would have been three years old this month.

It was a horrible act—unthinkable—but it was also carefully deployed to incite public outrage at addict-villains whose lineage reached back to Anslinger's child-raping-widow-killing marijuana fiends. The article didn't present any addicts suffering, just an addict killing a baby. Daren was unemployed, too busy copping drugs to make any cabinets, and his girlfriend wasn't letting her habit get in the way of her determination to abuse the welfare state. Like a piece of exotic travel writing, the article ushered middle-class readers into an illicit underworld, summoned by suggestive ellipses: "'Crack it up, crack it up,' the drug dealers murmur from the leafy parks..."

The crack scare managed to combine the narratives of addiction as disease and vice by imagining crack as a predatory "epidemic" spread by black addicts who were morally responsible for what they carried. These scare tactics invited the narrative thrill and ethical imperatives of combat. As a director of the DEA's New York office noted, "Crack was the hottest combat reporting story to come along since the end of the Vietnam War," and by the mid-nineties, the metaphor of war had turned into something more concrete. Police departments got millions of dollars in military equipment from the Pentagon: bazookas, grenade launchers, helicopters, night-vision goggles. They got military training and SWAT teams. They were allowed to confiscate the cash, cars, and homes of everyone arrested in drug busts.

But many of the people waging that war hated it. One politician would call government antidrug policies the legislative "equivalent to crack." They would offer a short-term high, he argued, but would be catastrophic in the long run. One San Francisco judge wept on the bench after imposing a ten-year sentence on a shipyard worker who'd carried drugs to help a friend.

The public stories told about addiction had consequences. Between 1980 and 2014, the number of incarcerated drug offenders increased from just over 40,000 to almost 490,000, and the majority of those incarcerated were people of color. A 1993 study found that only 19 percent of drug dealers were African American, but they made up 64 percent of arrests. Michelle Alexander put it like this: "By waging a war on drug users and dealers, Reagan made good on his promise to crack down on the racially defined 'others' — the undeserving."

When Nancy Reagan launched her famous Just Say No campaign in 1982, its slogan didn't offer advice so much as implicit recrimination: *Just say no* meant also, *Some said yes*. As George H. W. Bush's National Drug Control Strategy would put it a decade later: "The drug problem reflects bad decisions by individuals with free wills." In its insistence that addicts not be seen as victims, U.S. drug policy continued to echo Anslinger's frustration with the "altruists" who called addicts sick. When Reagan signed the Anti-Drug Abuse Act of 1986, he implemented mandatory sentencing for first-time drug convictions, and put in place the infamous 100-to-1 ratio — which mandated vastly disproportionate sentencing for those caught with crack rather than powder cocaine, a policy that converted the racial scare tactics of the War on Drugs into actual prison terms.

One 1995 survey asked participants: "Would you close your eyes for a second, envision a drug user, and describe that person to me?"

Even though African Americans constituted only 15 percent of the nation's drug users, 95 percent of the respondents pictured someone black. This hypothetical drug user was the product of decades of effective storytelling.

The story I got to live was a different one: throwing up during blackouts, bruises on my shins from stumbling up stairs, coke dusted under my nose like powdered sugar from a slice of coffee cake, these legible residues of fairly unremarkable dysfunction. Some parts of my drinking life have become comfortable grooves in memory—whiskey shots, reckless nights—but those months with my dying grandmother aren't comfortable to remember. It's the resentment I regret most, the ways I wished myself away instead of being where I was; the ways I resented showing up to make her oatmeal each morning.

One night after coming home from my night shift at the inn, I drank my bottle of room-temperature wine and watched a movie on my laptop—about a man who had squatted in an abandoned bus in the Alaska woods, then gotten stuck there when the creeks swelled during spring thaws. By one in the morning, I was imagining myself into his trailer, wishing myself alone though that was hardly the moral of the story.

During those days in California, I discovered that I actually preferred drinking alone. It was easier without anyone watching how much I was drinking, or expecting me to produce anything—wit, good cheer, or explanation. "I enjoy it much more, because I don't go to bars," Berryman once said. "I just order it in and settle down with it."

One night, my sister-in-law and I came home to find my grandmother lying naked on the tiles just inside the front door. She told us she'd fallen on her way to the bathroom, but she wasn't anywhere near the bathroom. She was talking about my grandfather, from whom she had been divorced for decades. I couldn't remember the last time I'd heard her say his name. My sister-in-law called 911 and I went into the bathroom to try to gauge which of her pills she'd been taking, because the Lifeline calls had taught me they'd probably ask. But all her pills were spilled across her counter, and in her sinks.

When the EMT guy arrived, he asked me who took care of her on a regular basis. "You're twenty-three, and this is a lot for you," he said. "But she deserves more."

After Dell was admitted to the hospital, once she was sleeping in her room, my sister-in-law and I went to an IHOP across from the hospital and got chocolate chip pancakes. I emptied an airplane nip of rum into my coffee, in silent conspiracy with my sister-in-law — this was a time it was okay to drink, understandable — but I longed for another kind of drinking: a bottle of wine alone, in selfish privacy.

Dell had a heart attack a few days later. She died in a bed in the ICU, her body cluttered with tubes until they took away the life support and there was just the morphine and her swollen face and fingers, puffy with pooling fluid.

Near the end, she had spoken not about her own physical discomfort but mainly about my father and my aunt, the two children who remained in her life, and how fiercely proud she was of them. She had been a good mother for almost seventy years — and that duration, that constancy, was staggering to me, all those packed lunches and worried nights. I tried to imagine the pain she must have died with, knowing she'd tried as hard as she could with her middle daughter but had somehow lost her anyway.

After the memorial, my family found an address for Phyllis in Montana and sent her a letter saying that her mother had died. We got a letter back from Phyllis, who said she was living alone in a cabin at the end of a dirt road. She thought it might be a good place for the whole family to gather during end times. There was something in that gesture — the idea she still wanted to provide for us, the ones she hadn't seen in years or hadn't ever met—that moved me, even as it suggested the ways she was still ill.

The novel I was working on began to change its shape. Phyllis was creeping into it—or the idea of Phyllis, anyway. In the novel, the young woman who is taking care of her grandmother begins searching for an aunt she has never met, a woman named Tilly who has been estranged from the family for years. She finds Tilly drinking herself to death in a trailer in the middle of the Nevada desert.

The plot wasn't my life, exactly, but a hypothetical version of my life that I hadn't lived. Tilly was loosely based on Phyllis, which is to say I wrote to fill the blank space of what I didn't know about Phyllis. But writing from Tilly's perspective gave me the chance to articulate an alcoholic's obsession without fully claiming it as my own. Tilly was pointedly *not me*. While I stole cheap Chardonnay from my job and drank it on a futon, Tilly stole cheap booze from her catering gigs and drank it in a closet—a ghost of the college closet where I'd stepped on a scale every morning. But I described her swollen face by looking in the mirror at my own, hungover in the morning: puffy, slack-jawed, glassy-eyed.

I was careful to put up some fences between us: I made Tilly like gin most, because I preferred vodka. She binged in a dark closet, full of rotten food and empty bottles, and I drank white wine, got rid of my empties every day, and showed up promptly, with clenched knuckles and determination, for tutoring gigs where I let my teenage clients flirt with me—just a little bit—while I coached them on the crude logic of analogy: *Bandage* is to *blood* as *cast* is to *injury*? Or *Pinot Grigio* is to *loneliness*? Or *fiction* is to *diary*?

I purposefully sketched Tilly's life as more extreme than my own—a type of situational ventriloquism, throwing my own voice across distances—but I gave her all the parts of myself that were just coming into focus, not just my bone-deep desire to get drunk every night, but my growing sense of drinking as the most important part of my life, my central relief, as well as a clarified vision of how I wanted the drinking to happen: alone, without rules or witnesses, without shame.

Though of course there *was* shame. There had been many kinds of shame: tensing up whenever my manager took inventory in the pantry at the inn, worried that she would get suspicious at how many bottles of wine we'd gone through; or reaching for a stick of gum whenever guests returned, so they wouldn't smell the Chardonnay on my breath. Every Friday, when people put out their recycling bins on the street for pickup, I dropped a plastic shopping bag full of my own empties into a stranger's bin. Each time it was like I'd gotten away with something. They couldn't be traced back to me.

As Charles Jackson told countless AA meetings, writing a book about drinking didn't keep him from doing it. He had been sober for eight years by the time *The Lost Weekend* was published, in 1944, but he relapsed three years later. His stints of sobriety—sometimes grudging, sometimes passionately committed, always fraught— punctuated the ongoing catalog of wreckage that his life became: a slew of benders and hospitalizations, a growing tally of alienated friends and unpaid debts. His wife had to sell a mink coat to pay the coal bill. He spent decades smoking four packs of cigarettes a day on one post-tubercular lung. His suicide attempts were so frequent they became, if not casual, at least horribly familiar.

But from certain angles, in the dim lighting of certain midtown bars, Jackson's drinking carried the gloss and polish of legend. His archives include a bar tab four pages long. A fellow patient at the sanitarium where he went for his tuberculosis remembers waking one morning to find Jackson's footprint outlined in a dried puddle of wine.

Jackson first stopped drinking at the age of thirty-three, using something called the Peabody Method. It was an approach grounded in pragmatism rather than psychoanalytic excavation, spirituality, or fellowship. It stressed honesty and reparations. Jackson worked with

an unlicensed therapist named Bud Wister on rigorous daily schedules of self-improvement. "We regulate our lives in orderly and profitable fashion without benefit of Freud," Jackson wrote in one progress
report. "I have lately acquired…a sound responsibility based on
sobriety and my true self."

But *The Lost Weekend* offers another "true self" in its pages, or
asks us to recognize that any self is always plural. You can sense a
sober Jackson drinking vicariously through his protagonist: Don
drinks whiskey in an uptown bar and a downtown bar, then settles
into his favorite drinking pose of faux sophistication, curled up in a
leather chair with a full tumbler and some classical music.

During the years I spent writing this book, about my own
drinking—from the vantage point of four years sober, then five years
sober, then six years sober—I sometimes sank into the old memories
as if they were a comfortable couch, collapsing under the old spell of
eerie muted longing. It wasn't just predictable flavors of nostalgia—
the sepia-toned glow of the Advocate's wooden floor, sticky with gin—
but more surprising ones: those restless early-morning hangovers,
parched and sour-mouthed, dog tired but unable to sleep. Even *that*
discomfort had started to carry its own shabby glow.

The Lost Weekend regards even drunken embarrassment with an
oddly tender nostalgia. Jackson makes Don drunk-dial F. Scott
Fitzgerald, as Jackson himself once did, to tell him how much he loves
his work, only to be politely rebuffed: "Why don't you write me a letter about it? I think you're a little tight now."

Making his protagonist call Fitzgerald in the middle of the novel
was a poignant confession of Jackson's own literary aspirations and
insecurities. He wanted to include himself in the ranks of the Great
Drunk Writers, but he didn't know if his own portrait of alcoholism—
untethered from Tragic Meaning—was good enough to join the
canon. When Don imagines the novel he will write, he conjures a
winding yarn full of events punctuated by alcohol ("the long affair
with Anna, the drinking"), but eventually the plot is overwhelmed by

booze, even in hypothetical outline, until even the commas between binges disappear: "the books begun and dropped, the unfinished short-stories, the drinking the drinking the drinking."

Jackson was actually doing something revolutionary in refusing to make his character's drinking a symbol of psychic complexity, by letting Don dismiss the question "Why do you drink?" as irrelevant: "It had long since ceased to matter Why. You were a drunk; that's all there was to it. You drank; period." Don doesn't want to falsify the story of his drinking by ennobling it with overblown causes, though he's also worried about the story that remains without them: *It wasn't even decently dramatic. It was nothing.* Except it must have been *something*, because hundreds of thousands of readers were engrossed by a book that kept telling them they should probably put it down. *The Lost Weekend* is enthralling in an aggressive sense of *thrall*—a state of servitude or submission. Against my better instincts, I found myself rooting for Don to get his hands on the booze. I appreciated the frustrating force of his desire, and wanted him to stop serving it. But I also wanted to see it satisfied.

We love our drunk heroes intoxicated. We don't want to watch them get sober. When critic Lewis Hyde wrote about *The Dream Songs* three years after Berryman's death, he railed against the ways people had romanticized Berryman's drinking. "I am not saying that the critics could have cured Berryman of his disease," Hyde wrote. "But we could have provided a less sickening atmosphere." Hyde hated the vision of Berryman conjured by his "Whisky and Ink" profile in *Life*—the drunken poet as icon, holding court in Dublin pubs. Hyde resented the people who had seen Berryman's body as a symbol, with his windblown beard and a cigarette between his fingertips, his liquor as proof of his wisdom rather than the sick, glugging heart of his disease.

For his part, Berryman loved the *Life* profile. It showed him a side of himself he wanted to believe in — a prophet surveying his kingdom of empty shot glasses — and fed the delusions that were feeding his drinking. The *why*-less drinking that Charles Jackson had proposed in *The Lost Weekend* would have been harder to absorb. That type of buffoonish drinking — with its vaguely comic desperation — didn't strike the same appealing pose as the poet with his quivering psychic antennae pointed toward death.

Hyde's essay on Berryman is a fascinating artifact of anger. It's an attack on *The Dream Songs* waged in Berryman's own name. "It is my thesis here," Hyde argues, "that [a] war, between alcohol and Berryman's creative powers, is at the root of the Dream Songs." Hyde resists the ways these poems can be interpreted "under the fancy handle of 'the epistemology of loss,'" insisting they were really just sung by "an alcoholic poet on his pity pot." If the poems stage a war between booze and creativity, Hyde insists, it's the booze that wins: "We can hear the booze talking. Its tone is a moan that doesn't revolve. Its themes are unjust pain, resentment, self-pity, pride and a desperate desire to run the world. It has the con-man's style and the con-game's plot."

Hyde wasn't blaming Berryman for his disease, but he was angry at the sheen Berryman's sickness had acquired — and angry because he wished Berryman could have gotten better. He wanted a different ending to the story: not Berryman jumping off the Washington Avenue Bridge in a bitter Minnesota winter, but Berryman living One Day at a Time into the future. "It would not have been easy," Hyde speculates. "He would have had to leave behind a lot of his own work. He would have had to leave his friends who had helped him live off his pain for twenty years."

When I first read Hyde on Berryman, a few years into my own sobriety, I whispered a secret "Amen." I wanted to believe that giving up booze didn't mean giving up electricity, and Hyde was suggesting that the fruits of alcoholic composition weren't glorious but deeply compromised. Here was someone saying "Fuck off" to a mythology that I'd come to see as corrosive and misguided. I loved Hyde for pushing back against the toxic filters that turned addiction into romance, and I loved him for articulating a version of the anger I carried toward a prior version of myself, consumed by self-pity that had come to seem grossly self-indulgent.

It would be easy to dismiss Hyde's piece as shrill or puritanical, the rambling ad hominem attacks of a teetotaler stick-in-the-mud—like a girl pacing around a swimming pool, as I once did, shrill-voiced, telling everyone to get out of the Jacuzzi because it just wasn't safe to be there stoned. (I was stoned too.) But that's what I loved about Hyde's essay, its unfashionable indignation—its insistence on the horrors of drinking, rubbed bare of their gloss, and its conviction that these horrors weren't the engine of creativity but its straitjacket.

Where had all Hyde's anger come from, anyway? At the start of the essay, he confesses that for two years he worked as an orderly in a detox ward. He spent time in the trenches. That's part of why he needed to acknowledge that behind the photograph of the poet with his whiskey, there had been an actual man. Berryman's mythology offered its own supernatural alchemy—whiskey was the fluid he ingested and ink was the fluid he produced, both were alternatives to ordinary human blood—but Berryman was full of ordinary human blood, blood that his drinking slowly poisoned, and his life was full of fluids that weren't ink: the sweat of tremors and withdrawal; the vomit of illness, the piss and shit on his pants. Behind the mantra of whiskey and ink, those lyric parallels, there was a man with bruised shins living half his life in blackouts. His liver was so swollen with toxins it was palpable through his skin. This wasn't drinking as swagger or farce. This was drinking as seepage toward death.

Billie Holiday was an addict whose life staged the collision of two addict myths: the romantic notion of the tortured artist, and the morality tale of the deviant junkie. She was worshipped as a gloriously self-destructive genius, but she was also persecuted as a criminal. As a black woman raised poor in Baltimore in the 1920s, dogged by the justice system's double standards all her life, she wasn't granted the same unfettered access to the same mythologies as windblown Berryman.

From the beginning, however, Holiday's legend was similarly tied up in the gloss and heat of her hurt, as if the beauty of her singing rose off her pain like steam off boiling water. The writer Elizabeth Hardwick was enchanted by Holiday's "luminous self-destruction," while Harry Anslinger, during the late thirties and early forties, made Holiday one of his personal crusades. One of the federal narcotic agents assigned to her case called her a "very attractive customer," because he knew it would be great publicity for the Federal Bureau of Narcotics if they could bring her down.

When Holiday started shooting heroin, in her mid-twenties, it gave her back a stronger sense of herself. "I got a habit and I know it's no good," she wrote, "but it's the one thing that makes me know there's a person called Billie Holiday." A friend said she had a "shyness so vast that she spoke in practically a whisper," but when she sang, her voice made her a legend in the jazz clubs of Manhattan. She was told nobody could sing the word "hunger" like she sang it. She sang the clubs on West Fifty-second, tucked into brownstone basements, and loved Jimmy's Chicken Shack, where the whiskey was served in tea-cups. Holiday gave gin to her Chihuahuas, Chiquita and Pepe, and it was rumored she shot up her little boxer, Mister. Hardwick marveled at the "sheer enormity of her vices," admiring the powerful alchemy by which Holiday was able to transform them into her extraordinary art. It was as if Holiday had risen to the occasion of her own pain. "For the grand destruction one must be worthy," Hardwick wrote, in awe of Holiday's "ruthless talent and the opulent devastation."

For Harry Anslinger, the enormity of Holiday's vices offered another type of opportunity. Her self-destruction wasn't luminous but criminal, and her celebrity was a convenient hook upon which he could hang the racist scripts he'd already been writing for years to bolster his crusade against drugs. His vendetta wasn't just about constructing the addict-villain but constructing the *black* addict-villain, since at the same time he was hunting Holiday, he was busy telling Judy Garland that she should get over her heroin habit by taking longer vacations between movie shoots.

Anslinger assigned several agents to Holiday's case during the late 1940s, and they busted her on multiple occasions, including the 1947 conviction that sent her to Alderson Federal Prison Camp, in West Virginia, for almost a year. At Alderson, Holiday got Christmas cards from more than three thousand fans all over the world. When her whiskey cravings got bad enough, she made moonshine from potato peelings in the commissary.

Jimmy Fletcher, one of the men Anslinger assigned to track Holiday, ended up becoming quite fond of her. They once danced together at a club, and another night he sat with her and Chiquita, talking for hours. Years later, he remembered their relationship with regret. "When you form some sort of friendship with anybody," he said, "it's not pleasant to get involved in criminal activities against that person." The first time Fletcher busted Holiday, in the spring of 1947, she was staying at the Braddock Hotel, in Harlem. Fletcher pretended he was delivering a telegram. During her strip search, Holiday forced Fletcher to watch her pee: a way of demanding that he face the degrading, invasive nature of his work.

Some forty years after that bust, in July 1986, ABC News introduced the American public to Jane—an addict with a five-hundred-dollar-a-day freebase habit—and her premature twins, who each weighed two pounds three ounces. In October 1988, NBC News introduced Tracy, Erocelia, and Stephanie: Erocelia was recovering on a hospital bed after giving birth to her premature baby. Stephanie had left her baby at the hospital and was headed for a crack house.

Tracy smoked crack on national TV. As criminologist Drew Humphries argues, the media effectively created the "crack mother" as a sensational character, almost exclusively targeting minority women although the majority of pregnant addicts were white. Occasionally contrite but frequently shameless, the crack mother was almost always black or Latina, and she was invariably a failure at the primal task of motherhood.

The problem with media scripts about the crack mother wasn't that crack addiction wasn't devastating individuals and communities (it was) but that the public outrage around crack mothers effectively redirected public notions of addiction away from disease and back to vice. This indignation offered a convenient scapegoat for the deeper ills fueling addiction — urban poverty, trickle-down economics, systemic racism — and obscured the science itself. Dr. Ira Chasnoff, whose early reports on the effects of cocaine in utero had fueled the press frenzy, eventually pushed back against what he called the media's early "rush to judgment," explaining he had "never seen a 'crack kid'" and doubted he ever would.

The figure of the crack mother sharpened to a vindictive blade the notion of addiction as something you were guilty of, rather than something you suffered from. A crack mother wasn't just damaging herself; she was damaging another body inside her own. "If you give drugs to your child because you can't help it," said Jeffrey Deen, one of the prosecutors who eventually put a crack mom on trial, "that's child abuse." Deen's phrasing held a contradiction he couldn't acknowledge: *you can't help it* suggested illness, but *child abuse* was a crime.

It wasn't just that crack mothers were portrayed as irresponsible, it was that they appeared to have the wrong feelings about motherhood. "Instead of showing shame, Tracy was defiant in the face of obvious censure," Humphries writes. "Instead of revealing remorse, Stephanie was indifferent to the baby she had left in the hospital." As opposed to those male geniuses whose addictions were understood as badges of psychic complexity or inner anguish, these women were portrayed as emotionally stunted or deformed by their addictions; or else guilty of some latent emotional deficiency that their addictions had exposed. And when white pregnant drug addicts were covered in the media (rarely), they were usually powder cocaine users depicted in states of contrition and recovery, and were often shown bathing or otherwise caring for their babies. But minority crack mothers fit neatly into preexisting racist stereotypes. Now they weren't just part of the "undeserving" poor, welfare junkies who were corroding the civic body; they were actively destroying their own children.

Crack mothers weren't just criticized for their addictions; they were prosecuted for them. Unlike most addicts, they entered the criminal justice system through the hospital, where doctors were asked to start turning over their pregnant patients to the legal system. Prosecutors twisted familiar laws in new ways: They sought an indictment for Melanie Green on manslaughter charges after her infant daughter, Bianca, died during the first week of her life. Jennifer Johnson was convicted of delivering a controlled substance to her unborn child. In Johnson's case, the prosecution claimed that Johnson had effectively been "trafficking" cocaine to her newborn, rewriting the umbilical cord as a state highway and their shared blood as a drug deal. "Maybe sending a woman to jail is like killing a fly with a shotgun," said one judge. "But I had other concerns. I had concerns about an unborn helpless child to be."

The crack mother was the negative image of the addict genius: She wasn't someone whose dependence fueled her creative powers. She was someone whose dependence meant she'd failed to create the way she was supposed to.

When Billie Holiday told her own story—in *Lady Sings the Blues*, her 1956 autobiography—she wasn't interested in peddling either of the addict myths that had been projected onto her: luminous self-destroyer or depraved villain. She was mainly interested in telling people heroin wouldn't do them any favors. "If you think dope is for kicks and for thrills, you're out of your mind," she wrote. "There are more kicks to be had in a good case of paralytic polio or by living in an iron lung."

Holiday's coauthor, journalist William Dufty, thought addiction would be a good "gimmick" to help them sell the memoir to publishers. But its account of addiction was actually remarkably unsensational, more concerned with tiring logistics than luminescence. "I've been on and I've been off," Holiday explains. "I've spent a small fortune on the stuff." She was less interested in waxing lyrical about her own pain than in honoring the maddening back-and-forth of addiction, its reversals and regressions, its tedium and stubborn siren call. With every relapse, she called herself No Guts Holiday. Rather than presenting her addiction as proof of psychic depth, she wanted to confess the ways others had suffered because of it: "A habit is no damn private hell." And she was clear on one point: "Dope never helped anybody sing better, or play music better, or do anything better. Take it from Lady Day. She took enough of it to know." It wasn't just a moralizing persona constructed for the pages of her book. To her pianist, Carl, she once said: "Don't you ever use this shit! It's no good for you! Stay away from it! You don't want to end up like me!"

Holiday genuinely wanted to stop using—plenty of oral histories attest to that—but she had nothing but disdain for a system in which the cure was little more than a cloak for punishment. "I want you to know you stand convicted as a wrongdoer," one judge told her. But Holiday wanted to know: Would he treat a diabetic like a criminal?

Holiday had been treated like a criminal for as long as she could remember. She was born just a month after the Harrison Act came into effect in 1915, targeting the use and sale of opium and cocaine, and it was as if she'd been fated to a life bound up in its ongoing legacy. For a citizen like her, poor and black, the law was more likely to punish than protect. When she was almost raped at ten, she was treated as a criminal—arrested for solicitation and then sent away to a disciplinary school. When she spurned a customer as a teenage call girl, she got treated as a criminal—sent away to jail for prostitution. When she got sick as an addict, she was treated as a criminal—sent away to Alderson. In *Lady Sings the Blues*, Holiday wrote that she wanted her country to "wake up" to its narcotics problem "for the sake of young kids whose whole life will be ruined because they are sent to jail instead of a hospital." But this plea was made in 1956, the same year Congress passed the Narcotic Control Act, mandating more drastic minimum sentencing.

In the face of increasingly harsh drug legislation in the 1950s, another figure started to gain a cultish appeal: the unrepentant addict. William Burroughs's *Junkie*, subtitled *Confessions of an Unredeemed Drug Addict*, was published in 1953, the same year as Anslinger's *Traffic in Narcotics*. The cover was pure pulp: a man in wild disarray, necktie flailing, restraining a blond vixen as she reaches for her dope works. (Though, in truth, Burroughs's junkie didn't try to keep anyone away from her dope.) The novel's antihero isn't interested in going along with the establishment's redemption narratives. "Given cooperation," the narrator knows, his doctor "was ready to take down my psyche and reassemble it in eight days." But he doesn't want to play along. Elizabeth Hardwick's vision of Holiday as an addict with "no pleading need to quit, to modify" was another version of this figure. "With cold anger," Hardwick wrote, Holiday "spoke of various cures that had been forced upon her."

The allure of the unrepentant addict has endured. When Amy Winehouse's single "Rehab" became a hit in 2007, half a century after Holiday published *Lady Sings the Blues*, it tapped into our running obsession: *They tried to make me go to rehab, I said no, no, no.* It's a great song—straight up and flat out, jaunty and sublime—with Winehouse's singular voice all acrobatic and vaulting and rich, like vinyl and leather; the chorus blunt and surprising, full of defiance where you might expect to find the keening croon of self-pity. Refusing rehab becomes its own statement of power: *When I come back, you'll know, know, know. No* turns into *know:* Resistance becomes knowledge. This isn't just refusal; it's a declaration of presence, and the success of "Rehab" as an anti-rehab anthem was attached to the appeal of Winehouse as an un-rehabilitated woman. At one concert on the Isle of Wight, drunk and slurring her words, she ended "Rehab" by throwing a plastic cup full of wine. An arc of crimson sprayed across the stage. *No, no, no,* she sang. She wouldn't go to rehab. She was doing this instead.

The online clips of Winehouse's concerts, especially the ones that show her visibly intoxicated or tweaking onstage, have thousands of comments. People offer judgment: *So many people dream of being a Singer and being on stage and Amy just threw it all away.* Or else self-congratulatory sympathy: *I see someone with a broken heart.*

After her final concert, in Belgrade, which she spent muttering senselessly into the mike, one newscaster wondered: "Why do they keep putting her on stage? Surely they know she has a problem." Another said: "This was supposed to be a comeback, and she TOTALLY. BLEW. IT." Something about her addiction made people angry. But their anger wasn't simple. The woman who wrote *Amy just threw it all away* had a story of her own. *As for accidentally OD'ing that's bullshit. My dad didn't have a fucking accident when he overdosed on heroin. Me and my brothers just stood and watched as the paramedics revived him.*

Someone else asked: *Does she want to go back to rehab now :P*

It was a fantasy that Winehouse never tried to get clean (she went to rehab four times) just as it was a fantasy that Holiday had no need to quit or modify, as if the only alternative to a woman completely victimized by her addiction was a woman who had no desire to live past it. Though Holiday spoke "with cold anger" about the "cures that had been forced upon her," as Hardwick put it, it was more that Holiday was angry about the *forcing,* and the punishments disguised as "cures," rather than the idea of a cure itself.

The unrepentant addict pushes back—in thrilling, necessary ways—against rabid moralizing rhetoric and the kinds of social control that often masquerade as rehabilitation. Her open-ended story is an appealing antidote to the bow-tied conversion narrative. But fetishizing the unrepentant addict can also ignore her genuine desire to get well. It might have been appealing for Hardwick to imagine Holiday as a woman facing the wreckage of her life with unrepentant grandeur, but it's no accident that a white woman called Holiday's self-destruction luminous while Holiday didn't see it that way at all. She was too aware of the price.

After my grandmother died, I spent five months working two jobs, tutoring and innkeeping, to save the money I needed for an airplane ticket to Nicaragua and a month's rent once I got there: a room with a single bed in a small yellow house. I craved luminosity—the glimmering constellation points of a life told as anecdotes—and a world removed from the home where my grandmother had died. In a city called Granada, I volunteered at a two-room schoolhouse during the day, pretending to bite off my own fingers to teach second-graders subtraction, and drank at night, more recklessly and more dramatically than I ever had before. This drinking looked more exotic than it had at my grandmother's house, when it had been about lukewarm wine bottles on a bare futon mattress, but it was still daily and necessary, still the relief I woke up craving.

My first diary entry from Nicaragua began, *No thoughts. Just things.* Piles of burning trash along the road from Managua. Salsa music wailing from a stereo perched in front of a miniature bouncy castle. Tiny pancakes bubbling on hot griddles outside the church. The mohawk spine of fur along a dog's back. I made sandwiches on shriveled bread with mashed avocados from the market, and shook big flakes of salt into my cupped palm to sprinkle on top of *campesino* cheese purchased from clattering carts. I used a liter soda bottle with the top cut away to pour water for my laundry. I never killed the cock-roaches in my room because someone had told me that if you crushed a pregnant cockroach, all the eggs inside her belly would hatch. I was sure the stray dogs could smell my period when it came.

In Granada, I was part of an ongoing ecosystem of tourists and parachute do-gooders and locals. Whenever a man stole a purse from one of the cantinas on Calle Calzada, a small flock of expats exploded after him, their flip-flops scattering to the side of the road; and then another man carefully collected these flip-flops and lined them up again, hoping for a tip, checking our discarded Toña bottles to see if any had a few drops of beer left. I fell in with a crew of Dutch girls who were older and more cosmopolitan than I was. My Spanish was better than theirs, but it was my second language and their fourth. We passed an afternoon in hammocks by the Laguna de Apoyo, with cold beers and a warm breeze, eating whole fish roasted over flames, swimming in a volcanic basin with ribbons of chilly water and hot water swirled together like scarves. After a day in the ragged sunlight I dreamed about fever, and then a few nights later I got one. I could feel it strok-ing my bones. I turned twenty-four by candlelight and woke up with the sour taste of the last night's sangria in my mouth, my clothes smelling like smoke.

Every afternoon I drank Toñas with the Dutch girls and every night we drank rum. I wasn't a huge rum fan. But it was all you could get in Nicaragua, so I drank it: Flor de Caña, the local favorite. Or Nica Libres, which were just rum and cokes, like Cuba Libres, as if the revolution had been a little sibling, formed in its elder's image. Those were the early days of Ortega's second lease on the dream, and it went black for hours at a time each night. The government was figuring out how to make electricity a public industry. When *la luz se fue*, the light left, we watched flame jugglers outside the cathedral. Boys pushed their baskets of cashews into our elbows. A caustic man from Quebec wondered what they did with all the fallen mangoes every morning. The warm darkness fell over my buzz like a blanket fort at dusk. We bought tamales from the woman at the corner of the *parque central* and ate them somewhere with candles, or without candles— just fumbling with our hands—and some nights we piled into unmarked black taxis and rode down the lake to Oscar's, where people danced and snorted lines of coke, where little black flies lifted in a fluttering scrim over the water at dawn. There was a traveling magician on crutches who came around most nights; he was missing one leg from the knee down. He was clearly a drunk. I remember thinking: *You should take better care of yourself.*

At the school where I volunteered, I ran an Uno game during recess. I learned how the kids played: Leticia was merciless, and impatient with anyone who wasn't. One Gloria played fast; the other Gloria played slow enough to give the others a chance to plead their cases about which color she should choose: *Amarillo! Rojo! Verde!* She liked the power. My students colored between the lines on their paper *payasitos*, little paper clowns. From the woman who stood beside the rusted metal swings, they bought plantain chips and something that looked like toothpaste made of sugar. After I saw lice crawling through Sol's hair, I went to the dim concrete box of our local *farmacia*—where I mimed the bugs crawling across my scalp to make sure I got the right little brown bottle of poison.

For the first time in my life, I started getting real hangovers: a sour mouth and twin heartbeats of pain in my temples; a head stuffed with crumpled-up pieces of paper like a trash can, all of them rasping against each other whenever I nodded. *Nursing a hangover:* You have to care for the aftermath, like a child you've given birth to.

I started drinking with a guy named Felipe, from Managua, and whenever we got drunk he talked about being alcoholic. The way he put it, being alcoholic wasn't anything that made him special. It was just true for him and for a lot of the guys he'd grown up with. He wasn't packing up his drinking and taking it on an international flight or to his job at a Santa Monica inn. He wasn't busy blaming his frequent-flier father. He didn't feel particularly sorry for himself—this was just a way of being, and it wasn't his alone.

Felipe and I got blind drunk and went dancing at Oscar's by the lake, kissed as dawn brightened the sky. A mist of flies rose off the greenish water and fluttered around us in the early light. Felipe told me things in Spanish that it would have embarrassed me to hear in English: *Quiero tu boca, quieres mi boca?....* I started to translate—"I want your mouth, do you want my mouth?"—until I forced myself to let go, to stop translating, to lean into his body and into the drunkenness itself.

My drinking was still winding its tentacles into everything, as it had in Los Angeles, and Iowa before that, but now it was happening on a different stage set, with dark cobblestone streets and mangoes six for a dollar, with unreliable electricity and candlelight that wavered like a voice about to break into crying. There was more narrative action in this play than there had been when I drank on a futon, in front of movies on my laptop, but the central themes were the same: wanting it, getting it, wanting it again. One night I was walking from one bar to another—drunk, on a quiet street—and got punched by a stranger, who took my purse after breaking my nose. The blood splattered all over my skirt.

There was a night with a stranger named Mackey. I can't remember if that was his last name or just a nickname. My memory is a pile of scraps, sodden and souring. I remember riding in an unmarked black cab, my knees against other knees, voices filling the small car, jostling over rutted roads, with the jutting rebar of unfinished second stories profiled against the night, barbed fences and trash piles catching stray vectors of street light. I remember sitting on his lap, in a huge group of strangers, and feeling him push his fingers into me and not wanting them there but being too drunk to tell him to stop—and too embarrassed, somehow, as if my drunkenness had invited them.

I don't remember asking him to come back to my room, though I do remember him taking off my clothes in an open courtyard outside my bedroom, and realizing that the night guard was standing nearby in the shadows—not because he wanted to be there, but because it was his job.

At a certain point we were on my bed and I didn't want to fuck him—but I was too drunk and too tired to figure out how *not* to fuck him, so I just lay there, still and quiet, while he finished. The situation would sharpen into awareness, in fleeting moments, and I'd think, *This isn't what I want*, and then it would dissolve into soft focus again.

I remember lying there afterward, going in and out of sleep, not wanting to sleep with him there next to me, not knowing what he'd do—but deeply tired, flattened and confused by where the drunkenness had taken me, with the terrible insect whirring of my fan going on and off as the power cut out and came back. I remember cool air prickling the sweat on my back. Then he tried to turn me over and fuck me again, and I rolled away and fell asleep, and then he woke me up and turned me over again and then I pushed him away again and then he woke me up and turned me over and then I pushed him away and then—I'd be lying if I told you I remembered how many times he rolled my drunk body over and tried to fuck it again. I can tell you that I just lay there for a while afterward with my mind swimming far away from my body, and I prayed for him to leave.

I had fucked him because it was easier than not fucking him, because it seemed hypocritical to stop what we'd started—like I'd already promised him something just by letting him come back to my room, like I owed him something as payment for the meager gift he'd given me, the affirmation of wanting to fuck me in the first place. My rum-blood believed every man's desire was a gift he gave to me, and a promise I made to him. But there was also this, beyond and beneath each *because*: It happened because I was drunk, and because he didn't stop.

The next day, the night guard told me: "No more visitors," and I thought of what we'd done in front of him, how rude and blind it had been.

I went to school. I taught subtraction. I played Uno. My hangover pounded at my skull like it wanted out. The heat was impossibly thick. I stood in a dry gully behind the classrooms and felt sick, chugged orange Fanta and felt sicker. I apologized to one of my Dutch friends for getting so drunk the night before and she shrugged, not in a bad way, more in a *your life, not mine* way. I was apologizing to her because it seemed like something had happened that required an apology, and maybe I could get it out of me by apologizing to someone, anyone, enough.

— IV —

LACK

During my dry-mouthed mornings in Nicaragua, hangover after hangover, I touched something in myself that wasn't right, something unguarded and sweat-stained and sloppy. So when I moved back to the States that fall, to start a doctoral program at Yale, I decided to drink differently: no more beer, no more rum. Only clear liquor, which seemed purer when I imagined it traveling through me, and white wine. A lot of it. I lied to the guy at the wine shop on Orange Street—"I'm throwing a little dinner party, what's good with salmon?"—knowing full well I was drinking alone that night. I might eat some crackers from the box. "We'll be eight," I'd say. "Do you think I should get two bottles or three?" Pretending the *we* of myself, cracker-crumbed and sour-breathed, was a moderate crowd. Pretending I wasn't used to these kinds of calculations. The nights I actually did have people over, I had to get even more.

One of my first friends in New Haven was a graduate student named Dave—a charming, gregarious poet. When I'd visited Yale as a prospective student, I'd stayed with him and his girlfriend in their apartment on Humphrey Street, a warm, lamp-glowing place with hardwood floors and endless bookshelves, nothing like my bare room back in California, with its futon mattress and empty wine bottles tucked in a plastic bag in the closet. Dave's girlfriend was a few years older than us, almost thirty, and their life seemed intoxicating in its domesticity and its *adult*-ness: granola for breakfast, overdue library books, weekend hikes.

Oddly enough, I realized I'd actually already met Dave—almost ten years before, when we were seniors in high school, on opposite sides of the country—at a national arts program, a scholarship that had funded twenty high school students to attend a week of classes at a hotel in Miami. "I remember you," I told him. "You had a goatee! You played your guitar in the lobby!" What I did not say: I'd watched him from the shadows, behind a potted plant—as he'd played to a group of people, all laughing and talking—before disappearing back into my hotel room, too shy to join them.

"Of course!" he said. "Amazing!" He seemed delighted by the coincidence, though I was stunned he remembered me at all. Although the program had only twenty students, I was sure I'd been invisible.

The week after I moved to New Haven, I invited Dave and his girlfriend over to my apartment for dinner. They were my first guests. I drank while I cooked, as usual—preparing the same risotto I'd made for my grandmother's memorial service, cooked with cheddar and Corona, her favorite beer. Slicing pears for a salad, I used my roommate's mandoline, with its fearsome horizontal blade, to shave layers of fruit so paper-thin I could see their veins. After the third glass of wine, I sent my thumb over the blade. It was less like a cut, and more like a section of my thumb had been removed—a sliver of flesh-colored fruit, salad-possible. I texted Dave: *Can you bring a Band-Aid???* And then: *actually, a couple.* And then: *I promise I didn't bleed in your food!!!!* And then, thinking the whole series looked a little suspect, a final message that was just: *!!!!!!!!!!!!* In the meantime, I wrapped wads of toilet paper around my bleeding thumb and tightened the toilet paper wrapping with a hair band. It looked like a little ghost.

Dave and his girlfriend arrived with Band-Aids and an olive oil cake. Who knew such a thing existed? I accepted their Band-Aids but was afraid to unwrap my thumb because I didn't want it to start bleeding again; it had taken long enough to stop the first time. We sat at a round table under my living room skylight, crouching under my slanted attic roof, and I held the stem of my wineglass with four fingers and one puffy white pillow. It stayed numb all through dinner.

New Haven was a grayish, contradictory city, full of massive brick housing projects and side streets full of quaint Victorian cottages;

Gothic dorms and imposing concrete buildings built in the style called Brutalist, with windowless flanks like faces without eyes. You could sense the invisible borders where vegetarian cafés and scruffy secondhand bookstores gave way to dollar shops and methadone clinics; where the botanical garden edged onto an abandoned rifle factory. After getting my nose broken, I was afraid to walk alone at night—though I was also ashamed of my nervousness.

That fall, I fell immediately, greedily, into a consuming relationship with a man named Peter, another graduate student. In the same way that drinking white wine in an attic apartment seemed safely distanced from stumbling rum-drunk through dark Nicaraguan alleys, getting involved with a whip-smart Henry James acolyte seemed safely removed from letting strangers fuck me on sweaty sheets. Peter and I spent our mornings at a local coffee shop, describing our dreams and splitting muffins the size of softballs; then we parted ways so we could spend the rest of the day writing each other emails about the parts of our dreams we'd forgotten to describe earlier. Sometimes I'd delay reading his message just to keep its unread potential like a warm glow in my gut, not unlike the glow of imagining the first drink. Knowing when I would see Peter again was in fact the same thing as knowing when I would drink again, always *that* night, because we always drank when we were together. We bought cheap magnum bottles of Shiraz and fixed plates of cheese and crackers and often never even cooked dinner. Falling in love was the only sensation that had ever truly rivaled drinking—for buzz and transportation, sheer immersive force—and with Peter they came conveniently entwined.

Peter was tall and reserved, but his observations were full of caustic, witty judgment. His eyes were blue and crystalline, adamant, their beauty piercing and skeptical. It felt like victory to be admired by him. He was one of the most intelligent people I'd ever met. His mind was precise and relentless, his phrases like scrimshaw, whittled to intricate perfection. His ability and willingness and actual compulsion to dissect himself at all moments were the only instances of self-consciousness I'd ever encountered that struck me as more obsessive than my own. We were like two twenty-four-hour archeological digs happening side by side—just when you thought we'd pause for lunch, we went deeper.

It was no wonder we got drunk so much; we just wanted a fucking *break*. Booze let me live inside moments without the endless chatter of my own self-conscious annotation. It was like finally going on vacation somewhere beautiful without having to pose for photographs the whole time. Magnums helped us get simple and sloppy. Self-awareness burned off like fog and there we were, watching *America's Next Top Model* on his Ikea bed, or my Ikea bed, and speculating about the possibly anorexic identical twins: Who would get kicked off first? How would the other cope?

The depth and intensity of our relationship provided the perfect alibi for drinking. Peter certainly wasn't fucking my drunk senseless body when I didn't want him to. He was figuring out his dissertation, and bringing me baked goods—rum cake and peanut butter chocolate chip cookies. For a year we basically drank, and ate dessert.

Sometimes we met at an Irish bar on State Street—with baskets of peanuts on the tables, broken shells all over the floor—and drank vodka tonics till we stumbled home through the sharp autumn cold. I started getting there early enough to drink one vodka before Peter arrived; then early enough to drink two, and then three. And then once Peter came we always had so much to talk about: every thought I'd ever had about Victorian illness memoirs, or the stuffed tiger my dad had given me as a kid, or the etymology of the word "render." I was never out of class, always trying to impress. There was no amount of myself I could give Peter that seemed like too much. He wanted every observation, every impulse. After several years of men who'd wanted a night, or a month, this was like a homecoming. I wanted to deposit myself inside him, like putting myself in a vault for safekeeping. We wrote enough letters to sustain a long-distance relationship, but we lived only three blocks apart.

It was hard to imagine we were trying to escape anything, much less each other; but in truth I was escaping something subtler: the possibility of any distance, any fissure, any silence, any seam. We talked about everything, including how maybe we drank too much. So we decided we wouldn't drink on Mondays. I grew to dread Mondays. Then it wasn't *every* Monday. That was better. Then it was forgotten entirely.

All my life I had believed—at first unwittingly, then explicitly—that I had to earn affection and love by being interesting, and so I had frantically tried to become *really fucking interesting*. Once I hit the right relationship, I planned to hurl my interestingness at it, like a final exam I'd spent my whole life studying for. This was it.

The theorist Eve Kosofsky Sedgwick argues that addiction isn't about the substance so much as "the surplus of mystical properties" the addict projects onto it. Granting the substance the ability to provide "consolation, repose, beauty, or energy," she writes, can "operate only corrosively on the self thus self-construed as lack." The more you start to need a thing, whether it's a man or a bottle of wine, the more you are unwittingly—reflexively, implicitly—convincing yourself you're not enough without it.

For much of my twenties, I scribbled different versions of the same question in my diary, always when I was drunk: *Am I an alcoholic? Is this what it's like to be an alcoholic?* My shame about drinking wasn't mainly about embarrassment at what I did when I was drunk; it was about how much I wanted to get drunk in the first place. Intoxication had become the feeling I was most interested in having. In "Dream Song 14," Berryman's speaker remembers what his mother told him when he was young: "Ever to confess you're bored / means you have no / Inner Resources." Wanting to get drunk—at least, as much as I wanted to get drunk—seemed like a similar confession.

Years later, I interviewed a clinician who described addiction as a "narrowing of repertoire." For me, that meant my whole life contracting around booze: not just the hours I spent drinking, but the hours I spent anticipating drinking, regretting drinking, apologizing for drinking, figuring out when and how to drink again.

It's nothing new, the desire to disrupt consciousness—to soften it, blunt it, sharpen it, distort it, flood it with bliss, paper over its disenchantments. The desire to alter consciousness is as old as consciousness itself. It's another way to describe the act of living. We just keep discovering things we can put into our bodies to change ourselves more dramatically, more suddenly: to feel relief or euphoria or the dulling of anxiety, to feel *different*, to feel the world made strange, more spellbinding or simply more possible. The temperance movement called liquor "demon drink," a way to externalize the desires— for escape, for weightlessness, for euphoria, for extremity—that seek fluid or powder forms beyond our bodies.

Addiction doesn't surprise me. It seems more surprising that some people aren't addicted to anything. From the night of my first buzz, I didn't understand why everyone in the world wasn't getting drunk every night. Addicts often describe every high as chasing the first one—the purest, the most revelatory—trying to recapture, as psychiatrist Adam Kaplin puts it, that first time going "through the turnstile." Dr. Kaplin told me that one of his alcoholic patients, an artist, remembered his first cup of vodka as warmth filling his entire body, scalp to toes—the unmistakable feeling of coming home.

Scientists describe addiction as a dysregulation of the neurotransmitter functions of the mesolimbic dopamine system. Which basically means your reward pathways get fucked up. It's a "pathological usurpation" of survival impulses. The compulsion to use overrides normal survival behaviors like seeking food, shelter, and mating. It's the narrowing again: *this, only this.*

A chart from the early years of AA frames alcoholism as reckless bookkeeping: "FACTUAL GAIN AND LOSS CHART ON UN-CONTROLLED DRINKING." It's composed of two columns presented side by side: "Assets" and "Liabilities." Every asset has its corresponding liability, which is to say: its price. The "pleasure of disregarding conventions" sits alongside the "Penalty of Indiscretions," and the "Satisfying Flight from Reality" produces the "Fear of Being Sober Enough to See Depleted Self in True Light." The liabilities column grows wider and wider near the bottom of the page, representing the progress of the disease, forcing the assets column to grow narrower and narrower, and the whole thing ends in capital letters and exclamation points: "WET BRAIN. INSTITUTIONS. DEATH!!!"

Neuropharmacologist George Koob, director of the National Institute on Alcohol Abuse and Alcoholism, would call this vertical disintegration a "spiraling distress/addiction cycle" comprising three interconnected stages: preoccupation/anticipation, binge/intoxication, and withdrawal/negative effect. In one popular-science volume about addiction, the chart explaining the spiraling distress/addiction cycle looks like a tornado with an arrow pointing straight down through the middle. In a nearby illustration of neurotransmitter activity, the neuron receptors look cheerful, just waiting to get activated. They have no idea what's ahead.

It's a strange type of double vision to rewatch certain moments of my own life with the subtitles of biology playing underneath, like watching a thriller once the trick ending has been explained. I can understand sniffing lines of coke off a boy's coffee table as the activation of a receptor that blocked dopamine reuptake, so the dopamine stuck around longer in my synapses. But I felt that blocked dopamine reuptake as the surge of my own voice. It was the sloughing of a snakeskin, the shedding of fear.

When I look back at a night with a stranger in Nicaragua, I can say the GABA receptors in my neurons were activated by the rum in my veins—an agonist, they say—and the dopamine accumulated in my nucleus accumbens and my amygdaloid complex, these parts of my brain that sound like foreign lands, even though they're where large portions of my sense of self resides. When I look back at sweaty bedsheets, I can see the disinhibition the booze produced when it depressed my prefrontal cortex. I can see the hangover I woke to — the jittery, anxious, guilty headache — and see the unrestrained glutamate that made me irritable and restless, trying to remember what he'd done to my body, sick to my stomach, sick of myself, uncomfortable enough to crave another drink.

Part of the bind of coming to depend on drinking is that it becomes nearly impossible to imagine a life without it. Inevitability becomes an alibi, or an excuse. "When I'm drunk it's all right," says one of Rhys's heroines. "I know that I couldn't have done anything else." The drunk self becomes the self revealed rather than the self transformed, an identity that has been lurking inside all along: needy, desperate, shameless. When I saw the night guard in Nicaragua, the morning after I'd fucked a stranger in front of him, I believed he'd glimpsed a version of me that was truer than the self I showed the world. It was a version of myself I was usually too cautious or prudent or fearful to reveal: a self with no limits, all hurt, always grasping.

It's more accurate, I think, to say that booze expresses and creates this self at once. Getting drunk didn't reveal the self I *was*—in some absolute, static, categorical way—but a version of myself I feared becoming. When I was drunk, I believed I was nothing but need.

When I talk about that man in Nicaragua — which isn't often, and usually happens in the context of how and why I got sober — I always say, "I mean, it wasn't rape." I was giving him certain signals of consent, like the absence of its stated opposite. But consent when you're drunk means something I still don't have a good language for. It was as if I'd already made myself available as someone without pride, and it would have been hypocritical to become someone different. By that point, getting drunk was usually about reaching a point of giving up on myself. That time, it just happened with him.

After nearly a year with Peter, I found myself drunk in a Bolivian courtyard, about to sleep with someone else. It was the day before the country's gubernatorial elections. Because it was illegal to buy booze during election weekends, we'd already stocked up. We were mixing orange soda with singani, a local brandy made from grapes grown high in the Andes, to make something unholy called Chuflay.

I was ostensibly spending the summer in Bolivia to improve my Spanish, to satisfy one of the requirements of my doctoral program—and I suppose I was doing that, too, I was certainly using some of my program's funding—but the trip was also my way of getting away from a dynamic with Peter that had turned claustrophobic. Our life back in New Haven had begun to seem quarantined by the same routines that had been pleasingly dependable at first: nightly banter about aspiring models on reality television, not enough dinner and too much dessert, endless pictograph wallabies leaping across seven-dollar bottles of Yellow Tail Shiraz. I couldn't even count all the hours of my life I'd devoted to discussing Peter's dissertation on Henry James, an author who seemed mainly interested in what his characters *thought* about feelings. They never actually seemed to feel anything. I was hungry for something that might cut through this web of calculation—like actual emotion, which I defined as sudden, extraordinary, and overpowering, not the daily grind of knowing someone else's favorite muffin. Peter was utterly committed to me, which gave me a sensation not entirely unlike nausea.

The trip to Bolivia wasn't something I could fully afford, despite help from my program, and I'd borrowed money to make it possible. Peter was supposed to join me after a month—down in Sucre, the city where I was staying. Then we'd travel together, and the travel was supposed to deliver our dynamic to broader horizons: the salt flats, the Andes, the jungle.

Now, a week before Peter arrived, I was seeking some absurd

approximation of these broader horizons with someone else, this Irishman, who'd gotten plenty of singani because—like me—he understood that you needed to think ahead when there were days you couldn't buy booze. Sundays in Connecticut had taught me that. The Irishman was telling me all about his motorcycle voyage across Latin America, and I was imagining the ways I might someday tell someone else about a man telling me about his motorcycle voyage across Latin America, and I was telling him—in the meantime—that maybe I needed a bit less soda, and a bit more singani.

This Irishman's hair was long and reddish, falling in corn-silk flaps that framed his pale face. He limped because he'd broken his collarbone and one of his legs in a bad bike accident in rural Chile. His bike was taking longer to fix than he was. That's why he was hanging around in Sucre. The first spark with him was like a match lit under the kindling of my year with Peter, a year soaked with booze but also dulled and flattened by routine, framed by Ikea bookshelves and uninspired seminar response papers. This election and its injured Irishman were more like the flush and fever of Nicaragua, more like a story unfolding. At the time, I thought this appeal had to do with the boldness of seeking novelty; but in retrospect it looks like something far more ordinary—a fear of familiarity.

Sucre was the old colonial capital, a city of cobblestone alleys surrounded by rolling brown hills frosted with sharp Andean light. I was staying in a little room above a fern-filled courtyard and eating *salteñas* for breakfast, cracking holes in their pastry shells to get the meat stew inside. It was cold. We were high in the mountains, and it was winter in the Southern Hemisphere. At the market on the edge of town, I went looking for a coat, walking among street vendors selling fried dough and dishwashers from tarp-covered stalls clustered in a system of old storm drains, hawking tubs of lizard-skinned custard apples and pale salty cheese in sweating blocks the size of dollhouses.

Once we were good and drunk, the Irishman asked me if I wanted to see the top floor of the house where he was staying. There was a room in the attic that had been rented to an Argentine boy who'd died a few months before. The boy's family hadn't come to get his things, and the landlord hadn't known what to do with them, so they were still there. It was a gruesome sort of tourism—stepping into this dead boy's room, with his soccer photographs taped to the walls—like slowing to look at a car accident. I stood there wondering if I had it in me to actually go through with what I was about to do. It's not that I wouldn't have cheated if I hadn't been drunk. It was more like I got drunk so I could cheat. I drank myself toward zero gravity, what Hemingway called "rum-brave" and Lowry called "tequila-unafraid." Our Chuflay eventually gave way to straight singani, which just meant we'd run out of soda.

I woke up in a strange bed, in a bare white room, physically ill, the liquor curdling in me. I wanted to turn my body inside out and wring myself free of everything, like a piece of wet laundry. I was surprised that I'd actually cheated on Peter. *Can I do this?* you think, and then watch yourself: *I guess so.* It was less like becoming a cheater and more like discovering that I'd been one all along. The singani had wiped away my upper layers, dissolving their varnish to show the grimy truth below. It didn't escape me then, the notion of inheritance—what might run in the blood.

In retrospect, this random cheating—with someone who meant nothing, inside a relationship I wasn't obligated to stay inside of—seems explicable and unextraordinary. It was a way of choosing the drama of a minor train wreck over the more mundane work of recovering a relationship that had gone stale. The loud volume of my guilt was a buffer against the quieter actuality of uncertainty. I ducked into dusty Internet cafés and wrote oddly punctuated notes to friends back home, doomed by unfamiliar keyboards: *What have I done}*

Many scientists prefer the phrase "chemical dependence" to terms like "addiction" and "drug abuse." Once Berryman started to identify as an alcoholic, he put it like this: "We're all dependent people. Take our chemicals away, we have to find something else to depend on." But we're *all* dependent people, literally all of us — anyone human. So what primes you for a particular chemical dependence?

You could say I'm made of need. You could say everyone is. You could say my dad's absence for stretches of my childhood created need, or else inspired a certain relationship to men that kept creating need. You could say that my dad drank, and his sister drank, and their dad drank before they drank. You could point to the twenty-year study that found chromosomal patterns in more than 2,255 families "densely affected by alcoholism," and conclude that certain brains are more disposed to the neural adaptations that enable chemical dependence. You could say it all depends on how your neurons respond to the neuromodulators in your system; that it all depends on a complicated constellation of particularities in your genotype, and that how these responses are treated or punished depends on the money you have, and the color of your skin — and all of these explanations would be true, and none would be sufficient. What often seems truest is the confession of every explanation as partial and provisional, a possible shape to fill the empty space of *why?*

Whenever I was drunk, I could tell you exactly why I drank. The reason was rarely the same river twice: because I deserved relief from the burden of my own self-consciousness, the endless chatter of my inner monologues and self-appraisals; or else because there was something dark and broken at the core of me that I covered up with excess functionality, and getting drunk was the only way I could acknowledge it. Drinking was self-escape or else it was self-encounter, depending on the story I was telling myself.

But I was also interested in the ways these stories weren't sufficient. In the novel I was writing, there was no good reason that either of my characters was so sad. In early drafts, there were no explicit traumas in the narrative that produced their self-destructive impulses.

The mystery of these impulses was what I wanted to explore, the possibility that you might damage yourself to figure out why you wanted to damage yourself—the way exhaling into cold air makes your breath visible. "In so much of your writing," one boyfriend told me, "there are so many hooks to hang the pain on, but no explanation of where the poison coat came from." He was right. It can seem dishonest to attach certain kinds of pain to the syllogisms of cause, to pretend you can source the fabric of the poison coat.

That's part of why I loved *The Lost Weekend*—for its rejection of the idea that you could easily or automatically turn drinking into meaning. It insisted that you couldn't always trace the self-destruction back to a tidy psychological myth of origins: *It had long since ceased to matter Why. You were a drunk; that's all there was to it. You drank; period.* Jackson's account suggested that drinking was more mysterious than that, and maybe less noble, a wreckage less fully constituted by the Grand Profundities.

In "A Drunkard," a poem left unpublished in her lifetime, Elizabeth Bishop traces the origins of her drinking to the aftermath of a fire she witnessed as a toddler. "The sky was bright red; everything was red," the speaker remembers, "I was terribly thirsty but mama didn't hear / me calling her." Mama was busy giving food and coffee to strangers whose homes had been destroyed in the fire.

The next morning, sifting through the charred debris from the fire, the little girl picks up a woman's stocking: "Put that down!" her mother says. This moment of scolding is identified as the seed of a desire that will haunt the girl for years:

> But since that night, that day, that reprimand
> I have suffered from abnormal thirst—
> I swear it's true—and by the age
> of twenty or twenty-one I had begun
> to drink, & drink—I can't get enough...

All this rings true to me: the idea that thirst might rise from an abiding longing for the one who would not come, that hunger becomes constitutional in the shadow of absence or departure. Compulsion might find its roots in reprimand—from a sense of being scolded by the world, or found wanting by it.

But it's really the final lines of the poem that interest me most, not the ones that explain but the ones suggesting that any definitive explanation would be futile:

> ...as you must have noticed,
> I'm half drunk now...

> And all I'm telling you may be a lie...

One critic calls this a "half-hearted disclaimer," but to me it's the point of the poem—the way it calls out the instability of any thesis statement about need, and recognizes the desire for clear-cut causality as another powerful thirst: *The drinking came from my mother, from my mother's absence, from this moment, from this trauma.* Instead, the poem withholds the clarity of that origins myth, suggesting that the drinking (*I'm half drunk now*) has invented its own domino trail of causes.

"Why do you drink?" Berryman once asked himself in a note, then wrote: "(Don't really answer)." But he answered anyway: to "animate boredom...calm down excitement...dull pain." He listed other reasons:

> Insecure grandiosity self-destructive: I am just as great, and as
>   desperate, as Dylan T., Poe etc etc
> Delusion: "I need it" for my art
> Defiance: Fuck you. I can handle it.

He didn't believe in any single reason. He believed in all of them, and also none of them. *Don't really answer.* But what else could he do?

Returning to his reasons was one of the things he kept doing, in hopes that it would help him stop.

Gabor Maté, a Vancouver clinician who spent more than a decade working with addicts on skid row, traces every addiction back to childhood trauma — drawing neat boundaries around its thrall like a chalk outline at a crime scene. In *Grand Central Winter*, Lee Stringer's memoir about his days as a homeless crack addict living in the subterranean tunnels of New York's Grand Central Station, Stringer frames the causes of his addiction as a three-act play anchored by the death of his brother. He puts the whole thing in italics: *Act I, Act II, Act III.* The form allows him to connect his addiction to his grief while still acknowledging the crafted nature of this connection — how it imposes its neat structure on a much messier root system of craving.

Stories of addiction are full of this insistence that addiction can't be fully explained. It's a trope of the genre. "I told him I drank a lot," Marguerite Duras writes, describing a young man she'd just met, "that I'd been in hospital because of it, and that I didn't know why I drank so much." As Jackson put it: The question of *why* stopped mattering a long time ago. In *Junkie*, Burroughs anticipates the questions — "Why did you ever try narcotics? Why did you continue using it long enough to become an addict?" — but refuses to answer them: "Junk wins by default." Most addicts, he writes, "did not start using drugs for any reason they can remember."

These refusals aren't statements of objective truth. They're descriptions of the texture of experience. In resisting definitive explanations, they testify to the way addiction creates its own momentum, its own logic, its own self-sustaining warp speed; the ways it can seem autonomous and untethered, born of itself. These refusals resist the simplicity of syllogism, any neat one-to-one correspondence between trauma and addiction, insisting that the self is always more opaque than we're prepared to imagine. There is no simple key to turn the lock of *why*.

When I posed the question of *why* to Dr. Kaplin, the psychiatrist and Johns Hopkins professor who had described an addict's first time going "through the turnstile," he expressed frustration with the limited psychoanalytic accounts that held a monopoly on the medical establishment's ideas about addiction for much of the mid-twentieth century: *bottle as breast*. Dr. Kaplin wasn't dismissing the importance of childhood, or the enduring desire for affection. He was simply resisting the cookie-cutter simplicity of a single predetermined psychological story line, just as Stringer's italics questioned the origin story of his addiction even as he offered it.

When Burroughs refuses to answer the question of *Why*, he's also refusing the demands of respectability politics. He won't give the doctors — the ones who want to dissect him in order to heal him — exactly what they want. Burroughs doesn't want to be broken into explanations and reassembled into well-being. He wants to stand behind his subtitle: *Unredeemed*. The syllogisms of cause and effect dangle the prospect of transformation, but he's not interested in that kind of redemption.

By the end of my summer in Bolivia, I'd made my way to an island called Isla del Sol, in the middle of Lake Titicaca — where I got drunk each day, alone, by early afternoon. I spent a week in Yumani, a settlement on the south side of the island, where I had a concrete room with a lidless broken toilet, clogged by toilet paper soaked in the urine of strangers. Isla del Sol was quite possibly the most beautiful place I'd ever seen, but its beauty was merciless: The water glittered like shards of glass. The blue sky was so bright it hurt. The dry light left you with chapped skin and sun fever. Llamas humped each other in wooden-fenced pens on the terraced hills.

After Peter had come down to join me in Sucre, we'd spent a terrible month together. I hadn't told him about cheating on him, but it seeped into our weeks anyway — through my irritation and the nettles in my voice, my ways of pushing our dynamic toward breakage because I was tired of its tense sedation and distances. I thought of myself as selfish, and this had become a familiar vein of self-deprecation, but the underside of my selfishness was stitched with fear. I'd never thought of myself as someone with a fear of intimacy, because I loved talking about feelings—it seemed I was rarely doing anything else. But there were other kinds of intimacy I was scared of: tension, tedium, familiarity.

And I was scared of silence, wherever it found us: in the bar where we watched the bartender teach his ten-year-old son how to make sangria with crushed strawberries and red Fanta; or in the dirt-road town called Sipe Sipe, where we hiked up hilly trails to ruins littered with broken Taquiña bottles and looked for shacks marked with the white flags that meant they sold *chicha*, a type of moonshine made from fermented corn that people had chewed to a pulp in their mouths. At one of the white-flag shacks, an elderly woman dipped two clay bowls into a blue plastic vat maybe four feet high. We drank standing on the dirt. It was the old familiar wash of relief. It didn't matter if I got it from a vodka tonic in a sconce-lit bar, or a room-temperature bottle of wine on a futon mattress, or a clay bowl on a dirt road, drinking something straight from the inside of a stranger's mouth. It was the same softening: *Okay. Here it is. Here we go.*

At a dusty cantina outside of town, we drank Taquiñas and ate a massive platter of *pique a lo macho*—chopped steak, silky disks of chorizo, boiled eggs, and fried potatoes—underneath a pair of empty whiskey bottles hanging on the wall: one dressed in a tiny wedding dress, the other in a tux. We took an overnight bus to Cochabamba, and around three in the morning I got off to pee on the side of the road, in the full glare of the headlights, and then leaned against Peter for the rest of the ride, bleary and tired, grateful for his presence. He seemed safe. His mind glowed bright. I wanted to feel a different way than I did. We watched a circus in a battered little tent on Avenida

Ayacucho: dancers in silver bells and silver thongs, a clown in a pink unitard who looked hungover. Lots of people look hungover when you're hungover.

Certain parts of Peter began to repel me: his insecurities about our relationship and about himself, his hunger for my reassurance. These parts of him echoed the parts of me that had been hungry for reassurance all my life; that was probably why they disgusted me. But I couldn't see that then. I could only see that he'd gotten the same lip balm I'd gotten; he hadn't even been able to choose his own brand.

This double bind with men wasn't anything new. It was an enduring pattern: I gave myself utterly to the pursuit of what seemed unattainable, convinced myself I wanted their full devotion, and then got claustrophobic once I got it—restless without the vectoring purpose of pursuit. As Dr. Kaplin said: *You keep seeking the first time through the turnstile.* It was a pattern that had started with my high school boyfriend, the minivan-driving, kindhearted mushroom eater: I was heartbroken he didn't want to stay together for college, but once he changed his mind, I immediately started imagining our breakup.

For an endless stretch of days—specifically, three—Peter and I stayed in a cabin on the shores of the Rio Beni, in the Bolivian Amazon, without booze or electricity. I lay on our bed, cloaked by mosquito netting, shrinking from his touch, watching huge cockroaches scuttle across our floors. I was restless. I was *bereft*, because there wasn't anything to drink. I went to see if we could buy booze at the front desk of the lodge, but we couldn't. There was just a wooden cabinet full of Kotex and Pringles.

We trudged onward through the sober days. It was only once booze was literally out of reach—miles downriver—that I realized how essential it was. Now we were raw and unaccompanied. We ate a cousin of the piranha for lunch: stewed chunks of its white meat wrapped in banana leaves. We pushed an old wooden sugarcane press while baby pigs squealed around our feet, the size of muddy little apples. All of it was dirtied by our constant pull-and-tug, his desire and my withdrawal, and by my constant desire to drink: missing it, wondering why I missed it so much. Everything else was just a shoddy substitute. Beehives the size of dogs hung from the trees. My discontent found fault with ridiculous beauty: We hiked through the jungle and I became convinced my socks were full of ants. We went swimming in an idyllic secluded grotto and I started to notice a swollen mosquito bite on my ankle. I'd read about the botfly—a parasite that deposited its egg via mosquito, then hatched into a maggot under the skin—and became convinced I had one. We were made fools of by the macaws, who mated for life. They looked so impossibly regal, streaking twin arcs of color across the sky.

I finally ended things with Peter in a humid motel room with a broken fan. It was the worst possible time—we were literally stranded in a tiny Amazonian village, with three days until the next flight to La Paz—but it was also a relief. Something was broken and now at least we weren't trying to pretend it wasn't. We had days to wait together, but at least we had a thatched-roof bar that served a drink whose name loosely translated as "Eye-Closing Dusty Road." We started drinking early. We swatted flies from our eggs and played cards all day. My numbness confused me then—*We just broke up*, I told myself, *I should be sad*—but doesn't confuse me now. The drinks were called eye-closing for a reason.

When Peter flew home, I took a bus and a boat to Isla del Sol. There weren't any liquor stores on the island, but there were cafés that would sell you a bottle of whatever they served. Around noon each day, I'd buy a bottle of Bolivian wine and drink it all. Then I'd go back to my concrete room and pass out on my hard bed. One day I actually ate lunch: trout from the lake, charred until its skin crackled.

It was ridiculous good fortune to see this strange, cold, beautiful part of the world—a ragged Andean island, on borrowed cash—but I couldn't even bring myself to stay awake for it. When I woke up in the early evening, I regretted that I hadn't gotten drunk enough to stay passed out for longer. I would immediately check under my wool sock to touch my mosquito bite, now a hard cone on my ankle. An obscenely swollen ant bite on my other leg had collapsed into a deflated red circle, like a tiny fallen soufflé, and this actually made me even more panicked: Other bites were following their natural life cycles, why not the one on my ankle? There *must* be a botfly maggot in there. There was no other answer, logically speaking. I hadn't talked to another human being in days.

There weren't any computers on Isla del Sol, so I couldn't obsessively Google "symptoms of the human botfly," as I'd been doing in dusty Internet cafés on the mainland. Thinking ahead, I'd copied these symptoms onto a piece of paper and folded it into the back of my passport. *Pin-shaped breathing hole?* Check. I'd pull down my socks to check the bite every hour: *Is this hole more pin-shaped than it was an hour ago?* The first stabbing pain came like a little knife in my ankle. I'd read about old wives' remedies: You were supposed to smoke out the worm by burning cigarettes near the skin, or suffocate it with Vaseline until it got weak enough to pluck out with tweezers.

I told myself to stop thinking about my possible botfly. *Feel sad about Peter,* I told myself. But when I woke up every day at twilight—bleary and chilled and still half drunk, scalp scratchy under my alpaca wool cap—I just wanted to fall asleep again.

I returned from Isla del Sol to the Bolivian mainland to find an email waiting from Peter saying he'd gotten sick on his way home. I wrote him an email that spent about three sentences saying, *I hope you are okay. Drink water. I am imagining your fever,* and about twenty-three sentences saying, *I really think I have a botfly maggot living in me.* I was so self-absorbed there should have been a different word for what I was. Of course I would have loved that, if there had been a different word for what I was.

It was when I got back to New Haven—hungover from months of heavy drinking, my ankle swollen from whatever was growing inside it—that I finally saw the maggot: a flash of white that bobbed out of my ankle and then quickly disappeared under the skin again. It was just past midnight. I took a cab to the ER, where the intake nurse asked if I'd recently taken any mind-altering substances. I thought: *I wish I had one now.* The on-call doctor told me that he'd never heard of botfly, that there was nothing he could do for me. Actually, maybe there was *one* thing he could do for me. I took his Ativan with gratitude. It gave me a lovely swimming sensation, and my only regret was that such a gracious feeling was being wasted on the beige cubicle of an ER exam room. When I turned my head, the motion was slow enough to hold the thought *I am turning my head,* as if the words were rippling through my muscles. Things were easy and liquid. There was a worm living in my ankle, sure, but that was just one truth out of many truths.

A dermatologist eventually cut the botfly maggot out of my ankle, but almost immediately I grew convinced there was another botfly left inside—still moving around under the messy skin of the open wound. I wondered how much I'd have to drink before it curled up dead inside me.

Now that we were back in New Haven, I told Peter I wanted to get back together. But he was wary. He thought, reasonably enough, that we should talk about what was happening. We had spent a year doing little besides explaining ourselves to each other, but these choices—splitting up, getting back together—weren't things I wanted to explain. I responded to discomfort in sweeping, categorical ways: If it didn't feel right to be together, I wanted to be apart. If it didn't feel right to be apart, I wanted to be together. It was harder for me to stay inside a situation and repair it from the inside or wait it out. This was also the instant alchemy of drinking: It replaced one state with another, no questions asked.

I'd purged something in Bolivia, I told Peter. I'd gotten something out of my system. Now we just had to get this second worm out of my ankle. My boundless self-absorption was seeking something bounded. It was easier to focus on the body of a hypothetical parasite than on the more nebulous question of why we'd spent so many nights crying in humid Bolivian motels. So we filled a vitamin-jar cap with Vaseline and duct-taped it over my ankle, left it there overnight, and then clutched a pair of tweezers in the morning, ready to extract the woozy botfly that I was sure would emerge, nearly suffocated, from its glistening prison. When no botfly emerged, I didn't feel relief—only disappointment. If it had been there, I could have removed it.

— V —

SHAME

A few weeks after my return from Bolivia, I went out for drinks with Dave—whom I'd first seen years earlier, with a guitar and a goatee, and who'd become one of my closest friends in New Haven since that first dinner party with my bandaged thumb. He got a single Red Stripe that night. It's been almost a decade and I still remember it clearly, that single beer, because I limited myself to one drink as well—too self-conscious to get another if he wasn't going to get another, but thinking, *This is all we get?*

That summer, Dave had recently broken up with his girlfriend and moved out of their beautiful apartment—the one where I'd stayed as a prospective student, where his girlfriend had said, "We have a few different breakfast options." Their life had seemed like the epitome of what it meant to be an adult, eating artisanal granola in a sunlit linoleum kitchen, and the opposite of my own: filling plastic bowls with cigarette butts and watching laptop movies on a mattress, waiting till trash day to dump my empties in strangers' recycling bins.

After the breakup, Dave told me that their life had come to feel claustrophobic—but at the same time, when I stayed with them, it had seemed sophisticated and seamless—utterly enmeshed, the kind of stable unit I longed for. Of course a life never looks the same from the inside. "We were in these stable grooves of domesticity," Dave explained. "It had gone stagnant."

Though I was trying to repair my relationship with Peter, I was also interested in the sense of electricity that lived with other men, in other conversations—a species of possibility whose natural habitat was a dim bar with good midweek specials. When I told Dave about breaking up with Peter in Bolivia, I tried to make myself sound reckless and dramatic, someone who was desired more than I desired back. That was my working definition of power: being wanted more than you wanted. I had less to say about why Peter and I had gotten back together.

That fall Dave started inviting me over to his new apartment for dinner, and I started staying late, eating his massaman curry and his crème caramel. We did not admit to ourselves what we were doing, but we were doing it. In early November, he invited me to come on a road trip to Virginia to canvass for Obama with our graduate student union. We were going to swing the state blue for the first time in forty-four years. I framed the trip in terms of good-citizenship, but it wasn't solely about that. It was also about the buzz I got in my gut from the guilt and thrill of imagining what might happen.

This buzz blocked out everything else—like the fact that I still loved Peter, but didn't know how to stick around in a dynamic that had become tense and opaque. It was easier to break the thing with a hammer and start over. I'd grown up in a family where almost everyone had gotten divorced at least once. It seemed like a law of nature that love would go rotten or run out, eventually. You did what you could, and then you fled the premises. This inherited blueprint made so much intuitive sense to me it had gone transparent. It seemed inevitable.

The night before our first day of canvassing, Dave and I sat in a carpeted basement den, on a pullout couch, and watched a nature documentary called *Animals Behaving Badly*: the spitting frogs, the rampaging llamas. I drank water from a glass with a crab on it, glass after glass, as we crept further past midnight. It was an hour before we finally turned toward each other. When we kissed, he felt solid and alive. Guilt thrummed inside me like another pulse. This electric moment—crossing that first threshold, confessing desire—made me feel the same way a dirty martini did, so crisp and deadly cold, like it would leave you cleaner than it found you. I craved that sense of inner purge and renewal, no matter whom it hurt. It's nothing I can blame on my drinking, but it came from the same place drinking came from.

As we knocked on doors across the county the next day, and gathered with other union members in the motel lobby that night, I kept watching for a sign from Dave, that he didn't regret what had happened the night before—kept watching him laughing in crowds, talking to others, and by the time we finally kissed again, I was desperate for that kiss as confirmation. I took a train back to New Haven from Newport News, Virginia, and somewhere on that train ride, somewhere near the bowels of Penn Station, at three in the morning, I got a strange pain in my jaw that wouldn't go away, like something was burning all along the bone. It stuck around through Obama's victory, and through the night after, when I broke up with Peter over a casserole dish of vegetables I'd roasted—withered broccoli, dark and crispy, as we liked it, red onions burnt to charred wisps, spindly fingers of carrot—and white wine, our old familiar magnum.

Instead of guilt, I had a jaw on fire. The sensation endured for days. I was helping one of my graduate advisers organize a conference on postwar American literature, and when I drove up to the Hartford airport one night to fetch a hotshot young professor, my jaw burned all the way up I-91. After I met him at baggage claim, I pulled small talk out of my mouth like it was a nail I'd swallowed. Dave came over at two that morning. We ate grapes. Our newness was consuming. The next morning Dave sat with me while I smoked on my back steps, so Peter wouldn't see. I hadn't told him about us, and he still lived three blocks away. There was something I liked about that: the backyard smoking, the secret.

I went to a doctor and told her about my mysterious burning jaw. She might want to check for lupus, I suggested. I'd been doing research on the Internet. She said it didn't sound like lupus. She asked if I was getting enough sleep.

My adviser gave me a French press as a gift for helping to organize the conference. I'd done great, she said. And there was leftover wine. I should take it home, if I wanted.

In his diary, Berryman once wondered, in all capital letters, "WHETHER WICKEDNESS WAS SOLUBLE IN ART." He believed his flaws might become engines of beauty, and he trusted that self-awareness was one of the key ingredients in this alchemy. Alcoholic self-pity wasn't the secret engine of *The Dream Songs*, as Lewis Hyde had it, so much as their explicit subject. "You licking your own old hurt," Henry tells himself, inflating his self-pity so he can puncture it:

> What the world to Henry
> did will not bear thought.
> Feeling no pain,
> Henry stabbed his arm and wrote a letter
> explaining how bad it had been
> in this world.

This figure of a man stabbing his arm and "explaining how bad it had been," using his own blood as ink, lives inside the wound and also mocks it. This is what *The Dream Songs* do: They play with the pain. They sing it. They tease it. They don't dismiss it, but they know better than to take it at face value. Berryman asks us not to take everything so damn seriously.

In "Dream Song 22," we hear the disease announcing itself:

> I am the little man who smokes & smokes.
> I am the girl who does know better but.
>
> . . . I am the enemy of the mind.
> I am the auto salesman and lóve you.
> I am a teenage cancer, with a plan.
> I am the blackt-out man.
> I am the woman powerful as a zoo.

Drinking is an enemy. (It harms.) It's a salesman. (It convinces.) It lóves. (It offers solace.) It blacks out. It smokes and smokes. (So did he.) It knows better. (But.) Its power isn't the power of any single thing but the power of a menagerie, powerful as a zoo.

In many ways, Berryman knew himself better than his own mythologizers did, or at least he was wise to the appeal of certain mythologies. When he describes Henry as being "in the mood / to be a tulip and desire no more / but water, but light, but air," he acknowledges the appeal of transcending physical craving—just as *Life* would praise his "true intellectual's indifference to material things." But he promptly deflates the fantasy. "Suffocation called," he says, and confesses the "sirening" allure of his "dream-whiskey," always beckoning. The man who wants to live on nothing but water is called back to another thirst. That desire never shuts up. The girl knows better, *but*.

Henry is rarely proud of what he's done. In "Dream Song 310," he is *"all* regret, swallowing his own vomit, / disappointing people, letting everyone down / in the forests of the soul." Henry doesn't just *have* regret, he's made of it. It's all of him. He's swallowing the aftermath of a binge.

Lewis Hyde's critique of *The Dream Songs* assumed a certain binary: that Berryman was either guilty of his drinking, or else his wounds were deep enough to sanction it; that he was either exploring the "epistemology of loss," or else was just an alcoholic on his pity pot. But why are these mutually exclusive? Pain includes the pity pot. Pain spends time on the pity pot. Self-pity doesn't mean the pain isn't also real, and pain isn't less painful for being self-inflicted.

Nearly two decades after his critique of Berryman's self-pity, Hyde wrote a critical sequel to his reading of *The Dream Songs*, looking back at his own anger and calling it "the anger of anyone who has been close to an active alcoholic and gotten hurt." He called it "anger toward an intellectual community that seemed unable to respond to the wounded one in its midst."

Things got very bad for the wounded one, eventually. Describing his physical condition just a year before his suicide, Berryman wrote:

Diet: *poor.*
Weight: *bad.*
Digestion: *often bad.*
Other functions: *vomiting daily for weeks.*

This is no poem, just a set of replies to questions Berryman's body was forcing him to answer. He was sick of letting everyone down, sick of wandering through the forest, sick of the forest itself. He was sick of the sickness in his mouth, where the words came from.

D ave and I never decided to be together, we just were, eating scrambled eggs on long winter mornings. He was handsome in a way that was passionate, extravagant, sexual—not chiseled or pristine. He told me I should take calcium supplements so my bones didn't break when he fucked me. How can I describe him? I could tell you about the dark mess of his curls, his big nose, his full lips. I could tell you he was olive-complexioned, wiry and athletic, just shy of six feet; wore button-down flannel shirts and jeans that cost more than he liked to admit. But what do these descriptions do? Better to say that my desire for him felt luxuriant, like a rippling piece of fabric folded over and over itself. Better to say that his eyes nearly closed every time he laughed. When he laughed that hard, it was an event. His pleasure—at the world, at other people, at the play and electricity of a single conversation—was sincere and contagious.

A few weeks after we'd started seeing each other, I took a late train back from New York, where I'd been meeting with an agent about the possibility of sending my novel out to editors. I texted Dave to see if it was okay to take a taxi straight to his apartment from the station. I was eager to see him. I was always eager to see him. When he didn't text back, I started getting anxious: Was this too much? I checked my phone on the escalator that led up to the main concourse: a soaring marble cavern with massive windows and dangling amber lamps. The station was empty at midnight, echoing and dim, but as the escalator rose, I could see Dave sitting cross-legged on a blanket he'd laid across the marble floor, spread with fruit and cheese, a piece of cake, dark chocolate broken into triangles. "I made you a picnic," he said. He handed me a tiny bowl of pale vitamins. "For your bones."

When I was a child, one of my favorite chapter books was about a group of cousins who discover an enchanted tree. Every time they climb it, they find a different land waiting for them at the top: The Land of Goodies, the Land of Birthdays, the Land of Take-What-You-Want and Do-As-You-Please. Now I'd ridden the train-station escalator up to a strange new land.

It seemed destined: Dave and I had met all those years ago, as teenagers, and now we were together. We announced the size of our feelings however we could. We stood alone on a Connecticut beach, kelp-strewn and shadowed by jagged rocks, and took a picture of ourselves kissing in the cold salt wind. My scarf looked lifted by a ghost. We posed in front of the Origami Holiday Tree at the Museum of Natural History and Dave texted a photo to his mom. "Just what every Jewish mother wants," he told me. "Her firstborn in front of a giant Christmas tree with his new shiksa girlfriend."

There was a problem with our giddiness, though, a niggling loose tooth: Dave didn't like to get drunk. He drank, sure. He'd even gone to weekend bartender school, where he'd been timed on his Hairy Navels and his Harvey Wallbangers. But he drank the way people were supposed to drink, or the way I'd heard people sometimes drank. He had a beer, *singular*, with a friend. Or he tried a new cocktail for the taste. He wasn't expecting to get drunk every night. Even if I'd known in the abstract that some people drank like that, being close to it was endlessly confusing. Didn't he like being drunk? If so, why didn't he want to get drunk every single night? Being drunk seemed the only logical conclusion of drinking.

I wasn't using the word "alcoholic" with other people, wasn't describing myself or my drinking that way, but those were the years when I started writing it in my diary, secretly, often during blackouts, syntax out the window: *Is this what an alcoholic?* The messy scrawl of that drunk writing looked prophetic and absurd at once, as Lowry described it: "half crabbed, half generous, and wholly drunken," with lower-case *t*s "like lonely wayside crosses save where they crucified an entire word." It was as if a child just learning how to write had crawled inside my diary and called me by my name.

One night I went to Dave's apartment and sat in his living room for twenty minutes while he puttered in his kitchen making me a Cosmopolitan. I thought, *Can't I have a drink while I wait for my drink?* He'd set out a tray spread with pomegranate seeds and a delicate creamy hunk of Taleggio cheese, single jewels of fruit glistening in the candlelight and olives slick against my fingers. This was food for another type of person. I wanted to turn the plastic spigot on some box wine and eat six lemon bars and a slice of cake.

Dave's drinking set up a shimmering reality alongside mine: a way of being that was less fully saturated by need. His way of drinking was elegant and restrained; it plucked single pomegranate seeds. *Take it or leave it* is what they would call it — years later — in recovery. While I wanted to get drunk and dissolve into the evening, every evening, he honestly didn't care if we drank or not. His moderation switched on certain calculations inside of me that hadn't been happening before, that certainly hadn't happened with Peter. I started to keep track of how many times I'd suggested we find a bar, how many times I'd suggested a second round, how many times I'd suggested we stop at the wine store on the way home. Sometimes I drank a few glasses of wine before we met up, to give myself a head start, and on those nights, when I got to his place, I turned my face to let him kiss me on the cheek so he wouldn't smell it on my breath.

In the middle of December, after our graduate-student stipends had been deposited into our bank accounts, we drove up to Stonington, the coastal town where James Merrill—a poet Dave admired—had conducted Ouija board sessions to contact the spirit realm. We stayed at a bed-and-breakfast just a few blocks from the sea and used our own Ouija board on a rug by the fireplace. We filled our claw-foot tub with so much bubble bath that glistening foam flooded the bathroom floor like a snowdrift. We were excessive, and proud of our excess. When we went downstairs and saw the inn had laid out evening wine and cheese, I was relieved that the booze hadn't been my idea. Now I could enjoy it without having to show how much I'd wanted it. They filled our big wineglasses all the way to the top.

Years later, I heard an apocryphal anecdote about the comedian W. C. Fields, an anecdote Berryman had loved, about how Fields always requested a pitcher of martinis on the set of his movies, and called the pitcher his "pineapple juice." One day a clueless assistant actually filled the pitcher with pineapple juice and Fields exploded: "Who's been putting pineapple juice in my pineapple juice?" Just by drinking normally, Dave was exposing my drinking as something else.

At a party, Dave could go to the kitchen intending to grab another beer and I'd find him an hour later still chatting in the living room. He'd never made it to the fridge. He'd run into so many people on the way! If I headed to the kitchen for a drink, I'd end a hundred conversations if necessary. But Dave could leave a glass of wine half full in front of him for hours, and he was someone who'd probably see it that way: half full. Half full, half empty, whatever. I couldn't understand why you'd ever drink half of anything.

When I think of those early days with Dave, I think of a song he always used to play in his white clapboard apartment on

Cottage Street, how it boomed and vibrated, surging with synth and the sound of clapping hands: *There isn't much I feel I need, a solid soul and the blood I bleed.* One night we danced on the bar at a dive downtown—jukebox crooning, stepping between foam-lipped glasses; another night we smoked pot and stayed naked for twelve hours straight. The next morning he told me, "I feel like I cheated on you with the person you were last night," or I told him that. Certain joint-custody phrases lived between us for years. His mind was the mind I wanted filtering my world.

The first time we had to be apart, just for a week, we set up profiles on JDate and used them to communicate to each other in secret code. *My Ideal Relationship: Green eggs and ham, maybe a séance,* he wrote. *I am looking for a woman who shows me her scars like so many city monuments. My Perfect First Date: Animals Behaving Badly, all night long.*

That fall, Dave applied to poetry MFA programs. He was tired of training to be a scholar. He wanted to write poems and he wanted a new town. He'd been in New Haven too long: at that point, almost eight years. One of the programs he'd applied to—the one he was most excited about—was the Writers' Workshop in Iowa. Though I'd never imagined moving back, it seemed reckless and wonderful to picture us moving back together, dropping everything to start a new life. I'd just sold my novel, and gravity seemed to be bending its rules. My agent gave me the news while I stood in Dave's kitchen, running my fingers along bottles of specialty liquor that were mostly full because they weren't getting ruthlessly guzzled. It was surreal, an impossible thing—to think that the world wanted the novel that had begun during those lonely days when my grandmother was dying.

Dave and I started talking about moving for a year to Nicaragua, if he didn't get into Iowa, so he could write poems and I could write a novel about the Sandinista revolution. When I'd taught down in Nicaragua, an old woman on Calle Calzada had told me about the early years of the Sandinistas, looking me straight in the eyes, her hands folded across checkered oilcloth. The idea of writing something far away from my own life appealed to me—writing about people who'd committed their lives to something much bigger than private emotion or personal happiness, the driving forces I seemed to obey so absolutely.

It didn't take long for Peter to find out about me and Dave; it happened at a party at the old corset factory by the railroad tracks, a huge industrial building that had been converted into loft apartments. Peter cornered me in a doorway and asked if it was true what he'd heard, had I been seeing Dave? I nodded yes, and tried to explain—but he wasn't interested, and what was there to explain? It was ordinary and painful. It was also shamefully gratifying, sensing the pain I'd caused him. For me, that hurt was a measure of his desire.

That night in bed Dave told me he actually had no memory of me from that time we'd met in high school. He'd been playing guitar in the lobby, and I'd been—as I'd always feared—completely invisible. Or that was what I told myself: a story about lurking in the shadows then, to justify why I needed so much affirmation now.

That Thanksgiving, I went to a cabin by a lake with my brother and sister-in-law. It surprised me to realize that one of my first thoughts about the trip was one of anticipation: It would be nice to drink without Dave. Without my quite realizing it, every feeling about another person was also becoming a feeling about drinking.

At the lake, we stocked up on supplies for whiskey sours, and I started making them at noon. The first drink gathered all the threads of the day so nicely: the wind on the lake, rippling the water; red leaves gathered like snowdrifts outside; the sense of chill out there, somewhere else; the booze going down like candy. In *Under the Volcano*, the Consul senses "the fire of the tequila run down his spine like lightning striking a tree," and then, "miraculously, blossoms." The whiskey lit me up. This new thing with Dave glowed inside me, a talisman.

The glow dimmed as the night progressed. I drank whiskey sours until I was yellow-tongued and sticky-mouthed, checking my phone constantly to see if Dave had texted. When he didn't, I read it as verdict: He mattered more to me than I mattered to him, or at least he needed me less. My stomach ached and sloshed. The sugar of the whiskey sours was like a layer of algae inside me. When I was good and drunk, I lay back in bed and closed my eyes against the spins, curling into my guilt about cheating on Peter, which was dark and familiar. I got fetal inside it.

My life played as ticker-tape allegory against the back of my eyelids: I was GUILTY but I was also FALLING IN LOVE and all my feelings were THE BIGGEST FEELINGS and they existed in CAPITAL LETTERS. The cheating had been WRONG but this new man was AMAZING and our new thing was HUGE and I was the WORST person but also the BEST person, because this new love was ENDLESS, even if the wages of LOVE had been SIN, and the wages of SIN should be MISERY. Everything was the best or the worst. Selfhood was a deck of superlatives I kept reshuffling. I didn't want just part of someone, I wanted *all* of him. I wasn't just bad, I was the lowest. I had the *most* fickle heart. I was the whiskey-sour scum of the earth. Some part of me actually enjoyed the guilt, which capitalized my ordinary life and granted it the shrill inflection of high drama. If wickedness was soluble in art, I needed wickedness.

In recovery, years later, when someone described self-loathing as the flip side of narcissism, I almost laughed out loud at the stark truth of what she'd said. This black-and-white thinking, this all-or-nothing, it was cut from the same cloth. Being just a man among men, or a woman among women, with nothing extraordinary about your flaws or your mistakes — that was the hardest thing to accept.

A month after Peter and I broke up, a friend of mine told me she'd spent the night with him. She was sheepish about it. (*You should be!* I thought, from my precarious moral high ground.) She also told me he wasn't doing well. When he was with her, he'd had a black eye from falling down drunk the night before. I got that. It made a lot more sense than taking half an hour to make a cocktail.

Malcolm Lowry understood the siren call of superlatives, and *Under the Volcano* exposes its antihero, the Consul, as a man dependent on the twin gods of booze and melodrama. Lowry himself was rabidly committed to the idea of writing not just a novel about alcoholism, but the Best Novel Ever Written About Alcoholism. He believed his drinking could be redeemed only if it was transfigured into epic, writ large across a sweeping dramatic canvas. That was the hope he pinned on *Under the Volcano*: that it would redeem the wreckage of his life. As he described it later, he wanted to turn "his greatest weakness...into his greatest strength."

Everything was outsized—his motivations, his ambitions, his dysfunction, his plot—and when Jackson published *The Lost Weekend*, in 1944, Lowry was devastated and indignant. He had been working on *Under the Volcano* for almost a decade, sustained by the idea that he would write the first truly groundbreaking account of alcoholism; and he was heartbroken by the fact that Jackson had beaten him to the punch, not to mention the fact that Jackson's novel had achieved such instant success, hitting bestseller lists immediately. Lowry judged Jackson's book for its absent layers of Higher Meaning—deeming its vision of boozing (tedious) an insult to his vision of boozing (tragic)—but this snobbery was cold comfort: Jackson had still belittled his masterpiece by making it unoriginal. Lowry wanted a monopoly on tragedy, even though his novel exposed the foolishness of a drunkard's need to do just that.

Published in 1947, *Under the Volcano* takes place on the Day of the Dead, as the Consul drinks himself into the "swift leathery perfumed alcoholic dusk" of a fictional Mexican town called Quauhnahuac.

(Based on Cuernavaca, where Lowry himself had lived, and gotten grotesquely, ongoingly drunk.) The Consul has been left by his wife, Yvonne, and has spent the past year longing for her return. But once Yvonne arrives, all the Consul can talk about is the bender he went on in Oaxaca after she went away. He has been hoping that her return can save him from himself, but it only ends the illusion that he could be saved by anything at all.

The novel's plot, despite its fever-dream pulse, is surprisingly faithful to the smallness of a drunk's life: We see the Consul trying not to drink, sipping a strychnine concoction from a doctor, hunting for his hidden booze, trying to fuck his wife, failing to fuck his wife, trying not to drink, drinking anyway, passing out. Rather than offering some sentimental vision of whatever homes we make in the darkness, *Under the Volcano* illuminates these delusions from the inside. The novel does offer the drunkard as martyr and symbol, his booze a dark communion — the Consul drinks as if he "were taking an eternal sacrament," and laments a world "that trampled down the truth and drunkards alike!" — but the Consul's melodrama invariably gets exposed and chastised. As another character puts it: "Do you realize that while you're battling against death, or whatever you imagine you're doing, while what is mystical in you is being released, or whatever it is you imagine is being released, while you're enjoying all this, do you realize what extraordinary allowances are being made for you by the world which has to cope with you?"

When other characters chastise the Consul, it's also Lowry chastising himself for the extraordinary allowances made on his behalf. The book reads like a drunkard's grandiosity punctured by an author who wants to exorcise the fantasies fueling his own drinking. The Consul's drunk body constantly interrupts his lyrical indulgences: "The will of man is unconquerable," he explains, then falls asleep. He is "suddenly overwhelmed by sentiment, as at the same time by a violent attack of hiccups." Drinking is a thwarted flight into transcendence; like a dog chained to a post, barking at the sky.

When the Consul delivers a rhapsodic monologue about the enchanted splendor of a "cantina in the early morning," Yvonne interrupts to ask if their gardener has left for good. The garden is a mess. The Consul remains undeterred. He has nothing but love songs for the ragged divinity of barfly living: "How, unless you drink as I do, can you hope to understand the beauty of an old woman from Tarasco who plays dominoes at seven o'clock in the morning?" One senses that—to the Consul—the woman playing dominoes at the bar is still beautiful at eight in the morning, and nine in the morning, and ten at night. One senses that the Consul wants to believe he is the only one who can see it: "Ah none but he knew how beautiful it all was, the sunlight, sunlight, sunlight flooding the bar of El Puerto del Sol, flooding the watercress and oranges." The "Ah" becomes a recurring textual street sign: *Beware melodrama ahead.* But the Consul's insistence on the singularity of his own drunk vision is perpetually undermined by the sleeve-tugging queries of the practical world: the messy garden, an attack of hiccups.

The Consul's tragedy isn't the tragedy of Higher Meaning, it's the tragedy of *absent* meaning—the fact that his suffering might not mean anything at all. Critic Michael Wood calls it "a great book about missing grandeur, about the specialized tragedy that lies in the unavailability of the tragedy you want." The Consul is constantly imagining the epic stories that might include him: "Vague images of grief and tragedy flicked in his mind. Somewhere a butterfly was flying out to sea: lost."

Lost! One imagines the newspaper headlines playing like ticker tape inside the Consul's tipsy sense of history: SMALL ORANGE BUTTERFLY NOT SURE WHICH WAY IS NORTH; MAN GETS DRUNK AND FINDS EVERYTHING PROFOUND.

Under the Volcano ultimately granted Lowry a certain literary pedestal, garnering lasting acclaim that Jackson never received, but Lowry's drinking only got worse after the novel made him famous. "Success may be the worst possible thing that could happen to any serious author," he wrote to his mother-in-law. He was a wreck when he came to New York to celebrate his reviews. "He is the original Consul in the book," observed someone who saw him on that trip, "a curious kind of person — handsome, vigorous, drunk — with an aura of genius about him and a personal electricity almost dangerous, demon-possessed." His delirium tremens got so bad he couldn't hold a pencil. Lowry's intelligence could see the drinking from every angle, but he couldn't find a way out of it.

"A little self-knowledge is a dangerous thing," says the Consul's half brother, not so fond of sobriety himself. We see this self-knowledge lodged in the novel like a worm at the bottom of a tequila bottle. It didn't save anyone.

Dave and I threw a miracle berry party that January. This meant everybody got a little purple pill that made everything turn sweet. We served lemons and limes and grapefruits. You could bite into them whole, like apples. They tasted like candy. It was the middle of winter, and my kitchen was hot with the bodies of graduate students. I drank beer that tasted like chocolate, and wine that tasted like syrup, and at a certain point the night flickered into blackout. People were there and then they weren't; it was just me and Dave in bed. Then it was me and Dave in bed, but it was morning. This was the first real blackout I'd had with him — the first time I'd let myself go that far.

After a blackout, memory deals out bits of the night before like a partial poker hand. You get pieces of the picture, but never find out exactly what hand you played. I asked Dave what had happened: Had I embarrassed myself in front of everyone, or was it only obvious after they'd gone?

"Only after they'd gone," he said. "I think."

This was good news.

"I was scared," he said. "You weren't making sense."

Dave wasn't usually someone who said things like *I was scared*. But there it was. I'd been muttering, upset, incomprehensible. When we got up to clean the kitchen, it was cold, and my backyard was glazed with frost beyond my attic windows, glinting in the pure harsh light of winter. A squirrel had gotten himself to the top of a telephone pole and didn't seem able to get down again. I thought he looked terrified. Dave thought maybe he was just triumphant. The winter light was gorgeous, sharp and crystalline, but I didn't feel entitled to it. It was like the Consul, as Lowry described him: "He had lost the sun: it was not his sun."

Meanwhile, the kitchen was a mess. Everything that had been sweet was simply itself again, shriveled or crusted. Plastic red cups were everywhere. When Dave lifted a spoon from the table and the paper plate beneath it lifted as well, sticky with wine, it looked like the plate was floating in air. Dave saw the floating plate; I saw the stain of wine. He wanted to take a picture: *Levitation!* I was already thinking: Will I drink again tonight? And where? And when?

When I pictured Peter's black eye, from his fall, I tried to imagine how he'd struck his face, or where else he was bruised, and wondered who was taking care of him. I wondered if he'd taken a night off getting drunk — maybe a Monday. It was as if Peter and I were still inside something together, something that had to do with the drinking. In that way, we were more alike than I would ever be like Dave.

I was pregnant when we threw our miracle berry party, though I didn't know it yet. When I took a pregnancy test a few weeks later, in a bathroom tucked deep in the labyrinthine corridors of a massive Gothic castle on campus, the plus sign made something bloom in me: joy and terror at once. Dave met me after one of my seminars, which I'd spent twitchy and distracted, listening to other people talk about postcolonial departures from traditional lyric forms. It was early February: flinty skies over weathered stone, grass trodden and defeated under patches of snow. Dave took my gloved hand in his gloved hand

and asked me what I wanted to do. He said: "I will stick by you no matter what you choose."

It surprised me: not that he would stick by me, but that he was approaching the moment as a choice. I couldn't imagine having a baby—not right then, just a few months into our love, when everything was just beginning. The fact that Dave was willing, that he was saying he would summon himself for that, for a lifetime of parenting together, made the possibility actual: I pictured him teaching a small floppy-haired boy to play the guitar. I pictured him listening to our daughter's make-believe story, asking her questions: *How did the little squirrel learn to be less afraid?* Once I talked to him, I was more aware of the loss than I had been on my own: the loss of a creature we had created with our bodies and then created again, with our conversation that day in the brittle chill, putting our imaginations toward the possibility of a shared life.

Once I realized I was pregnant, I was repulsed by how much I'd been drinking. I pictured a not-yet-baby built of gin, with little fin feet and cauliflower hands, pickled inside me. But I didn't stop. If I was going to have an abortion, what difference did it make? It still made me sick, picturing the fetus like a tiny ice cube cloaked in whiskey. I was nervous about the recovery—afraid of seeming needy, or unappealing; afraid of being wanted less. How long would we have to wait to have sex again?

On the morning I got the abortion, Dave held my hand as we walked past the protesters outside Planned Parenthood—elderly, in lawn chairs, holding the same poster board they always held, a webby mess of tissue and blood. I was angry at them, for all the women they'd spooked and shamed, but I also felt a sorrow I couldn't account for. It had to do with the way they spent so many of their days on these lawn chairs, grieving.

When I got out, three hours later, I was grateful for Dave's hand, grateful for the smell and solidity of him—the grain of his beard stubble against my cheek. He hugged me, hard, for long moments, in the middle of the waiting room. Years later, he wrote a poem that ended with that same memory of our bodies together: "They kiss each other in the middle of a waiting room and cry, / because they are not thinking / of how they will be seen." I couldn't remember kissing in the waiting room, or crying, but I could remember precisely what it had been like: not thinking of being seen. I could remember his embrace as enfolding, absolute.

A month after the abortion, I had heart surgery to correct persistent tachycardia—episodes of rapid, gratuitous heartbeats that I was told would slowly wear out my heart before its time. I wasn't going to fall down dead if it wasn't treated. But I might not live as long. This was interesting to me: I wasn't saving my life now; I was giving more years to a future version of myself. I was preserving her. It was the second time I was asking Dave to take care of me, right on the heels of the abortion—after nights I'd spent lying awake in bed beside him, twisting with the hot swirled knot of a pain I hadn't quite expected. When he woke, he rubbed my back, and whispered into my neck. There was something I liked about the dynamic: being cared for, being understood as vulnerable. But it made me ashamed to find any part of it appealing.

The night before the surgery, I was careful to drink only a few glasses of wine. This seemed prudent, to make sure there wasn't too much stray booze running through my system when I went into surgery the next morning. Before we went to bed, I told Dave I was nervous: What if it didn't work? What if something went wrong and I ended up with a pacemaker? I'd been told this was unlikely but possible.

What I saw on Dave's face then was an expression I hadn't seen before: a hardening, as if the blood had cooled into a solid gel beneath his skin. "You shouldn't worry," he said. "What good would it do?"

I was suddenly embarrassed, like I had done something wrong by worrying, or burdened him by speaking it. I didn't say anything more.

After I woke up from surgery, the surgeons told me it hadn't worked. My cardiologist came to my hospital bed with a bottle of pills—a beta-blocker called Sotalol—that I was supposed to start taking instead. The drug was strong enough that I had to stay in the hospital for three more days while they tracked its effect on my heart. When I noticed a little martini glass on the side, with an *X* through it, I immediately hid my dread behind casual questions: Was this pro forma? I asked hopefully. Just a generally-not-a-good-idea-to-be-drinking-on-medication situation? Or was it serious? I wanted the cardiologist to bottom-line it: Could I drink or not?

The doctor suggested I not drink for a few months and we'd see how it went. Sure. And maybe I could also spend a few months never using my hands. I was frustrated not just by the prospect of not drinking (*anything at all??*), but also by the idea that this wouldn't be a big deal, that we could just "wait and see."

Dave spent nights with me in the hospital. He brought me bread pudding, our two plastic forks sticking out of the wobbly vanilla loaf, and he learned which drawer at the nurse's station held extra stashes of the graham crackers I liked. He made them sacred, those hospital days. But there were certain things that confused me. When I was discharged and he came to pick me up, for example, he called from the car. "Can you just meet me down here?" he said. "I don't want to park." I'd been in a hospital bed for five days, but didn't want to ask for extra help; it seemed like I'd already asked for too much of it. So I hoisted my duffel bag on my shoulder and came down—had to sit down in the elevator, right on the cold dirty floor, so I wouldn't faint. When I got in the car, I said nothing. I could remember the look on Dave's face when I'd told him I was scared—before the surgery—and I didn't want to see it again.

Once I got home from the hospital, I decided the doctor's advice about not drinking was just *advice*. She would have been more adamant and less casual if it wasn't. It was advice I decided not to follow. We could just *see*, I thought. This meant trying to cut back on drinking, failing to cut back on drinking, and not taking my heart medication whenever I'd drunk a lot, which seemed like due diligence. I also Googled "Sotalol" alongside every type of alcohol I could think of, to see if I could find reassurance that it was okay, or else a warning dire enough to make me stop drinking entirely.

About a month later, my cardiologist ordered something called a Holter monitor to test if my medication was working. It was a box I wore around my neck for twenty-four hours, attached to EKG monitors stuck to my chest that measured my heart rate. I told myself I wouldn't drink for the day I was wearing it. I didn't want to fuck up the results. I was stuffed with Internet wisdom: "Drinking alcohol affects how well Sotalol works," the New Zealand Medicines and Medical Devices Safety Authority had said—in bolded letters, quoting the drug company—and I believed them. If I drank with my Holter monitor, I imagined the data would be incriminating evidence, my heart rate spiking around twilight. But then I went to a reading on campus and it seemed weird, almost ungrateful, not to have one glass of wine afterward—it was free!—and before I knew it, I was sitting at a bar downtown with a friend, drinking a martini with my weird little heart contraption dangling around my neck.

A week later, my cardiologist called to say the Sotalol wasn't working. I had to stay in the hospital for another three days while they tested the new drug, whose bottle *also* had a little martini glass with an *X* over it. So I switched drugs, kept drinking, kept Googling— this time with a new drug in the search bar: "Flecainide + alcohol + death."

That spring, Dave found out he had been accepted at the Writers' Workshop, and we flew to Iowa to look at apartments—giddy at figuring out the contours of our new life in a new town. We'd been together about five months, and his acceptance felt like fate cosigning on our giddiness. For Dave, a child of the Boston suburbs, it was his first time west of the Mississippi. We rented a second-floor apartment in a white farmhouse down the street from the local Co-op, only a few minutes' walk from where I'd lived five years earlier, for that first year of bonfires and blackouts. This was a different sort of thrill, making a home together so quickly—like putting down a huge bet on a promising pocket pair in Texas Hold'em before you know the flop, the turn, or the river. I was ready to return to Iowa with the things I'd wanted, back when I lived there the first time: a man and a bit of success, two measures of value I'd always understood as linked. Dave was elated at the thought of spending two years writing poems—as opposed to writing *about* poems, which he'd been doing in our doctoral program— and excited to move to a town that didn't hold eight years of his past.

In those days I was editing my novel, still drinking, and still writing my heavy-drinking character as a woman with whom I had nothing in common. My editor told me she wanted the novel to dramatize the possibility of recovery—as narrative tension, even if it got thwarted. What if I included an AA meeting, or even a stretch of sobriety?

I'd never been to an AA meeting, and couldn't really imagine one. I pictured folding chairs in a church basement, Styrofoam cups of steaming coffee. That was it. But I didn't want to go to one for research. Perhaps some part of me was nervous about what I'd hear. So I summoned a vague sketch, and wrote about Tilly watching people who were part of something—making coffee, trading phone numbers, swapping life stories—and deeming herself a failure in comparison, because her sobriety consisted of memorizing the TV schedule and watching the clock. That was all I could grant sobriety. Even Mondays without drinking had been bad enough.

Tilly goes to the AA meeting with her adult son, who walks out partway through because he doesn't want to be there. I didn't want to be there either—in the scene, or writing it. As Tilly watches her son leave, she thinks about the difference between them: that he could walk out of the room because he didn't live in the world she lived in, a world defined by ceaseless longing. I wasn't yet sure which world I lived in, whether I was someone who could stand up and awkwardly pick her way between the folding chairs, walk out on thirst like a lover I was done with, or whether I had to stay in the room—a room full of people who had to do something about their constant wanting.

In his book *In the Realm of Hungry Ghosts*, Gabor Maté—the clinician who worked with skid-row addicts in Vancouver—compares addicts to "hungry ghosts" on the Buddhist Wheel of Life: "creatures with scrawny necks, small mouths, emaciated limbs, and large, bloated, empty bellies." Their bodies are physical expressions of that "aching emptiness" that drives addiction, what Maté describes as a search for "something outside ourselves to curb an insatiable appetite for relief or fulfillment." But for Maté, addicts don't have a monopoly on the quest: "They have much in common with the society that ostracizes them. In the dark mirror of their lives, we can trace the outlines of our own."

To argue that addiction holds a dark mirror up to more universal hungers isn't a denial of its physical mechanisms—neurotransmitters and their adaptations—or a denial of chemical dependence as a discrete phenomenon with its own physiological reality. It's simply an acknowledgment that the operative urges of addiction aren't unrelated to desires that show up in everyone: the urge to court bliss, to dull pain, to find relief.

For decades, much of the scientific research on addiction suggested a certain inevitability in its mechanisms—as if it operated outside of context, compelled by its own unique velocity. From the late sixties to the late eighties, the scientific studies that got the most press (and often the best funding) were the ones where caged animals were trained to give themselves drugs until they did so compulsively. One laboratory joke maintained that the definition of a drug was any substance that, when given to a rat, produced a journal article. Rats pushed the cocaine lever until they died.

These journal articles eventually turned into household wisdom and after-school specials: "Cocaine Rat" was the title of a 1988 PSA video that showed a white rat gnawing pellets in desperation until it keeled over, its little claws fumbling in the air, its matted fur shadowed by the bars of its cage. "It's called cocaine," said the voice-over, "and it can do the same thing to you."

But the voice-over didn't explain that these rats, the ones that pressed the coke lever until they died, were kept alone in bare white cages. They had injection apparatuses implanted in their backs. They were often starved. A few scientists eventually wondered: What if they were given some company? What if they were given something else to do? In the early eighties, these scientists designed Rat Park, a spacious plywood habitat painted with pine trees and filled with climbing platforms, running wheels, tin cans for hiding, wood chips for playing, and—most important—lots of other rats. The rats in that cage didn't press the coke lever until they died. They had better things to do. The point wasn't that drugs *couldn't* be addictive, but that addiction was fueled by so much besides the drugs themselves. It was fueled by the isolation of the white cage, and by the lever as substitute for everything else.

Most addicts don't live in barren white cages—though some do, once they've been incarcerated—but many live in worlds defined by stress of all kinds, financial and social and structural: the burdens of institutional racism and economic inequality, the absence of a living wage. The original cover of George Cain's *Blueschild Baby* featured a drawing of a black man tying off his arm with a strip of the American flag, popping out the veins for his next dose of heroin.

"What was it that did in reality make me an opium eater?" Thomas De Quincey wondered in 1821. "Misery, blank desolation, abiding darkness."

Most addicts describe drinking or using as filling a lack. I once met a woman who described herself as a bucket that had sprung a leak, and she kept trying to fill it—with liquor, with affirmation, with love. David Foster Wallace once called booze "the interior jigsaw's missing piece." The leaky bucket and the missing puzzle piece are visions of Sedgwick's "self thus self-construed as lack." Though these circular statements of cause—you drink to fill the lack, but the drinking only deepens it—all raise the same question: Where does the lack come from?

I could tell you a thousand and one stories about mine. I could tell you a story about the men in my family, as I've already started to— about my frequent-flier father, my godly brothers and their powerful reserve—and how a self comes into its shape by seeking. This is the depth-psychology fairy tale, airplane ticket stubs as smoking gun: *Aha!* But I've always distrusted the neatness of this story—dime-store psychoanalysis, turning wounds to tarot cards—or the ways it seemed to blame my relationship to substances on people who have spent my whole life loving me. My childhood was easier than most, and I ended up drinking anyway.

Maybe I need to tell a different story about lack. Maybe it wasn't about my father's life on airplanes so much as his wiring, the parts of his genetic code he passed along to me, the chromosomal variations we shared that made our neural systems more primed to coax dependencies. I imagine tracing our chromosomal inheritance back through generations—my father, his father, who knows how many fathers before him, all the way back through the whiskey-strung branches of our family tree. I can't even count how many free shots of whiskey our surname has secured for me over the years, as if my alcoholic ancestors were raising a glass in my direction.

Or maybe the lack is systemic: I was born into late capitalism, an economic system that sold me on the notion that I was insufficient so it could sell me on the notion that consumption was the answer to my insufficiency. It's true that people loved getting fucked up long before capitalism, but it's also true that one of the core promises of capitalism — transformation through consumption — is another version of the promise addiction makes. *Make something of yourself:* This is one of the secular articles of faith in the American gospel of productivity. So I spent years making as much as I could, as well as I could. But at the end of the day — more specifically, at the end of *each* day — I was exhausted by all that making, and wanted the chatter of these exhortations quieted. So, gin. So, wine.

If we imagine the story of the lack as something encoded within us, an internal set of blueprints for a sense of absence, then it's a story that is still being written. The Collaborative Studies on Genetics of Alcoholism is an ongoing research project, running since 1989, that has interviewed and sampled blood from more than 17,000 members of over 2,200 families, trying to illuminate the specific genetic factors that put people at risk for alcoholism, trying to substantiate — in a broader sense — my father's conviction that drinking was more dangerous for us.

The COGA study has linked certain phenotypes (observable characteristics) to specific DNA regions on various chromosomes: the "low level of response" phenotype (i.e., you need to drink more to feel the same thing) and the "alcohol dependence" phenotype were both linked to the same region on chromosome 1, while the "maximum number of drinks…ever consumed in a 24-hour period" phenotype (usually 9 or more was a sign of trouble) was linked to a region on chromosome 4. The evidence supporting a genetic basis for alcoholism is pretty much indisputable.

Which is to say: We're all dependent, but some people are more dependent than others, and different forms of dependence deform our lives in different ways. My drinking had something to do with my family, and something to do with my brain, and something to do with the values I was raised to worship: excellence, enchantment, superlative everything. All these tales of *why* are true and also insufficient. A state of insufficiency is part of being human, and I responded to my particular state of insufficiency by drinking—because I was wired for it and groomed for it, because once I started doing it, it was so eloquent in its delivery of a particular bodily guarantee: *With this, you will feel like enough.*

Drinking promised a version of consciousness that didn't mean endless twisting and turning in the bedsheets of myself, tangled and restless, aching for dreams. Booze promised relief from the default state of needing something from men. It was an object I could always make available. But when it broke these promises, again and again, it also sharpened the need that made me crave it in the first place. It was a bait and switch: It promised bliss and offered shame. It promised self-sufficiency and offered dependence. It also felt really fucking *good*. But it was always just a temporary flight. When I returned to myself each morning, the groove of lack had just grown deeper, more stubbornly etched—like a skip, skip, skip in the song.

The summer before we moved to Iowa, I turned twenty-six in a little town called Riomaggiore, on Italy's Ligurian coast, where Dave and I were spending our final graduate-student stipend checks—impulsively, romantically, unwisely—on a little apartment overlooking the Mediterranean. Riomaggiore was arranged around a single steep road running from the hills down to the sea, where fishing boats bobbed around a wooden ramp jutting into the waves. Tall narrow houses crowded the road like crooked teeth, painted shades of fuchsia, buttercream, tangerine, mint, and rose. For some reason, all the window shutters were painted green. Dave and I sat on the rocks by the water, baking in the sun, and made up stories to explain why they'd all been painted the same color.

"Well, it definitely had to do with a woman," Dave said.

"Maybe an affair?" I suggested. We imagined a woman with

pistachio eyes and the mayor who couldn't have her—so he made a rule that all the town's shutters had to be painted the same shade as her eyes, as an oblique homage to his hidden love.

That week was full of play: pinning notes to each other on the clothesline outside our kitchen window, next to my salt-crusted bikini; and cooking a local dish called Octopus in Hell, which involved tomatoes, olive oil, and patience. The restaurants in town served wine in pitchers, the way restaurants back home served water, and being on vacation somewhere beautiful made it less awkward to get tipsy every night. I'd never told Dave I wasn't supposed to drink on my heart medication, so he never bothered me about it. But every once in a while, lying in bed at night after too much booze, my heart went wild—hammering under my ribs.

Dave loved a local cake called *torta di riso*, made from rice and orange rind, and convinced himself that the elderly woman who ran a bakery near the dock was going to teach him how to make it.

"She's not just going to invite a stranger back into her kitchen," I told him.

"We'll see." He shrugged, smiling, and the next thing I knew, he was standing over a flour-dusted butcher-block table in the woman's ancient kitchen, learning how to simmer the rice in milk steeped with orange peels and a single, monstrous brown vanilla pod. Dave thought he could charm his way into everything. Most of the time, he could.

One afternoon we were lying in bed after sex, talking about Milton's *Paradise Lost*—one of the books I had to prepare for my oral exams that September—and I was busy defending Eve. She'd been framed.

"Well," he said, "you can't really say Eve *wasn't* responsible for the fall."

"If you were made from someone's fucking *rib*," I said, "you might want to eat from the tree of knowledge too."

"The serpent was preying on her vanity," he said. Somehow our voices grew edgier. I didn't like that I was naked, and pulled the sheets tighter around my body. It was less about the argument itself—Eve was guilty, Adam was guilty, the serpent was guilty; no one was clean, that was the whole point—and more that neither one of us could let go. Both of us needed to be right.

For my birthday, Dave told me he was going to teach me how to ride a bike. From the moment he realized that I'd never learned, he'd been determined to teach me. "It'll be amazing," he said. "You'll always remember this birthday as the one where you learned to ride a bike."

"Okay," I said, because I didn't want to disappoint him. But in truth, I didn't want to spend my birthday learning how to ride a bike. I wanted to lie on the rocks in the sun, and make up stories about window shutters, and drink red wine from ceramic pitchers.

We rented a bike and took it to a dirt path running through the hills above the town. The sun beat down, and for hours I kept trying and tipping over, and trying and tipping over. Dave steadied the bike and pushed me from behind. "Just pedal!" he said. "Just trust it!" But I couldn't trust. "Being afraid of falling is what makes you fall," he said, which only made the whole thing seem like a verdict on my character.

For an hour we tried: me pedaling, the bike tipping, him bewildered and amused. My nerves gave way to a brute physical frustration that eventually made me kick the bike, like a kid throwing a tantrum. I started crying. "Can we just stop?" I said.

"It frustrates you to not be in control," he said, dead calm.

"I just want to stop," I said.

"After a few more tries," he said, the disappointment plain across his face.

When I looked at it from his perspective, my reaction seemed absurd: He'd planned this whole afternoon to celebrate my birthday, and I'd ruined it by getting upset. But my fear of disappointing him was a raw panic in my gut—not something I could control. I just wished he could have said: *You hate this. Let's stop.* So much of our play—the stories we made up, the notes we exchanged, our little fights about books — was about impressing each other. Sometimes it got exhausting.

On our last night, we sat in rickety wooden chairs on our balcony and ate melon wrapped in fatty prosciutto, pocked with sea salt; drank wine from mugs; watched lightning crack in sharp sudden knife blades over the water. The bike lesson was just an absurdity in the rearview mirror. Why had I been crying? There was music coming from a church on the hill. We got up and danced, took off our clothes, felt the cool salt air and the warmth of each other's bodies.

In Milan — on our way home — we drank martinis by the green canals, strolling past antique stores selling junked gilded birdcages, and cafés where women smoked long cigarettes through frosted pink lips while Serge Gainsbourg played from secret speakers. Woozy and drunk — grateful for the world as stage set and soundtrack to our love — I was sure we'd get married someday, and our life would be made of nights like these.

This was what drinking felt like when it still felt good. It felt good to drink cloudy pastis in a pub that summer, playing cards with Dave and his brothers, staining our mouths crimson with cheap house red. It felt good to drive out to a friend's cottage and pass a bottle of whiskey around a bonfire, toasting marshmallows over the flames and wrapping garlic bread in tinfoil to make it bubbling hot. It felt good to drink cold Red Stripes on the porch of our new apartment in Iowa, to drink white wine in the humid kitchen, *our* humid kitchen, while I garnished plates of risotto, the first meal I'd ever cooked for him, that night I'd sliced my thumb. These were the nights — on the balcony, in the pub, by the bonfire — I carried as proof, saying *See, it can be perfect*, wanting so badly to believe that the drinking could electrify everything without price.

At first, life with Dave in Iowa was luminous: late-summer evenings on our wooden porch, eating sweet corn and zebra tomatoes tossed into crude, perfect salads with Amish goat cheese and ripped hunks of baguette. We spent afternoons playing pinball in dim bars, giving ourselves faint mustaches of beer foam as silver balls pinged through the sticky quiet hours. We went for brunch at a friend's cottage by the river, found him frying bacon in the kitchen, smoking a cigarette over the stove. That morning smelled like coffee and smoke, tasted like the sizzling salt heat of the bacon; glinted like sun off the river.

Dave loved the world of writers in Iowa City, the community and bohemian allure of it — the vaporlike quality of Iowa socializing, how it would expand to fill as much time as you wanted to give it — conversations spilling across the edges of hours, nights ending where you hadn't expected them to end: walking the visiting poet back to where he was staying as dawn broke over Dodge Street, or riffing about parataxis on someone's busted brown corduroy couch. Dave had left the dry, airless corridors of scholarship to live a more expansive life, to live another version of the early twenties he'd spent more domestically, in a four-year relationship with an older woman. But I was growing tired of home-pickled vegetables and drunken poetry recitations. These potlucks are *ridiculous,* I thought. Who could attend so many in a week? Part of me just felt excluded. The poets had their seminars by the river, and their bar nights after class — and I had early shifts at the bakery where I'd started working, three or four days a week, to pay my share of the rent. I woke at six in the morning and walked a mile to a little yellow house by the railroad tracks, owned and run by a woman named Jamie: funny, efficient, demanding; someone with no time for bullshit. When I came in to ask for a job and she asked if I had any bakery experience, I'd said, "Not really," then "Not at all," and she hired me anyway.

In a cramped kitchen with an eight-foot double oven and a walk-in freezer stocked with frozen slabs of dough, we made chocolate-raspberry cakes and sticky buns and banana bread, all our bodies moving in a fluid choreography between the prep counters and the cake island. The floor mixer was as tall as a little man, and had four speeds and a gear transmission, like a car. "It's a Hobart," my boss told me, as if I was supposed to understand what that meant. My beat was sugar cookies in seasonal shapes—leaves and pumpkins during my first few months—as well as front of the house: running the register, busing tables, pulling espresso shots. I loved the job. Jamie intimidated me—around her, I felt timid and meek—but it was nice to have a place where I was needed, if not exactly skilled.

The bakery was also introducing me to a different version of Iowa City than I'd known the first time around, when I hadn't had a single number in my cell phone with a 319 prefix, the local area code, because everyone in my life was from somewhere else. Now I got texts from my boss asking me to pick up shifts, or from the head baker—a guy my own age with a massive unfinished tattoo on his biceps, a sense of humor perched between sarcasm and cheesiness, and two kids, a toddler and a baby—who texted me photos of his perfect meringues, to brag. When my boss brought her five-year-old daughter into the shop, I would pull over a stool and ask her to help me wash dishes in the industrial three-tub sink in the back; we'd both get our arms fully soaped.

At the workshop, everyone was basically between the ages of twenty-two and thirty-five, stylish and sharp, but the people in my world at the bakery wore less black and smiled more. I got to know the couple in their fifties who came in every day at seven-thirty and ordered coffee and morning biscuits—like scones, with a dollop of strawberry jam—and asked how my book was going, and I lied and said "Great," when in truth I hadn't begun it.

Back home, in our white farmhouse at the corner of Dodge and Washington, life with Dave wasn't exactly unfolding as a parade of midnight train-station picnics. It was often spent arguing about something in the kitchen, like where to put the rolling dishwasher with only three wheels, the one Dave had insisted on bringing with us; or who should wash the pile of dishes in the sink, because the dishwasher was too much trouble to roll anywhere. (It only had three wheels!) Our life was spent scheduling the Internet guy, and scanning the right documents to get me enrolled as a domestic partner for health insurance. Life was the rent, and the fickle vacuum cleaner, and the slow creep of silence, a silence I wanted to understand as intimacy, but couldn't help reading as decay, as we sat quietly at our kitchen table, over godly tomatoes: *Have we run out of things to say?* These changes were only ordinary, but I'd never stuck around to watch love become daily.

I was afraid Dave would regret the life we'd made together, afraid I couldn't constantly produce a version of myself that he'd like enough to choose over everyone else—which I believed was a requirement of love. Wasn't that the difference between love and compromise? When I drank, my fears attached to objects of fixation that seemed petty when I spoke them out loud: Dave flirting with other girls; Dave making plans without me. Every time Dave stayed out late, or seemed distant or bored, or simply *quiet,* I got nervous. Was this a sign that he was slightly less invested than he'd been? Slightly less entertained? I was haunted by the words he'd used about his last relationship: *Grooves of domesticity. Claustrophobic.* The only person in my family who had never gotten divorced was one uncle who lived on a farm in New Mexico, where his wife trained sheepdogs and sunset fired their alfalfa bales with scarlet light. But they seemed superhuman. Dave was not a farmer and I was not a trainer of dogs. We could barely get the three-wheeled dishwasher across the kitchen to our sink faucet.

We spent much of that first Iowa autumn flying to other people's weddings, where we were inevitably asked when we were planning to get married ourselves—as if we'd entered hunting range during open season. We bought the cheapest plane tickets we could find and ended up in deserted midwestern airports at ungodly hours. I fell off the end of a moving sidewalk in St. Louis at four in the morning and Dave helped me up, both of us laughing. We were inside some pocket of time and space that was just ours, full of empty moving sidewalks— an odd dream we were building together.

During that first autumn in Iowa, I watched Dave for signs that our relationship had been tarnished by proximity and tedium. I watched his poems, wondering if the *she* was always me. I watched his phone, wondering who was texting him. The workshop itself had become a rival, something he might love more than me.

When he was in the shower one afternoon, I finally did what I'd been imagining doing for weeks: picked up his phone — palms sweating, afraid of what I'd find, or that he'd catch me finding it — and scrolled through his texts. All I wanted was the complete inventory of his heart and mind — that was it, nothing more. "I need a pipeline directly from my brain to yours," he'd told me once. I wanted that, too, so I could convince myself that I'd never have to doubt anything — that uncertainty wasn't native to love, and I wouldn't ever have to reckon with it.

I found a long swath of messages he'd exchanged, over the course of several weeks, with a girl in the workshop named Destiny. She was twenty-two, or something close, the same age I'd been at the workshop five years earlier, and when I saw a poem he'd texted to her line by line, I got sick to my stomach. It was one he'd just written — I knew, because he'd read it to me — but I thought I'd been the only one he'd shared it with. Their messages were daily and affectionate, and sometimes, I could tell, they'd been meeting up: *At Java House now?* And then: *Will be there in 10 min!* Or: *See you at G's tonight?* With a little punctuation face at the end: ☺ Their aliveness, their daily-ness, their back-and-forth energy, came like a sudden slap, a confirmation of my fears: He would always crave the sharp tingling sensation of falling for someone, rather than having her.

That's what I told myself then, when of course I was afraid that *I* needed these things — needed newness and thrill. That's part of why I imagined he couldn't live without them.

When Dave got out of the shower, I stewed in miserable, sullen silence until he finally asked if we should talk. We sat on the steps of our front porch, side by side, staring at the little gazebo in the park across the street.

"I looked at your phone," I told him.

He glanced at me. "Did you find what you were looking for?"

"I saw your texts to Destiny."

I paused. He said nothing.

"You texted her that whole poem," I said. My words sounded plaintive to my ears, pathetic.

"Why were you checking my phone?"

"I'm sorry," I said, and I was. But I also felt righteous—like he should be apologizing to me. "I shouldn't have," I said. "I know. But—"

"But what?" he said. There was an edge to his voice.

"But I was right," I said, starting to cry. "I mean, that there was something happening."

"Nothing's happening," he said. His calmness was deliberate and sure-footed.

"When you flirt like that with someone," I said, "something is happening."

"I have the right to friendships," he said.

"I promise you," I said, "she doesn't think this is just a friendship."

"Whatever she thinks, I know where the lines are," he said. "I haven't crossed them."

"Remember how you texted me?" I asked. "Before we got together?"

During the weeks before Dave had finally kissed me, our texts had thrilled me—their constant back-and-forth, like tin-can phones stretched between two bedrooms. I could remember getting out of Peter's bed to check for them.

"I wasn't the one in a relationship," he said, and of course he was right. "Now I'm with you."

"Exactly!" I said. "When you're with someone, you're not supposed to be this way with other people."

"This way?" he said. "What's that, exactly?"

His voice was chilled and steely, almost a shield, as if he were tucking himself behind it. The icier he got, the shriller my own voice became. "Flirting like this!" I said. "Texting every day. Making her—"

"You call it flirting, I call it friendship," he said. "How do you define flirting, anyway?"

"You just know it!" I said. "You know it when you're doing it."

"The real issue," he said, "is why you wanted to read my texts in the first place."

I didn't answer, couldn't even look at him—glanced down, instead, at the splintery wood of our porch steps beneath us—but we both knew: I was afraid.

"Watch out," he said. "Your fear will make the things you fear come true."

The fight we had that night was like many of the fights that would follow, circling around certain questions—*What counted as flirting?*—that became our ways of talking about freedom and fear. "You can just feel it!" I repeated, yelling now, knowing I sounded ridiculous, but thinking, *Can't you?* I hurled myself against his refusal to apologize—apologizing myself, for violating his privacy, though my apologies always returned to some *but:* Didn't he understand why a woman wouldn't want her boyfriend texting poems, line by line, to another woman?

Eventually he said we should try to fall asleep. It was three in the morning. We'd been fighting for hours. I splashed cold water on my face—watermelon-splotchy, swollen from crying—and tried to imagine him looking at this face, degraded by insecurity and need, and loving it anyway, and I couldn't imagine it at all.

In bed, Dave fell asleep quickly. Fighting made him tired. But I was wide awake, on high alert from conflict, and hated sensing the stiffness of his body beside mine, the gap between our limbs. Fighting sent a surge of adrenaline through me, when all I really wanted was to retire from consciousness for a while. I went into my office to drink, because I couldn't sleep, and kept drinking until I could settle into numbness. Things were still ugly, but their ugliness didn't much bother me.

This started to become a pattern: drinking alone, in my office, after Dave was asleep. In the morning, I'd check my Sent folder to see if there were emails I'd sent during blackouts. Once I saw I'd written to my sister-in-law:

> Do you ever feel like you are completely outside outside our life? I feel so lonely. does this make sense to you? it probablty doesn't. it doesn't make sense to anyone as bad as i am. i want so much for your to understand this place. i love you.

Whenever I was drunk, the stakes were *huge*—all those capital-letter feelings. My darkness was the darkest. *Outside outside:* so true I wanted to say it twice.

That October, we went to the wedding of one of my best friends, back in New York—held in the garden apartment of her brownstone, rooms full of fashionable people flitting between beet burgers and carrot spears from her husband's farm-to-table restaurant. The charcuterie and cheese tables were luxuriant, like Dutch still lifes, and Dave went to fill our plates while I sat on the staircase with my friend.

About twenty minutes later, my friend asked: "Where did Dave go?"

When we surveyed the room, we saw him in an animated conversation with the woman manning the cheese table, who was laughing at something he'd said. She was beautiful, even in her ridiculous apron-smock, with a messy blond bun.

"I'd lose my shit if my boyfriend spent twenty minutes talking to another woman like that," my friend said. "You're a saint."

But I wasn't a saint. I was humiliated. My gaze kept flicking back to Dave—over and over again, though I tried not to—and I kept taking quick, stubborn gulps of wine. I hated the idea that I'd somehow become the woman whose boyfriend was always flirting with other women. By the time he finally returned, triumphantly presenting me with a plate of cave-aged Gouda and sheep's-milk Manchego, a switch had flipped in me. I was spoiling for a fight.

"Let's go outside," I said. "We need to talk."

We stood on the sidewalk—on a crisp fall night, on a block of brownstones like a movie set—and my wine breath made little puffy clouds in the cold air when I spoke. "Do you know how embarrassing it is for me?" I asked. "The way you flirt?"

He bristled at the word "flirt"—and his body stiffened. "I don't want to be policed," he said.

I got more insistent, almost frantic: "It's not just me!" I said, reporting what my friend had said, that it would drive her crazy.

"This isn't about her," he said, "this is about you."

Am I being absurd? I thought. *Am I totally fucking insane?* But I couldn't get the image of them out of my mind—both laughing, her messy bun, that massive parchment-colored mound of Gouda rising behind them, the whole thing like a meet-cute from a romantic comedy. I could imagine the voice-over: *So I was at this wedding with my girlfriend, who was actually pretty drunk*...

"This is my best friend's wedding!" I said. "I don't want to spend it on the sidewalk, fighting with you."

"It was your idea to come out here," he said—which was, maddeningly, accurate.

When we went back into the party, the first thing I spotted was a bar counter covered with orderly rows of brimming wineglasses, big and cold, sweating with beaded moisture. I grabbed one immediately.

"Are you sure that's what you need?" Dave asked.

And yes, I was sure. It was.

At a party we threw back in Iowa that fall, I got so drunk I had to lock myself in our bedroom and slap myself—hard, across the cheek—to get myself undrunk again. It didn't work. I sat with my back against the wall, staring at our bed piled with fall coats, and breathed deeply over the hiccups rising under my ribs. I went down to our front porch and found Dave holding court—laughing, animated, gesturing with a three-quarters-full beer he hadn't bothered to drink—and found myself missing Peter, who'd seemed irritatingly insecure while we were together but now seemed simply comprehensible, a human full of chinks and needs, while Dave seemed horribly untroubled. He seemed like the human embodiment of not-needing itself. I was very drunk. I wanted to go home, but it was my house.

Holding a big red Solo cup, full of whiskey to the brim, I walked across the street—to the gazebo in the park—where I sat on the cold stone floor and called my mother. She listened patiently as I told her about Dave's neglect, how he was probably back there flirting right now with this twenty-two-year-old poet he was friends with. Probably *right at this very moment.*

Where was I, exactly? my mother wanted to know. She said I should go home.

"But my house is full of *people*," I told her. She said I could ask them to leave.

I took another gulp of whiskey—felt it burn, held it down, then took another, tasting the sour tang of righteousness in my throat. My mother clearly didn't understand the difficulty of my situation, the conspiracy of forces, the immovable obstacles. Everyone was *happy* all around me.

The hiccups returned—jolting my whole body, turning my obstacles to slapstick. I told my mom I had to go, hung up, and sat there in the dark, breathing as hard as I could, gulping air. Eventually I crossed the street. As I approached my own house from the darkness of the park, someone on the porch asked where I'd gone. "I had a *call*," I said, as if I'd been consulting on a hostile corporate takeover.

By the next morning, the rest of the night had splintered into patchy blackout: a beeline for the bathroom, crying over the toilet, throwing up or wanting to throw up, voices in the hallway and then no voices in the hallway.

I told Dave "I'm sorry," and asked him what had happened the night before.

"You kept saying, 'I'm sorry,'" he said. "You said 'I'm sorry, I'm sorry, I'm sorry.'"

We made coffee and Dave scrambled our eggs like he did, with herbs and cheese and just the right amount of milk. But my face was swollen. My mouth felt crusted with nicotine, like I was gently forking his well-scrambled eggs into an ashtray. Everything beautiful was nothing I deserved. "For shame is its own veil," Denis Johnson wrote, "and veils the world as much as the face."

Although *Blueschild Baby* is a novel about a heroin addict named George Cain getting clean, George Cain was using heroin the whole time he wrote it. It reads like a book-length reckoning with dependence and rebellion, an attempt to exorcise with fiction what Cain couldn't purge from his body.

The novel takes place in Manhattan during the summer of the 1967 Newark riots, evoking New York as an orchestra of noise and need and possibility, all din and overwhelm: projects buzzing with hawkers and flapping curtains and ice cream truck bells; alive at night with dope fiends trying to cop and young couples kissing in doorway shadows; Sam Cooke lilting from a kitchen radio: *It's been too hard living but I'm afraid to die.* The novel is a love song to Harlem and also a primal cry of despair, a picaresque of scoring and trying to quit. George seeks out "Sun the Pusher" in his drug den just off Amsterdam and shoots up in the bathroom of a Newark courthouse before meeting his parole officer, walking past the "marks of rebellion" on Springfield Avenue, blackened storefronts and broken glass. He spends the night with his toddler daughter and her white mother in Greenwich Village before running into an old friend named Nandy, taking her to a jazz club and deciding he wants to get clean for her. (His parole officer has also threatened to send him back to prison if he fails a urine test in seventy-two hours.)

The novel closes with George recalling the first night he shot heroin, when "a strange moon hung in the sky" and he was first swallowed by that "calm, terribly sudden and infinite," before he renounces it for good. Cain resists respectability politics at every turn—by presenting a character who is smart and full of yearning, but often acts aggressively, even callously—in order to suggest that someone doesn't need to be blameless to deserve care.

The arc of *Blueschild Baby* stages a conflict between various narratives of addiction—addiction as repressive political rhetoric, addiction as social rebellion—but it never forgets addiction as a bodily reality: jangling nerves and dry skin, gaunt bodies and sweat, the sensation of "bones scraping against one another inside." Over the course of the novel, Cain dramatizes a shift away from his old political justifications for using—as a *fuck you* to the social order, a way "to live life unhindered" by rebelling against white power structures or the tyrannical demands of racial upward mobility—and ultimately resists the siren call of extolling addiction as social protest. When George sees a crowd of "nodding junkies" on the street, listening to a man who is calling for support for "victims of the Newark rebellion," he sees them "no longer [as] the chosen driven to destruction by their awareness and frustration, but only lost victims, too weak to fight."

If Cain's novel resists those easy alchemies that might fetishize addiction as rebellion, refusing to ignore its human cost, then his own life thwarts the impulse to narrate self-awareness as salvation. Cain's lived addiction brought together several driving forces—the allure of the tortured artist spinning darkness into gold, and the stress of being a black man in a country that had consigned on the notion of his criminality before he was born—but dissecting these motivations in his novel wasn't enough to liberate him from the physical imperatives of dependence itself.

When I asked Cain's ex-wife, Jo Lynne Pool, if she ever tried to get him to stop using, she said simply: "I knew better."

Pool was surprised I'd even tracked her down, surprised that anyone still cared about her husband—whose genius had largely fallen in obscurity, as his life dissolved into addiction—but she was glad to talk to me about his troubled brilliance. Pool told me that he started shooting heroin after dropping out of college, operating under the notion, as she put it, that "writers needed conflict and adversity. So he deliberately went out to find some." After dropping out of Iona College, a Catholic school in New York where he'd been given a basketball scholarship, lauded as a triumph of upward mobility in a way he found suffocating, Cain headed west through Texas, and eventually spent six months in a Mexican jail on marijuana charges. When he got out of jail, Pool said, "he had the makings of a book."

By the time Pool first met Cain, in the late sixties, he was already a full-blown addict, though Pool didn't realize it. She'd come to New York from Texarkana, Texas, to study at Pratt, and she'd never met "a dope fiend, or a heroin addict, or any other kind of addict." She was immediately drawn to Cain, with his "green snake eyes" and his evident and overwhelming intelligence. He always walked around with two or three composition books tucked under his arm, full of notes for his novel. "He never let them out of his sight," she said. He even took them up to Harlem whenever he went uptown to buy drugs.

After Pool and Cain had their first child, it was like he lived two lives. In one life, he was trying to be a more present father. He became a Sunni Muslim and joined a mosque that was like a surrogate family. But he would also disappear for days at a time—go up to Harlem and come back glazed. He'd nod out in the middle of dinner. One time he had a few friends over and while Pool was in the bathroom, his friends took off with half her clothes and armfuls of their baby supplies. Cain had to chase them down the street to get it all back.

When *Blueschild Baby* was published, the *New York Times* called it "the most important work of fiction by an Afro-American since *Native*

Son." In his review, Addison Gayle Jr. interprets Cain's recovery story as a narrative of racial self-possession, as he "redeem[s]" himself in the "72 hours of living hell" that constitute his withdrawal. "In that time," Gayle writes, "George Cain, former addict, emerges phoenix-like from the ashes, as George Cain, black man." In this interpretation, sobriety — rather than addiction — becomes the way he resists white oppression.

The publication of *Blueschild Baby* brought Cain the buzz and affirmation he had been craving — that sense of arrival. His publisher, McGraw-Hill, threw him a party in a beautiful loft down in SoHo. A few days after getting his first royalty check, he ran into one of his friend's little brothers on the street and took him to a record store nearby — told him to choose all the records he wanted and Cain would buy them for him. James Baldwin invited himself over for dinner, requesting fried chicken, though he never came. "People assume black women can cook," Pool told me, "so I thought, 'I have to figure out how to fry chicken.'" Everyone loved the book; Cain's mother was only disappointed she couldn't recommend it to her friends from church. The affirmation of this reception quieted something in Cain, and for a few years, at least, he was using less.

But by the time he got a temporary appointment at the Iowa Writers' Workshop, on the merits of the book and its success, and moved to Iowa City with Pool and their infant daughter, Cain was restless without easy access to drugs. He started flying back to New York every weekend. When Pool told him they couldn't afford his commutes, he took a bus to Davenport — about an hour away, right by the Mississippi — and didn't come back for days. Eventually Pool took a bus there herself, with their baby in tow, and when she asked a cabbie to take her to the junkie part of town, he pulled up to a run-down building where she found George inside and "dragged him out by his ear."

But his using kept getting worse. Back in Brooklyn, after his temporary appointment at Iowa was over, Cain kept trying to commit himself to a second novel. He didn't want to fall into the "one and only" trap to which he thought so many black writers had succumbed. He was using more because his writing wasn't going well, and his writing wasn't going well because of all his using. He was juggling a full-time teaching gig at Staten Island Community College and a full-time addiction, an infant son in addition to his young daughter. For Pool, their marriage ended the night she picked up the phone and heard a woman tell her that Cain had gotten her pregnant; he'd told her he lived with his sister.

Pool left Cain without telling him where she was going—she needed distance—and ended up moving to Houston with their two kids. After years, Cain found them and came out to visit. But he didn't like it out there. "He said the sky was too open," Pool told me. "He felt like God could see him."

When she spoke to me about Cain, Pool's voice was full of respect and even tenderness. It was clear she'd been through a lot with him, *for* him, but she didn't regret it. She mainly regretted how his life had turned out. He died in poverty, his work basically unknown. She told me about his last apartment in Harlem, where their kids went—just once, as teenagers—to stay. It was a basement unit that smelled like sewage.

Dr. Kaplin told me that when he first meets a patient struggling with addiction, he asks: "What were you like when you were doing well? Don't you want to be that person again?" When Cain was doing well, he kept company with his heroes; he was in fellowship at his mosque, he carried his notebooks with him everywhere. But when the *New York Times* ran an obituary for Cain after he died of complications from liver disease just shy of his sixty-seventh birthday in October 2010—forty years after the newspaper's glowing review of his novel—the article described Cain as a promising voice whose potential was never realized: "Drugs dashed these hopes."

When I spoke to Pool, she told me that the mutual friend who'd introduced them felt guilty about connecting a "pure-souled country girl" to a Harlem junkie, but she told him there was nothing to apologize for. "How many people get invited to cook chicken for James Baldwin?" she asked me. In our conversations about Cain, she used the word "genius" more times than I could count. She wasn't bitter about their marriage. She'd just done what she had to do.

"I'm not upset," she told me. "I just needed to make sure we survived George."

The first time I told Dave that I might have to stop drinking, we were still living back in New Haven. I'd woken up from an ordinary blackout, sick of them, and framed the possibility in hedging terms: maybe just for a little while. I knew that something was wrong inside me and feared that other people would eventually be able to catch whiffs of it—like a decaying tooth you can faintly smell when someone opens her mouth to laugh, or that you can taste when you kiss her.

Dave said he trusted my judgment: If I thought I had to stop, I should stop. But he was careful not to tell me what to do, and I read this care as a sign that I wasn't a *real* alcoholic. This was a relief. It meant I would be able to start drinking again, maybe after a few weeks, without having to convince him it was okay. By stopping for a while, I would prove—to him, and to myself—that I didn't need it, which would justify starting again. I drank again after three days.

The second time I tried to stop drinking, it was six months later, during that first fall in Iowa, right before I drove back to New Haven to take my oral exams. These exams were my swan song in academia before I put my doctoral program on hold for two years and plunged fully into my new life with Dave in the middle of the country. I would sit in a room full of professors firing questions at me about Shakespeare and American modernism and Chaucer's "Parliament of Fowls." It made me sad to think of passing the exams sober, because I had no idea how I'd celebrate.

When I told Dave that I thought I needed to stop drinking again—maybe for good this time—even saying the words out loud was terrifying: *for good.* The sober future looked like a lemon squeezed dry, all the juice gone, just the wrinkled mess of rind left behind. Dave's face looked different than it had looked the first time. It held the memory of more drunk nights, more drunk fights. I wondered if it also held the suspicion: *Can't you just drink better?* He said he could also imagine other ways to moderate. Maybe I could limit myself to two drinks a night. Maybe we could agree that I'd only drink at a party if he brought me a drink. That sounded like hell.

Driving back to the East Coast, sober and raw, I sent Dave lists of daily wonders I'd seen—as a way of reminding myself that the world without booze wasn't just flat champagne. I told him about a truck bed full of lamps. I told him about the woman in a gas station with fake blue eyes the color of sapphires. I told him about meeting a ninety-year-old woman who kept a scrapbook full of death announcements pasted next to the marriage announcements—for the same people—that she'd pasted in fifty years earlier. My reports to Dave were heavy with unreleased desire, like soaked sponges, desperate to find something good enough to replace how good drinking had been. When I tried to explain how much I missed booze—even a day without it—Dave said my honesty was like clean air. He said, *Keep your eyes open for those wonders.*

After I passed my orals, I went to a party where I moved miserably from room to room, watching other people drink. What good was it to nail Satan's self-begetting unless you could obliterate yourself afterward? This was just serving in heaven, and I wanted to reign in hell.

After orals, I stayed alone at my brother's apartment in Boston—he was out of town—and didn't see another human being for days. I was supposed to start the novel I was planning to spend the next two years writing, but every morning I woke up and thought: *Don't drink. Don't drink. Don't drink.* So I didn't drink for one hour, and then I didn't drink for another one. Nothing got written. I sat on my brother's green couch and cried. I called Dave, who said he'd stayed out till two in the morning singing karaoke. I cried more. He asked why I was crying, his voice full of love and confusion. I didn't know how to explain how hard it was to go through a single day without drinking, to ponder the possibility of going through every day without drinking. Every hour. Another hour. I thought I might lose my mind.

At a museum I visited, largely to get away from myself, I watched a video installation tucked behind a curtain: It showed a woman giving birth, and the footage got close to the mess of blood between her legs. She was screaming, but at least her pain was doing something useful. I thought: *If I hadn't gotten the abortion, I'd be having a baby this month.*

In the addiction section of a bookstore in Harvard Square—the same bookstore where I'd spent hours during college, reading books to distract myself from how hungry I was—I picked up a memoir with a wineglass on the cover and sat on the floor, consuming it: her obsession with the moisture on a wineglass, her nights alone slicing green apples into thin-as-paper pieces. I missed drinking so much, it almost slaked my thirst to read about it. The book was subtitled *A Love Story.*

The clerk at the checkout register was a middle-aged man with balding hair and a soft voice. "What's this?" he asked, laughing nervously. "An ode to alcoholism?"

"I think it's more like a warning," I said. Something in my tone, or my face, made him catch my eye. Some strange voltage passed between us.

"Maybe the next time you're in the store," he said, "you can let me know what happens." It seemed like he was trying to say: *I know why you are reading this, because I want to read it too.* It was like he'd been able to recognize me, as if my insane hours alone at the apartment, *not drinking not drinking not drinking,* had left some visible residue.

By the time Dave flew out to Boston—so we could drive up to Vermont, to the wedding of a friend who'd been in his band in college—it had been ten days since I'd had a drink. An hour into the drive, I told Dave I was pretty sure I could start drinking again. In fact, I was pretty sure I could start drinking again *tonight*. It was easier to say these things without looking him in the eye, while we were both staring at the highway. I could already imagine the wedding: champagne, red wine, dancing, relief. It would be the end of whatever this horrible week had been.

"I can do this," I told Dave. "It's no problem." And it wasn't, that night.

But soon enough, back in Iowa, we were back to ugly fights—where I accused him of giving too much of himself to the world, and not enough to me. Describing Dave to a friend, I invoked that scene from *Out of Africa* where another character explains what's charming and infuriating about Robert Redford as a big-game-hunting, impossibly restless lover: "He likes giving gifts, but not at Christmas."

Dave said it would be easier to give me the things I wanted—attention, affection, time—if only I weren't demanding them so fiercely. Certain parallels haunted me: If only I didn't need proof of his love so badly, then I could have it unstintingly. If only I didn't need to drink so badly, then I'd be able to drink well.

My relationship with Dave was also the first time I'd let myself be known in boringness and tedium and irritation, in those moments where I felt tired and unalive—and booze made it easier to mistake that exposure for injury. "Last year our drunken quarrels had no explanation," Robert Lowell once wrote, "except everything, except everything."

After every bad drunk fight, I would spend the next morning composing the most eloquent apology note I could muster. I often ended up recanting everything I'd said the night before, not because I hadn't meant it but because I was ashamed of how I'd said it drunk. If I could just *explain* myself well enough, if I could make sense of these fights—extract a certain meaning from them, just *get to the bottom* of them—then we'd be okay. But the fights weren't helping us get to the bottom of anything. The specific content of our fights—how much he flirted or didn't flirt, how much we planned our schedules around each other—was less essential than the tidal flow running beneath them: I was always reaching for more of Dave, grasping for something. He told me once that it felt like he was pouring his heart down a drain: It was never enough.

I was haunted by my first memory of Dave, playing his guitar with a crowd of people gathered round, and the reductive truths I'd extracted from it: that he was happiest at the center of an adoring collective gaze, and that I couldn't be that crowd for him, multiple and always new. But this myth of our origins cast Dave in a limited role— the crooner, the charmer, full of self-assurance that pressed on all my bruises—and made it harder to see that Dave was full of his own insecurities. It was just that he didn't express them as I did, by drinking himself silly, as if that were the only emotional currency I recognized. His sources of anxiety were quieter: working on a project for months—a review, a poem—missing one deadline after another. He was exacting and perfectionist, prone to revision and delay. He once showed me a note his school psychologist had written about him at the age of seven: *Because he considers many possibilities, it often takes him longer to finish what should be a short simple answer.*

When my heart skittered after a night of too much booze, I wondered if it was the booze interfering with my medication or just my anxiety about whether it might be. I started dreaming about a man with red hair who pointed to the plastic cup in my hand and said: "I know what you are." What I definitely was: a woman showing up puffy-faced and swollen-eyed to 7 a.m. bakery shifts; and drunk in my kitchen at home, like a slapstick cooking show, accidentally slicing off bits of myself with the mandoline, or gouging my palm with the ragged edge of a tunafish-can lid, checking the food for blood.

Now that I'd talked about how bad the drinking had gotten, it was trickier to do so much of it. If I knew Dave was getting home at seven, and I was getting home from the bakery at six, it might go like this: In that hour I'd pour myself as much gin as I thought I could get away with, just enough to get drunk without looking drunk, and then I'd listen for his key in the door, at which point I'd have just enough time to swallow whatever was left, rinse the cup, and duck into the bathroom. Then I'd brush my teeth as hard as I could, gargle the Listerine until it hurt. This was satisfying, like burning the evidence of my guilt in an incinerator—torching the corpse. I'd come out and kiss him quickly, without opening my mouth. Then we'd each have a glass of wine, just like reasonable nonalcoholics, and I'd tell him all about the day's wonders.

In 1939, a man named Ervin Cornell sat down and wrote a letter to the U.S. Bureau of Narcotics, telling the government how much he wanted to stop using:

> *Dear Sir:*
>
> *This is a funny letter because I do not know who I am writing to. The Doctor wanted me to write to you and see if you can get me in [the] Kentucky Hospital. Would it be possible for you to call at my home and explain to me what I have to do. I would very much like to get away from this morphine habit. If possible I wish you would let me know right away. Thanking you for your kindness.*

The "Kentucky Hospital" was another name for the Narco Farm— the infamous prison-hospital for addicts that had opened near Lexington in 1935—and Cornell was desperate to get in. He wasn't the only one. It was an odd prison in that way: Despite its barred windows and strict regimens, nearly three thousand people showed up to its locked doors each year requesting entry. Photographs show them walking up to the main prison gates with suitcases in hand, sunlight glaring behind them.

At a certain point in the life cycle of an addiction, this is what desperation could look like: begging for anything that might deliver you from your own worst impulses, sending messages in bottles. *Do you ever feel like you are completely outside outside our life?* "If theres any way in the world to be cured I wont to try it [*sic*]," wrote J. S. Northcutt, of Mississippi. Milton Moses was even more urgent:

> *I have been smoking marijuana cigarettes for six years. Baltimore City is full of these cigarettes and I know where they are all located. I beg of you to come and see me. I sure would like to be on the narcotic Farm for a cure... for Gods sake have a heart and do something for me I am sure suffering in this place. I hope I can depend on you, and please dont fail me.*

Paul Youngman of Chicago wrote on December 1, 1945:

> *Dear Sir,*
> *I would like very much if you wold [sic] send me papers so I could go to Lexington, Ky. (U.S.P.S.) to take a treatment for drug addiction as I am about fed up with it and will do my best to stay away from it as it is very hard to obtain it any more and will do my utmost to quit it all together and will do my very best to quit it all together.*
> *Thanking you in advance,*
>
> > *Yours truly,*
> > *Paul Youngman.*

Youngman's desperation is palpable in his repetition and his contradiction. The drugs are getting harder to find, he says, *and* he wants to stay away from them.

Chester Socar wasn't patient enough for the postal service. He sent a telegram:

PLEASE SEND APPLICATION FORMS FOR ADMISSION TO FEDERAL
NARCOTIC FARM LEXINGTON KY AT EARLIEST POSSIBLE MOMENT.

The Narco Farm was a three-year construction project and a four-million-dollar compromise: an art deco prison with locked doors and a bowling alley. To appease progressive reformists, it offered a program of rehabilitation. To appease frustrated wardens, it offered space for the addicts who had been crowding federal prisons. The press called the Narco Farm a "new deal for the drug addict" and, less enthusiastically, a "million dollar flophouse for junkies." Before it opened, a Lexington newspaper ran a contest to get suggestions from local residents about what it should be named, and the suggestions varied from awestruck ("Courageous Hospital," "Beneficial Farm") to ruthlessly ironic: "Big Shot Drug Farm," "Dream Castle," and "US Greatest Gift to Lift Mankind Sanatorium."

In truth, the prison-hospital-Big-Shot-Dream-Castle was still figuring out *what* it was. For starters, it was a working farm with ninety dairy cows. (Physical labor was supposed to be good for recovering addicts.) For inmates who got transferred, it was a step up from federal prison. One inmate from Leavenworth said the "courteous treatment that we discovered at the farm seemed too good to be true," and one photograph shows elderly addicts—hardened by years of addiction—getting their nails trimmed and buffed by a crew of beautiful young nurses. Manicures and pedicures were part of "the cure" for which Lexington became famous: a blend of physical treatment, talk therapy, structured recreation, and therapeutic labor. Inmates got dental work on the teeth their heroin habits had wrecked (4,245 teeth were extracted in 1937 alone) and vocational training. They worked as tailors, making "going home suits" for the guys who were doing just that, and picked tomatoes—canning fifteen hundred gallons in a single day.

The patients also had fun. Or at least they were supposed to. That was the idea. That was the rhetoric. It was a strange type of fun: institutional fun. Which meant that the institution was shaping it and keeping track of it. When a magician named Lippincott performed at the Narco Farm, "practically the entire population of 1100 patients" came to enjoy themselves, said one newspaper clipping stapled to the top of a monthly report sent to the surgeon general, as if to boast: *See! These guys are having a great time.* In 1937, the hospital logged 4,473 collective patient hours of horseshoe tossing and 8,842 hours of bowling. Just as there was some cognitive dissonance about who came to the Narco Farm (were they prisoners or patients?) there was some cognitive dissonance about what was supposed to happen to them once they got there: Were they supposed to work themselves right again, or rediscover pleasure?

Kentucky Ham, a novel about life at the Narcotic Farm written by Billy Burroughs Jr.—whose famously "unredeemed" father had spent time at the Narco Farm before him—describes the unofficial pleasures of resistance. The novel's "banana-smoking epidemic," for example, prompts farm officials to take bananas off the menu while they test if bananas can actually get anyone high. After that, the prisoners start smoking "everything we hated like Brussels sprouts."

So many musicians ended up at Lexington—Chet Baker, Elvin Jones, Sonny Rollins—that it became an informal jazz academy. At one point there were six different jazz combos practicing inside. One night an orchestra composed of Narco Farm patients performed for the nation on *The Tonight Show.*

Despite its transcendent claims, the Narco Farm was deeply enmeshed in an early war on drugs that was punitive and inhumane—Harry Anslinger's three-decade crusade to demonize the addict—and its "cure" was also a Trojan horse hiding a darker impulse: to contain addiction without calling it imprisonment. The Narco Farm rhetoric promised you could take a broken man and send him back out into the world as someone whole, but the line between rehabilitation and reprogramming was porous. "The treatment is, for the most part, a skillful rearrangement of the intangibles that go to make up human existence," said an article in the *Chicago Daily News.* "A man comes to them with one destiny. They figure out its trade-in value and give him a new one. It's as simple as all that." It was a strange definition of simplicity: taking all the intangibles that composed a man, and then rearranging them; tossing out his old destiny and giving him a new one.

Clarence Cooper's novel about his time at Lexington, *The Farm*, includes a scene in which his narrator (also named Clarence) refuses to play along with its scripts of rehabilitation. When the doctor asks how he feels, Clarence says, "Not very much," and when the doctor tries to nudge him back toward the right line — "You mean Not Very Well" — Clarence insists: "I mean not very much."

Some addicts hated the Narco Farm's hypocrisy, while others craved the cure it promised. Some felt both: the craving and the betrayal. Even if there was something false about the Narco Farm's promises, there was nothing false about the desperation of those who craved the rehabilitation it promised: *If theres any way in the world to be cured. I am sure suffering in this place.*

In its institutional contradictions, its categorical confusion, and even its architecture, the Narco Farm manifested a more legible version of the same cognitive dissonance that defined America's relationship to addiction. The intake form of every "vol" mapped out an arrangement of intangibles, a patient who had to present himself as seeking rearrangement:

Name: Robert Burnes
Place of Birth: Hallettsville, Texas.
Personal Description: Age 47, Build slender. Green eyes, neat
    dresser.
Means of livelihood: Salesman.
Reason for addiction: To avoid monotony of living.

I t was autumn in the corn belt and I was thinking about booze all the time. I woke up trying to figure out if it would be an easy night to get drunk or a hard night to get drunk: Was there a party? Was I seeing a friend? Was it a friend who liked to drink? At six in the morning, I got in the shower and thought about relief. At six forty-five, I put on my apron in the bakery bathroom and thought about relief. At seven-fifteen, I flattened cookie dough — ran it through the sheeter and back again, back again, back again — and thought about relief. At eight, I punched out squirrels and thought about relief. At nine, I frosted the same squirrels — with a brown swirl on their tails, and white whiskers — and thought about relief. At noon I ate a sandwich and thought about relief. At six in the evening, while I mopped the floor, I could almost taste it. The day was a tight skin that only booze could help me wriggle my way out of.

Nights out turned into endless calculations: How many glasses of wine has each person at this table had? What's the most of anyone? How much can I take, of what's left, without taking too much? How many people can I pour for, and how much can I pour for them, and still have enough left to pour for myself? How long until the waiter comes back and how likely is it someone else will ask him for another bottle?

A few months after our move to Iowa, Dave showed me a poem he'd put up for workshop. My stomach thrilled at the dedication, *for Leslie*, then knotted with shame at how it began: "Last night I spoke in anecdotes. Other people / were parking meters ticking quietly with vague / smiles, while you drank alone behind the house." I couldn't even pay attention to how the poem continued — with the speaker putting chipotle pepper in the French-toast batter, or breezing through a video store to pick up the cowboy flick his lover wanted — or how it ended, with an invitation: "Hey partner, whatever story you're about to tell, I've never heard it before. My umbrella / is small, and cheap, and I swear by it."

To me, the poem seemed to be about two people who were in love but also lonely — disconnected, even if they were struggling to be otherwise. Dave told me he'd meant it as an affirmation of our relationship, and meant the ending to suggest he would love me even if he'd heard all my stories before; that he would share his umbrella, even if it was small and cheap. But shame veils the world as much as the face, and I could see only what I was ashamed of: drinking alone behind the house.

Every time I was talking to someone then about anything that wasn't drinking, I felt like I was lying. But I was overwhelmed by pre-emptive grief whenever I tried to imagine life as a procession of sober nights—blank, bland, unrelenting: Dave and me sitting at our kitchen table, drinking fucking *tea*, trying to think of things to talk about.

One night back in New Haven, a few months into our relationship, I'd been in a terrible mood after we'd come from a party: drunk and insecure, lashing out at Dave, sitting on my futon with my legs clasped to my chest. "It's like underneath all my efforts to perform," I told Dave, "if I let them all drop—there's nothing there."

That night, he put his arms around my legs and said: "I want to get inside your head and fight that way of thinking until one of us dies."

In Iowa, I kept asking him for more intertwining of our lives—landing on that word, "intertwining," to describe whatever sense of connection we lacked—but this request was driven as much by fear as it was by desire: the fear of being left, or deemed insufficient. And in truth, another part of me had stopped wanting intertwining entirely, had started to prefer the nights we spent apart. If Dave came home late, I could drink alone; or if he was asleep when I got home, then I could keep drinking on my own, without having to explain why I was so drunk or why I wanted to keep getting drunker. Drinking was easiest in the room we called my office, where he couldn't walk in without at least a knock. I loved Dave, more than I'd ever loved anyone. I just wanted him on one side of the door, and me with my whiskey on the other.

That autumn was a series of lunges from one unremarkable drunk night to the next. The air was crisp. The wind rustled the brittle yellow leaves and layered them into patchwork quilts across the grass. I was sick with shame. Each morning I showed up to work at seven with a puffy face and pulled my uniform out of a locker, punched three hundred leaves from a thin blanket of cookie dough, and restocked giant bags of sugar from the basement. Sometimes these trips to the basement were convenient opportunities to cry. Sometimes Jamie, my boss, saw the look on my face and said, "What do you need?" and I told her I needed to dip two hundred ghosts into melted white chocolate and not say anything to anyone.

My first fall at the workshop, five years earlier, still glowed in memory: smoking cloves on a wooden porch, wearing thin jackets with fur trim and imagining my nights unfolding as a row of sparkling question marks, tingling with all the drama crackling through the chilly air around me: gossip, talk of so-and-so's line breaks, talk of fellowships, the gazes of men. All of that seemed stupid and perfect, looking back.

Drinking was no longer electric. It was musty routine, little more than a claustrophobic shell game: Will there be a fight at the end of this day or not? I kept drinking wine until my teeth turned red; kept drinking whiskey until my throat flamed; kept crouching in bathrooms with the hiccups, my vision blurred liquid, my back leaned against cool wallpaper, knees tucked into my chest, thinking, *When will it stop?*

The final night was just the last ounce of pressure on something already broken. I came home from a bar—already drunk, but looking to ride the buzz even further, to run it straight into the ground—and Dave was asleep. I was relieved because I didn't have to summon myself for him. I just wanted to keep feeling this righteous sadness at what I'd become, and I wanted to keep feeling it alone. So I filled a big red cup with straight whiskey, maybe eight shots, and took it into my office.

After that, there are patches of time I don't remember. I remember panicking when I heard him knocking on the door. I remember putting the cup behind the futon, where he couldn't see it. But it was clear I was drunk, sitting on this futon with my arms wrapped around my knees. I couldn't hide what I was doing, and I was too tired to try. He asked me what was wrong, and instead of trying to explain, I just picked up the cup from behind the futon. It felt so good to show him it was there.

— VI —

SURRENDER

The night of my first meeting, I drove across the river to an address near the hospital, crying all the way across the Burlington Street bridge, tears streaking the streetlamps into bright white rain. It was almost Halloween: cobwebs on porches, hanging ghosts made from stuffed sheets, jack-o'-lanterns with their crooked grins. Being drunk was like having a candle lit inside you. I already missed it.

The first two times I'd stopped drinking, I hadn't gone to meetings, because it seemed like an irrevocable threshold. Some part of me had known I would drink again, and I hadn't wanted voices from meetings chiding me. But this time I wanted to cross a line; to make it harder to go back. It was like taking out an insurance policy against the version of myself—days from now, weeks from now, months from now—who would miss the drinking so much she'd say: *I want to try again.*

I wasn't quitting because I wanted to quit. I had woken up that morning, just like every other morning, wanting to drink more than I wanted to do anything else. But quitting seemed like the only way I would ever arrive at a life where drinking *wasn't* the thing I wanted to do most when I woke up. When I imagined a meeting, I pictured grizzled men in a church basement talking about their DTs and their time in detox wards, gripping their Styrofoam cups with trembling hands. I pictured what I'd seen on television—slow claps and nodding heads, earnest *mmm-hmms*. But I didn't know what else to try.

When I reached the gravel parking lot of the address I'd copied down, it was just a clapboard house, not a church. But the lights were on. For ten minutes I sat in my car without killing the engine, heat blasting, wiping my snotty nose with the back of my wrist, jamming my fisted hands into my eyes to make them stop crying. I was searching for a story I could tell myself that would take me back home: *Maybe I'll come back tomorrow, maybe I don't have to be here, maybe I can do this on my own, maybe I don't have to do it at all.*

The meeting itself—once I willed myself out of the car, into the cold, and through the lit doorway—was just a bunch of strangers gathered around a huge wooden table, past a kitchen tracked with footprints, old linoleum curling upward at the edges of the room. People smiled like they were glad to see me, almost like they'd been expecting me to come. A sheet cake on the table was frosted with muted sunset tones. A man named Bug was celebrating an unthinkable amount of time without booze. I tucked myself quietly in a corner. I wasn't sure what to say but my name. Which, as it turns out, was enough.

Bug talked about staying in his apartment for forty days straight—without leaving, without going anywhere, like Christ in the desert of a low-rent Iowa condo—and getting big handles of vodka delivered to his door. I thought: *I never got that bad.* And then: *Vodka delivery actually sounds pretty great.* When Bug described how he'd gotten there—starting with the ritual of a vodka tonic with the six o'clock news, his whole day built around it—I thought, *Yep.* When I got a white chip to mark that I was in my first twenty-four hours of sobriety, it summoned those shacks marked by white flags down in Bolivia: the giddy anticipation of knowing what they sold. Imagining the rest of my life without that relief made me sick to my stomach.

But in that room I felt a different relief, just an inkling: the eerie immediacy of hearing myself spoken out loud. These people didn't know anything about me, but they knew one part of me—the part that thought about drinking all day, every day—better than anyone else. While I'd been outside telling myself that I didn't have to be here, maybe I could do this on my own, maybe I didn't have to do it at all, someone inside might have been saying, *I remember when I tried to tell myself: Maybe I don't have to be here, maybe I can do this on my own, maybe I don't have to do it at all.*

No matter how long you sit in the car, somebody is waiting in that wooden building. Maybe he will tell you through his silver mustache, *Your disease is patient, but so are we.* Maybe he will look like a farmer, or an ad exec with a sharply creased suit; or maybe she'll look like the annoying sorority girl who lives down the block, or a tired supermarket clerk with bitten fingernails. Maybe he's called Bug, or maybe he has a name you can't pronounce. Maybe he likes that sunset cake or maybe he can't stand it. Maybe he's just another old-timer you confuse with all the other old-timers, except for the moment when he opens his mouth and says something that gets you absolutely right.

That first winter, sobriety was the smell of oranges and wood smoke. It was the rabid, dangerous glare of sunlight on snow, and the warmth of car vents. It was insomnia. It was a woman at a meeting telling me she'd gotten custody of her son but they were still living in her van, and me standing there, hurting for her, grateful for the common currency of a phrase like *Take it one day at a time*, which seemed stupid until it didn't. Sobriety was brittle and uncomfortable, and it was also the only thing I hadn't tried for the long haul, so I was trying it. It stripped the world to a series of hours I had to get through. It made me raw. My nerves were open. Radio commercials made me cry.

I'll always associate sobriety with a quality of light that I've only ever seen in the broad winter horizons of Iowa: hard, expansive, exposing. It came from huge and frozen skies, their dwarfing blue, and glinted off snow mounds the size of bedrooms. I was nothing but naked in it—a brightness so clean and uncluttered it hurt.

In those early months, I was grateful for the structure of my bakery work. Its regularity offered relief. It wasn't supposed to be pleasurable, it just needed to happen. Every morning, no matter how I felt, there was a production list stuck to the cooler with my name on it. I was so lost in my head most of the time, so agitated and elegiac without booze, that just *doing* something—frosting an acorn, or a hundred—gave me a way out, for a moment, standing in my apron and sending the dough along the sheeter belt, back and forth, thinner and thinner, punching out shapes that strangers might enjoy.

On my days off from the bakery, I went to a second job, at the hospital, where I worked as a medical actor—play-acting various ailments for medical students to diagnose. I envied the actors playing DUI car-crash victims, who got to splash themselves with gin like it was cologne, when all I got was fake appendicitis.

On the days I had off both jobs, I tried to write and usually couldn't. So I went on long drives through the cornfields, or past the ugly strip malls across the river—a self-imposed exile. I'd gotten sick of how melodramatic I was when I was drunk, but now sobriety seemed to come with melodrama of its own: I was a martyr. For what larger cause, I wasn't sure. My breath curled into a sky so cold it felt like an insult. In those days I took everything personally, even the weather.

Dave was glad I'd started going to meetings. This was the third time I'd told him I had to give up drinking, and twice now he'd seen me start drinking again. He could see that my drinking carried me to terrible places, though it was hard to explain to him what *powerless* felt like, that word meetings had given me—hard to bring him inside its obliterating constancy.

I tried to charge sobriety with energy. For Halloween, a week after I stopped drinking, I made a graveyard cake with chocolate pudding and crumbled Oreo soil and cookie tombstones and gummy worms feeding on the graves. But all of it felt dull and dry, like getting kissed by a pair of chapped lips. When Dave and I went to a costume party dressed as vampires, I repurposed my yearly Girl Scout costume with badges in coffin making and blood mixology. But I seethed with resentment the whole time, pulling a Diet Wild Cherry

Pepsi from my purse, embarrassed to expose it, and watched Dave across the room, enmeshed in conversation with Destiny or just about to be enmeshed in conversation with Destiny. To me, it seemed she was always lurking just outside the frame, her body a vessel for ordinary fears—about getting left, or fallen out of love with—that didn't have much to do with her.

With Dave, I tried to attach my vast desire to particular requests: nights together at home, texting more, coordinating plans, not spending parties apart or losing each other to the room. These requests seemed trivial as I made them, grasping at tallies or logistics, but they were the only ways I knew how to ask him to make me feel less alone now that I'd lost the thing that had made consciousness seem possible. ("Need you with me for three days, need you every minute," George tells Nandy when he's getting clean, "can't be out of sight for any time cause I'm not strong enough without you.") My requests were just scratching the surface of what I really wanted, anyway—a guarantee that Dave would never stop loving me. A promise we would never end.

Three or four days a week, I went to a noon meeting full of bikers and housewives, businessmen on lunch breaks, a few farmers. Participating was called "sharing" or "qualifying." The verb itself, "qualify," made me anxious. Had my drinking been bad enough? They called speaking "earning your seat," but they also said that all you had to do to earn your seat was to believe you needed it.

Meetings worked all kinds of different ways. Some had a speaker who gave her story, and then other people shared in response. Others started with everyone taking turns reading paragraphs of an alcoholic's story from the Big Book, or with someone choosing a topic: Shame. Not forgetting the past. Anger. Changing habits. I began to realize why it was important to have a script, a set of motions you followed: First we'll say this invocation. Then we'll read from this book. Then we'll raise hands. It meant you didn't have to build the rituals of fellowship from scratch. You lived in the caves and hollows of what had worked before. You weren't responsible for what got said, because you were all parts of a machine bigger than any one of you, and older than anyone's sobriety. Clichés were the dialect of that machine, its ancient tongue: *Feelings aren't facts. Sometimes the solution has nothing to do with the problem.* Maybe stopping drinking didn't have to do with introspection but paying attention to everything else.

Heading downstairs into church basements made me remember that first party in an Iowa basement—when we'd gathered in a circle and performed our lives for one another, when I'd mimed riding a gentleman just to get a few laughs. This was another vision of story-telling altogether, not about glory but survival. Though at round-robin meetings, where we shared in a circle, I grew anxious if I was sitting next to someone who usually gave powerful shares—not resentful, exactly, but aware of trying to follow forceful words with my own cobbled offering.

At the end of most meetings, someone stood up and handed out poker chips for sobriety birthdays: Thirty days. Ninety days. Six months. Nine months. It was powerful to see old men and women walk up for sixteen years—or twenty-seven, or thirty-two—and know they'd once been the person who'd just walked up for sixty days, the guy who'd just thanked his sponsor and then awkwardly hugged him, flannel to leather, arms locked firmly and without equivocation.

Every Sunday evening, I went to a lottery meeting where I took a poker chip with a number on it. It worked like bingo: Maybe your number would get called, to come up to the podium and share, or maybe it wouldn't. That was hard for me, because I liked being in control of when I was going to speak, and it was good for me, because I liked being in control of when I was going to speak. I always worried I didn't have anything useful to say, but usually something just rose up and asserted itself: "I worry every day that there will never be anything that feels as good as drinking felt." I said that once. I said that more than once. And every time I heard someone else say, "I'm so anxious about talking tonight, maybe I don't have anything useful to say," I thought: *Thank you for saying so.*

B ill Wilson, the founder of AA, was a man whose life became myth—a stockbroker turned bathtub-gin drinker turned sober savior—but he didn't trust his own mythology. He was uneasy with the burnished legend his life became, how much grit and difficulty it elided, even as he understood how useful it could be for a recovery movement to have an anchoring tale of origins. He never wanted his own story to become more important than the stories of others, even though the fact remained: His sobriety was the original legend.

His story was the first chapter of *Alcoholics Anonymous*, the Big Book, first published in 1939. The narrative tracked his descent into chronic alcoholism as a stockbroker drinking his way through the booming stock market of the mid-twenties, then his crash into unemployment and round-the-clock dependence after Black Tuesday, in 1929. His story confessed many unsuccessful attempts to stop drinking: Willpower couldn't make him stop, love couldn't make him stop, medicine couldn't make him stop. When he went to a hospital and his condition was finally explained to him, he was sure that "this was the answer—self-knowledge." But it wasn't. He kept drinking anyway.

What eventually *did* save Wilson was the arrival of an old friend named Ebby, whose candor about his own drinking, and his newfound spirituality, opened Wilson to the possibility of belief. At first, Wilson wasn't convinced. "Let him rant!" he thought. "My gin would last longer than his preaching." But something shifted during their talk, and after it was done, Wilson went to the hospital to be "separated from alcohol for the last time." As he wrote in the Big Book: "I have not had a drink since."

This switch to present perfect—"I *have* not had"—is how his readers know that *this* time was different from all the other times he stopped. Those times were all doomed to the past tense, the endless cycle: *I still thought I could control the situation...there were periods of sobriety...Shortly afterward I came home drunk...I had written lots of sweet promises...In no time I was beating on the bar asking myself how it happened...I told myself I would manage better next time...*

At the hospital where he went to dry out, Wilson had a moment of intense connection with God: "I felt lifted up, as though the great clean wind of a mountain top blew through and through." But the Big Book doesn't frame Wilson's moment of sublimity as the turning point in his sobriety—this visionary moment of being blown through by the mountain wind. It frames his turning point as the conversation with Ebby, when he saw eye to eye with a friend at his kitchen table. That's the moral of the story: This communion is what made the mountain wind possible.

AA itself began not when Wilson got sober, but when he helped another man get sober, an Akron doctor named Dr. Bob, who would become famous, too—as the stranger Wilson saved, the first of many.

Early in my sobriety I met a stranger I wanted to save. Dave and I had a few people over one night, and I was trying hard to be a good host, unloading pink boxes from work full of jam-oozing scones and caramel cinnamon buns that had been gooey at breakfast but were harder now, stale cardboard approximations of their morning selves.

When I came back from the kitchen with the pastries arranged on plates, I found a girl in a gold Lycra bodysuit holding court in our living room. Everyone assumed someone else knew her, but no one did. We were all getting to know her, or at least we were learning that she was looking for this party where her friend was supposed to be. She was very drunk. She'd just wandered through our unlocked front door and come upstairs. She'd heard voices and thought perhaps this was the party she'd been looking for. Her Lycra bodysuit was truly astonishing.

"We're playing a board game," someone explained to her. But she wasn't interested in our board game. She was interested in her friend's party. Her face was glazed, her eyes rolling around like marbles. I offered to drive her home, already imagining how it would play out: We'd have a conversation in the car—about drinking, where it had gotten her, where it had gotten me. Maybe I'd take her to the Sunday-night meeting, or maybe I'd just tell the story of her there. It would be my first act of sober heroism. I went to the bedroom to get my keys.

But when I came back, she was gone. She'd just wandered off, the others said. Just like she'd wandered in. I got in my car anyway, and cruised the dark streets looking for her shiny gold suit shambling through the shadows. But I never found her.

Every meeting was a chorus. You got to know the regulars. A man named Mitch remembered waking up one morning—after a bender, in a car that wasn't his, in the middle of a field—to see a cow sticking her nose through the open window. A woman named Gloria described taking long "naps" when her daughter was young, drinking alone in her bedroom and answering, groggy and irritated, whenever her daughter knocked on the door. A man named Carl remembered drinking thermos after thermos of instant coffee—compulsively, into jittery oblivion—as a boy in elementary school. A man named Keith, in his polyester tracksuit, was usually quiet, but one day he said simply: "When I drink, hope dies in me." A man named Felix, an aging heroin addict in a red beanie, said he loved being hungry. It was his body telling him it wanted to live.

A woman named Dana had half her hair shaved, with purple streaks in what was left. She rarely smiled those first few months after she got off heroin. The way she glared at me sometimes, I was sure she found me tiresome and long-winded. But one day she laughed so hard at something I shared about tuning the car radio to NPR before turning off the ignition, so that when Dave started the car he would think I'd been listening to NPR, because it seemed like I *should* listen to NPR, rather than the ridiculous pop music I played instead. It was a trivial thing, but also not; it was about lying to give the world what we wanted it to see.

"That's *me*," Dana said. "That's totally me."

When I started giving her rides to meetings, we never played NPR. After a few months clean, she really bloomed: You could see it in her eyes and body, how tightly she hugged other women. One morning I picked her up during a huge snowstorm, with the roads nearly empty. My car was shit in the snow. I blasted the heat and clenched the wheel. We fishtailed all the way but made the meeting. We had a time now, the two of us. We had a story: *That day we drove through the snow; that day we weren't sure we'd make it, but then we did.*

Bill Wilson told the story of his sobriety different ways depending on where he was telling it, or to whom. While the Big Book version of his story featured his kitchen-table conversation with Ebby as an unequivocal epiphany — "My ideas about miracles were drastically revised *right then*" — his autobiography confessed a few more binges after this visit. It was only after the wind on the mountain, he said, that he stayed sober for good.

The disjunction between these two versions wasn't a question of vanity or authenticity so much as pragmatism. For the Big Book, Wilson wanted to stress the importance of what AA offered, which was identification and fellowship, rather than pinning sobriety on the type of intense spiritual experience that some people might never have. He didn't alter his story out of self-concern but from a nearly opposite impulse — he understood his own life as a public tool rather than a private artifact.

Wilson's story was a complicated tool, because it created certain pressures of its own. What about the reader who didn't stay sober for good after his first conversation with a sober friend? Perhaps that reader relapsed six more times, called his sober friend drunk, and said, *Sorry that I can't stay sober like that guy in the Big Book.*

That's why Wilson wanted to put out a book that reflected the structure of a meeting — that held the stories of others, not just his own. He gave the Big Book a fitting subtitle: *The Story of How Many Thousands of Men and Women Have Recovered from Alcoholism.* The single story of the whole book held the plural population of its many tales. Wilson didn't want his story to become binding archetype or narrative legislation: *You must be sober like this.* He wanted to make room for everyone who hadn't found great winds on mountaintops, or deliverance in a single conversation. He wanted to "play the foundations of this movement down," because he thought it worked better "without too much sanction from the top."

Wilson didn't want to become a saint, but he found himself the "number-one man" in a movement he'd sculpted to resist the whole notion of being number-one anything. At an AA conference in 1958, he told the crowd: "I am like you... I, too, am fallible." He wrote a letter to an AA member named Barbara explaining that a perch had been constructed for him that no human man could possibly occupy. That was part of why he hated the idea of writing an autobiography: the fear that it would elevate his perch even further. "Of course I have always been intensely averse to anything autobiographical being done in print," he wrote in the foreword to an autobiography that was eventually published after his death. Titled *Bill W.: My First Forty Years*, it was actually a series of transcribed conversations Wilson had conducted with a fellow sober friend named Ed Bierstadt in 1954. The book's structure replaced the standard one-man show of memoir with the conversation of fellowship.

The book framed itself as an inoculation — an attempt to preempt the hagiographies that might follow — and during its conversations, Wilson is constantly reckoning with the question of his own ego. He's worried about the ways that telling his story might threaten to inflate it, that he might take too much pride in his old sins, or his new redemption. "Ed and I just had a good laugh about the Wall Street days of the last record," he confesses at one point; "it is all too clear that I reverted to type. The whole tone of the thing sounds like I was in a barroom pounding on the bar, talking big deals, financial omnipotence and power."

It's a narrative relapse. For a moment, Wilson's voice loses its sobriety and reverts to drunken self-aggrandizement—bragging about his financial escapades. For a moment, self-exposure lapses into its dark alter ego: self-promotion. This is an occupational hazard when it comes to conversation narratives. What if your pleasure in telling stories about the old prodigal days betrays that part of you still wants to return to them? But Wilson confesses it—the slip, the creep of pride—and by confessing that his old drunk ego has momentarily hijacked the story, he trusts he can reclaim it.

One of the first major media features about AA, Jack Alexander's 1941 article for the *Saturday Evening Post*, was skeptical about the dramatic storytelling habits of its members. They "behaved like a bunch of actors sent out by some Broadway casting agency," Alexander wrote. But he happily reproduced a catalog of their tales:

> They tell of the eight-ounce bottles of gin hidden behind pictures and in caches from cellar to attic; of spending whole days in motion-picture houses to stave off the temptation to drink; of sneaking out of the office for quickies during the day. They talk of losing jobs and stealing money from their wives' purses; of putting pepper into whiskey to give it a tang; of tippling on bitters and sedative tablets, or on mouthwash or hair tonic; of getting into the habit of camping outside the neighborhood tavern ten minutes before opening time. They describe a hand so jittery that it could not lift a pony to the lips without spilling the contents; drinking liquor from a beer stein because it

can be steadied with two hands, although at the risk of chipping a front tooth; tying an end of a towel about a glass, looping the towel around the back of the neck, and drawing the free end with the other hand, *pulley fashion, to advance the glass to the mouth*; hands so shaky they feel as if they were about to snap off and fly into space; sitting on hands for hours to keep them from doing this.

What Alexander begins to realize, or at least frames as a realization for his article, is that these sober men aren't telling their stories as performance pieces — to play the parts of feckless dilettantes or sanctimonious altruists. They're offering their stories as cures, for other people and for themselves. Of course it's not an either/or. Someone can be trying to seduce a crowd and save their lives; can crave glory and earnest utility at once. Alexander insists that AA members are like diabetics, with "drunk-saving" as their insulin. He doesn't build them up as selfless saints, but as people whose self-preservation involves making themselves useful. They don't just tell their stories as cocktail party anecdotes (*see what I've lived!*) or wound badges (*see what I've suffered!*) but so they can reach people who need them.

Take Sarah Martin, who jumped (or fell) out of a window drunk, landed face-first on the pavement, and suffered through six months of dental work and plastic surgery. Now she "spends many of her nights," Alexander observes, "sitting on hysterical women drinkers to prevent them from diving out of windows." Sarah talks about jumping out of a window not because it distinguishes her, but because it doesn't.

Alexander's article was written with Bill Wilson's help, and it was published with his endorsement and his gratitude. "For many a day," Wilson wrote to Alexander, "you will be the toast of AA — in coca cola, of course!" In the first twelve days after the article was published, AA heard from nearly a thousand alcoholics who wanted help. By the end of 1941, the program had more than 8,000 members. By 1950, it had 100,000. By 2015, it had more than 2 million.

What does the concept of recovery mean? It can mean healing, repair, relocation, reclamation, or recuperation. French philosopher Catherine Malabou proposes three different visions of recovery, attaching each one to an animal: the phoenix, the spider, and the salamander. The phoenix represents a version of recovery in which the wound is utterly erased — "an annulment of the defect, the mark, the lesion" — just as the phoenix rises unscathed from the ashes, perfectly unblemished, precisely as it was before. It's like skin healing without a scar, and it's something close to the psychic opposite of AA, in which wounds are not forgotten but fundamental, their narration the glue binding every Sarah Martin and her flock of newcomers.

AA lives somewhere between Malabou's other creatures: The spider offers a model of recovery that involves something like an endless accumulation of scars spun into a web, like a text "covered with marks, nicks, scratches" that refuses the possibility of "taking on a new skin" without blemishes — while the salamander, Malabou's third recovery mascot, grows a new limb that is neither scarred nor identical to the one it had before. This new limb is not the spider's endless web of scars, but it's not a phoenix-style resurrection either, recovery bringing back an unchanged version of the former self, because the Salamander's new limb has a different size, shape, and weight. "There is no scar, but there is a difference," Malabou writes. "The difference is neither a form of higher life nor a monstrous gap."

AA's vision of regeneration proposes a sober identity that is neither a replica of the prior self, with the drinking excised like a tumor, nor a version of this self covered with calluses and scars, but a new organ entirely. The transformation is neither holy nor grievous. It's just a strategy of survival. The program's twelve steps have become famous, reaching from surrender to confession: admitting that your life has become unmanageable in the First Step; surrendering to a Higher Power in the Third; sharing an inventory of your resentments and character defects in the Fifth; making amends to those you've harmed in the Ninth; and reaching out to help others in the Twelfth: *Having had a spiritual awakening as a result of these steps, we tried to carry this message to alcoholics.* In this way—in this ongoingness—the steps are never done.

When I first heard the phrase "witness authority," it was like hearing someone say "Dihydrogen monoxide," and then thinking: *Of course. Water.* Dr. Meg Chisolm, a psychiatrist at Johns Hopkins, was telling me she recommends AA to patients mainly for its social infrastructure and for this witness authority, meaning the way other AA members offer—by sharing their experiences—a lived authority distinct from her own. *So that's what you call it,* I thought. I'd already been living on it for years: Bug getting me right that first night, or Dana saying, "That's *me*," as if her whole life had been spent listening to the wrong radio station. Dr. Kaplin told me that his patients often say to him: "You'd be doing heroin, too, Doctor. You don't know what it means to walk a mile in my shoes." He works with Baltimore addicts whose lives often differ sharply from his own, and part of what these patients find in recovery is recognition.

Both Dr. Kaplin and Dr. Chisolm told me that twelve-step recovery can be a delivery mechanism for effective behavioral treatments—like positive reinforcement and peer support—but it has no monopoly on them. It teaches coping strategies, facilitates community, and rewards abstinence with poker chips and birthday cake, with a room of people clapping for your ninetieth day, your first year, your thirtieth. "Meetings are particularly useful for people who need to hear themselves confessing," Dr. Kaplin said.

When I heard the sinuous, glimmering energy of recovery offered back to me in these clinical phrases—"contingency management" and "community reinforcement"—I got a sense of déjà vu. It wasn't unlike hearing about the dopamine-transport blockage responsible for the billowing sail of my coke high. Nothing was falsified or cheapened, only translated and specified—charted like a ship's voyage on a different type of map.

When Dr. Chisolm told me that she sometimes attaches a warning when she encourages certain patients to seek out AA, it didn't surprise me. "You're really smart," she tells them. "That might work against you." The idea of being "too smart for AA" immediately resonated with the part of me that sometimes found its truisms too reductive or its narratives too simple. But I was also aware that being "too smart for AA" could become its own siren call to the ego: considering yourself the exception to the common story, exempt from every aphorism — with a consciousness too complicated to have much in common with anyone else. I was even aware that my rejection of that ego trip was, in its way, also a revision of it: I was proud that I *didn't* feel too smart for AA, as if I deserved a gold star for resisting that arrogance.

In the early days of his sobriety, Charles Jackson dismissed AA wholeheartedly, calling it a group for "simple souls" and "weaklings" founded on a bunch of "mystical blah blah." He got angry when a local bookseller ("a bloody bore") pushed AA on him too forcefully. "You S.O.B.!" Jackson thought. "If you don't think I know what I'm doing by now, after *eight years* of sobriety on my own, then you don't know very much!" It's not surprising that *The Lost Weekend*, written in the thick of Jackson's AA skepticism, didn't present an optimistic portrait of fellowship-based recovery. In a 1943 letter to his publisher, a year before the book came out, Jackson describes the novel's relationship to the possibility of a "solution": it "is offered, so to speak, and then taken away, not used."

From a recovery standpoint, the problem with Jackson's antihero, Don Birnam, isn't simply that Don can't stop drinking, it's that he keeps telling the wrong type of story. He's interested in anecdotal humor rather than painful self-exposure. After his failed attempt to pawn his typewriter, for instance, as he staggers a hundred blocks along Third Avenue, Don's first impulse is to redeem the experience by transforming it into "anecdote." He imagines his audience would only want to laugh; they wouldn't "care to learn or hear of the real, the uncomfortable, the cruel and painful details behind the joke." If recovery is premised on the call to share the "cruel and painful details" of one's experience, then drunk Don reveals himself as a teller of anti-AA stories: stories that value anecdotal entertainment above the exposure of authentic difficulty.

Fifteen years after he published the novel, Jackson stood in front of an AA meeting in Cleveland and tried to tell a different type of story. By saying he was tired of being his own hero, and by telling a room full of strangers that his "definitive portrait" hadn't done him any good, Jackson was—of course—participating in the act of storytelling even as he questioned it. But storytelling in a recovery fellowship wasn't the same mode of storytelling as his best-selling novel. It was supposed to be less invested in himself, and more invested in others. "I couldn't get outside myself," he told the group. "I think this is the thing that plagues the alcoholic so much...I was too self-absorbed, too self-infatuated, and I drank."

By the time he addressed this AA group in 1959, Jackson had come a long way from his early dismissals. "I tell you, boy," he wrote one friend, "there is much, much more to AA than mere sobriety; there is happiness and a whole new way of life." Jackson first started going to meetings in the mid-forties—not as a member but as a speaker, somewhat grudgingly, at the behest of his publisher, to publicize *The Lost Weekend*. But at a Hartford AA chapter, he couldn't help trying to win over a crowd of six hundred by admitting that AA fellowship might have been just what Don Birnam needed.

It wasn't until Jackson bottomed out in 1953, one of many bottoms, that he finally wanted to join. "These people *knew* about me," he said, "these people had been where I had been and had something I didn't have. And I wanted it." This was during a stint at the Saul Clinic, an alcoholic ward in Philadelphia run by a doctor who—years earlier—had written Jackson a personal letter imploring him to write a sequel describing Don's recovery: "I am thinking solely of the responsibility that is yours and the great good that you can do," Dr. Saul had written, "as every alcoholic, his friends, and his family await the sequel to *The Lost Weekend*." But by the time Jackson arrived at the Saul Clinic nine years later, the irony was palpable: Jackson was asking for help getting better from the doctor who had wanted him to help others get better by writing the story of how he'd already done it himself.

At first Jackson was worried he wouldn't be among "intellectual equals" in AA, but as he spent more time in meetings, he grew less convinced that intellectual kinship was what mattered most. When he called one AA chapter in Montpelier, Vermont, for more information, they asked if he wanted to come join them as a speaker—but he said he'd rather just show up and listen. Through his sponsor, he grew increasingly enamored with a quote from G. K. Chesterton: "How much larger your life would be if your self could become smaller in it. You would find yourself under a freer sky, in a street full of splendid strangers." Jackson had found a crew of splendid strangers, or splendid enough, sitting on folding chairs in church basements all over New England and swapping stories, trading drunken abandon for another kind of liberty.

One evening in the dead of winter, I went to a sober ladies' night in a big house in the middle of an Iowa subdivision. The house belonged to a woman named Nell, and it was immaculate—with a brown leather living room set and a white shag rug. It was eerie, the clean and polish of everything, the hanging metal saucepans gleaming in their dangling rows. It seemed lonely. From her shares in meetings, I knew that Nell's husband was struggling with her relapses.

We were having game night. Someone had brought Balderdash. Someone had brought Apples to Apples, where one player dealt a card with an adjective (*Expensive, Useful, Rich*) and everyone else had to play a noun from the cards in her hand (*Switzerland, Igloo, Bank Robber*). A woman named Lorrie had made banana muffins, still steaming in their basket, wrapped in cloth. A woman named Ginger brought turkey pot pie, and Val brought something called Chicken Surprise, made of five different kinds of beige: cream of this, cream of that, milk and grated cheese and mayonnaise.

I could remember sweating straight rum onto my sheets, kissing a man at dawn with coke crackling through my veins, getting woozy on a lawn full of fireflies. That was *living*, I'd been so sure of it. This night was several kinds of casserole.

I'd brought cookies from the bakery — wherever I went, I brought cookies from the bakery — in a pink box speckled with tiny archipelagos of grease. Nell took them from me, excited, and I felt like a child, so pleased by her pleasure, by the primal buzz of food passing from my hands to hers. It was nice to be useful, even in the smallest way.

Nell's husband was a lawyer who worked long hours, and had always wanted a kid, though Nell's drinking was making it hard for them to imagine having one. As Nell showed me around, she pointed out her old hiding spots for bottles: a paper bag under the kitchen sink, behind the cleaning supplies; an old camping bag in the garage, where she'd rolled them in blankets. I remembered listening for Dave's key in the lock, drinking the last of the gin, brushing my teeth so hard my gums bled.

That night we played charades. We played it hard. We played Apples to Apples. We drew *Trustworthy* and someone put down *Canadians*, then someone won with *Whiskey*, a wild card that had been added, handwritten. We drew *Desperate* and I wanted to put down *Board Games*. We poured our Diet Coke from liter bottles. Middle-aged women in pastel cardigan sweaters talked about shooting heroin into parts of the body I didn't know it could be shot into. We talked about how to get through a day without the old horizons of relief, and there was relief in that — in hearing another human being say how fucking *hard* it was, for her as well, just the simple act of living in the world without anything to blunt its edges. The longer I spent in Nell's house, the more amazing she seemed to me, just getting up each day in a home full of the ghosts of her old hidden bottles, facing up to the husband she'd disappointed, trying to own the pieces of her life again, trying to do — as I was hearing people say in meetings — *the next right thing.*

Driving home, I imagined me and all these women getting drunk together in a bar somewhere, totally sloppy, doing the one thing that connected all of us but that we'd never do together. I wanted to meet the people these women had been when they were drunk. The din and revelry of that impossible night was like noise from another room, something muffled behind a door.

I recognized whatever remained in Nell that made her want to point out exactly where the bottles had been: *under there, up there, tucked in there.* I imagined her back in her empty house, in its dark subdivision — sweeping up pastry crumbs, wiping down surfaces that were already clean, fighting the swallowing quiet. One part of me was sorry that she couldn't just grab a vodka bottle from the camping backpack and sink into that sweet clean stupor, but another part of me believed in this aftermath, its daily accumulations.

"Don't leave before the miracle happens," another woman told me, and I thought, *Sure, okay,* but also wanted to know: *When?* I wanted to know the exact date of the miracle — day, month, and year — for me and for Nell, so I could tell her, *Just hold out till then.*

At least there was this: When Dave and I sat down to eat our corn-and-tomato salads, I was no longer trying to hide the wild animal of need, no longer trying to keep from saying, *Let's drink another round, can we pour another glass?* Now we drank sparkling water with lime. As a sobriety gift, Dave gave me an antique seltzer carbonator, a beautiful glass-and-wire contraption that could make soda from syrup: raspberry, ginger, vanilla. I loved him so much for that gift, for the way he was brightening the landscape of the great dry forever of sobriety. We just had to get a little cartridge to carbonate the water.

We were trying to launch ourselves back into the wonder of our relationship in its early months. On a bright cold winter day, we drove in search of a place called the Maharishi Vedic City, a town founded by a guru in the middle of cornfields, where every building faced east and had a golden spire on its roof. It even had its own currency: the raam. Its transcendental meditation halls were called yogic flying chambers. I'd seen online videos of yogic flying: people bouncing across mats with their knees crossed. It looked awkward but joyful, and I wanted to believe that the flurry of their effort was a sign of transcendence, rather than its absence.

Dave and I drove through snowy cornfields and kept our eyes peeled for golden spires. What we found was a desolate dirt road, patchy with unplowed snow, and a building the color of sour cream where vegan brunch was being served, lentils and curried cauliflower, though Dave wasn't even hungry since he'd eaten so much jerky on the road. But he ate anyway, because we were doing this together. He pointed out a small red fox trotting gracefully across the crusted snow, leaving a trail of delicate prints in its wake. We had no raam, but it turned out we could pay with a credit card.

After brunch, full of lentils, we went looking for the yogic flying chambers. We nearly ran our car into several snowdrifts. We were trying so hard to have a good day. When we found the flying chambers, they were empty. We stood at the threshold and peered inside. Where meditating bodies should have been, their knees flapping like bird wings, there was only silence, and a stillness so solitary it made me want to touch the man next to me—fox spotter, copilot—and so I did, I touched him, and then we left.

Loving Dave was like this: It was his jeans against my tights when we kissed in our kitchen, my hands still soapy from the dishes, and the tornado siren wailing outside. It was eggs and coffee on our orange couch, with mounds of snow outside our windows—domed over the cars, in drifts like hills over the park—as we shivered with gratitude for our home, this living room, this warmth. It was the way we delivered the world to each other, how he told me about cedar waxwings landing just down the block from our house, in the middle of their migration, their breasts yellow like yolks stirred into milk, their little crested tufts like arrowheads.

Loving Dave meant going to Gabe's, a club downtown that smelled like stale beer and other people's sweat, and watching a woman layer drum loops with her ukulele, listening to her alto voice full of gristle and yearning, sensing the hum of Dave's excitement beside me, as this woman captured her chorus with her foot pedal and played it back with a difference, how excited he was by the sheer act of *making*. It meant hearing a teenage girl in the library talking to her friend—*When Brian and I were going out and he would wall me like, I like you so much I don't even have words*—and knowing I had found one with all the words, but I still felt walled. Loving him meant getting thrown onto our bed and tickled—our fierce play—and then lying in bed for hours, the next night, waiting for him to come home, picking his dark curls off the pillows to remind myself he slept here. This was our bed. It smelled like the smell that lived in the crook of his neck.

Dave taught me a quote from Gertrude Stein—"Dirt is clean when there is a volume"—and I wanted this to mean there was something on the other side of all our accumulated friction, how we clashed against each other and then came back to say: *It's you I want.* When I watched him sleep, with one arm flung across his face, love ached through me so hard I had to ball the sheets in my fist.

As an exercise in surrendering control, Dave asked his students to write collaborative poems. "When this happens," he wrote once, describing the assignment, "you can feel the boundary between self and other flicker, each an organ to some larger being." He gave me a poem he'd written about a flock of birds lifting off from the park across the street: "As if touching the same being made them part of the same dream." Though I saw us living in binary—Dave wanted to be free, and I wanted to be certain—in truth we were asking so many of the same questions: what it meant to let your edges dissolve, to be surprised, to touch some dream or being larger than yourself.

Charles Jackson's wife, Rhoda, who arguably had even greater reason to celebrate Jackson's recovery than Jackson himself, wrote gratefully about the camaraderie he found in AA: "It's all so easy and natural and no posing or anything. Everyone likes Charlie, but it's all on an even footing and he responds to that very happily.... He has no resentment of the fact that he really couldn't meet many of the members on any other terms—that they're not very bright or interesting or anything." Rhoda acknowledged that her husband's fellowship in recovery didn't glitter like his literary company, but she still celebrated what it was giving him: even footing, naturalness, ease.

Jackson worried that people might think he'd gotten boring in recovery. He was anxious it would leave him lusterless, make him terrible company at cocktail parties, replace his electric charms with what he later called "vegetable health." In an aside to a friend, when writing about how much he'd come to love AA, he added an anxious addendum: "Please don't squirm at this."

But Jackson also loved the way he'd been embraced by AA. Going to a meeting with him, one friend observed, was "like visiting a birth control clinic in the company of Margaret Sanger." As Blake Bailey, his biographer, has observed, part of the zenith of Jackson's AA involvement—the second half of the 1950s—was also an artistic dry spell for him. The church basements of AA gave Jackson affirmation as a storyteller during years when he was creatively blocked. Jackson loved showing up late somewhere and telling friends that he'd been speaking at a meeting and "the members simply wouldn't let him go." He loved being the expert and the "star pupil" at once. It was his "new addiction." He loved going out with AA folks for ice cream.

But loving this admiration didn't preclude being drawn to recovery for other reasons—for the sense of connection and leveling Rhoda described. People are nothing if not multiple vectors of desire, drawn to behaviors and communities for a thousand reasons at once. Jackson was certainly aware of his own hunger for affirmation, and how it was part of the fabric of his AA life, even though it worked against the AA ethos of humility. But when he spoke in meetings, he confessed these ulterior motivations rather than trying to deny them. Yes, he wanted to be an AA star, but he also wanted AA to give him a way to get outside himself. Both yearnings were authentic: AA fueled his ego, and it offered him relief from his ego's tyrannical engine.

It was certainly true that the success of *The Lost Weekend* was part of why Jackson found himself so beloved in the rooms. Even though the novel wasn't a celebration or validation of recovery, it was still a clear-eyed portrait of the disease. As Bill Wilson wrote to Jackson in 1961:

> *My dear Charlie,*
>
> *Thanks for your thoughtfulness in sending me the new edition of "The Lost Week-end." To have an autographed copy from you is to have a very real keepsake— a remembrance also of your demonstration in the later years of all that is AA.*
>
> *Please be assured of my constant affection and friendship.*
>
> *Always devotedly,*
> *Bill.*

Wilson's letter gently acknowledged that Jackson hadn't always been an AA fan. But after he got deeply involved, in the early fifties, Jackson was eager to share his enthusiasm publicly. Just five months after his stay at the Saul Clinic, in December 1953, Jackson landed a commission with *Life* to write a two-part article about AA. Part 1, the story of his disastrous drinking, came easily. Part 2, called "Possible Answers," proved more difficult. Jackson tried to explain the philosophy and practice of AA, but his editor found the piece disappointing and wanted Jackson to "dramatize" more, the very thing that Jackson would later chastise himself for doing too much in his early AA spiels. For *Life*, the story of a drunken train wreck was more interesting than the story of its redemption, and the piece never ran. Its aborted trajectory was an early manifestation of the creative dilemma that would haunt Jackson for the rest of his career: Would he ever be able to tell another story as well as he'd told the story of falling apart?

During my early months, recovery did not seem like a compelling story. It was like moving through water rather than air. Effort saturated everything. "I know what will happen if I drink," another sober alcoholic said. "I don't know what will happen if I don't." This was a promise I desperately needed the world to make good on. I was trying so hard to find something wonderful in the world that I hadn't seen before, to make the sobriety worth it. At the Art Institute in Chicago, willing myself toward beauty, I looked for it in the Chagall windows, all those bunchy bodies curved upward into flight; and the Giacometti statues, so thin they'd disappear if you squinted. I clutched at everything, not really caring about anything. I cared about *drinking*, and how I wasn't doing it. "Look at these flakes of sunlight," I wrote about some painting, "falling from wrong-colored suns."

At the bakery, I was often distracted, forgetting about cookies in the oven while I was pulling espresso shots in the front of the house. We had to dump trays of burnt snowflakes in the trash, parchment paper and all. I was easily rattled by almost everything. Just before Thanksgiving, I'd handed a woman her order—forty gingerbread turkeys—and she had a meltdown, right there at the counter: They were supposed to be sugar cookies, she said, asking: "What am I supposed to do with these?" And then I had a meltdown of my own, sputtering "sorry" after "sorry," and it seemed like there wasn't a good answer to our situation, her anger and my hopeless apologies; my frantic attempt to figure out if *I'd* been the one who'd gotten the order wrong or if someone else had gotten the order wrong, and I was desperately trying to determine if her emotions were valid, or my emotions were valid; I wanted to slap her, or prostrate myself in front of her. It was like the apocalypse. And then my boss came out of the kitchen and told the woman we'd get her forty sugar-cookie turkeys in a couple of hours. I thought, *Oh.* That was another way of responding to a moment. Every time I imagined getting home and having a glass of wine, I remembered that I couldn't. Already it was starting, the nostalgia. Drinking had been the honeyed twilight sun falling over every late afternoon, softening everything to amber.

In December, my oldest brother was planning to run a hundred-kilometer race called Hellgate. It was supposed to start at midnight in Virginia, and I decided to run with him—not in Virginia but in Iowa—timing my run to align with his start. It would be an act of solidarity. I imagined my new life in sobriety as something that might seem zany and inspired: *Oh, I used to get drunk every night but now you never know WHAT I'm going to do! I might go for a nighttime run in the arctic cold!* I was convinced that if I did things I wouldn't have done before I got sober, then sobriety would be worth it. Jamie, my boss at the bakery, told me she'd put out a thermos of hot cocoa in her backyard for me.

I bundled up: long underwear, sweatpants, wind pants, a sweatshirt and a ski jacket. Dave had some friends over and I told them what I was doing and they were like, *Okay,* but I could see they were a little confused. In my mind they were trying to figure out whether this plan had anything to do with my sobriety, but in truth they probably didn't even realize I'd stopped drinking, or didn't really care, because most people weren't obsessed with drinking or not-drinking the way I was obsessed with both.

When I started jogging, that swelling music I'd been imagining as soundtrack didn't start. My nose was so cold it went numb almost instantly. I was aware of myself as someone you might cross the street to get away from. It was eleven at night, and I was running through the cold in layers, track pants swishing with every step, fingers going numb under my gloves, thinking— *This is great, right? This is really SOMETHING, right?*

When I reached the thermos in my boss's backyard, two miles later, I took a sip and realized the cocoa had booze in it. I spit it out onto the snow.

When I met other alcoholics for coffee or sugary pastries, the vices still available to us, I began to spend those dates imagining how the drinking might work a little better than it had before. Reading the Big Book with another woman over night-discounted muffins, I was secretly concocting a plan: If I drank again, I'd only drink three nights a week. The restriction would make me look functional to Dave, and hopefully keep my tolerance low enough that I'd be able to get just the right buzz from only three drinks (maybe sometimes I'd need four), and maybe the buzz could stay perched right there, at just the right level, and those other four nights would be great nights, sober nights, *great sober nights!*, and on those great sober nights I would of course have the nonsober nights to look forward to. If other people wondered about my drinking I could just point at my non-drinking nights, how *not* a big deal they were, how much I enjoyed them. It seemed like this plan could work. It actually seemed pretty straightforward.

That's when we hit the beginning of the Big Book's next chapter: *The idea that somehow, someday he will control and enjoy drinking is the great obsession of every abnormal drinker.* Yes, that. Check.

It wasn't just the Big Book that made me feel seen-through and chord-struck. When a sober friend, Emily, sent me a Carver poem about drinking called "Luck," I saw myself reflected in the speaker, a nine-year-old boy wandering through an empty house full of half-drunk drinks, on the morning after one of his parents' parties. The boy drinks a leftover lukewarm whiskey, then another. It's unexpected manna, all this booze and no one around to keep him from drinking it:

> What luck, I thought.
> Years later,
> I still wanted to give up
> friends, love, starry skies,
> for a house where no one
> was home, no one coming back,
> and all I could drink.

Those lines spoke the coiled longing at my core, the desire to disappear into the velvet depths of a solitary drunk with no one around to stop me. The poem said it so simply, without pretense or explanation. Just *of course*. That thirst. It made me think of Bug getting his vodka delivered. I'd never gotten that bad. Part of me still wanted to.

Bill Wilson recognized that every sober alcoholic might reach a stage in her sobriety when she wanted to start drinking again. "Alcoholics get to a point in the program where they need a spiritual experience," he told Betty Eisner, a psychologist, "but not all of them are able to have one." This was twenty years into Wilson's own sobriety, and with Eisner's help he had just taken his second acid trip—in February 1957, at Eisner's home in Santa Monica—an experiment that was part of his broader exploration into the various ways LSD might be useful in recovery.

Describing his first trip to a friend, Wilson compared it to his early visions of AA as a "chain of drunks around the world, all helping each other." For Wilson, acid summoned visions of collectivity and possibility, dissolving his boundaries and connecting him to forces beyond himself. He experienced his first acid trip as a "dead ringer" for the spiritual experience he'd had at New York's Towns Hospital two decades earlier, the mountaintop vision that catalyzed his recovery. Because acid had "helped him eliminate many barriers erected by the self, or ego, that stand in the way of one's direct experiences of the cosmos and of god," Wilson imagined it might do this for others — especially "cynical alcoholics" who hadn't had visions of their own.

The rest of AA didn't exactly embrace Wilson's exploration of hallucinogens. As his official AA biography puts it, "Most AAs were violently opposed to his experimenting with a mind-altering substance." But Wilson's fascination with acid was an organic extension of his commitment to one of the core principles of AA recovery: the elimination of the ego, that barrier between a self and everything beyond it.

Around that time, Wilson found another way around the ego — through a spiritualist practice called automatic writing. During these "spook sessions," Wilson believed he was taking dictation from visiting spirits, a process that effectively allowed him to inhabit his own voice and escape it at once. Automatic writing let the reluctant "number-one man" become an ordinary vessel — or at least, a more passive one. A listener.

In a 1952 letter to Ed Dowling, a priest who would eventually join the informal acid-dropping salon Wilson organized in New York, Wilson describes getting help from spirits in writing *Twelve Steps and Twelve Traditions*, his extended practical outline to the AA program. "One turned up the other day calling himself Boniface," he wrote, a "man of learning" who knew "a lot about structures." AA was nothing if not a structure, and Wilson granting credit to Boniface was the humbling logic of recovery writ large, across the astral plane, crediting the voices of others rather than his own. (Wilson also said

Boniface "checked out pretty well in the Encyclopedia.") Wilson liked the notion that the wisdom wasn't coming from his own mind. It fit with the ethos of interdependence that was central to his understanding of recovery. "I have good help, of that I am certain," he told Dowling. "Both over here and over there."

Records of this help remain in the AA aphorisms scribbled all over scraps of paper left in the wake of Wilson's spook sessions: "<u>first</u> things <u>first</u>," "God grant me the <u>serenity</u>," "take it easy." In automatic writing, Wilson found a cousin to the "surrender" of the First Step. Each session involved the logic of a blackout transplanted to sobriety: letting his body become the vessel for an agency he couldn't claim. It was a desire directed toward *otherness*—not the other voices in a meeting, but voices even farther out, voices beyond the room entirely. One of the longest fragments still remains on the back of page 164 of a Big Book typescript:

> *Are you going to stop smoking. Please do Bill as you are being prepared as <u>a chanel</u> [sic] for important things. You must believe us when we say that you are destined for tremendous development. Please, please, Bill, do this and do not fail us. So much more depends upon your attitude and actions. You are a link in a long chain and you must not be the weakest point. Do not fear contact by us...Go and lie down but please don't smoke any more.*

Wilson was a lifelong smoker—he kept it up in sobriety, with even greater fervor—and there was a tragic earnestness lodged in this moment of ventriloquized self-awareness. Wilson's own survival impulse announced itself from a celestial distance. He listened to a voice trying to persuade him to stop smoking, a voice he tried to convince himself belonged to someone else.

Wilson's spook sessions and his acid trips and his nicotine addiction aren't the parts of his story that sit most comfortably inside his legend, but for me they don't undermine the story of his sobriety, they humanize it. They speak to the raggedness of his recovery, or anyone's — the ways it might always yearn for something more.

You are destined for tremendous development. Are you going to stop smoking. He didn't, and died of emphysema at the age of seventy-five.

Wilson tried to project authority elsewhere, in these astral voices, but eventually came back to an assertion of his own singularity: *You are destined.* It was one of the peculiar paradoxes embedded in his sobriety, which ultimately wasn't like everyone else's — no matter how much he wanted it to be.

In February 1957, the General Service Headquarters of AA released a "Pattern Script" for radio and television appearances. It provided a script for any AA "John" to follow, stressing that he should limit himself to general points about alcoholism and fellowship, including only a brief personal interlude: "Suggested that at this point 'John' speak extemporaneously about two minutes, qualifying himself as an alcoholic, as he might do at an AA Open Meeting. Further suggested that, to minimize 'rambling,' comments hew closely to theme of how alcoholics hurt others while drinking." At one point, the script even prompted John to say "Naturally I can speak only for myself," even though John was following a script — one that was supposed to translate his story into something that could apply to every drunk who might be listening.

When I first saw the Pattern Script, it seemed to crystallize everything that was troubling about recovery narratives, their cookie-cutter conventions and the tyranny of their triptych structure: *what it was like* (your drinking), *what happened* (why you stopped), *what it's like now* (your sobriety). The flip side of resonance in meetings was the suspicion that this resonance was simply self-fulfilling prophecy — that we convinced ourselves our stories were all the same and then pressured one another to tell them the same way. Perhaps our platitudes were just sheepdogs herding us into neat clusters of oversimplified dysfunction: We were all selfish in the same simple ways, fearful in the same simple ways, escaping our own lives in the same simple ways.

Clichés were one of the hardest parts of my early days in recovery. I cringed at their singsong cadences. *Meeting makers make it. It's the first drink that gets you drunk. Take the cotton out of your ears and put it in your mouth.* At meetings, I hated when other people abandoned narrative particularity in their stories — *I accidentally crushed my daughter's pet turtle after too much absinthe* — for the bland pudding of abstraction — *I was sick and tired of being sick and tired.* I wanted crushed turtles and absinthe. Clichés were like blights, refusals of clarity and nuance, an insistence on soft-focus greeting-card wisdom: *This too shall pass,* which I once saw on a cross-stitch in the bathroom of a Wyoming meeting, followed by *It just did.* Long ago, I had learned that to become a writer I had to resist clichés at all costs. It was such accepted dogma that I'd never wondered why it was true.

Keep it simple was one of the clichés I struggled with most. I'd never thought there was anything simple about me, or anyone else. Simplicity seemed like disrespect, a willful evasion of the wrinkles in every human psyche, a failure to witness consciousness fully. If life wasn't simple in the first place, how could you keep it that way? The insistence on simplicity seemed like part of AA's larger insistence that we were all the same, which was basically a way of saying *fuck you* to my entire value system. My whole life I'd been taught that something was good because it was original — that singularity was the driving engine of value. *Make it new,* the modernists had said. It was impossible to imagine what it was to *be,* as a person or a story, without thinking in terms of difference. I'd always understood love in terms of singularity as well, an assumption I'd held so close it had become nearly transparent: *I'm loved because I'm not quite like anyone else.* Whenever someone talked about the unconditional love in the rooms of recovery, I always wanted to shout: *You can't love me! You don't even know me!*

Actually, when it came to love I had somewhat contradictory desires. I wanted to be loved unconditionally, simply because I *was*, but I also wanted to be loved for my qualities: because I was x, because I was y. I wanted to be loved because I deserved it. Except I was scared to be loved like this, because what if I *stopped* deserving it? Unconditional love was insulting, but conditional love was terrifying. This was something Dave and I had talked about—being loved for qualities, or else without conditions. He taught me the notion of love bestowed *stam*, as they said in Hebrew, for no earthly reason: because because.

D ave and I weren't fighting drunk anymore, but we were fighting sober—which was even worse, because I no longer had drinking as an alibi or an excuse. Without booze in the room to take the blame, these fights were between *us*—or between him and the brittle, vigilant version of myself I'd become. Honestly, I'd already been this person. But without drinking, I had no way to mute myself. Sobriety was like a merciless interrogation room, every detail lit by harsh fluorescence. I scanned everything Dave did for signs that he was tired of me, because I was tired of myself. When a friend told me it was difficult to imagine being with Dave, because he seemed to save all his charm and energy for everyone else, it confirmed my fear that I'd become little more than a burden.

I started staying home from parties because it was miserable to go to them without drinking. I was tired of keeping a Diet Wild Cherry Pepsi hidden in my purse. But staying home wasn't much better. When Dave went out, I would lie awake for hours wondering when he might get home. I'd watch the clock, then try to go to sleep so I wouldn't keep watching the clock; then I'd wake up and check for his body next to mine, sense an absence, and check the clock again, miserably awake, sober as a puckered wedge of lime in a glass of flat seltzer. A friend of Dave's offered to shave off his beard if Dave could finish a review he'd been struggling with, and when he actually went through with it—using an electric razor in the bathroom of the Foxhead—it seemed like just another epic night I hadn't been part of. Of course, it was also the mark of Dave accomplishing something that mattered to him. But I didn't think of it that way.

Dave came up with a gesture for moments when I got low, putting two fingers against my forehead to remind me that whatever I was feeling would eventually pass. It was true, what his fingers told me— and I loved their pressure against my skin, that sense of closeness, its electric charge—but it was hard to summon his fingers as sense-memory when he wasn't there.

Years later, when a clinician described the classic addict temperament as stubbornly focused on the present moment, I was immediately convinced that this addict personality type didn't have much to do with *my* addict personality type. What was I ever doing with my life, if I wasn't stubbornly fixated on the past or daydreaming about the future? But the more I thought about it, the more I realized this was a way of describing what Dave's two fingers had tried to resist: my conviction that there would never be an outside to the present moment.

It was frustrating for Dave, I think, to have our days consumed by my ongoing dramas: first the slurred sadness of my drinking, then the grand epiphanies of getting sober. Some mornings he just wanted to pour a bowl of cereal and sit down at his desk to write, while I was pounding on his door incessantly with one intensity after another: *I have to get an abortion! I have to get heart surgery! I have to get sober!* That was the movie that played in my head: my desires like barbarians at his door. I wanted his constant reassurance that my needs weren't too much for him—which was, of course, another need I laid at his feet.

When the earthquake hit Haiti, in January 2010, we read about people holding shirts over their mouths to keep out the smell of the dead, and a woman calling her brother's cell phone to see if she could hear it ringing in the rubble. We decided to host a fund-raiser to raise money for relief work—part of my desperate attempt to redeem the bereavement of sobriety with virtue. The bakery donated a hundred cookies and a cake, which I thought of decorating but didn't. It would have been like making a vanity plate for a catastrophe. The whole enterprise was muddled by my cloying, frustrated desire to justify my sober life: Is this *it*? Doing *good*?

I spent most of the party watching Dave talk to Destiny, following her body around the room, keenly aware of every moment they were standing together and laughing. I'd never felt so primal, like an animal tracking the movements of another animal—a mating rival. I'd never been so fully present in my own jealousy, without any numbing agent in sight. It was like waking up during a surgery I was supposed to stay unconscious for.

After everyone had left, we threw away the ruins of the cake and counted how much money we'd raised for Doctors Without Borders. The whole time I was fuming, until I finally just broke down and asked Dave if he realized how openly he'd been flirting. From Doctors Without Borders to this: Few subject changes could be more embarrassing.

"We're honestly on this again?" He looked disappointed, and, more than anything, exhausted. We both kept cleaning—putting sticky cups in big white trash bags, sweeping crumbs into our hands—because it was easier not to look at each other when we fought.

"It's humiliating," I said. "To see you standing there with her, especially after—"

"After what?"

"It's just this feeling I get about the two of you," I said. "An energy."

That's when he turned and looked at me directly, his voice cold and probing: "Did you read my journal?"

The molecules shifted in the room. I set down my trash bag and its mouth sagged open, showing red plastic Solo cups, crumpled napkins, cupcake sleeves still furred with crumbs.

"I need you to be honest," he said. "Did you?"

My gut dropped. I didn't even know he kept a journal. "What's in it?" I asked, hating my own shrill panic. "Why are you asking?"

"That's not an answer," he said.

"I didn't read it," I told him. "I didn't even know you kept one. But what were you afraid—"

"I don't believe you," he said.

After the texts, I knew I had no right to blame him. If I'd known he had a journal, I probably would have tried to read it too. Learning about a new type of privacy just made me want to violate it. We went back and forth for almost an hour. I kept begging him to tell me what was in the journal; he kept telling me he didn't know how to believe I hadn't read it. If I were him, I wouldn't have believed me either.

"I've never even seen it!" I told him. But part of me dreaded knowing what the journal looked like—afraid that if I knew, I'd be obsessed with the possibility of reading it, the same way I'd grown obsessed with his phone, which I constantly imagined picking up, just like I constantly imagined picking up the bottle of Bombay Sapphire in our freezer.

"It's on my computer," he said, and I could tell that maybe now he believed me, though I was already thinking, compulsively, about when and how I might read it: while he was in the shower, or at a bar. How would I cover my tracks, so it wouldn't show up in the list of recently opened documents? Trying to know him entirely was like trying to pick up a thousand grains of rice scattered across the sidewalk.

"Please tell me what you wrote," I begged him. "Something happened, didn't it?"

"The only reason I'm going to tell you," he said finally, "is that whatever you're imagining is so much worse than the truth."

We sat together on our orange couch and he told me there had been a night back in December, one of the nights I'd lain awake waiting for him, miserably sober, when he and Destiny had been sitting on a couch, just the two of them, at two or three in the morning, closing down a party. She'd been waiting for something to happen, he could tell.

"Of course she was," I said, thinking: If it's three in the morning and you're alone on a couch with a guy, and his girlfriend is at home, then something is probably going to happen. I remembered sitting on a couch with Dave, with my boyfriend at home.

"I told her something could have happened in another world," Dave said. "But not in this one."

"You told her *what*?"

"I told her nothing was going to happen."

"That's not what you said."

"The point is, I shut it down."

But that wasn't the point to me: Why had he been there in the first place? Why had there been something to shut down? To him, the story was proof of his fidelity, but to me it was proof that life was happening just as I'd feared: on couches somewhere else, with bottles all around. While I was home alone, sober, jealous and nervous and afraid, he was testing the limits of possibility, seeking the near edges of transgression. It made me sick, thinking Dave and Destiny both knew about this moment — a secret between them — and I hadn't.

"Why didn't you tell me after it happened?" I asked him.

"Because I didn't want this," he said, meaning the three-hour fight we were in the middle of. At three in the morning, on our couch, we didn't test the limits of what might be. We ran our scouring sponges over the surface of what was.

Couldn't he just pull back from his friendship with this woman, I asked him, because it was something I needed?

"What about my needs?" he said. "We never talk about those."

His needs — to connect with other people, to share a life with someone who was not constantly accusing him of something — were real, but they were hard for me to hear above the volume of my fear, which turned so quickly to blame.

At that point it was past four in the morning.

"Your fear isn't about me, or about this," he said. "It runs deeper."

He was dead tired and wanted to go to bed. I wanted to keep talk-ing until we worked it out. *Never go to bed angry*, I'd heard. It makes me smile now. As if you could avoid it. He went to bed angry, but I knew I wouldn't be able to sleep. It was the middle of winter, but I pulled on my coat and gloves and started walking the streets — past the sorority houses on Washington and Governor, past the shuttered Co-op, with its squashes on sale; down to the twenty-four-hour gas station on Burlington, where the sleepy college student behind the register blinked when I asked for Marlboro Reds. "Always thought they were nasty," he said with a shrug, but for me, that night, they were just right, and I smoked them in the freezing cold — on the street, in the park, on our porch — until I was finally tired enough to climb into bed with Dave, too scared to touch him, though I wanted to, very much.

A few weeks later, I found myself on the phone with my mother — crouched in the closet of my office, where I was sure we couldn't be heard — telling her I was convinced Dave was cheating on me. She said she couldn't tell me if he was or not. But she also said this: Every time she thought my father had been having an affair, she'd been right.

My paranoia about Destiny was a tangible, humiliating receptacle for a more nebulous set of fears about the opacity of other people, the possibility of wanting multiple people at once, the diminishment of love over time, and the lurking possibility of being left. Even on the days I believed Dave hadn't slept with her, I was still haunted by the possibility of his desire — by the way his long nights held electricity I couldn't offer anymore, certainly not with these claustrophobic arguments.

We never got a carbonation cartridge for the seltzer maker he'd given me. It stood there magnificent and untouched, while I still craved the booze it was supposed to help me live without.

— VII —

THIRST

As winter turned to spring, I kept taking long drives past strip malls on my days off work, through cornfields where snow was thawing into smaller patches of crusted dirty white. But these drives seemed empty, my life unbeautiful. I was just a woman jamming my fingers into the heat vents of my car. Everything glossy or buzzed or hot-blush-drunk in my life was gone. Only strip malls and that big fucked Iowa sky remained. On one of my routes, I passed an indoor water park, with a single curve of waterslide protruding from its stucco wall, and I fantasized about that pocket of warmth and rushing water—that chlorinated speed, its oasis.

When I was seven years old, I'd told my mom I was pretty sure I could make an apple crumble topping better than hers: a brown sugar crust baked with cinnamon and nutmeg. She gestured at the kitchen—unfazed, smiling—and said, "Go ahead." I made a disgusting concoction with too much butter and, for whatever reason, raw macaroni, and then, too proud to admit I'd failed, I sat there eating the mixture in front of her, pretending that I loved it. Sobriety felt like that.

Everything made me think about booze. Empty shower caddies for sale at the student store made me imagine the hypothetical undergrads who would someday use them to get ready for their sorority parties, and I envied all the drinking they'd get to do, still smelling faintly of vanilla body scrub. When I thought of my nephew in San Francisco, at the other end of I-80, I imagined all the drinking he'd get to do someday. He was just over a year old. One afternoon a stranger in my regular coffee shop, two tables away, sat with his beer half drunk in front of him for hours, and I thought, *Come on already!* The woman in front of me in line at the Co-op bought a split of wine, half of half a bottle, and I thought: *Why would you do that?* I watched *Leaving Las Vegas* and felt envious of Nicolas Cage because he got to drink as much as he wanted.

Sobriety was shaping up to hold precisely the blankness I'd feared it would. I woke up every day without anything to look forward to, except the hour I spent craning my face to get closer to the small blue UV lamp that was supposed to combat my winter gloom. It was exhausting to be around anyone, because I didn't have much inside — much energy or interest — so I had to portion it carefully across the day. Talking took effort. What was there to talk about? My family thought I might be clinically depressed, which wasn't particularly interesting to talk about either.

The question of producing interesting conversation in sobriety has always been tricky. In *Junkie*, William Burroughs describes the Narcotic Farm as full of patients who talk about nothing but drugs, "like hungry men who can talk about nothing but food." In *The Fantastic Lodge*, an "autobiography" published in 1961, culled and edited from taped interviews, an addict named Janet arrives at the Narcotic Farm to find it full of patient-prisoners talking about the drugs they miss: "There's just nothing to do, nothing — except talk about junk. All is junk, and that's all, you know; that's the way it is." Even Janet's grammar is saturated by obsession; she keeps saying the same thing over and over again — about how there's nothing else, really, to say.

By the end of *The Fantastic Lodge*, Janet has written a manuscript about her addiction and recovery, but it hasn't done her any good. "She had come to put great hope in getting this book published," says her psychiatrist in an afterword, and she "carried the manuscript with her wherever she went," in a brown paper shopping bag that nearly split open from its weight.

In meetings, I had been told that telling our stories would save us, but I wondered if this was always true. What if your story was just dead weight, a bundle of pages in a soggy paper grocery bag?

When the Narcotic Farm's annual reports classified discharged patients in terms of their suspected likelihood of relapse, the statistics did little more than suggest their own futility: "Cured, prognosis good (3) / Cured, prognosis guarded (27) / Cured, prognosis poor (10)." Another said: "good (23); guarded (61); poor (2)." The "guarded" category still loomed large: 61 out of 86, and 27 out of 40. Prognosis guarded essentially meant: We have no idea what will happen to him.

I'd envisioned the logic of sobriety working like a recycling redemption center, where I'd bring all the booze I wasn't drinking, and in return I'd get back my relationship as I'd known it in the beginning. This was the contract logic version of sobriety: *If I get sober, I'll get* x *in return.*

But now that I was sober, the main difference seemed to be that it was much harder for me to fall asleep after Dave and I fought. Our fights left me with so much restless energy—a vinegar tonic of anger and guilt—that I'd often leave the house at three or four in the morning and go walking like that first time, often to the same gas station on Burlington. It was strange to be out late without being drunk, strolling into the gas station utterly sober at four in the morning, as if I needed to explain myself to the clerk: *I'm not partying, just awake.* At a certain point, my mom—apologizing for even saying it at all—wrote at the bottom of an email: "If it were possible for me and you to have a conversation sometime about yours and Dave's relationship when it wasn't in response to an immediate crisis, I would really like that."

That winter, after months spent in a dull, zombie dream, I eventually went back home to Los Angeles and sat in a chair in the middle of a psychiatrist's office. He asked me if I ever felt like I was seeing everything through shit-colored glasses. I said: *Always.* He gave me a prescription for an antidepressant and said I should dose up slowly and watch for a rash. My mother and I drove to a convent where the trimmed grass was sliced into pieces by the gray ribbons of concrete pathways. We wrote our wishes for the year and burned them to make them come true. But when I tried to pray, nothing happened. It was like I was trying to edge my way into a conversation that had already begun without me.

B ack in Iowa, on the days I didn't work at the bakery, I trudged into my office at home—the room where I used to drink alone—and tried to work on the novel I wanted to be writing about the Sandinista revolution. Sobriety was supposed to mean you got beyond yourself, and I was drawn to the premise of the novel as a way to hurl myself as far away from my own life as possible. The novel itself was actually *about* the desire to give yourself to something bigger than your particular life: a revolution.

I started researching with frantic propulsion, from the subtleties of the Sandinistas' hybrid-Marxist doctrinal debates to the jars of blood thrown in protest against the white fortresses of Somoza's for-profit blood banks. I covered one wall of my office with grainy photocopied photographs: black-and-red FSLN flags waving above a crowded plaza; men in berets riding buses to Managua with their guns pointed against the sky. I wrote heated debate scenes that took place in cobblestone courtyards. Did the revolution depend on mobilizing the rural peasants or gaining the support of the urban elite? At least I had the courtyard down: candles tucked in the crevices between stones; their fluted, flickering light; the sweet stink of piss and flowers; the faint shushing of palm fronds in the wind overhead. Minor sensory details were all my imagination could muster, a sublimated nostalgia for my drinking days in Nicaragua. But the prose sagged under the weight of all my desperate research. *We must not forget the middle classes in Managua!* It was terrible. I gave my characters plenty of rum to drink, the same rum I'd drunk years before, to ease the burden of all the soapbox lecturing I was foisting upon them. I imagined all that rum running in tender spicy streaks down their throats. I could have described that rum for paragraphs, for pages.

Every once in a while, I would creep into my bathroom, get on my knees, and ask God to help me write the book. Then I'd correct myself, ask Him to help me do His will, and secretly hope that His will would be for me to write the best novel ever written about the Sandinista revolution.

In those days, I prayed grudgingly. My faith was skeptical and contractual. I wasn't sure God existed, but if He did exist, there were definitely a couple things He could do for me. It felt fraudulent to get on my knees in front of my own futon—right next to where I'd stashed the whiskey bottle under the frame—as if, by kneeling, I was pretending to have a faith I couldn't actually summon.

In order to convince myself that sobriety was worth it, I tried to write day and night. But most evenings I broke down and watched hours of reality television instead. I got especially attached to *The Gauntlet,* a reality-TV show where former cast members from better reality-TV shows went to beautiful parts of the developing world and competed in absurd gladiatorial contests. They dunked themselves in ice water and buried themselves in coffins. They ended up eating ice cream mixed with their own vomit. I was glad to see Trishelle get into a bike accident because I still hadn't forgiven her for choosing Steven over Frank back on *Real World: Las Vegas,* though she'd eventually hooked up with both of them. ("Everyone's cute after twelve cocktails," she said, and I couldn't disagree.) Sometimes I glanced up at my Sandinista wall and thought the revolutionaries must be gazing down at me, judging.

When my first novel came out that winter, the girls at the bakery made a cake decorated with a version of the cover—which showed a faceless woman in a mauve negligee, not my first choice—fashioned from pink and purple chocolate. The book didn't sell well. The high point was the day it reached ninety-something on the Alcoholism sublist on Amazon, far below the Big Book—translated into twenty different languages. My mom was excited to see it ranked on a sublist. She emailed me about it. *Thanks for letting me know!* I wrote back, as if

I hadn't been checking for myself. I read my online reader reviews obsessively, all ten of them. The most passionate one said that my descriptions of alcohol were so detailed I *must* be an alcoholic, and gave the book three stars out of five.

I was still trying to work myself as hard as I could—to prove to myself that sobriety was worth it—but mostly my writing felt like riding a stubborn horse, kicking it with spurs until it bled.

In *The Shining*, Jack Nicholson plays a dry drunk desperately punching away at his typewriter in an empty off-season resort—an embodiment of grudging sobriety, its maze of carpeted corridors haunted by the sinister ghosts of prior revelry. Jack hurls himself at his manuscript but ends up typing just one phrase for hundreds of pages, *All work and no play makes Jack a dull boy*, varied only by margins and typos: *All work and no play makes Jack a dull bog. All work and no play makes Jack a dull bot.* It's sobriety through a glass darkly. All work and no play—no booze—makes everything hopelessly dull. Life, prose, *everything*.

Jack starts drinking again in the movie, or at least he wants to drink so badly he hallucinates his own relapse. He gets a tumbler of bourbon from poker-faced Lloyd, a ghost bartender at the empty lobby bar. "Here's to five miserable months on the wagon," Jack tells Lloyd, "and all the irreparable harm that it's caused me."

Stephen King's novel *The Shining*, on which the Kubrick film is based, is the story of a failed recovery set in a twisted vision of rehab: An unhappily sober man relapses in an empty hotel perched high in the Colorado Rockies. Instead of the community of rehab, we get life in an isolation tank. When Jack Torrance takes a job at the Overlook Hotel, he no longer drinks, but he's still consumed by the resentment and anger that fueled his drinking. "Would he ever have an hour," he wonders, "not a week or even a day, mind you, but just one waking hour [without] this craving for a drink?"

After the winter's first major snowfall, the phone lines go down and the road that connects the Overlook to the rest of the world is closed. Jack and his family are utterly alone, left to the devices of their own unraveling. The hotel's walls are banked with fallen snow, its rooms full of rotting ghosts, its wallpaper stained with blood. The topiary animals come alive. The elevators fill with confetti and deflated balloons, the menacing afterlife of revelry. *The Shining* isn't just a relapse story; it's a story about the frustrations of a dry drunk — recovery-speak for someone who no longer drinks but isn't in any recovery program — a man literally white-knuckling his way through life. Jack's hands and fingers appear constantly throughout the novel's six hundred pages, "clenched tightly in his lap, working against each other, sweating," his nails "digging into his palms like tiny brands," or shaking, or balled into tight fists, contorted by "the wanting, the *needing* to get drunk."

Though Jack has been dry for longer in the novel than the movie — fourteen months, to be precise, not that he's counting every second of it — he's angry that he hasn't gotten enough credit for his own self-improvement. "If a man reforms," he asks himself, "doesn't he deserve to have his reformation credited sooner or later?"

Everything conspires to make Jack drink again. He pictures guests drinking in the gardens during summer: sloe gin fizzes and Pink Ladies. He wipes his handkerchief across his lips in longing. He starts chewing Excedrin just like he used to for his hangovers. He eventually finds himself facing Lloyd at the bar, asking for twenty martinis: "One for every month I've been on the wagon and one to grow on." Jack sits on his bar stool telling Lloyd about the trials of staying high-and-dry, the five months he's added to his sobriety during the long winter: "The floor of the Wagon is nothing but straight pine boards, so fresh they're still bleeding sap, and if you took your shoes off you'd be sure to get a splinter." Sobriety is Spartan and uncomfortable, sticky and joyless. It pricks you at every turn. The ballroom behind his bar stool fills with ghosts — ghoulish creatures with sagging skin wearing fox masks and rhinestone brassieres and sequined dresses—and they're all egging on his relapse, "looking at him expectantly, silently," as the bartender tells him: "Now drink your drink," a command that all the spirits repeat, in chorus.

Jack's relapse exists in a strange purgatory between hallucination and actual intoxication: "Jack brought the drink to his mouth and downed it in three long gulps, the gin highballing down his throat like a moving van in a tunnel, exploding in his stomach." Does he actually drink, or just imagine drinking? It gets him drunk either way.

After this fantasy has ended and its imagined bottles have disappeared from the shelves, Jack finds himself at the bar with his crying wife and their traumatized child, wondering: "What was he doing in a bar with a drink in his hand? He had TAKEN THE PLEDGE. He had GONE ON THE WAGON. He had SWORN OFF." It sounds like a temperance play—like my old all-caps superlatives, or Lowry's melodrama—and it sounds like one to Jack, too: "It was just before the curtain of Act II in some old-time temperance play," he thinks, "one so poorly mounted that the prop man had forgotten to stock the shelves of the Den of Iniquity." Jack is aware of his own self-dramatizing tendencies, but he's also aware—with keen disappointment, like a real alcoholic—that all the bottles are gone. His son, Danny, telepathically curses the hotel: "You had to make him drink the Bad Stuff. That's the only way you could get him."

The novel and film versions of *The Shining* both present bleak visions of the relationship between sobriety and creativity. In the movie we get a sober man without a story—his mind fallow and fumbling, typing the same words over and over again—but the book imagines a writer seduced by the *wrong* story. Jack becomes obsessed with the story of the Overlook Hotel itself, its history of depravity: murders and suicides and mafia scandals. One day while Jack is checking on the boiler in the basement—the novel's Chekhovian gun, spotted in the first act and fired by the last—he discovers a scrapbook full of articles about the hotel's violent past. His fascination quickly starts to sound like relapse, as he examines the scrapbook "almost guiltily, as if he had been drinking secretly," all the while worried that his wife "would smell the fumes on him." When Jack thinks about writing the story of the Overlook, he gets the same sensation "he usually felt… when he had a three-drink buzz on."

Whether he's working on a story that doesn't exist (in the film), or committed to telling a story of dissolution (in the novel), Jack's mono-maniacal focus on creation is what obliterates his decency. In the novel, he relapses because he finds himself drawn to the wrong tale, not a recovery narrative but something nearly opposite: the hotel's own sor-did drunkalog. The sinister revelry beckons, all the ghosts beckon: *Drink your drink.* It's a relapse writ large. The stakes are supernatural. When the boiler explodes and the hotel goes up in flames, there's no triumphant recovery, only finality: "The party was over."

When Stephen King wrote *The Shining*, in the mid-seventies, he wrote it "without even realizing…that I was writing about myself." At the height of his use, King was filling his trash cans with beer bottles and doing so much cocaine he had to stuff tissues into his nos-trils so he wouldn't bleed on his typewriter. *The Shining* was a night-mare written by an addict terrified of sobriety. "I was afraid," King wrote decades later, "that I wouldn't be able to work anymore if I quit drinking and drugging."

When I wanted to force myself to write, I spent my evenings at the Java House, a cavernous coffee shop stocked with fist-sized cookies—often stale—that I purchased with dogged determination, trying to tell myself that pleasure was still possible. I opened my laptop by the front windows and watched people walk into bars while I pecked at my keyboard, working on a short story called "The Relapse" that was supposed to be an inoculation against actually relapsing.

The story begins with a woman named Claudia binge-drinking while pregnant, just like I had. When I wrote about the clear sweet booze surrounding her fetus, I wanted to drink it. I wanted gills so I could swim through it. After Claudia decides to quit drinking, she meets a man named Jack at an AA meeting. This plotline was a way for me to dramatize one of my relapse fantasies: that I would meet a man in the program and throw everything away with him—my relationship, my sobriety, all of it. Claudia and Jack trade drinking histories the way other people might flirt by talking about their sexual pasts. Claudia isn't sure if she is using the possibility of alcohol to flirt with Jack, or the possibility of Jack to flirt with alcohol. Claudia tells Jack she wants to relapse so she can know—without a doubt—that she has absolutely lost control. Then she'll be able to get better.

In the first draft I wrote, Claudia and Jack got drunk together. Then I decided the ending was too predictable. I gave it away in the title! That version of the story seemed like a pathetic version of wish fulfillment, without any larger purpose in sight. So I revised: She didn't relapse. She stayed straight. But all this flip-flopping, draft to draft, was just another version of what I was doing every day in my own head.

"The fantasy of every alcoholic," says one textbook, "is that there is a nearby, possible world in which he discovers a decorous dosing regimen, and drinks like a perfect gentleman or lady." From the safe perch of sobriety, I started to summon a catalog of my finest drinking moments. Recovery wisdom said, *You can't turn a pickle back into a cucumber.* But I was busy re-cucumbering, marinating in nostalgia. I could still remember drinking on a balcony with Dave while the dark sea frothed and surged below us; or stumbling back to my college boyfriend's concrete high-rise dorm, exhaling puffs of frosted gin breath into the cold, falling into his twin bed on the nineteenth floor as the high tower creaked and moaned in the wind. I could still remember getting drunk during a work trip to Xi'an, on a clear liquor that a Chinese writer told me was white wine. But it wasn't white wine. It was fire. I could still remember picking up a fried scorpion from the pile of fried scorpions, under the watchful gaze of two birds carved from turnips, and making a joke with my chopsticks, acting like a total fucking idiot but not caring. That was the point: not caring. As if I'd been released from a contract. Drinking was plush and forgiving. It sparkled like backyard fireflies. It smelled like good meat and smoke. It was already happening in the nearby possible world. It said, *Come on over.*

In that world, I would drink like I'd always wanted to drink, except it would work out; it would be okay. I definitely wouldn't get drunk and stuff my face with old crusty leftover pasta from the fridge and tell Dave it made me *sick* to watch his compulsive attachment to affirmation, something I obviously knew nothing about. I definitely wouldn't start crying and wiping the snot from my nose with my hand and asking him why he couldn't even comfort me, why he was so repulsed by my sadness.

At a meeting, when I shared about how hard it was to be at parties, one woman suggested that in that case I might not want to throw so many parties at our house. But I was going to meetings less frequently, and we were throwing parties more often. Twenty-two-year-olds in heavy eyeliner were taking shots in my kitchen. At one I went to the fridge and found that my Diet Wild Cherry Pepsi, the one I'd tucked behind the soy milk to keep it safe, was gone. Dave had given it to a visiting poet, who was sober and thirsty.

"But I'm sober," I told him. "I was thirsty."

These things were both true. It was also true that I could have said, *Hey, let's not have sixty people get drunk at our house.* But I was wary of imposing another limit—already worried he resented the ones I'd tried to impose—and I liked imagining that I wasn't entirely banished from the realms of revelry.

After that party was done, thirty minutes after everyone was gone, a tiny poet climbed out of our hallway closet. We were picking up red plastic cups, still sticky with wine. "Where is everyone?" she'd asked. "Is it over?"

And I envied her, because she was drunk.

When Sasha finally decides to drink herself to death in Rhys's *Good Morning, Midnight*, she reflects on how easy it can be to disappear entirely: "You are walking along a road peacefully. You trip. You fall into blackness. That's the past—or perhaps the future. And you know that there is no past, no future, there is only this blackness, changing faintly, slowly, but always the same."

After publishing *Good Morning, Midnight*, in 1939, Rhys tripped and fell off the road herself—as if the novel had been prophecy. Rhys disappeared for a decade, publishing nothing, and no one knew where she'd gone. Rumors spread that she'd died at a sanitarium; that she'd died in Paris; that she'd died during the war. Occasional articles about her work referred to her as "the late Jean Rhys."

In 1949, an actress named Selma Vaz Dias put out a personal ad in the *New Statesman*, a weekly newspaper, to see if Rhys was still alive: "Will anyone knowing her whereabouts kindly communicate." She was interested in turning one of Rhys's novels into a radio play. By this point, Rhys was married (for the third time), to a disbarred lawyer named Max Hamer, a devoted but unstable husband who was convicted of fraud charges shortly after their marriage, in 1947. When Rhys saw Vaz Dias's ad, she was living alone near Maidstone Prison, in Kent, England, where Hamer was incarcerated. Rhys had been in jail for drunk and disorderly behavior several times herself. A local paper had recently run a headline about one of these run-ins with the law: MRS. HAMER AGITATED, ONLY HAD ALGERIAN WINE. When Vaz Dias wrote an article about "finding" Rhys, she framed the fifteen years Rhys had been lost to the world as an open mystery: "But who was JEAN RHYS and WHERE WAS SHE?"

Where was she? Mainly, she'd been somewhere drinking. Her days played the same tracks on repeat. Even her biographer got tired of it. "Jean's life," wrote Carole Angier, "really did seem to be the same few scenes re-enacted over and over." The drinking made Rhys plump, or else it made her scribble phrases on the wall: *"Magna est veritas et praevalet,"* she scrawled in lipstick. "Truth is great and it prevails."

After Hamer was released from prison, he and Rhys moved into a Cornwall summer cottage in the middle of winter, where she made a sign telling people to go away: "NO teas — NO water — NO lavatory. *No* matches. *No* cigarettes. *No* teas. *No* sandwiches. *No* water. Don't know where *anybody* lives. Don't know *anything.* Now Bugger Off." They eventually moved to a dilapidated cottage in a little village called Cheriton Fitzpaine, where the roof leaked and the walls were full of mice and the villagers thought Rhys was a witch because she once threw broken bottles at a fence in the middle of the night.

During the years of her "disappearance," Rhys also began working on the book that would eventually make her famous. It was a novel about the madwoman in the attic from Charlotte Brontë's *Jane Eyre* — an attempt to reclaim this woman from her villainy and her insanity, to write her backstory as a woman exiled from her Caribbean homeland and wronged by a man. Nothing like Rhys at all.

"I'm struggling with a new thing," she wrote a friend. "What a tiresome creature I was, or still am. But if I can do this book, it won't matter so much will it?"

The first spring of my sobriety, I got a month off work at the bakery so I could go to a place called Yaddo — a swanky writing residency in upstate New York. Half of me imagined this month as a creative whirlwind that could justify the dreary trudge of my sobriety, but the other half of me imagined it would be the perfect place to start drinking again: among strangers, far from anyone I'd ever told I was an alcoholic. I'd heard Yaddo described as a messy swirl of debauchery — infidelities and drunken rambles through the woods — and imagined slurred recitations of "The Raven" in a glossy wood-paneled library that would feel like the inside of a walnut shell, with tasseled brocade curtains and gleaming booze trolleys. "I am drunk every morning, almost, at Yaddo," Patricia Highsmith had written. "I am the God-intoxicated, the material-intoxicated, the art-intoxicated, yes."

Sobriety had disappointed me in almost every way I could imagine: It hadn't repaired my relationship with Dave. It made me feel drained and shy. It made my writing lifeless and effortful. I thought of it this way — as if I were a victim of my own life, as if sobriety were a snake oil salesman who'd made promises he hadn't kept. He had taken away the main thing I looked forward to when I woke up in the morning. He had launched me into a series of tiring days cloaked by a gray scrim that only my antidepressant seemed partially able to lift. Now that the grayness had given way enough to see around its edges, I was telling myself the drinking didn't have to be so dark.

There hadn't ever been a moment when I decided to stop going to meetings. It was more like I'd peeled away, a bit guiltily, surrendered to *not-feeling-like-it* for many days in a row, until I hadn't gone for several months. And without meetings, sobriety had turned into a weight I was carrying around for no reason at all.

Much of my train ride to Yaddo was spent deciding whether or not I should start drinking there. Eventually, I decided it would look too sneaky. If I was going to convince everyone in my life that it was okay for me to drink again, it wouldn't look good if I started on the sly. But I didn't want to tell anyone at Yaddo I was sober, either, because I was pretty sure I *was* going to drink again, sometime soon, and the fewer people to whom I'd introduced myself as alcoholic, the better. So I told people I was celebrating Lent late this year, *after* Easter, and I was giving up booze. I wasn't like *sober* or anything. People looked at me in confusion. "Okay, that's great." A few people asked, "Why didn't you do it *during* Lent?"

I said, "It's sort of complicated. Don't worry about it." I'm sure no one did.

Yaddo looked like an illustrated fairy tale — a grand mansion with terraces overlooking rolling green lawns, formal parlors upholstered with crimson fabric, a set of glimmering ponds called the "ghost lakes," a stone ice house where composers made landscapes of sound. With sheer brute force, I was hurling myself at my Sandinista novel. But the writing had no pulse. I was glad I didn't have Internet access so I couldn't spend my days checking to see if my novel had somehow miraculously climbed back into the top 100 on the Amazon Alcoholism sublist. Since there was no cell reception in any of the buildings, I had to wander down a dirt road—to a particular bend—until I could hear Dave's voice through the phone, at which point I usually spent our conversations trying to figure out if he'd seen Destiny, making feeble attempts to sound casual. "Did you hang out with anyone after the reading?" The suspicion was palpable in my voice and I hated it, just as I hated the tightness in his replies.

Nights were stiff and uncomfortable. While self-possessed performance artists were turning their studios into installation spaces and getting tipsy before our nightly games of pool—a variation called Pig where you had to jump on the table and push the balls with your hands—I was deeply sober, deeply stymied, and deeply worried about deer ticks, terrified of catching Lyme disease. One night I lay in bed while three artists drank and laughed in the living room just outside my door. It sounded like they were laughing right into my ear. I was coiled tight with resentment. It didn't even sound funny, whatever they were saying, though I couldn't quite make it out. I was ashamed of my prim, ascetic life without booze. I hadn't felt this far outside the world of others since junior high, back when I rocked suspenders holding up a floral skirt that twirled above my unshaved legs. I thought of asking the artists to be quiet, but couldn't stand the thought of breaking up a party I hadn't been invited to. *Isn't that the girl who doesn't drink?* They'd giggle. *We should let her sleep.* My own desires were cramped and joyless: I wanted to go to sleep early so I could wake up early and work, or punish my body by running around the ghost lakes in the cool dawn.

One day I came back from a run and spotted a tick stuck on my thigh. In a panic, I checked the "Tick Safety" pamphlet in my room. Was the tick partially engorged or fully engorged? I didn't know. It looked like *some* kind of engorged. It looked like an evil little button, capable of anything. I pulled it out with special tick tweezers, its fierce grip tenting my skin, and took a panicked ride to a local medical clinic. I went on antibiotics that day, which didn't seem like a compelling thing to talk about at dinner, but I didn't feel compelling — about ticks or anything else. I was just a chronic hypochondriac who'd been right a very small but unforgettable number of times. The other residents were natural storytellers who carried quivers full of anecdotes, drank good wine at dinner in our oak-paneled dining room, and then split into smaller cliques to drink harder stuff at night.

By the time I left Yaddo, I was determined to start drinking again. I spent much of the trip home thinking of how I would present this decision to Dave. *It was good to stop drinking for a while,* I'd say. *But I think I'm ready to start.* I had to make it persuasive. More than anything, I had to make it sound casual. I couldn't say it like someone who'd just spent an entire plane ride trying to figure out how to say it. I was nervous but eager. I was sure I had just the right phrasing.

— VIII —

RETURN

My first drink back was a Manhattan. It was May. The air was warm. I loved the cold sugared promise of the sweet vermouth gliding down the back of my throat. Dave made it for me in our kitchen, and I was happy to let him take his time. I'd waited seven months for it; I could wait another half hour.

Dave believed I could drink differently this time around, because I'd told him I could, and I needed his approval because I was ashamed of how desperately I wanted to drink, and how meticulously I'd crafted my excuses for starting again. This was exactly how I pictured normal drinking: a single cocktail with the man you loved, in a kitchen with a toaster and a rickety three-wheeled dishwasher.

The moment just before that first drink was the last moment I thought: *Maybe I don't need this. Maybe I just want it.* Then I drank, and needed it again.

I pointedly drank only one Manhattan that night. It was miraculous to get a buzz from just one. I told Dave I didn't want another drink, even though all I wanted was another drink. Like, six other drinks. But I wanted it to look good, this first drink back — controlled. The lie wasn't just saying I didn't want another; it was saying it *casually*, with such calculated weightlessness, when I knew exactly how drunk I wanted to get.

For the first few months, I tried to follow some of the rules I'd cooked up while daydreaming during Big Book sessions. It was clear to me from the beginning that I'd rather get drunk three nights a week than restrict myself to "a drink or two" every night. Without getting drunk, there was no point to drinking at all. Nights I didn't drink at all were trophies of restraint — enough of these sober credits in my pocket meant I'd earned a night of total abandon.

For my birthday that June, Dave took me to a water park in Wisconsin that called itself the biggest water park in America, where we spiraled around the open whirlpool of a funnel slide, its chlorinated hiss and rush, and then played laser tag, and then mini golf, and scored exactly the same, which was surely a signal from the universe — approving of our venture, and of my decision to drink again. We were bandits and brainstormers and coconspirators once more. We stayed at a B&B with sayings carved into decorative lawn stones, and somewhere in the middle of all that I turned twenty-seven. That night I had one margarita. Of course I spent a good chunk of the evening wondering *Will we get drunk? Can I get drunk if he doesn't get drunk? What will he think if he sees me trying to get drunk?* But we didn't get drunk, and we were happy anyway. Things were going to be better this time around, I was sure of it. I would drink like a person who never thought about drinking. On the way back home, we stopped in a little town called Solon and had pork tenderloins so big that their buns looked like little hats perched on top. The world was full of waterslides! Full of giant tenderloins wearing little hats of bread!

That summer I was doing wedding-cake deliveries for the bakery. Every Saturday, after my regular hours in the kitchen, I delivered three-tiers to barns strung with Christmas lights, their gemstone colors reflected in rows of glimmering mason jars. On these deliveries I thought mainly about two things: *Will Dave and I ever get married?* And: *Will I drop this cake?* I became obsessed with the Deepwater Horizon oil spill, its constancy, that unending dark bloom in the water: *right now, and now, and now.* At every moment I thought about the spill, it was happening. At every moment I didn't think about the spill, it was still happening. Until they finally plugged it up with enough mud and cement: a static kill.

Now that I'd disavowed the identity of being an alcoholic, I knew I was supposed to drink moderately, but I felt entitled to do just the opposite: My months of abstinence meant I deserved to drink everything. It was like the experiment where kids were rewarded with an extra marsh-mallow if they could restrain themselves—for a certain length of time—from eating the marshmallow placed directly in front of them. For seven months, I'd been sitting across from the marshmallow. Now I deserved some special reward, double what the other kids had gotten.

Dave was going to Greece for all of July on a writing fellowship, and I was secretly excited he was leaving because it meant I could drink as much as I wanted, alone in our apartment, with no one watching. *A house where no one was home, no one coming back, and all I could drink.* What a relief not to drink at bars. Fuck bars. Fuck the glacial pace of someone else's G&T, letting all the ice melt.

But I also imagined what the trip would hold for Dave: long late-night conversations with other women, moments they mistook for possibility, moments he'd eventually mistake for possibility as well. I'd always feared that my karmic punishment for cheating on Peter would be that I'd get cheated on. It took me years to consider the pos-sibility that maybe my punishment was the fear itself.

I was irritated that my mother—whom I loved deeply, and loved spending time with—was coming to stay with me for a week, because this would be a week I couldn't drink as much as I wanted. The night before she arrived, I sat down with two bottles of wine, ready to for-tify myself for a week of scripted functionality: *I WILL get the best kind of drunk tonight.* The last vestiges of syrupy light filtered through our beautiful westward windows and Chardonnay melted me into our orange couch. The gloaming was like wine itself, with a certain thick-ness and sweetness, getting into my blood and humming through me. Sometimes I pictured booze moving through my veins like the cathe-ter they'd used in my ablation surgery, threaded from my hips to my heart, attempting its miraculous, necessary work.

My story "The Relapse," about a woman who didn't, was published in July, two months after I did. Though I didn't think of my drinking as a relapse then, more like the correction of a category error: I'd gotten myself wrong. Now I'd figured it out. The recovery phrase *going back out* had always made me think of an Arctic explorer heading back onto the tundra without a compass. But I no longer believed that recovery phrases applied to me. I'd exited the circuitry of that system, and this was summer—with late sunsets and white-wine light.

While Dave was in Greece, we sent each other dispatches. He told me about watching the World Cup projected onto the white walls of the old fort on Corfu. I told him about hosting the bakery girls for pesto salad and rosé in our kitchen, about my boss wearing ripped white denim and taking us to a teen vampire romance at the megaplex in Coralville. He told me about memorizing a path through the cobblestone labyrinths to the gyros place, about eating in the warm night with tomato juice dripping down his chin. I told him about playing bingo at the Beef Days festival in Solon. He wrote to say he'd been swimming in the ocean, late at night, and he'd gotten a sea urchin spine stuck in his foot. I wanted to wash his foot and bandage it, and maybe also ask him: *Who were you swimming with?*

When my mom saw the wine in my fridge, she said, "You never told me you'd started drinking again," and I said, "Oh, I thought I had." I'd practiced the conversation with her so many times in my head, it was as if we'd actually had it. Now, I could see her trying not to say the wrong thing. I hated trying to justify that it was okay for me to drink, since the justification itself already suggested it wasn't. Stopping and starting again was a messy story. It meant I was either calling my past self a liar for saying I was an alcoholic, or making myself a liar now by saying I wasn't.

Part of the tremendous generosity of Lee Stringer's memoir *Grand Central Winter* is its willingness to let recovery be messy. You can call Stringer's story the story of a homeless man getting off the streets, an addict putting down his crack pipe, or a storyteller finding his voice, but it's certainly no mountaintop vision cleaving the world into before and after. Its opening scene might offer the promise of an easy conversion—Stringer finds a pencil on the floor of his basement boiler room while trying to smoke the last residue from his crack pipe—but the rest of his memoir insists on portraying his recovery in more complicated terms.

In this first scene, the book suggests itself as the triumphant conclusion of its own narrative arc: crack pipe traded for pencil. But that day he finds the pencil? He still smokes whatever resin he can. Even after he starts writing a regular column for the newspaper *Street News*, "there were *four* things [he] did every day. Hustle up money, cop some stuff, beam up, and write." For Stringer, there was overlap— he was writing and smoking. It was no easy substitution of the former for the latter. He sat at his computer with his mind out the window and his soul "in the pipe." He remembers the "yeasty anticipation" of wanting it, remembers cream-colored nuggets the size of lima beans and their "caramel-and-ammonia smoke," remembers the "yellow-orange glow" that "blossoms, wavers, recedes."

Even once Stringer finally does get sober, he relapses. There's the time he gets a craving and goes to see a movie instead of getting high; but also the time he steals five thousand dollars from an elderly woman to fund a three-week crack binge. Stringer even confesses going on binges with his book under contract; maybe *because* the book is under contract. When one of the counselors at his outpatient program asks if he'd be willing to give up his writing for his recovery, Stringer realizes that he has been "clinging to the idea of finishing *Grand Central Winter* the way a shipwrecked man clings to a reef." He observes a continuous ribbon of desire running through his life: not just his longing for the drug, but his longing for writing as its substitute. The rough edges of his recovery story resist the burden of providing a seamless arc: *Get addicted. Tell the story. Get better.* His book confesses that his story won't be over, even after it gets told.

The summer of my relapse, I did much of my drinking on crutches. The month after Dave returned from Greece, a car ran over my right foot, leaving the bruised imprint of tire tracks across my swollen arch. I'd been wearing flip-flops. At the ER, I mainly wondered which painkillers they'd prescribe. At home, in the aftermath, I tried to be as self-sufficient as I could — fetching things for myself, balancing coffee and plates while I crutched — because I hated the idea that I would yet again be asking Dave to care for me. Though of course, part of me wanted that more than anything.

Whenever I drank on crutches, I felt like a cartoon character. One night I tripped coming down the Foxhead stairs — crutches clattering as my palms braced against the asphalt — and thought of that one-legged magician back in Nicaragua. Back then I'd thought, *You should take better care of yourself.* Now I was the one hopping along, balancing my crutches against tables so that I'd have a free hand to hold my drink.

Most mornings, I faced my fictional Sandinistas with puffy eyes and a dry mouth, from the other side of a gauzy curtain. I'd hoped writing could burn off my hangovers — like sunlight burning off fog — but they were stubborn. The novel was still inert, which seemed like little more than a confirmation of my solipsism. Once I tried to write beyond myself, it seemed I had nothing to offer. As Charles Jackson lamented to a friend about his sober attempts to write "outside" himself: "As soon as I am not able to be <u>personal</u>, my writing falls apart." I would hit the end of a paragraph and stare into the blank space beyond it. *I could go anywhere,* I'd tell myself, trying to remember what *possible* had felt like. I'd think of what we had in the fridge: half a bottle of Chardonnay, three PBRs. I'd check the clock. How many hours till dusk?

It was impossible to do bakery work on crutches and I missed being useful in a simple, basic way. Jamie brought me little Tupperware containers of melted chocolate and cones of parchment paper so I could make cake decorations from home, where I sat on the floor —

next to our window-unit air conditioner, because every other part of the apartment was too hot for the chocolate to harden — and sculpted rows of little daisies.

Meanwhile, I tried to reboot my novel as magical realism, something I'd sworn I'd never do. Who wanted to see a woman in Iowa writing her magical realist account of a Nicaraguan revolution? Eve Kosofsky Sedgwick describes the way an addict projects "consolation, repose, beauty, or energy" onto his substance, what she calls "beauty delusively attributed to the magical element," and I was doing that in prose and life, looking for gods from the machine — asking drinking to supply my pulse, asking my jungle guerrillas to spot luminous beehives in the trees.

I spent long chunks of time in my hot apartment trying to tell myself I had the drinking figured out. It had gotten bad because of my depression, but now I was medicated. Or it had gotten bad because of me and Dave, but now we would work better. Or it had been recovery itself, convincing me I was alcoholic with the Möbius strip of its logic: *If you don't think you are an alcoholic, then you probably are one.* What bullshit was that? There was no way out of it. Sure, it *felt true* that I wanted a drink every fucking night, but maybe I just felt that way because I'd sat through enough meetings where people talked about feeling that way. I'd taken on the identity because it had been a useful way to sort out my sense of self at the time. Now I resented meetings for polluting my relationship to drinking. It was like the joke about two drunks who'd seen *The Lost Weekend.* When they came staggering out of the movie theater, the first one said, "My God I'll never take another drink," and the second replied, "My God I'll never go to another movie."

There was a little voice in me that considered the possibility that perhaps there were people who didn't spend hours every day trying to decide if their desperate desire to drink had preceded recovery meetings or been created by them. But it irritated me, that voice. I tried not to listen to it.

❖

The whole project of moderate drinking was maddening. The first time I ever heard the phrase *drinking to get drunk*, I actually found it humorously tautological. Of course you drank to get *drunk*. Just like you breathed to get oxygen. Which was part of why moderation was like constant acrobatic contortion.

After work one night, at a pub called the Sanctuary, the other girls from the bakery were ordering beer — the Sanctuary was known for its beer — so I ordered beer too, instead of something stronger. But I carefully checked the proof for every beer on the menu, so I could order the highest one. "I always go for an ironic name," I said, explaining why I'd ordered the Delirium Tremens, then added, "I hate beer," before ordering three more.

In August, I organized a birthday dinner for Dave at a farmhouse outside town where a French expat had a wood-burning oven in which she charred pizzas to black-blistered perfection: walnut and sage, blue cheese and mushrooms. We ate on her porch while a lightning storm lit up the cornfields, and it was insanely beautiful: that humid night breathing through the screens, crackling fingers of electricity across the sky, hot cheese and crisp dough in our mouths. I crutched across the rough-hewn floorboards, nearly fell headfirst on the way to the bathroom, and wondered: *Why do I have to get drunk to find this beautiful?*

For a long time, I'd thought of my drinking as the opposite of anorexia, as abandon rather than restriction. But I was beginning to see — during my days of attempted moderation — that my relationship with drinking was a direct extension of those restrictive days. Starving myself meant resisting an endless longing, and drinking meant submitting to it. But both times it was the obsession that shamed me, the sense of being consumed by a desire that was so limited in its object. When I restricted my eating, I was ashamed that there was nothing I wanted more than to eat — endlessly, recklessly — and when I drank, I was ashamed that there was nothing I wanted more than to drink. Trying to control my drinking only illuminated how deep that wanting went, like tossing a stone down a well and never hearing it hit bottom.

During one of her binges, Jean Rhys threw a brick through a neighbor's window. In her own defense, Rhys later said the woman's dog, "a killer and a fighter," had attacked her cat. The world Rhys lived in, or the world as Rhys lived in it, was always out to get her. One friend compared her self-pity to a gramophone needle stuck in a groove, "going over and over miseries of one sort and another." In a 1931 review subtitled "The Pursuit of Misery in Some of the New Novels," Rebecca West wrote that Rhys "has proved herself to be enamoured of gloom to an incredible degree." A profile of Rhys in the *Guardian* appeared under the title "Fated to Be Sad."

But Rhys didn't think of her work as particularly sad. She just thought it was the truth. She resented that interviewers always pushed her into a "pre-destined role, the role of victim." She'd often had enough of herself. She signed a woeful letter to one of her best friends "End of moan in minor." Everyone saw the characters in her books as victims, she told one interviewer, "and I don't like that. Everyone's a victim in a way, aren't they?" To Rhys it seemed more like she was the only one willing to speak plainly: "I'm a person at a masked ball without a mask, the only one without a mask."

Eventually, she put out a "Declaration of Rights" against her interviewers:

I am not an ardent Women's Libber
Or a Victim (eternally)
Or a darned Fool.

Rhys never wanted to be a victim (*eternally*). I love that parenthetical: She still wanted to reserve the right to be a victim sometimes.

Rhys's first biographer, Carole Angier, called her one of the century's greatest self-pity artists, but her second biographer leapt to her defense: "I do not see self-pity in Rhys's work or her life," wrote Lilian Pizzichini. "I see an angry woman who had good reason to be angry, and whose vision was bleak." But defending Rhys by saying her work and life held no self-pity is like defending a spider by claiming it never hurt a fly. The spider's grace comes from *how* it kills the fly, with its intricate web, and Rhys's grace came not from her refusal of self-pity but from her merciless portraits of its grip—always full of invention, never cluttered by apology.

Rhys was constantly dissecting self-pity by pulling apart the threads of its alibis. Her female characters were her hair shirts: through them, Rhys could pity herself, scold herself, humiliate herself, and martyr herself. She was still the little girl who'd smashed the face of her doll, then mourned it. Her self-pity wasn't a needle stuck in a single gramophone groove, because the song was always changing. One of her characters imagines her own face as a "tortured and tormented mask" that she can take off any time she likes, or wear under a "tall hat with a green feather." This isn't self-pity served straight up but with a twist, with a green feather perched over its unsightly features.

Defending Rhys's work by insisting it holds no self-pity already accepts the premise that self-pity must be entirely repressed— another version of Lewis Hyde's claim that *The Dream Songs* spent too much time on an alcoholic's pity pot. But both Rhys and Berryman refuse to ignore the pity pot, in its ugliness and shame, as part of pain itself.

Starting to drink again wasn't responsible for my self-pity—I'd managed to pity myself in sobriety as well—but booze certainly ignited it, and at a party that fall, it burst fully into flame. This was just before the start of our second year in Iowa. I'd been sitting on the kitchen stairs, with my crutches leaning against the steps beside me, talking to a poet who was looking at me funny.

"Which eye do you want me to look into when I'm talking to you?" he asked.

"What?" I said. He was drunk and I was drunk, but still.

He launched into a whole story about how he used to live in Boston and there was a guy he knew there with a wandering eye—how everyone had just pretended it wasn't there, his wandering eye, which only made the whole thing worse, and this guy didn't want to do that with me.

"But I don't have a wandering eye," I said.

He said, quite kindly: "It's nothing to be ashamed of."

I grabbed my crutches and crutched my way across the room to Dave, pulling him into the bathroom. "Tell me the truth!" I said. "Do I have a wandering eye? Have I *always*?" I felt betrayed. I fixed my gaze on him. "Is my eye wandering right now?" Then I called my mom from the porch, drunk and crying. "You have to tell me!" I said. "Have you been lying to me my whole life?"

"What are you talking about?" she asked. And then, after a beat: "Where are you? Are you okay?"

Although I didn't actually have a wandering eye, I became convinced I could actually *feel* my eyeball rolling around in my head, as if that's what a wandering eye would feel like. Maybe my eye wandered only when I got drunk enough, like a terrible poker tell. For days, I obsessed over it—this secret the whole world had been keeping from me.

I hated seeing people from meetings around town. But it was a small town, so it happened all the time. I did surgical strikes on the booze aisle of the Hy-Vee, in and out, so that nobody from meetings could pass by and catch me standing there: an abject failure, *just doing some research*. That's what people in recovery called it when you started drinking again. At the Java House one night, I saw a guy from meetings doing step work with his sponsee. Or rather, he spotted me. "How are you?" he asked, and I blushed instinctively, hearing, *Has your drinking gotten bad again?*

"I'm so *great!*" I said, then realized my voice was too loud — so made it softer, sincere. "I'm just really, really great."

After *The Lost Weekend* became a bestseller, everyone wanted Charles Jackson to write a sequel, a novel that would explain how Don "got out of it." As Jackson's former doctor put it, this sequel might "fall into the hands of someone whom it would help." Jackson tentatively titled this sequel *The Working Out*, but he wasn't enthusiastic about it. As he told an AA group, years later, he didn't think literature was meant "to solve psychiatric problems."

Also, there was the fact that Jackson hadn't entirely gotten "out of it" himself. He started taking pills a few years after *The Lost Weekend* was published, and then relapsed on booze in 1947, when he finally surrendered to the craving for an ice-cold beer while on vacation in the Bahamas. "What do you know," he told his wife, Rhoda, "I'm drinking again." Bud Wister, the counselor who had coached Jackson through the Peabody Method a decade earlier, died during a bender that same year, after swallowing broken glass from a whiskey bottle whose neck he'd smashed, drunk.

As the famously sober author of a wildly successful book about alcoholism, Jackson was under pressure to keep up appearances. "Nothing could make me take another drink," he wrote a year after his relapse, in a 1948 promotional brochure put out by his publishing house. "My house could burn down, my capacities could fail, my wife and children could be killed, and I still would not drink." But the truth came out anyway. AUTHOR OF LOST WEEKEND LOSES ONE HIMSELF ran one headline, after Jackson, driving drunk, drifted across a lane divider and crashed into another car head-on.

In certain ways, the success of Jackson's novel about alcoholism had made it more difficult to maintain his sobriety. After his 1947 relapse, Rhoda wrote in desperation to Jackson's brother, Boom: "I realized yesterday...how he managed to stop drinking. He held on to the fact that he was a great writer and he'd show everybody. When he got fame, that thing that sustained him all the time was gone—and he has nothing yet to replace it." Of course, *The Lost Weekend* hadn't exactly promised a happy ending. At the close of the book, Don pours himself a drink and crawls into bed: "No telling what might happen next time but why worry about that?"

Jackson was so committed to ending Don's story without any guarantee of salvation that he fought vehemently against the closing shot of the movie version—Billy Wilder's Oscar-winning 1945 adaptation—which shows a sober Ray Milland stubbing out his cigarette in a tumbler of whiskey, finis to *that*, and sitting down at a typewriter to begin composing the story we've just watched. Despite all the film's awards—it won an Academy Award for best picture, Milland won for best actor, Wilder won for best director, and he and Charles Brackett won for their adapted screenplay—Jackson was outraged by what they'd changed: "Chas. & Billy based their movie version far less on the book than on what they happened to know about me personally," he wrote to a friend, "and it's *false & untrue* at that, for the implication is that I overcame my drink-problem by writing a book about it & thus getting it out of my system." Jackson didn't just hate the fact of this happy ending, but the means of it. He hated that the movie peddled false faith in the idea of narrative as salvation.

That fall, four months after I started drinking again, I drove to another writing residency, this one in Wyoming. My relief at drinking far from home was almost ecstatic. Near the Badlands and their striated towers of rock, I found paradise: a tiny roadside motel, the neon VACANCY glowing, with nothing for miles but the only thing I needed, a small bar across the street. The bartender filled my tumblers with double shots, unprompted, in a glowing, cozy room with faux-log-plank rafters, and I knew no one, and only had to stumble across the street onto scratchy sheets; no apologies necessary.

In Wyoming, I drank with the artists in their studios—stumbled home across the cow fields one night and tripped face-first onto the metal bars of a cattle grid—and I drank with the writers at a place called the Mint Bar full of cattle-branded cedar shingles, marked by a glowing neon cowboy astride a bucking neon horse, where no one had ever heard me say, *I'm an alcoholic.*

On the drive back home through South Dakota, I was looking forward to one last anonymous night of drinking freely before I got back home to Dave; to stopping at the same motel and going to the same bar across the street, with its leather seats and green lamps, its wooden counters smooth as maple syrup. But I couldn't find the right exit, and eventually ended up at a Super 8 in Chamberlain, where the rooms faced the parking lot and I didn't feel like walking to the single bar I'd seen a mile down the road. So I drove to a gas station and bought two six-packs of Mike's Hard Lemonade, perhaps because it was the thing I'd be most ashamed to drink with anyone I knew.

The woman at the register eyed my two six-packs. "I can't drink this stuff," she said. "Makes me fucking *sick.*"

"My friends like it," I said, shrugging.

Something about the exchange peeled the skin off my evening and exposed the venture as pathetic. Why was I so hell-bent on drinking hard lemonade alone in a shitty motel in South Dakota? I brought the six-packs into my room but they regarded me accusingly, a sign of failure. I took the six-packs back to the trunk of my car, just to prove to myself that I didn't have to drink them, I didn't *have* to drink anything.

I sat in my motel room for about five minutes before I went back out to the car, grabbed the six-packs from the trunk and carried them halfway to the door, thought *This is crazy, why can't I just decide?* and then turned around and put them back in the trunk. Then I decided that if I was this obsessed, I should just go ahead and drink them, so I popped the trunk, brought the six-packs inside, turned on the motel TV, pulled the chain lock, and carried myself into the sweet, nauseating gauze of a hard-lemonade drunk.

❖

That fall, I put an incredible amount of effort into talking to my therapist about everything *but* drinking. I told her stories about my fights with Dave but carefully talked around the booze, a tumor I'd excised. I was also starting to cut myself again, like the holes you cut in the crust of a pie to let out the steam as it bakes. One day Dave caught sight of the cuts on my ankles and asked if I wanted to talk about it. I said I didn't.

The pages of my diary were filling up with drunken scrawls: *I believe there are things in me that are beautiful. When is enough?* Then farther down, the writing bigger and messier: *I know I've drunk a bottle and a half of wine an…*, the *n* trailing off. Another night: *I just want—I don't know…* and I didn't.

When I finally told my therapist about the drinking, it was because I was tired of running laps around it. "It gets so bad when I'm drunk," I told her, and started crying, and couldn't stop. I was already thinking about how our conversation was going to pollute my drinking that night, like a piece of hair stuck in the back of my throat.

I asked her what she saw when she looked at me.

"Shame," she said. "There is no other word for what I see on your face."

By the time Billie Holiday finally collapsed, she was forty-four and past the point of curing. This was the summer of 1959. Weakened by years of heroin abuse, and suffering acutely from cirrhosis of the liver, she was emaciated and covered with old track marks. Her legs were pocked with ulcers from injections. After getting checked into Metropolitan Hospital in New York, she told a friend, "You watch, baby. They are going to arrest me in this damn bed." And they did. Narcotics agents found (or planted) a tinfoil pouch of heroin in her hospital room, and handcuffed her to the bed. There were two policemen stationed by the door. Her mug shot and fingerprints were taken in that room at Metropolitan.

During the preceding years, Holiday's last few albums had met with mixed reactions. Some fans thought her late voice was a betrayal of its former glory: "an open wound…vocal cords flayed," husky from years of smoking and self-abuse. Others found this voice raw and moving, a distillation of her essence all along—the purest form of her. But almost everyone heard, in this late voice, a ledger of her trauma, an audible record of everything she'd endured and done to herself. While recording her last album, *Lady in Satin*, she drank gin from a water pitcher. Before one recording session, she pulled out a pint and said: "Now I'm going to eat breakfast!"

Ray Ellis, who did her musical arrangements near the end of her life, was disappointed when they first met:

> I had seen pictures of her ten years before and she was a beautiful woman. When I met her she was a repulsive woman.… She looked a little shabby, a little dirty…I was taken aback because I had this mental thing, like she turns you on and you can go to bed with her. But I didn't think I could have gone to bed with her at *that* stage for anything.

She was supposed to be beautiful and damaged, but instead—for Ellis—her damage had ruined her beauty. Her self-destruction was no longer luminous. When Studs Terkel saw her at a South Side Chicago club in 1956, he noticed "other customers were also crying in their beer and shot glasses," and insisted: "Something was still there, something that distinguishes an artist from a performer: the revealing of self. Here I be. Not for long, but here I be."

But the "self" Holiday revealed in her songs, the hurt and wounded self that people heard when they listened to her, the self they *wanted* to hear and in some part constructed for themselves—that self was only part of her. There were other parts, too. She'd always wanted a family, had fantasized about buying a farm in the country and taking in orphans. She tried to breast-feed her godson from breasts that didn't have milk, and tried to adopt a child in Boston. But the judge wouldn't allow her, because of her drug record. Pregnant as a teenager, she had spent eighteen hours in a mustard bath to try to end the pregnancy, because her mother didn't want her to have a baby before she was married, but she later told a friend: "The only thing I ever wanted is that baby."

While she lay handcuffed to her hospital bed, protesters outside Metropolitan held up signs: LET LADY LIVE. And on the July day she died, six weeks after she was admitted, Frank O'Hara wrote, "Everyone and I stopped breathing."

A year after my first AA meeting, I found myself drunk in a bathroom stall in Mexicali, snorting coke off the flat top of the toilet-paper dispenser. This was at a literary conference where I'd done some of my freest drinking in months—sitting on metal bleachers in the twilight, passing a flask back and forth with my new friend the Peruvian Novelist, dancing until three in the morning at a blacktop playground disco with a guy spinning records by the swings. At one point I thought: *If I'd stayed sober, I would have a year right now.*

Back home, Dave and I threw a party we called Octopotluck. It was October. It was a potluck. We were serving octopus. We bought it frozen in a big block of ice and handed out little paper cups, like shots, full of sautéed tentacles. We cooked it in Hell, as we'd learned in Italy, back at the beginning. In the two years since, we'd put so many kinds of fish in Hell: Tilapia in Hell, Flounder in Hell, Orange Roughy in Hell. If it was white and boneless, we'd probably put it in Hell. If Dave had proposed that first summer, I would have said yes. But Octopotluck was proof of the fallen world. Now our kitchen was full of the other girls he was flirting with, drinking gin out of my special teacups. "Those teacups are special to me," I muttered to no one.

Drunk, I started hunting for the old hurts with the heat-seeking missile of my fearful heart: Dave ignoring me, Dave and other women, Dave versus the hypothetical, impossible man who could plug whatever leak had sprung inside me. My heart skittered with accusations: *You cultivate your students' adoration. You cultivate their flirtation. You love that your enjambment lecture helps them understand their relationships with their fathers.* I never ate any octopus.

I woke to a familiar mess of fragments the next morning: bathroom wall, gritty linoleum, cool porcelain of the toilet throat, hallway slanting like a funhouse; me and Dave in the corner of our crowded kitchen; me accusing him of needing praise so badly, my voice dripping with venom; him saying "I think this is the alcohol talking," as I tried to open my mouth to explain that it wasn't.

Part of me still believed that real drinking stories demanded big tragedies: more broken noses and blood on the streets, fiery explosions you could see clearly against the horizon. My drinking wasn't that. I hadn't set off a bomb in the middle of my own life. It had just grown small and curdled. I lived with shame like another organ nestled inside me, swollen with banal regrets: remembering the chicken I'd half cooked drunk the night before, picturing the wet pink flesh at the core of each breast and imagining the spores of bacteria growing in our guts; or waking up five minutes before a seven o'clock bakery shift to find my windshield coated with thick ice, then driving to work with my head stuck out the window — glad for the cold wind ventilating my hangover.

Dave went back home to Boston for Thanksgiving and I stayed to help with the bakery pie rush. While he was gone, I often found myself at the grocery store buying large amounts of alcohol. There was always a reason. When I showed up at my best friend's house for Thanksgiving in the early afternoon, she was worried there wasn't enough booze. Could I go out and buy some? Sure, I said. But maybe someone else should drive. I said I'd had a glass of wine while I was cooking. I didn't say it was a giant plastic soda cup that I'd poured most of the bottle into, saving a bit so that I wouldn't have drunk "a whole bottle" before noon. Someone else drove. We picked up a thirty-pack of PBRs. I was happy we'd gotten beer because I didn't even *like* beer, and this made me feel less alcoholic because if I was *really* alcoholic I'd only be buying alcohol I was going to drink; this was just alcohol for other people—so they wouldn't drink the alcohol I'd gotten for myself.

At the meal, when I was bringing another bottle of wine back to the table, I knocked over my glass and it splintered into my food. Tiny shards of glass sparkled in my stuffing. My true self—clumsy, desperate to be drunker—had shown herself for a moment, like a wild animal peeking out from the underbrush, foolish and fumbling. I got another glass of wine but didn't bother to replace my turkey.

When I went to pick up Dave from the airport, I stopped at the recycling dump to drop off all my empties, then drove from one life to another: from the cold, stinking circle of dumpsters—with broken glass underfoot and bottles sliding out of my hands, shattering into their bins—to the warmth of our car, and Dave on the airport curb, scarf-wrapped and red-cheeked from the cold. I loved when we were apart and missed each other, but I knew he'd been missing somebody other than the person I'd become.

On my last night of drinking, we had Dave's poetry students over for dinner and I drank steadily in the kitchen, losing track of how many bouillon cubes I'd added to my chicken noodle soup. It ended up saltier than tears. A female student who sometimes texted Dave to see which bar he was drinking at ("Why did you give her your number?" I'd asked him once) sat on our orange couch and recited all of "The Love Song of J. Alfred Prufrock" from memory. I was swollen with booze and indignation: *It's so totally predictable to memorize "Prufrock"!*

That's MY orange couch. I couldn't wait for his students to leave, but couldn't kick them out. They left one by one, impossibly slowly. When Dave took the last stragglers down to the front porch to smoke, I thought, *Finally!* And carried a big plastic cup of whiskey to my office.

I don't know how long I was in there before he came in. I remember he showed me an email he'd just gotten from one of his students, who had written him—clearly drunk, after getting home from wherever she'd been drinking after she'd been at our house—to say she was depressed. She needed help. All this is blurry. Months later, this same girl would leave a drunken voice mail on Dave's phone saying she was in love with him, and wanted to kill herself, and he called 911, because he was afraid she would. That night he just wrote back to her—and to the dean of his department—to say he was worried. I don't remember if he asked me what he should do, or if he just did it. I remember thinking some people in the world were crying out for help, and other people were giving it—and I wanted to be one of the people giving it, but I was one of the people crying out for it instead.

I also wanted Dave to realize I was bottoming out, and somehow this other girl had stolen my bottom. I told him the drinking had gotten bad again, and I didn't know what to do about it; and I was sorry for the way we fought—I didn't want to fight, I hated fighting—and he sat beside me on the futon and wrapped his arms around me and I buried my face in his chest, which seemed more honest than trying to say anything. I made weird little animal sounds against him and tried not to wipe my nose with his flannel shirt.

"We're not having a fight tonight," he said. "You were wonderful tonight."

Sometimes it hurts to remember how selfish I was, how completely cocooned, and how good he was to me.

The rest of the night went fuzzy. At some point I was stumbling down the hallway. At some point he told me his student was okay. I thought, *Great.* At some point I stood over my pot of soup on the stove and picked out noodles and clumps of shredded chicken with my fingers, stuffing them into my mouth, then knelt by the toilet for a while. I'm not sure if I threw up or not. I know I went back into my office with more booze. I thought: *This has to be the last night.* It was just like the other one, the last night I'd already had—holing myself up with a big red cup of whiskey. Except this time I brought the bottle too, just to be safe.

—IX—

CONFESSION

The first day of my second sobriety, I crashed my friend's car into a concrete wall. I'd borrowed his car because ours wasn't starting and I needed to get to my morning shift at the hospital so that medical students could diagnose my fake appendicitis. It was a frozen December day and I was jumpy and nervous, hungover and jittery: *I need to stop. I don't want to stop. Stopping didn't work last time.* My hands were having trouble staying still. And then I pulled into a parking space and hit the accelerator instead of the brakes and slammed right into the concrete wall. I remember thinking, *Oh shit.* And then I wondered if I could pretend it hadn't happened. *Do I definitely have to tell him?* And yes, I did, because the front bumper was dangling like a loose Band-Aid and one of the headlights had been cracked into a glass web. My immediate impulse was simply to back out and pull into another parking space, as if that would give me a do-over.

I was trying to *do the right thing*, after all — get sober again — and today was supposed to be my big watershed, the first day of the rest of my life. Now my reward, for those intentions, was this battered station wagon? I was indignant. If I was going to stop drinking, I was supposed to discover a spectacular new version of myself, or at least recover the presence of mind not to accelerate into a concrete wall. But sobriety didn't work like that. It works like this: You go to work. You call your friend. You say, *I'm sorry I crashed your car into a wall.* You say you'll fix it. Then you do.

"Why do you deserve another chance?" one drug-court judge asked his defendant, an addict trying to explain his latest relapse.

"There's hope," said the defendant.

"What makes you think you have hope now?"

The defendant said he was getting clean for his kids. He had to give a reason it was different *this time*.

"How is life different?"

"I have better coping skills and listen more."

"Do you still know everything?"

"No. I'm open-minded now."

"Humble?" the judge asked. "Willing to *listen* now?"

The defendant laughed and shook his head. "It's been a personal challenge," the defendant admitted. "I thought I knew everything."

It's an uncomfortable ritual: the addict asked to perform his humility, expected to regard the judge as both therapist and punisher. It's just one of many ways that drug courts—the American legal system's main concession to the possibility that there might be something to do with addicts besides locking them up—still live imperfectly inside their ideals, one of the ways they still treat addiction as a form of failure.

In drug court, the judge and defendant are meant to collaboratively construct the person the defendant is supposed to become—not just someone recovering but someone who sincerely *desires* this recovery. But sociologists find that drug courts are full of "tongue lashings" from judges: "I'm tired of your excuses!" "I'm through with you!" Some defendants are treated as "salvageable" while others are deemed "irremediably deficient."

Part of proving that you're truly ready to recover—in drug court, in a meeting, in a memoir—involves admitting that you don't know if you can recover at all. Part of getting into the right narrative involves admitting you can't see the end of it. Like the Narco Farm reports: Prognosis guarded. In *Lady Sings the Blues*, Billie Holiday warns her readers against believing her own tentative happy ending: "There isn't a soul on this earth who can say for sure that their fight with dope is over until they're dead."

In the afterword to *Beautiful Boy*, a memoir about his son Nic's recovery from meth addiction, journalist David Sheff confesses that

Nic relapsed again after the book was published. "Yes, Nic relapsed," he writes. "Sometimes I tire of the convoluted, messy truth." Sheff's afterword doesn't just disrupt the provisional happy ending we've just read, it disrupts the possibility of *any* certain ending. This is a staple of the addiction memoir genre: the afterword, the epilogue, the "author's note" confessing that since first publication, things have not gone entirely as hoped. But confessing uncertainty outright—saying *no soul on earth can say for sure*—isn't cynicism. It offers an honest hope that doesn't depend on something impossible: knowing the end of the story before it comes. It's more ragged than Bill Wilson's mountaintop vision, and it's a more frustrating story to tell—just as so many stories I heard at meetings, over the years, involved countless cycles and repetitions. That's how humility gets built into hope. Old-timers sober for forty years say, "With any luck I'll stay sober till the end of one more day."

When I came back to my first meeting, I said: "When I started drinking again, I promised myself I'd never come back to a meeting. Now I'm here."

I owa City is a small town. When I returned to meetings, I knew I'd see the same people. It made me anxious. They would remember how I'd walked in a year earlier, full of desperation and pathos, and then quit their solution. Now I was back: my sadness stale, my case compromised. It made me picture Civil War deserters branded with a *D* at the hip, or forced to wear wooden signs proclaiming their cowardice.

But everyone was happy to see me. People said: "Glad you're back." Some said: "It was like that for me, too." A woman I'd known the first time around knelt on the floor next to my chair and said, "You never have to drink again," and I thought, *Never HAVE to?* Drinking was all I wanted to do. I wanted to do it right then.

Years later I looked back and saw the truth of what she'd said: that

I'd taken one step away from that tight crawl space full of endless scheming and apologizing, deciding and redeciding. But that first night back, the trap was still the thing I desired most. It made me anxious that the first thing I'd heard didn't ring true at all. Had it been a ridiculous mistake to come back? But I was crying, I was a wreck, and that woman had seen that whatever I was in the middle of, I was desperate for relief from it.

Relief came from sitting still and listening. That night, a man talked about getting drunk for the first time when he was twelve, babysitting his little sisters one night, how he broke into his parents' liquor stash, then ate a whole bag of licorice and woke up in a puddle of his own black vomit. He talked about how his diabetic wife had died of a blood infection six weeks after he left her. She'd stepped on a piece of glass, drunk—had to get her toes amputated, and then her foot. Then she died. That really sent him off. *Survivor's guilt*, he said. He also had that from working in the Marriott World Trade Center on 9/11. After he made it home that day, he turned on the news and drank a whole bottle of wine—then checked how many bottles he had left, in case the world was ending.

Hearing his voice in that church basement, above the scrape of metal chair legs across linoleum and the percolations of the coffee-maker, I listened to his story as a writer—for its themes and climax—but I mainly heard it another way: as a woman who still wanted to drink more than she wanted to do anything else.

During the zenith of his involvement in AA, during the mid-1950s, Charles Jackson started to believe that recovery was inspiring him to write in a new way. He had a new angle on the book he was writing, an approach committed to simplicity and honesty, and wrote to one friend that his "stopping-drinking and...enormous interest in AA" had "a lot to do with this new attitude." At that point,

Jackson was working on the book he imagined would become his magnum opus: an epic called *What Happened*, a "novel of affirmation and acceptance of life" that would tell the story of his old antihero, Don Birnam, once he'd left all his lost weekends behind him.

The epic's first installment, titled *Farther and Wilder*, would begin with a two-hundred-page overture constructed around the central event of a massive family reunion. Don "would be host to the gathering, they should come to him and be his guests, and he would not only take care of them all but be able to take care of them all." Jackson wanted to write a different Don than the one the world knew from *The Lost Weekend.* This Don would be stable and affluent, not only taking care of his family but *able to take care of them.* The syntax is poignant in its repetition.

Jackson had been stymied by the book for years—his biographer Blake Bailey has observed that Jackson was a master of "working on every conceivable thing *but* [this] novel"—but in the months after Jackson got involved in AA in 1953, he was finally able to generate more than two hundred pages. As he wrote to a friend:

> it's far & away the best thing I've done, simpler, more honest, and, for the first time, out of myself—that is, not self-tortured or -absorbed or -eviscerated. No, it's about people—life, if I may say so....My stopping-drinking and my enormous interest in AA, if you'll pardon the expression, have a lot to do with this new attitude—well, everything to do with it, I think.

The novel was anchored in the ordinary texture of a sober alcoholic's daily experience. "I can put it best," Jackson told his editor, Roger Straus, "by saying the story <u>happens</u>, is happening—taking place, like daily living—on every page." He wanted to write a novel that humbled its content—by taking up the topic of ordinary people and ordinary living—as well as its style, by resisting the siren call of virtuosic performance. These were both ways of trying to write away from his ego. In another letter to Straus, Jackson described his approach: "It is really wonderful, simple, plain, human, life itself—nothing in the dazzling intellectual class...but unless you are James Joyce, the 'relaxed' novel is good enough."

Jackson wanted to believe his novel could be wondrous in its attention to ordinary human life. But he was also worried. You can hear the doubt seeping into his justifications. Although he argued that the novel "can do just about what it pleases," and announced, "I please to make it plain, like everyday people," his underlined "I" suggested a fragile sense of his own prerogative. It was as if his social self-consciousness about his AA fellows (who were, as his wife said, "not very bright or interesting or anything") had its corollary in his anxiety about whether this new style would seem ambitious or intellectual enough. At times, he openly confessed his anxiety that this approach of "life unfolding moment by moment" could seem "careless and rambling," or just marked by a "total lack of originality"—the very lack of originality that AA was teaching him to embrace. Jackson's conflicted attitude toward the project had everything to do with the split he perceived between the spheres of literature and recovery. How could he write a novel that would satisfy the demands of both? He feared the judgment of a shrewish literati that wasn't much like the crowd at his AA meetings, people whose ethos of fellowship had asked him to imagine himself into their "everyday" lives and away from his own.

If Jackson had gotten drunk because he couldn't get outside himself, as he would tell AA crowds, then getting *out of* himself in the novel translated this newfound sense of sober purpose into prose. As he wrote to one friend, he wanted "all of it underline{outside} of myself—outside!" It was a curious claim for Jackson to make, that his project—another semi-autobiographical novel—was somehow leaving his own life behind. The AA ethos was key to these paradoxical ambitions: the belief that every person was simply a vehicle for delivering a story, and the faith that illuminating your own life was a way to be of service beyond yourself.

That first winter of my second sobriety, my sponsor gave me a chart to fill out for my Fourth Step, which involved making an inventory of all my resentments.

"Just that?" I joked. "How long do you have?"

She smiled patiently and said: "Trust me, I've seen worse."

My sponsor—Stacy—was a funny, generous woman who'd gotten sober before she was legal. She was nothing like me, except that neither of us had ever wanted to drink any other way besides a deep dive into drunk. She was matter-of-fact about her own experiences, and listened patiently to my rambling, comprehensive monologues, nodding but not particularly impressed, often distilling them to their core urgencies: *So you were afraid of being left?* Her distillations weren't reductions. They captured something it was useful for me to see starkly, without the webbing of so much language. Every time I thanked her profusely for taking the time to meet with me, she told me the same thing: "This keeps me sober, too."

When I first got into AA, I had been told to choose a sponsor who "had what I wanted." I sensed this didn't mean a Pulitzer Prize. I eventually chose Stacy not because she reminded me of myself, but because she didn't. She moved through the world with assurance— helpful without seeming righteous, humble without excess apology. It felt viscerally good to be around her ease, like silk against the skin. She was not ashamed to confess the size of her love for her Pomeranian. We shared a sense of humor, both laughed at the part of Bill's story in the Big Book where he said he'd never been unfaithful while he was drinking, out of "loyalty to my wife, helped at times by extreme drunkenness." We liked that he confessed the less-than-noble reason, too.

Stacy and I had worked together before my relapse, and when I decided to get sober again, she and her fiancé had taken me to my first meeting back. "Thank you for giving me another chance," I'd gushed, thinking it was all about our connection.

"Of course," she'd said. "That's how the program works."

When it came to my Fourth Step, I was anxious about the format of the list—a spreadsheet with extremely narrow columns—because I wasn't sure how I'd tell the full story of each item I was listing. "Some of my situations are pretty complicated," I explained.

"So are everyone's," my sponsor said. "I'm sure you'll manage."

The Fourth Step was supposed to include all my "harms and resentments," but I asked Stacy if I was supposed to list people I resented, even if I hadn't caused them any harm. She smiled. I was clearly not the first alcoholic who had asked this question. "Anyone who gives you a knot in your gut," she said. The chart had a column asking me to link each of my resentments to a motivating fear—*fear of conflict, fear of abandonment*—and I filled it out dutifully, always a model student. (*Fear of inadequacy.*) I hadn't done an inventory during my first sobriety, and it was part of my attempt to do things differently this time around. The inventory wasn't about asking for absolution for my sins; it was about bringing discomfort into the light, all the toxic grudges that might make me want to drink again. Listing them was like emptying a cluttered drawer.

When I looked back at what my drinking had been, I saw someone hurling herself at the world—asking it to give her back to herself with some edges. I saw myself standing in a man's doorway, my body thrilling with coke and already smarting with disappointment, practically begging him to kiss me. My sister-in-law had once asked me, "Would you rather have no bones or no skin?" and at first it made me picture a creature without bones, a shapeless dough-blob of flesh; and then a creature without skin, a taut sculpture of glistening nerves and muscles. How would you describe the creature without either? Just totally fucked? Sometimes I suspected I had no structure; at other times, no boundaries. I looked back at the girl in the doorway, waiting to be kissed, and wanted to clap a hand over her mouth—to shake the coke from her nose and drain the vodka from her stomach, to say: *Don't say that, don't drink that, don't need that.* Except I couldn't, because she did—say that, drink that, need that.

She wasn't the only one with needs. This was part of my inventory, too, accepting that I wasn't the only victim of my insecurities. In the chart called "Sexual History Inventory," the most telling column was this one: "Whom did I hurt?" It wasn't just telling because it was full of names, but because most of them were followed by question marks. I'd rarely paid enough attention to know whether I'd hurt them or not. My insecurity had convinced me I didn't have the power to hurt anyone.

By the time I was ready to go over my chart with Stacy—this was the Fifth Step, talking about the Fourth Step inventory with someone else—I was in the recent aftermath of another surgery, a procedure to fix residual damage in my nose from the time I'd been punched. I'd shared about the surgery in a meeting, hoping for sympathy, but the main thing I got was: "Be careful with your painkillers." It turned out to be good advice. I was surprised by how much I looked forward to the drugs that would knock me out, and the ones I'd get afterward; by how obsessively I'd imagined the possibility of laughing gas or Valium. It was like a surge through my belly, this anticipation—unbidden and unexpected. In meetings, people sometimes said: *Your disease is always waiting for you outside. It's out there doing push-ups.* I pictured alcoholism as a small man with a mustache and a wifebeater.

It turns out I didn't even get the pre-op stuff I'd been hoping for, nitrous oxide or Valium. All my anesthesia did for me was make me vomit after the surgery into a bucket Dave held beside me. He'd been there for me—over and over again—and in sobriety it was getting easier to see that; easier to tell him I was grateful for that tenderness.

The night before I was supposed to do my Fifth Step, my face was still bandaged. I hadn't taken any Vicodin, too scared of how much I wanted to take them all—or at least enough to make the whole world swim. I was on a zero-salt diet to bring down my swelling, subsisting largely on a mixture of Cheerios, walnuts, and dried cherries, like a vain little squirrel. I texted Stacy suggesting that maybe we should postpone our session for a few weeks.

"Are you physically able to speak?" she asked.

I told her I was.

"Then let's do it," she said.

So the next day we sat across from each other at my kitchen table. I put out a little bowl of Cheerios and cranberries. I poured us glasses of water. My chart lay on the table between us, its boxes reductive and true. It felt useful to look at my regrets in terms of fear rather than selfishness. Perhaps it was just a question of seeing how often selfishness, mine and everyone's, was motivated by fear.

I started explaining the first situation on my inventory, in all of its nuance and complexity, its layers of guilt and shame and—

"Just the short version," she said. "Keep it simple."

Through the course of his attempts to stay sober, Berryman took many personal inventories:

1. What has bothered me most about myself all my life?
   Whether I would be a great poet or not.
2. What bothers me most about myself at the present time?
   Poverty of love for others.
3. What bothers me most about myself in relation to the future?
   Whether I can overcome this.

No surprise, perhaps, that Berryman's final book of poetry was called *Love & Fame*. During the last four years of his life, he went to rehab four times, detoxed at hospitals, went to countless meetings, and even chaired one at a local prison, inviting the prisoners to have dinner at his house when they got out. (One took him up on it.) He read piles of AA literature. He filled out charts and checklists. Every one of his monthly inventories from Hazelden was full of check marks and *x*'s. He put little crosses next to "Self-Importance," "Dishonesty," and "False Pride." Next to "Resentment," he wrote: *Hurts oneself. Always for the unchangeable.* He underlined the "Immoral" in "Immoral Thinking." He was immersed in the so-called Minnesota Model (what we now call rehab) in the heart of Minnesota, residential treatment in the land of ten thousand treatment centers.

The AA First Step that Berryman completed the first time he first arrived at St. Mary's Hospital in Minneapolis gives a sense of the wasteland his drinking had become:

Wife left me after 11 yrs of marriage bec. of drinking. Despair, heavy drinking alone, jobless, penniless....Seduced students drunk....My chairman told me I had called up a student drunk at midnight & threatened to kill her....Drunk in Calcutta, wandered streets lost all night, unable to remember my address....Many alibis for drinking...Severe memory-loss, memory distortions. DT's once in Abbott, lasted hours. Quart of whisky a day for months in Dublin working hard on a long poem....Wife hiding bottles, myself hiding bottles. Wet bed drunk in London hotel, manager furious, had to pay for new mattress. Lectured too weak to stand, had to sit. Lectured badly prepared....Defecated uncontrollably in a University corridor, got home unnoticed....My wife said St. Mary's or else. Came here.

There's a palpable heartbreak not only in the devastation of Berryman's drinking, but in his surprising regrets—not just shitting in a hallway but also lecturing badly prepared. He was preparing better for recovery. Hence the piles of reading, the dutiful charts. In one Fourth Step, he made a list of his "Responsibilities":

(a) to God: Daily practice, submission of will, gratitude (I agree it's one of my few life-long virtues), well-wishing others

(b) To Myself: determine what I want (life, art); seek help.... never deceive myself. Look for the wonder + beauty.

(c) To my family: cherish them. They look to me for love, guidance

(d) To my work: "above all seek balance"
"Personal acclaim is the alcoholic's poison"

(e) to AA: "to God and AA I owe my deliverance"

At the bottom of the list, he wrote instructions to himself: "Be careful how you live. You may be the only copy of the Big Book other people ever read." When Berryman started to consider writing a novel about recovery, he imagined a book that would function not as great literature but as a Twelfth Step— *We tried to carry this message to alcoholics*—bringing recovery to those who hadn't found it yet. He scribbled ideas for what this book might become: "make a book of these notes—useful 12th step work—probably hardly worked up at all, only expanded and glossed, with some background...on Hazelden and St Mary's last spring."

This wasn't another lyric dream song. It was something else, *hardly worked up at all*, not meant to be beautiful but useful. In considering his book "useful 12th step work," Berryman was following the desire he'd articulated on his inventories: to replace the ambition to be "a great poet" with a creative life committed to "love for others." He thought of calling the novel *Korsakov's Syndrome on the Grave* but found he preferred *I Am an Alcoholic*. ("Like better," he wrote next to this simpler title.) Eventually he just called the book *Recovery*. He wanted to donate the profits: "Give half my royalties to—who? Not AA—they won't take it, perhaps just lend it privately to AA's in despair."

Berryman kept his notes in a beige notebook labeled RECOVERY NOTEBOOK, stained with coffee. His life no longer ran on whiskey and ink but on caffeine and graphite, less godly fuels. He wanted *Recovery* to constitute an act of gratitude. In an early draft he imagined his dedication:

This summary & deluded account of the beginning of my recovery is devoted to the men & women responsible for it (the founders of Alcoholics Anonymous, physicians, psychiatrists, counselors, clergymen, psychologists, transactional analysts, [group leaders, inserted], nurses, orderlies, in-patients, out-patients, members of AA) and to its primary divine Author.

In the spring of 1971, less than a year before his death, Berryman taught a course at the University of Minnesota called The Post-Novel: Fiction as Wisdom-Work. This was what he was attempting in *Recovery*, as well: something like wisdom-work.

Though Jean Rhys was never in recovery, she once wrote an imagined courtroom scene—called "The Trial of Jean Rhys," scribbled in spidery script in a plain brown notebook—that looks remarkably like the "fearless moral inventory" of an AA Fourth Step. After the Prosecution lists the major themes of her work ("Good, evil, love, hate, life, death, beauty, ugliness") and asks Rhys if they apply to everyone, she replies: "I do not know everyone. I only know myself."

When the Prosecution persists, "And others?" she confesses: "I do not know others. I see them as trees walking."

That's when the Prosecution pounces: "There you are! Didn't take long, did it?"

Part of Rhys's torment was that her self-absorption wasn't complete enough to make her unaware of its effect on others. But in the trial, confessing her solipsism doesn't count as repentance; it just confirms her guilt. The Prosecution continues its line of questioning:

> *Did you in your youth have a great love and pity for others? Especially for the poor and unfortunate?*
>
>   Yes.
>
> *Were you able to show this?*
>
>   I think I could not always. I was very clumsy. No one told me.
>
> *Excuse of course!* (Prosecution shouts.)
>
> *It is untrue that you are cold and withdrawn?*
>
>   It is not true.
>
> *Did you make great efforts to, shall we say, establish contacts with other people? I mean friendships, love affairs, so on?*
>
>   Yes. Not friendships very much.
>
> *Did you succeed?*
>
>   Sometimes. For a time.
>
> *It didn't last?*
>
>   No.
>
> *Whose fault was that?*
>
>   Mine I suppose.
>
> *You suppose?*
>
>   Silence.
>
> *Better answer.*
>
>   I am tired. I learnt everything too late.

Rhys's trial echoes Berryman's inventories: *What bothers me most about myself at the present time? Poverty of love for others.* Even when Rhys articulates some faith in human possibility ("I believe that sometimes human beings can be more than themselves") the Prosecution still objects: "Come come, this is very bad. Can't you do better than that?"

After that exchange, the trial transcript just reads: "Silence." Objection sustained. But Rhys did believe there was a way she could surrender herself to something larger than her claustrophobic sadness: "If I stop writing," she told the court, "my life will have been an abject failure...I will not have earned death."

The fantasy that brilliant writing might redeem a flawed life—*If I can do this book, it won't matter so much will it?*—didn't belong solely to Rhys. When Carver was brought to court in 1976—accused of collecting unemployment while he was employed—his first wife, Maryann, showed the court his first collection of stories as a defense on his behalf, presenting the brilliance of his work as an excuse for the disappointments and deceptions of his life.

Perhaps it's not enough. For the critic A. Alvarez, Rhys's "monstrous" life made a "powerful argument against biography itself." The effect of Rhys's first published biography was "to make the reader doubt if any book, however original, however perfect, could be worth the price Rhys and those close to her paid."

Neither of Rhys's biographies made me want to spend a long weekend with her, but I'm not interested in the question of whether her work is "worth the price," to us or to anyone, because it was never our choice to make. Her life was. The work is. We can't trade either back. There's no objective metric for how much brilliance might be required to redeem a lifetime of damage—and no ratio that justifies the conversion. Whatever beauty comes from pain can't usually be traded back for happiness. Rhys kept hoping anyway, not for relief but for the possibility of an assuaging beauty—that by voicing her thirst well enough, she could redeem the damage it had caused.

When Berryman scrawled down a daily plan for writing *Recovery*, he was also outlining the healthier life he imagined the novel ushering him into:

> Write 8 or 9–1 pm in study (aim at 2 pp a day, with next sentences drafted)

Walk! Drive!

Libr[ary]: Immunology, Alcoholism — journals!

Exercise + yoga
24 hr. book [AA lit]
1 or 2 short biog's — esp famous alcoholics: Poe!! H. Crane.

His notes betray a tone of self-exhortation — *Walk! Drive!* — and willed excitement: *Journals!* He wanted to do his homework. He wanted to do yoga. He wanted to ground himself in a tradition of other drunk writers: *Poe!!* His exclamation points hold a certain heartbreak: *Walk! Drive!* He wanted to believe in rituals and intention. He wanted to believe in showing up for a life you'd chosen.

In his novel *Kentucky Ham*, Billy Burroughs Jr. wrote about working on a fishing trawler after his time at the Narco Farm. "We worked like I never did at Lexington," he wrote. And he liked it. For him, work was the opposite of addiction: "You know what work does? It provides a constant. It structures time...I realize that a fix has to get done also and no two ways about it, but a fix goes *in.* To FIX. To adjust, to focus. But what I'm talking about goes *out* and in a choosy way rearranges reality."

For me, too, the drinking was always about taking something *in,* drinking something down — solace from the outside that could, for a time, be misunderstood as strength. And if the drinking had gone in, the work went out, just as Burroughs had said. As I got drunk and got sober, I liked that my bakery shifts stayed constant. It was always the same drill: Show up at seven. Work my production list. It was always: *Pick up the pace on those squirrels.* The routines of the bakery worked like another ritual, like the comforting structure of meetings — another shape I didn't have to invent, a way of being useful. We marked the seasons with hundreds of cookies each week: frogs with tiny love letters for Valentine's Day; ice cream cones for summer and glittery swirled leaves for autumn; snowmen in December with tiny orange triangles for noses. It was ridiculous, maybe, but they gave me a way to say, *I did that*—brought some small, undeniable pleasure to another person.

The camaraderie of the kitchen was surprising and often humbling. One of our bakers made a light saber from frozen cinnamon buns, and ate green bell peppers for lunch—cradling each one in his palm, whole and crunchy like an apple. Another one liked to tease me about my general ineptness, so on his days off, just to irritate him, I texted him photos of the doughnuts I'd made in our miniature deep-fry, which looked like giant mutant shrimps, captioned "Quality Control." For a Planned Parenthood fund-raiser, I made a cake with thirty circular cookies stuck around the top like birth control pills. I was trying to adjust, to focus.

That first winter of my second sobriety, I got my first down jacket. For years I'd felt personally persecuted by winter—a martyr to its bitter chill, my numbness epic and inevitable, the air little more than an external companion to my interior weather. But as it turned out, wearing a good jacket made you less cold.

For Valentine's Day, Dave and I drove north to Dubuque, an old river-money town perched on bluffs over the Mississippi. We played roulette at the riverboat casino and marveled at an octopus at the aquarium—swirling its legs like scarves in the water, purple and pearl-white, its suckers making little moons wherever it squished them against the glass. Dave was someone who could get excited about an octopus, or a dilapidated boomtown, and the fact that he could bring out that sense of wonder in me made me want to give it back to him. That was part of why I'd planned the weekend in Dubuque, though it was bittersweet, everything delicate. We were careful with each other.

Not long before the trip, while I was cleaning our apartment, I'd found a messy pile of notes stacked on Dave's dresser—all the apologies I'd written, all the mornings after we'd fought—each one acknowledging how many had come before it. A few days later, I'd asked if he was interested in coming to a meeting, something I hadn't done the first time around. I wanted to invite him into this new version of my life, rather than blaming him for not already being in it with me.

When he came, he was eloquent and thoughtful—moved by the things other people said. Three elderly women came up to me afterward and said, "He's so charming." It was like the time we'd gone to see a couples therapist, a middle-aged woman who ran sessions from her house in the suburbs and leaned over when Dave went to the bathroom: "Well, *he's* certainly charming." My face must have looked shocked, because she quickly said: "But I can imagine he's a real Jekyll and Hyde."

In Dubuque, we went to a Bavarian pub for dinner and ordered head cheese and goulash. There were approximately three hundred thousand beers on tap. I was desperately determined to enjoy the head cheese. Maybe I wasn't drinking beer but I was trying something *new*. At a certain point the bar broke into song. Strangers belted out drinking anthems in German, though the message was clear enough across the language gap: *Drinking is awesome and more drinking is more awesome and most drinking is most*—The head cheese was disgusting.

Dave and I went back to our bed-and-breakfast full of decorative plates and watched *Dune* on VHS—watched the fat man fly around with his little jets, deformed and degraded by the spice, his drug, totally slave to it. We curled up under our quilt and I thought, *Maybe this can be saved.*

— X —

HUMBLING

Everyone shared at meetings, but "telling your story" meant speaking in a more structured way—*what it was like, what happened, what it's like now*—usually at the beginning of the meeting, for anywhere from ten to thirty minutes. People had different philosophies about how to approach it. "I'm not going to give you my drunkalog, because all our drunkalogs are the same," some people said, and launched straight into sobriety. But I loved drunkalogs. I couldn't get enough of them. They were like getting dessert before dinner. Sure, they were all the same. But they were all different, too—insofar as every particular life manifested and disrupted the common themes in its own way. Drunkalogs were also useful because they reminded me of certain absences it was easy to take for granted after they'd been absent for a while: not waking up early with a hangover, or not thinking about booze every minute, every hour, every day; a type of progress that depended on not being aware of it.

The first time I spoke—the time I got heckled by an old-timer, *This is boring!*—it was in the basement of a school, a gym with gleaming hardwood floors and bleachers pushed into the walls and a wooden stage where we laid out grocery-store cookies in their plastic trays next to a tarnished silver coffeemaker. For the Monday speaker meeting, the folding chairs were laid out in rows, probably forty of them, with an aisle down the center—like a literary reading, or a wedding. The night I had agreed to speak I wore a shiny black shirt that wouldn't show the sweat under my armpits.

Fifteen minutes before the meeting began, there were only a scattering of people—mostly people I knew, friendly faces: the therapist who was in the midst of a divorce, the man whose infant daughter had died six years earlier. But the crowd was sparse, and I began to worry it was because word had gotten out that I was speaking. This was typical thinking: imagining the world as a conspiracy of forces directing their attention toward me, when it was more likely people were just picking up their dry cleaning, or watching the *Bachelor* episode they'd been looking forward to all week.

When more people started arriving, I realized I'd also been relieved at the low turnout, and immediately started to imagine how everyone who'd shown up might be disappointed by what I said. Before the meeting began, I poured a scalding cup of coffee and grabbed a brittle chocolate chip cookie, took one bite and then put it down in front of me—on the folding table I sat behind, facing the crowd, beside the meeting's chairperson, a woman I trusted. She had short-cropped gray hair and a teenage daughter, and she spoke with matter-of-fact warmth. She was honest about her mistakes but not exhausting in her regret.

My half-eaten cookie stared up at me as I told my story, which ended up focusing less on narrative drama and more on things I was surprised to find myself talking about: waking in the middle of the night worried about my meds, with a racing heart like a bird trapped in the cage of my ribs; and finding that stack of apologies on Dave's dresser.

It was right about then, just when I'd just started to feel pretty righteous about moving away from narrative interest and toward emotional candor, that the man in the wheelchair started shouting, "This is boring!" After he started shouting, I started unraveling—heat in my eyes, swell in my throat, voice starting to crack open—and struggled to finish the thought I was articulating about prayer. "It's like picking up a heavy box," I said. "I mean, prayer is like putting *down* the heavy box, but then I kept trying to pick it up again." I started crying fully. Again, the man yelled: "This is boring!"

He wasn't a bad person. He was just losing his grip on whatever part of us keeps us from shouting at strangers. And maybe, also, he was bored. I wiped my eyes with the back of my hand. What was my other thing I had to say about prayer? I had another thing to say about prayer. Multiple women in the audience reached for tissues in their purses. After the meeting, one of them came up to me immediately. "It was so moving to see you cry," she said, "when you started talking about prayer."

Then another woman, the chair of the meeting, put her hand on my arm and said: "You just told my story. Thank you."

Malcolm Lowry's greatest nightmare was being accused of telling someone else's story. That's why he was so outraged by the success of Jackson's *Lost Weekend*, and by its publication in the first place — by the idea that someone else had told his story before he'd been able to tell it. Years later, in his unfinished final novel, *Dark As the Grave Wherein My Friend Is Laid*, Lowry offered a thinly fictionalized account of his own anger: a scene in which a novelist named Sigbjørn Wilderness discovers that his alcoholic magnum opus has been scooped by a terrible book called *Drunkard's Rigadoon*. "It's purely a clinical study," Sigbjørn's wife assures him, "it's only a small part of yours." But Sigbjørn is crushed. If his alcoholism hasn't helped him produce an original masterpiece, what good has it been? He was sure he'd been "achieving something that was unique," but instead is told — by his agent and several publishers — that his book is "merely a copy."

When a dismissive 1947 review in *Harper's* magazine accused *Under the Volcano* of being "a long regurgitation [that] can only be recommended as an anthology held together by earnestness," little more than a patchwork "imitating the tricks" of better authors, Lowry defended himself in a passionate letter to the editor. Though critic Jacques Barzun had given the novel only a paragraph in his review, saying its characters were "desperately dull even when sober" (*This is boring!*), Lowry's rebuttal was twenty-two (indignant) paragraphs long. It closed with a postscript suggesting which line Lowry truly couldn't forgive: "PS: Anthology held together by earnestness — brrrrrr!" It's as if the charge of redundancy was so grave that it had banished Lowry to the cold, a merciless literary exile.

But an anthology held together by earnestness? It's one of the most apt descriptions of a recovery meeting—its particular beauty— that I've ever heard.

More than thirty years after he wrote *The Shining*, and twenty years after he got sober, Stephen King started to wonder whether a more fulfilling sobriety might have been possible for Jack Torrance, the dry-drunk writer who blew up the Overlook Hotel. "What would have happened to Danny's troubled father," King asked himself, "if he had found Alcoholics Anonymous?"

King's 2013 novel, *Doctor Sleep*, was an attempt to answer this question. The plot follows Jack's son, Danny—now grown up into a drunk like his dad, but finally clean and sober—as he fights an anonymous collective called the True Knot, a band of RV-dwelling supernatural monsters who chant in circles before they "drink pain" harvested from their unfortunate victims. The True Knot looks like a sinister version of AA, a fellowship of suffering where pain has become—quite literally—a form of sustenance. The novel's climax, however, is not Danny's triumph over the True Knot but a scene directly afterward, when Danny finally confesses his true "bottom" to an AA group at his fifteenth sobriety anniversary. He describes the morning he woke up in bed with a coked-up single mom and stole money from her wallet while her diapered son reached for a pile of leftover coke on the coffee table, thinking it was candy. (*Leftover coke?* The addict in me was dismayed. But the shame was familiar.)

After Danny confesses his terrible truth, the moment of honesty that the whole book has been building toward, he gets...very little in response: "The women in the doorway had gone back to the kitchen. Some of the people were looking at their watches. A stomach grumbled. Looking at the assembled nine dozen alkies, Dan realized an astounding thing: what he'd done didn't revolt them. It didn't even surprise them. They had heard worse." The narrative doesn't just insist on the moment as anticlimactic; it insists that this anticlimax has still been meaningful.

As it turned out, my own sobriety held the same double moral as a second-act Stephen King novel: You've spoken your truth, and now everyone is making a beeline for your sober-birthday cake. Your story is probably pretty ordinary. This doesn't mean it can't be useful.

When I finally read the manuscript of Charles Jackson's unfinished novel *What Happened*—the pages he had written under the influence of recovery, unpublished in his archives—I brought so much desire with me. It was like the desire poet Eavan Boland confesses when she asks for poems with women in them who aren't beautiful or young: "I want a poem I can grow old in. I want a poem I can die in." I wanted a story I could get sober in.

This made it disappointing to confront the manuscript of *What Happened*, which offered a tedious, convoluted narrative I found difficult to keep reading. "I can only write the human, meanderingly," Jackson had written to a friend, confessing his fears about his long-awaited epic, and I started to understand what he'd meant. I'd been glued to *The Lost Weekend*, unable to put it down, and I wanted *What Happened* to be like that—only better! about functionality!—but it wasn't. Mostly, it was hopelessly abstract:

> What life means, it came to him (or he seemed to overhear it), it means <u>all</u> the time, not just at isolated dramatic moments that never happened. If life means anything at all, it means whatever it means every hour, every minute, through any episode big or small, if only one has the awareness to sense it... each step, the dramatic and the humdrum alike—every fleeting second of the way.

The thing was, I actually agreed with what Jackson was saying. I'd come to believe that life happened every hour, every minute; that it wasn't made of dramatic climaxes so much as quiet effort and continuous presence. But I could also see how Jackson's desperate desire to deploy his recovery wisdom had crippled his story. His own words about the book now played back to me like an omen: "with scarcely any 'plot' but much character...I'm proud to be so objective and detached, *finally*."

The manuscript bore out some of my worst fears about sobriety: that it was destined to force you into a state of plotless abstraction, a string of empty evenings, a life lit by the sallow fluorescence of church-basement bromides rather than the glow of dive-bar neon signs. The reckless readability of *The Lost Weekend*—the momentum of Don's escapades, and the roaring engine of his thirst—had been replaced by stasis.

If Jackson was afraid he would only ever be known for *The Lost Weekend*, then Lowry carried a similar fear that he would never write anything as good as *Under the Volcano*. (Even his fears were unoriginal.) But after several rounds of brutal "aversion therapy" to treat his alcoholism in the mid-1950s, Lowry embarked on a major round of edits on the book he hoped might someday surpass his alcoholic magnum opus. *October Ferry to Gabriola* was a novel about the happiest years of his marriage, spent in a squatter's shack north of Vancouver. In critic D. T. Max's account, Lowry wrote furiously in the aftermath of his aversion therapy—new pages that examined "what he called the 'alcoholocaust' of his life, and the way that drinking had affected his art." Lowry took apology letters he'd written to his wife, Margerie, over the years and pasted them directly into the draft. He was trying to fill the book with the texture of his regret, to make it not just a transcript of harm but also the process of reckoning. This kind of salvage made me imagine crafting a book from my own apology notes.

The response from others was a bit less enthusiastic. Lowry's editor at Random House canceled his contract for the book because the manuscript sent to him was "just about as tedious as anything I'd ever read." After Lowry's death, Margerie added her own comments to the manuscript. "Rambling notes," she wrote. "Seems like a dissertation on alcohol. Nothing useful here."

When I read the manuscript of Jackson's *What Happened*, I grasped at its meager glimmers of plot: "He had the impulse to pull the car over to the side of the road and give himself up to introspection, a kind of self-inventory....Leaving nothing out." *Okay, he's in a car,* I thought. But where was he going? Would something finally happen there? I perked up at the mention of an inventory, like the AA Fourth Step, because maybe that meant I would get to read about how Don had fucked up. But then I felt guilty for wanting the train wreck. I was supposed to be rooting for the underdog story—the story of sobriety—but instead my own lapsed attention was just proof that this story would never be as interesting as the story of getting drunk. It was like sitting at a meeting and hoping the drunkalog would never stop, thinking *yeah yeah yeah* at the part about a newfound connection to a Higher Power. I didn't want to think *yeah yeah yeah* about sobriety, didn't want my eyes glazing over at its even-keeled horizon line. I was afraid that loving the drunk story best meant some part of me still wanted to keep living it. And of course, some part of me did.

During those first few months after I quit drinking the second time, sobriety often felt like gripping onto monkey bars with sweaty metallic palms, just praying I didn't fall. When an arts cooperative in a small Iowa farm town offered me a week in their workshop—a converted tofu factory in the middle of soybean fields, offered as barter payment for judging a student contest—I spent my days trying not to think about the kitchen counter in the nearby farmhouse where I was staying, and the bottles of red wine someone had left there. I asked Dave if he wanted to drive over from Iowa City and stay with me, share the tofu factory, but he said he was behind on a deadline (he was often behind on a deadline) and needed to stay at home.

Once he said he wasn't coming, it became even harder to stop fantasizing about drinking. It would be so easy to get drunk out in these ghostly soybean fields, all alone—to sink into that blooming warmth and not tell anyone. So I tried to distract myself. Because I was afraid to go back to my farmhouse at night, to those three bottles I could picture so clearly, I stayed up till three in the morning trying to work in the converted tofu factory. It was barely converted to anything— still full of broken machinery, tackle boxes, and rusty metal lockers, with loose screws rolling down the concrete loading dock. The worst night, I sat at my big slab of a desk until five in the morning and watched a BBC miniseries about just-industrialized nineteenth-century Manchester, snow falling on mill strikes, and then started *re*watching it, and then watched the "Making Of" special about it—all so I wouldn't have to go back to the farmhouse and reckon with those bottles of wine.

The next morning, I looked online for a list of meetings in town. At noon I showed up at the address I'd found: a brick church with a stained glass window that looked dull in the sunlight. The front door was locked. But when I circled around to the back, where two bikers in full leather were standing with a white-haired woman in a mint-green pantsuit, I knew I'd come to the right place. It was just the four of us, until a woman in sweatpants showed up, a single mother who lived on a farm nearby with her son. It was only her second meeting, she said.

One of the bikers, smiling, said, "The journey begins."

"I hope so," she said. "I can't even imagine tomorrow."

It turned out the back door was locked and the person with the key hadn't come, so I thought maybe we'd all go our separate ways, but no—we all went to a gazebo in the park instead, and sat in the dappled sunshine on splintered wooden benches.

The woman in the pantsuit was a local librarian, and the bikers were just passing through. The single mother was ten days sober and totally falling apart. Her son had seen her crying two days in a row. Their llama was going through puberty and acting like a little shit. When it was my turn to speak, I told everyone about rewatching the BBC miniseries just to keep myself from drinking, and one of the bikers—a huge man with a snake tattooed around his neck—nodded so vigorously I was sure he'd say he'd seen that miniseries too. He hadn't. But he knew what it was like when craving tugged you like a puppet. He told us about his first drink, and when he paused to describe the smell of that bourbon, he spoke straight to my gut, straight to those terrifying bottles in the farmhouse pantry. It wasn't his words so much as his pause, how it held him for a moment, the memory of that bourbon smell—how it stopped him in his speech.

A few days later, I met the single mother for coffee. She brought me bratwurst made from her goats, and I told her I didn't know what it was like to be a single mother, or any kind of mother—but I did know about crying every day, and I also knew that the ninetieth day of my sobriety had been pretty different from the tenth one.

The second time I got sober, I started praying with a sense of purpose. It was impossible to picture the clear outline of any god, but praying regularly was a way to separate my second sobriety from my first one. Back then I'd only prayed haphazardly—when I wanted something, basically. This time around, I understood arranging my body into a certain position twice a day as a way to articulate commitment rather than a bodily lie, a false pretense. I prayed in the bathroom—by the toilet, under the dirty skylight over our shower—where Dave wouldn't see me. He wasn't judgmental; I was just embarrassed. It was easier to be alone with my fumbling faith, and it felt good to kneel on the bathroom floor for different reasons than I'd knelt on them before: not throwing up or getting ready to throw up, but closing my eyes and asking to be useful. I'd been told to pray for people I resented, so I prayed for Dave and for every girl he'd ever flirted with, for every man I'd ever hated for not wanting me. I even liked the physical residue of these morning prayers, the tangled red pattern on my knees from the bath mat we didn't clean enough.

When I was younger, I'd gone—reluctantly—to a regal Episcopal church in Inglewood. My mother had started going to church after she and my father divorced, and she'd asked me to come with her. The church was stunning, with massive copper lanterns hanging from the wooden beams, and jeweled light stilled by the stained glass windows on Sunday mornings: angels with red-tipped fiery wings. The golden altar held a pale statue of Jesus with a sculpted triangular beard and ruthlessly serene eyes, his finger raised as if he were just about to say something. But what? Going to church meant feeling something just out of reach—a sense of connection to this pale man, or the sermon, or the songs—the ecstatic faith that seemed to swell inside everyone else. I wasn't sure I believed in God, so wouldn't it be lying if I prayed to him? The premise of the miracle at the heart of everything, that impossible resurrection, made me feel miserly with disbelief, like my heart was a locked storefront shuttered against sublimity. I was shy and uncomfortable in my own body, kneecaps bruised by wooden kneelers, afraid of the vulnerabilities of belief— afraid to find anything too beautiful, or fall for it.

Because I wasn't baptized, I couldn't take Communion, so I either sat alone in my pew while everyone else walked up to the altar, or else I went forward and knelt on the velvet cushion, arms crossed over my chest, while the priest placed his palm on my head and said: "I bless you in the name of the Father, the Son, and the Holy Spirit." But I didn't believe in any of them, and it seemed dishonest to take a blessing in their name. The more you had to *make* yourself believe, I was sure, the more false your belief was.

Years later, recovery turned this notion upside down—it made me start to believe that I could do things *until* I believed in them, that intentionality was just as authentic as unwilled desire. Action could coax belief rather than testifying to it. "I used to think you had to believe to pray," David Foster Wallace once heard at a meeting. "Now I know I had it ass-backwards." For a long time, I'd believed that sincerity was all about actions lining up with belief: knowing myself and acting accordingly. But when it came to drinking, I'd parsed my motivations in a thousand sincere conversations — with friends, with therapists, with my mother, with my boyfriends — and all my self-understanding hadn't granted me any release from compulsion.

This ruptured syllogism — *If I understand myself, I'll get better* — made me question the way I'd come to worship self-awareness itself, a brand of secular humanism: *Know thyself, and act accordingly.* What if you reversed this? *Act, and know thyself differently.* Showing up for a meeting, for a ritual, for a conversation — this was an act that could be true no matter what you felt as you were doing it. Doing something without knowing if you believed it — that was proof of sincerity, rather than its absence.

I didn't know what I believed, and prayed anyway. I called my sponsor even when I didn't want to, showed up to meetings even when I didn't want to. I sat in the circle and held hands with everyone, opened myself to clichés I felt ashamed to be described by, got down on my knees to pray even though I wasn't sure what I was praying to, only what I was praying for: *don't drink, don't drink, don't drink.* The desire to believe that there was *something* out there, something that wasn't me, that could make not-drinking seem like anything other than punishment — this desire was strong enough to dissolve the rigid border I'd drawn between faith and its absence. When I looked back on my early days in church, I started to realize how silly it had been to think that I'd had a monopoly on doubt, or that wanting faith was so categorically different from having it.

When people in the program talked about a Higher Power, they sometimes simply said "H.P.," which seemed expansive and open, a pair of letters you could fill with whatever you needed: the sky, other people in meetings, an old woman who wore loose flowing skirts like my grandmother had worn. Whatever it was, I needed to believe in something stronger than my willpower. This willpower was a fine-tuned machine, fierce and humming, and it had done plenty of things — gotten me straight A's, gotten my papers written, gotten me through cross-country training runs — but when I'd applied it to drinking, the only thing I felt was that I was turning my life into a small, joyless clenched fist. The Higher Power that turned sobriety into more than deprivation was simply *not me*. That was all I knew. It was a force animating the world in all of its particular glories: jelly-fish, the clean turn of line breaks, pineapple upside-down cake, my friend Rachel's laughter. Perhaps I'd been looking for it — for whatever it was — for years, bent over the toilet on all those other nights, retching and heaving.

When Charles Jackson reread *The Lost Weekend*, years into his inconstant sobriety, he "was most of all impressed by the sense that, in spite of the hero's utter self-absorption, it is a picture of a man groping for God, or at least trying to find out who he is." He understood the old patterns as driven by the same hungers: the hunger for booze as the hunger for God, all this groping as part of the same journey.

At times, it seemed my relationship wasn't to a Higher Power but to the act of prayer itself — a ritualized cry of longing and insufficiency — as if my faith were a catalog of places I'd gotten on my knees, a hundred bathrooms where I'd knelt on cold tiles with thin ribbons of grout under my shins; or crouched on a foot-worn bath mat, facing the eye-level skyline of my mother's bubble bath, jars of pearly peach and vanilla. In those bathrooms, God wasn't faceless omnipotence but proximate particulars, grout and soap — the things that had always been there, right in front of me.

During the spring of my first sobriety, I had embarked on a different type of writing project than I'd ever pursued before: I drove to the Tennessee wilderness to write about an ultramarathon my brother was running, a 125-mile race through briar-cloaked hills and hollers around the outskirts of a deserted federal penitentiary. The runners spent days in the woods, circling back to a central campsite after every loop to fill their fanny packs with candy bars and pop their blisters with sewing needles. I'd never done anything like this, conducting interviews and gleaning observations to write about the lives of strangers, and the sheer plenitude thrilled me—how much was all around me, just waiting to be gathered.

I slept in my car and filled a notebook with details: one runner's tale of seeing a wild boar on the trail, the dead-tired glass of his eyes and the mud on his legs; rain pattering on the roof of my Toyota all night, sliced by the lonely cry of bugle taps played whenever a runner dropped out of the race. I ate chicken slathered in barbecue sauce, roasted over a campfire in the smoke and chill of early spring, and asked these runners why they pushed themselves past the limits of what they thought they could endure. What community was made possible by a shared confrontation with pain? Even this attempt at reportage was turning into autobiography. But it was still something new—inspiring and awkward. Before interviews, I got nervous. My armpits dampened with sweat. My pulse spiked up. I was a terrible interviewer, at first, too eager to prove myself, and so busy saying, *Yeah, I know exactly what you mean,* that I never gave people enough room to speak. Often I stuttered when I asked my questions, and cringed whenever someone shrugged or squinted in reply. But it surprised me, my own ability to make eye contact. Meetings had trained me. Whenever someone shared, you had to look at her—so that if she ever locked eyes with you, you could give what she was saying a place to land.

By the time Berryman started working on his novel *Recovery,* he had come to see the notion that he needed to drink in order to write as a delusion. "So long as I considered myself as merely the medium (arena for) my powers, sobriety was out of the question," he wrote in 1971, in a handwritten note he later adapted for use in the novel. "The even deeper delusion that my art *depended* on my drinking, or at least was *connected* with it, could not be attakt directly. Too far down. The cover had to be exploded off."

Several years earlier, in a 1965 review in the *New York Times*, Charles Jackson had questioned the mythic figure of the "tormented" artist: "Are we really all that tormented? Or is it something we hang onto, foster, even cherish, till it becomes an end in itself, full of self-defeating interest?" In this review of Lowry's *Selected Letters*—a review that would have infuriated Lowry, if he'd been alive to read it—Jackson wondered what Lowry might have been able to write "if by some supreme effort, some mystical or psychological shifting-of-gears, the tormented man had been able to get on another level and get outside of himself." Jackson was probably thinking more specifically about recovery, something he wasn't willing to name explicitly, perhaps thinking about what he'd told an AA meeting six years earlier—"I couldn't get outside myself"—or his own unfinished novel, his attempt to get "for the first time, *out* of myself."

Marguerite Duras certainly wrote drunk, but she didn't harbor any delusions about what the drinking did for her work. "Instead of drinking coffee when I woke up," she wrote, "I started straight away on whisky or wine. I was often sick after the wine—the pituitary vomiting typical of alcoholics. I'd vomit the wine I'd just drunk, and start drinking some more right away. Usually the vomiting stopped after the second try, and I'd be glad." Her pragmatic approach to this particular oblivion—the "typical" and totally *un*-singular vomiting, the relief when her body stopped resisting the booze—dismissed myths and opted for something more matter-of-fact: "Drunkenness doesn't create anything....The illusion's perfect: you're sure what you're saying has never been said before. But alcohol can't produce anything that lasts. It's just wind."

Duras's critique of the "illusion" of drunken creativity is also a critique of the illusion of singularity: the idea that *what you're saying has never been said before,* one of the precise notions that recovery pushes against. In my own sobriety, I'd given up on that impossible ideal of saying what had never been said, but I also believed every unoriginal idea could be reborn in the particularity of any given life. As my sobriety continued, my writing turned toward interviews and journeys: asking a long-distance runner in a West Virginia prison what it felt like to be trapped in one place, asking a woman at a Harlem community center about the way her obsession with a mysterious whale helped her recover from a seven-week coma.

Duras herself was never involved in any organized recovery, though she did undergo three brutal "disintoxication" treatments at the American Hospital of Paris. Their physical toll nearly killed her, and brought on terrible delusions: a woman's head shattering like it was made of glass, or "exactly ten thousand tortoises" arranging themselves into formations on a nearby roof. Duras even dreamed a vision of the communal salve she never actually experienced: "The sound of singing, solo and in chorus, would rise up from the inner courtyard under my windows. And when I looked out I would see crowds of people who I was sure had come to save me from death."

After one of his admissions into detox, Berryman wrote a poem addressed to his fellow patients Tyson and Jo:

> take up, outside your blocked selves, some small thing
> that is moving
> & wants to keep on moving
> & needs, therefore, Tyson, Jo, your loving.

The poet teaches what he most needs to learn, and Berryman was constantly finding ways to recommit himself to the lives of others. In the margins of a *Grapevine,* an AA magazine, next to one prompt—"Have I a personal responsibility in helping an AA group fulfill its primary purpose? What is *my* part?"—Berryman wrote: *To listen.* Next to "What is the real importance of *me* among 500,000 AAs?" he wrote: *1 / 500,000th.* There were 500,000 AAs for Berryman to love, every one of them moving. Recovery was about understanding himself as one tiny numerator, a blocked self, above the larger denominator of a community. Many communities. As part of his step work, Berryman listed all the groups he was part of:

> *My groups*
> K and Twiss
> AA
> Friends and poets (Cal etc.)
> Common Cause!
> HUM, all of M
> Shakespearians
> Students
> The church
> "America"
> the human race

K and Twiss were his wife, Kate, and their daughter, Martha; Cal was Robert Lowell; HUM was his division (Humanities) at the University of Minnesota; Common Cause meant protesting the war in Vietnam. He wanted to love his colleagues and his school; he wanted to love strangers halfway around the world, strangers his country was bombing in the name of its democratic vision. Hence "America" in scare quotes. Hence *the human race.* AA was the group that asked him to face his responsibilities to all the other groups on the list. Writing his novel was not only an opportunity to offer something to these communities ("useful 12th step work") but also a way to dramatize the difficulty of becoming part of one: the struggle to humble himself, to submerge his own voice by making himself 1/500,000th of the chorus rather than its soloist.

The protagonist of *Recovery* is a renowned former professor of immunology named Alan Severance—almost amusingly revered, as if celebrity immunologists are nothing out of the ordinary—who struggles, as Berryman did, to reconcile his acclaimed professional life with his identity as a debilitated alcoholic. From his room at rehab, Severance sees the spires of the college campus where he teaches: "Towers above the trees across the river reminded him he was University Professor Severance not the craven drunk Alan S who had been told by an orderly that his room smelled like a farmyard."

At rehab, Severance is constantly reaching for the part of himself capable of something besides self-concern: "His own hope was to forget about himself and think about the others." These are the same instructions that Berryman gives Tyson and Jo: *take up, outside your blocked selves, some small thing.* Who can Severance take up? There's a man named George, who is still seeking the approval of his dead father, or a woman named Sherry, who isn't interested in anything—until, to Severance's great delight, she gets interested in the history of North Dakota. There's another woman, named Mirabella, who tells the group that she hasn't wanted to do anything but scream for years. "You don't remember a time when you didn't have it?" her counselor asks, and she replies, "Drinking sends it away." The core question of *Recovery* is whether something else might send it away instead. Perhaps other people might. "In hospitals he found his society," Berryman's friend Saul Bellow wrote about his stints in rehab. "About these passioning countrymen he did not need to be ironical."

When George finally accepts that his dead father had good reason to be proud of him, Severance is so moved he finds himself "fighting sobs." And when George climbs onto a chair to announce his joy—"I DID IT. I DID IT."—Severance catches his exuberance as contagion:

"Cheers from everybody, general exultation, universal relief and joy. Severance felt triumphant."

But *Recovery* is also canny about the ways that resonance can become self-involvement, an absorption in the strength of your own emotional response. When George is having his breakthrough, it's actually difficult for Severance to hear him because his own empathy gets so loud: "There was more, but Severance was fighting sobs and didn't hear it." When the group recites the Serenity Prayer, Severance hates that "his rich, practiced, lecturer's voice had dominated the chorus, giving him no pleasure." Even when he forces himself to say the same words as everyone else, he still yearns to be loudest. One woman who had been at rehab with Berryman remembered that "he couldn't ever be wholehearted about belonging with the rest of us." He was "constantly retreating into his uniqueness," she said. "He really thought it was all he had that made him worth anything."

G oogling the phrase "just another addiction memoir" yields several pages of results, mostly blurbs insisting that a certain book isn't "just another addiction memoir," an author insisting his book isn't "just another addiction memoir," or an editor insisting she didn't acquire "just another addiction memoir." This insistent chorus reflects a broader disdain for the *already-told* story, and a cynical take on interchangeability: the idea that if we've heard this story before, we won't want to hear it again. But the accusation of sameness, *just another addiction memoir*, gets turned on its head by recovery—where a story's sameness is precisely why it should be told. Your story is only useful because others have lived it and will live it again.

By the time James Frey published his infamous addiction memoir, *A Million Little Pieces*, in 2003, addiction narratives had become so familiar, so *trite*, that more melodrama was required to purchase certain levels of attention. People had already heard the one about the crackhead; now they wanted to hear the one about the crackhead who had run over a cop, spent three months in jail, and gone through a root canal without anesthesia. Frey's editor, Nan Talese, said she'd almost passed on his manuscript because—as one account put it—it seemed like (yes) "just another addiction memoir," but she reconsidered after reading the first few pages because "the grim subject matter fascinated her."

When the memoir's distortions first came to light—Frey spent only one night in jail, he never hit a cop with his car, he probably *did* get anesthesia for that root canal—the call for reparations spread like wildfire. Oprah, who had chosen the memoir for her book club, brought Frey onto her show to stage an almost ritualistic public shaming. Twelve indignant readers filed a lawsuit on behalf of indignant readers everywhere. The book had given them hope, they said, and what did that hope mean now that they knew it wasn't based on truth? A social worker who'd recommended the book to her clients filed a lawsuit seeking ten million dollars on their behalf. Frey's distortions became a stand-in for the "truthiness" of his times, his book linked to the political deceptions and overblown narratives that had justified the war in Iraq.

"My mistake," Frey wrote in a public apology, was "writing about the person I created in my mind to help me cope, and not the person who went through the experience." He acknowledged that the changed facts were lies, but insisted they were products of a story he'd told himself to get better. Frey's fabrications weren't simply a product of his imagination, however, they were a product of the marketplace—in this case, a marketplace of sentiment and trauma already swollen by inflation, an economy that demanded increasingly elaborate forms of abjection to keep readers interested.

I've often wanted to defend Frey, not because I find his alterations defensible but because I find them comprehensible. Perhaps this is only because I project a certain desire onto them: Frey sought the objective correlatives of high drama—prison time, violence, even *dental work without Novocain*—because he was clutching at things that could communicate the huge stakes of how it felt to need drugs like he did. Perhaps I projected this desire onto him because I've often had it myself: this hunger for a story larger than my own, with taller buildings and sharper knives.

A t meetings, my stories were hardly the best ones in the room. It was like a picnic where I'd brought the plastic forks instead of the fancy Brie or a key lime pie. But I also knew my presence was one small part of what allowed the meeting to happen at all—my body in a room along with everyone's. "Exceptional case, my ass! I was just another junkie, period," Janet tells herself in *The Fantastic Lodge*, describing her time at the Narco Farm. "This disappointed me horribly, naturally."

People weren't dazzled by anything I had to say, or how I said it. They just listened. "Yeah, I've gotten punched in the face while I was drunk, too," one guy said. I wasn't supposed to tell my story because it was better than anyone else's, or worse than anyone else's, or even that different from anyone else's, but because it was the story I had—the same way you might use a nail not because you thought it was the best nail ever made, but simply because it was the one lying in your drawer.

When I got sober for the second time, the messy story I'd had so much trouble telling before—about getting sober and then starting to drink again—was something I could offer other people: *Yep! I also had trouble convincing myself I couldn't drink.* My return was not unique; it just meant I was present again, and I could tell the story of what it was like to be gone. In one of his haikus, the Japanese poet Kobayashi Issa writes: "The man pulling radishes / pointed my way / with a radish." I pointed the way with whatever radishes I'd lived: whiskey tucked behind a futon, wine bottles in a purse, apologies piled on a dresser. At three days sober, you can tell someone on her first day what the second day was like for you.

Could be anyone. Could have been anyone's story. These were phrases

I often heard in meetings, but they struck me as erasures. Giving up on singularity was like giving up on the edges of my own body. What would I *be*, if I wasn't singular? What was identity if it wasn't fundamentally a question of difference? What defined a voice if not distinction? I was still a little girl at the dinner table, trying to prove myself by coming up with something better than a few clichés balled up in my throat. Recovery started to rearrange these urges. Whenever someone else said something simple and true, I felt it bodily. "I got sad and ate a cookie," one woman said, and an electric current surged between her body and mine.

In early drafts of the AA Big Book, "you" was often changed to "we," which effectively turned assumptions into collective confessions. "Half measures will avail you nothing. You stand at the turning point" became, in waxy red pencil script, "Half measures availed us nothing. We stood at the turning point." In moving from *you have to stop drinking* to *we had to stop drinking*, the grammar implies a certain humility: *We can't know your story; we can only speak our own.*

The paradox of recovery stories, I was learning, was that you were supposed to relinquish your ego by authoring a story in which you also starred. It was a paradox made possible by the acknowledgment of commonality: *I happen to be at the center of this story, but anyone could be.* When Gilles Deleuze wrote that "life is not personal," he was getting at this, too, that an individual story is both more and less than self-expression. A 1976 AA pamphlet called "Do You Think You're Different?"—its cover full of black circles, one thinner than the others—opens with an admission of delusion: "Many of us thought we were special." The plural subject already holds the argument: Even the belief in singularity is common.

In a book called *My Story to Yours: A Guided Memoir for Writing Your Recovery Journey*, Karen Casey offers a paint-by-numbers approach to writing your addiction story. The premise itself insists that our stories are the same, and that this isn't a bad thing. Casey structures her personal story around prompts designed to nudge readers back into their own: "What's the first memory you have of drinking? Did it include friends you could trust or strangers you realize now were not very savory?"

Casey's book is the epitome of everything programmatic about recovery narratives. It makes the blueprint explicit. But I loved its stark confession that our stories have common hinges, whether we want to admit to them or not.

"You might have some fond memories of the drinking days too, and that's normal. Share some of them if you like."

A balcony with Dave: the crisp tang and sugared nectar of Sciacchetrà, a local white, the wine Pliny called "lunar," with the big moon over us and the waves breaking below, the faith we'd get married, the church music from another hill.

"Do you believe in destiny?"

Yes, I do! I wanted to tell her. I wanted to shout it.

"If so, what do you see as yours currently? Are you content with it? If you had hoped for something different, why not write a letter to God, here and now?"

I wanted to write God a letter asking why Dave and I were still fighting. I wanted to hurl myself at Casey's trite questions like I'd surrendered myself to the tight columns of my Fourth Step. I imagined flinging myself off a cliff, onto their necessary humbling.

"We're all drama queens," my sponsor told me once. "Even in our sobriety."

That first spring of my second sobriety, I was reading applications for the Writers' Workshop to make some extra money—specifically, to help keep up with the coupon book of student-loan payments from my own days as a workshop student. I was supposed to rate these applications on a four-point scale. The fiction program got more than a thousand applicants a year and accepted around thirty. That meant someone had to rule a lot of people out. But meetings were teaching me to listen to everyone. I started to lose my bearings. I would read something trite and second-guess myself. *Was* it trite? Who was I to say? Maybe it was just a radish I couldn't recognize.

When you're hungry for wisdom, it's everywhere. Every fortune cookie had my number. "Why is the truth usually not just un- but *anti*-interesting?" David Foster Wallace once wondered. "Because every one of the seminal little mini-epiphanies you have in early AA is always polyesterishly banal."

I kept a notebook where I recorded at least one thing I loved from each application—because I wanted to honor each applicant, even if she would never get admitted. This slowed down my reading process quite a bit, and whenever I glanced back at my notes, they never looked as wise as they'd seemed when I copied them down: "Father realizes he must accept son for who he actually is." "All the cats are named after different vegetables." Someone could have written: *I wrote this application because I want to be accepted*, and I would have wanted to accept her. Something about desire itself, its naked and unartful articulation, had started to seem beautiful.

I'd grown suspicious of my own narrative tendencies: my desire for drama; my tenacious, futile pursuit of originality; my resistance to clichés. Perhaps this resistance to cliché was just one symptom of my refusal to accept the commonality of my own interior life. But I couldn't deny the way that certain platitudes struck me like a bronze bell and left me feeling rung—spoken, stolen, shaken.

I was never persuaded that clichés held the Full Truth of My Experience, or anyone else's. I'm not sure anyone else was, either. But submitting myself to the clichés of recovery was another way of submitting to its rituals—gathering in basements, holding hands in circles. Saying *This applies to me too* started to seem necessary and tonic. There was something illuminating, something even like prayer, in accepting truths that seemed too simple to contain me. They weren't revelations but reminders, safeguards against the alibis of exceptionality that masqueraded as self-knowledge. The word itself—"cliché"—derives from the sound that printing plates made when they were cast from movable type. Some phrases were used often enough that it made sense to cast the whole phrase in metal, rather than having to create an arrangement of individual letters. It was about utility. You didn't have to remake the entire plate each time.

I knew a man in meetings who spoke almost entirely in clichés, like a patchwork quilt of phrases sewn together in jagged veers of thought. *We had to quit playing God…every recovery began with one sober hour…every day is a gift, that's why we call it the present…sobriety delivers everything alcohol promised…the elevator is broken, use the steps… God will never give you more than you can handle.* These phrases had helped him survive his own life. Now he was presenting them in hopes that they might be useful to the rest of us—less like a sermon, more like a song.

—XI—

CHORUS

Several years after recovery started changing my mind about cli-chés, I wrote a newspaper column in their defense. I called them "subterranean passageways connecting one life to another" and basically pulled a Charles Jackson, smuggling recovery into my prose and praising its wisdom without naming it directly. A few days later, I got an email from a man named Sawyer, who said he'd come to appreciate clichés quite a bit himself—in recovery, he said, not just in AA but in this "rag tag" rehab he'd helped run in the early seventies: "We started with all-volunteer help in a little ramshackle hostel. Actually a sort of hot pillow place in a secluded spot on the banks of the Potomac." That's how Sawyer first told me about Seneca House, a converted fishing motel in Maryland, insisting that he thought there was a "great story to be told about Seneca House, with both bathos and pathos."

For two decades, before closing in the early nineties, Seneca had been a rehab full of ambassadors and bikers, Navy guys and diplomats' wives, long-distance truckers and oil executives, housewives with Valium habits; a Navy commander, a dentist, a Rhode Island gigolo, and an elderly hypochondriac who wore his shirt unbuttoned to the waist; all swapping stories of grit and regret. One housewife described her ready-made tall tale for wine-shop clerks: She was making beef Bordelaise in a vat, and she needed nine bottles of red. One guy said he used to strain his shoe polish for the alcohol. One woman said her Valium stash had fallen out of her cleavage and into her Thanksgiving turkey, at the table in front of everyone; another confessed she'd shot heroin straight into her vagina.

From the first moment I heard about Seneca, I wanted to tell the story Sawyer believed in. These were Berryman's passioning countrymen in full splendor. I loved the image of an old firetrap by a river, its glowing old neon MOTEL sign hanging above the battered aluminum smokers' table, its reflection glimmering in the water. I wanted to tell the story of a ragged little universe in an old wooden house, how living alongside other people facing their damage could make it easier to face your own. It would be like Charles Jackson had written: *The story happens, is happening— taking place, like daily living— on every page.*

When I pitched the story to a magazine editor I respected, he wrote back: "Hmmm...it would be a tougher sell here on account of the why-write-about-these-guys-and-not-some-other-guys question. If you have a good answer for that, I'd be game to run it up the masthead."

I had no good answer for that. I thought Seneca House was compelling not because it was different but because it wasn't—because these-guys had gotten drunk just like some-other-guys had gotten drunk, because these-guys had gotten better just like some-other-guys had gotten better. They'd shown up at a junky wooden shack and said, *This is done.*

How had Jackson put it? *It is really wonderful, simple, plain, human, life itself.*

His name is Sawyer, and he's an alcoholic.

He grew up in Vandergrift, a Pennsylvania steel town. His father died when he was two months old. His mother, who'd come from Lithuania at sixteen, cleaned the homes of steel-baron millionaires. She saved every nickel and dime so that Sawyer could go to prep school, which is where he really started drinking. He got kicked out for booze. Then his test scores got him a scholarship to Virginia Polytechnic, and he got kicked out for booze again. He went to Korea with the Army, where he worked as a land surveyor and drank triples of whiskey. His battalion was based in an old walled silk factory in

Yeongdeungpo, a district in southwest Seoul that looked like medieval times, with mules pulling honey wagons full of shit to the rice paddies. When a mule died en route they set up a meat sale on the road, right then and there.

Eventually Sawyer managed to build himself a life that looked good from the outside — wife, kids, career as a lawyer in D.C. — but he drank away his paychecks at the Jefferson Hotel after work and often left his family's electric bill unpaid. At home, his six kids ate peanut butter and jelly sandwiches for dinner by candlelight while Sawyer sang along to Louis Armstrong at the hotel bar. On a good night, the guys at the Jefferson put him in a cab, but on a bad night he'd end up drinking rotgut at some illegal place in Chinatown, maybe get picked up by the police, maybe get bailed out of jail by his law partner. Looking back, he saw that the drinking had been a way to evade responsibilities — the flock of kids with their jam-sticky hands, tugging on his pant legs, asking him to fix their wagons.

Sawyer finally got sober when his wife, pregnant with their seventh, told him she would leave him if he didn't. He'd just come home from drinking all night. His first AA meeting surprised him. He thought he'd see the same guys he saw in drunk court. Instead it was a luncheon full of businessmen who seemed to be doing better than he was. He got a sponsor, an Irish-American veteran named Buck who'd flown with the Flying Tigers in China, Chennault's Fourteenth Air Division, a guy who liked to say, "Being Irish isn't a prerequisite for being a drunk, but it's not an obstacle either." He had no patience for guys who couldn't give their all to AA. One time Sawyer missed a Friday-night meeting to attend his son's Boy Scout meeting, and when he told Buck why he hadn't been there, Buck got red in the face and said that in *that* case, Sawyer should give the Boy Scouts a call the next time he got drunk and wanted help.

Sawyer was thriving in sobriety — making good money as a personal-injury lawyer, known as "Sawyer the Lawyer" on the D.C.

AA scene—when he got a call from a hospital, where a man named Luther had listed him as next of kin. Luther was a client Sawyer had represented several months before, for a crosswalk hit-and-run: a sober alcoholic who was in the middle of a serious schizophrenic episode. Luther had listed Sawyer because he didn't have anyone else. "Poor son of a bitch," Sawyer told his partner, then went down to the hospital.

During the months that followed, Luther kept coming around to visit Sawyer at his office, saying he wanted to help other drunks get sober. *My barnacle* is how Sawyer started to think of him. It seemed like the only way to help Luther, the only way to get *rid* of Luther, might be to help him help someone else. Luther had money he could use—some from the hit-and-run settlement, some inherited from family. So when a couple of guys, both sober counselors, came to Sawyer and told him they were trying to convert a run-down old fishing hostel into a rehab, he immediately thought of Luther.

The place was right on the shores of Seneca Creek, just off the Potomac and the C&O Towpath. In the twenties, it had been an old motel where people from the city stayed for the weekend to catch sunfish and bass. By the late sixties, weekend fishing had long since dropped off and the building was falling apart—soft wood, soggy mattresses, everything grimy. But these two sober counselors saw possibility in junk: They had twenty-five filthy beds. They knew a shrink who would volunteer. All they needed was cash.

That's where Luther came in. His money helped them lease the building and get it fixed up. Sawyer filled the place with furniture from a secondhand shop he owned. Once it was up and running, Luther was a regular visitor. He would sit at the kitchen table for hours, almost always in silence, chain-smoking his cigarettes. People sat with him, telling him their stories, and he listened quietly, a silent chimney of trailing smoke. People swore they couldn't have stayed sober without him.

When it first opened, Seneca charged six hundred dollars for a twenty-eight-day stay. The manager, a former Marine drill sergeant turned carpet cleaner named Craig, made exceptions for guests who couldn't pay the full amount. He took one guy's junked old pickup truck in exchange for a month. He let a prostitute barter some of her jewelry. There were bills he never collected. Whenever a new resident came in—bloated and sick, throwing up or soiling himself—Craig gave a hard time to anyone who didn't pitch in to take care of the newcomer. He said, "We all have to be on the vomit line."

This was 1971, the same year Bill Wilson died and Nixon launched his War on Drugs. It was a year of cognitive dissonance. Addiction was the enemy, but it also needed therapy. When Nixon called for the "reclamation" of the addict, he made him a victim and a sinner at once.

At Seneca, guests did chores every day: painting the lawn furniture, emptying ashtrays, managing the rowboats the house rented for extra income. Craig gave people the duties he knew they hated—cleaning toilets or washing dishes—because he thought it was good for them. The house had its own septic tank and the toilets were temperamental. If you plugged in the toaster at the same time as the coffeemaker, it was anyone's guess. When the power went out, meetings happened by candlelight.

The place was a firetrap. Patients weren't supposed to smoke upstairs, in the maze of old corridors and attic rooms, but of course they did. The furniture Sawyer donated was frayed at the seams and the chairs sagged from years of anonymous bodies. The couches had to get replaced every time the creek flooded the first floor. Meals were basic: cheeseburgers and quesadillas served at tables covered in oilcloth. The walls were cluttered with posters: WE HAVE MET THE ENEMY AND IT IS US. Old Johnny Mathis records played on the stereo: *Look at me, I'm as helpless as a kitten up a tree.* There were meetings in the basement, which had been a pub back when the place was a fishing hostel.

Old guests showed up occasionally, but turned around at their first glimpse of the Serenity Prayer.

Even though everyone had to go through detox before they were admitted, people still arrived bruised and dazed. The first house nurse was a patient who started working on Day 29 instead of going home, because she had no home to go back to. At first the staff mainly consisted of volunteers who worked for fifty bucks a month, if they got anything at all. It was hard raising money for alcoholism back then. People didn't see it as something you should raise money *for*. Sawyer put it like this: "You don't ever go into a convenience store and see a big jar there that says, 'Donate to the clap fund.'"

Seneca residents were often assigned contracts. Sometimes these were phrases written on index cards they were required to read aloud at meals: *My "tough guy" mask is just a front for my deep fear. I have to trust you if I am going to get well. God doesn't make junk, and I AM SOMEBODY.* But there were other kinds of contracts, all specifically tailored: Residents who didn't let others speak had to stay silent for forty-eight hours. Residents who had trouble giving or receiving affection had to spend a week wearing T-shirts saying I AM HUGGABLE or OFFICIAL HUGGER.

The "Get Grubby" contract was for people who focused too much on how they looked. It meant they had to wear rumpled clothes for a week, or stop shaving or wearing makeup. This contract had started with a surgeon who wore only three-piece suits and got a contract saying he had to wear jeans. He didn't have any, so they got him sweatpants. The contract was meant to take away the things he thought made him worthy, to convince him he was okay without them. The "Fetch Me" contract was for patients who compulsively devoted themselves to taking care of others. It meant they had to ask someone to do something for them at every meal. People who were always late had to spend a week waking everyone up at seven in the morning. They had to be first in line at every meal, and no one got any food until they showed up.

Patients who were always serious had to carry around stuffed animals and make them speak. Patients who hated themselves had to look into a mirror and figure out what they liked. Tough guys had to read *The Velveteen Rabbit* aloud. Some of them cried when they read the words of the Skin Horse, praising the shabbiest stuffed animals: "Once you are Real you can't be ugly, except to people who don't understand." When you wanted resonance, it was everywhere. The Toys that became Real were the ones that looked most broken.

At Seneca, they knew that having fun without booze was something you had to learn how to do, like developing a muscle you'd never used. On Monte Carlo night, guests made bets with "Senecash" and sipped lemonade at the blackjack table. In summer, there was an ice cream truck; and in fall, guests picked out jack-o'-lanterns at the local pumpkin patch.

Some patients held funeral services for their addictions, burying bottles in the backyard—and later, once addicts started coming, syringes too. But sometimes the old thirst rose up. The house cook, an Irishman with a thick brogue who made eggs and waffles for breakfast, relapsed on a trip to visit his sister in California. Back at the house, trying to go cold turkey, he went into DTs and had to be driven away by ambulance. Lips Lackowitz—sober front man of the band Tough Luck, self-taught on the harmonica—came out to Seneca House to perform and relapsed a short while later, after fifteen years clean.

But Seneca House saw only three deaths during the twenty years it was open, all suicides: two in the building and one right outside of it, when a former patient showed up drunk and drowned herself in the creek. A priest was found in his room one Sunday morning with a dry-cleaning bag over his head, and a shrink stabbed himself with a dinner knife. Another patient came into the hallway and saw it sticking out of his chest. After he died, the house mutt—named Molly—went to every single room, offering whatever comfort she could.

Every spring the creek swelled with rain and snowmelt, but in the early days of Seneca, once-in-a-century floods came twice in two years. When Hurricane Agnes flooded the whole house, everyone had to move to a motel nearby. There was a bar in the lobby, but no one drank, which was a triumph. During bad storms, when the creek flooded Riley's Lock Road, someone had to take the rowboat out to the main road to pick up new residents. "You came here to dry out, did you?" they'd joke. "Well, get in the boat." It's easy to imagine how many times that joke got rolled out, washed off, and used again. During the spring floods of 1984, an Australian named Raquel was the one who took out the rowboat to pick up the new residents. She loved the adrenaline rush, a boozeless thrill.

When Raquel first arrived at Seneca House, she was so nervous she was actually shaking—in a way she hadn't since she was a kid, right before she was about to get hit. What was she afraid of now? She was afraid that if she opened her mouth, she'd start screaming; and afraid that if she started screaming, she wouldn't be able to stop. Instead she opened her mouth and started talking. Craig said if something haunted you, you should talk about it three times: The first time would be almost unbearable, and the second time would still be pretty bad, but by the third time you'd finally be able to say it without breaking down entirely.

Simple, plain, human: The story of Seneca was the story of twenty years of cheeseburgers and vomit lines, meetings that felt like salvation and meetings that felt like dental drills; twenty years of popsicles from the general store down the creek and forbidden sex in the bushes and thighs covered in angry little red-ant bites; twenty years of lemonade at barbecues, and women wondering how they'd fuck their husbands sober, men wondering how they'd go back home and face everyone they'd disappointed, wondering how their roommates would go back home and face everyone *they'd* disappointed—twenty years of starting to believe it might be possible.

More than four thousand people came through Seneca over the course of two decades. They weren't famous. Their drinking wasn't famous. They hadn't turned their pain into dream songs or best-selling novels. They'd just arrived craving relief: a social worker named Gwen, who drank room-temperature vodka and Kool-Aid while hosting her son's Boy Scout troop; a journalist named Shirley who showed up after hurling all her mother-in-law's crystal against her dining room walls; a crack addict named Marcus, who claimed he'd flown all over the world, but had bottomed out working for his uncle's trash business. When he showed up, he was utterly emaciated. His dirty linen suit hung off his skinny body like a coat on a rack.

At Seneca, people put their past lives in chorus in order to craft new plotlines for themselves. Residents often stayed in touch after they left. "I'm all alone," one wrote from Cairo. "I need fellowship." So they sent him letters. Whatever those letters said, they always said one thing beneath everything else: *We are here.*

At my own meetings in Iowa, the chorus came as relief. Greg had followed dirt roads into the hills of North Carolina, to cinder-block houses where the moonshiners drank and sold. Chloe was a grandmother in periwinkle fleece, who said simply, "My drinking broke so much." Sylvie had torn jeans, red eyes, and a daughter sitting at her feet, cutting out paper snowflakes. My friend Andrea had to puff into her Breathalyzer before she drove me to lunch. Getting drunk had always carried me deeper into myself, into that velvet apathy, but listening to another person speaking—whatever he was saying, whatever she remembered—was the undeniable opposite of that descent.

AA skeptics often assume that its members insist on it as the only answer. But an AA meeting was the first place I ever heard someone say AA isn't for everyone. Dr. Greg Hobelmann, a psychiatrist in twelve-step recovery who was once an anesthesiologist with an opiate habit, put it like this: "There are a hundred ways to skin a cat."

For me, no skinning was quite like this one. When people spoke at meetings they were real about what hurt—maybe they were still angry at their mothers, or the IRS, or the jobs they hadn't gotten—but they were showing up anyway, to listen to other people's problems, and other people's hope. Many addiction researchers predict that we'll eventually be able to track the impact of meetings on the brain itself. The sheer fact of putting your body in a room—a hundred rooms, a thousand times—and listening hard, or hard enough, can neurally reconfigure what addiction has unraveled.

Dr. Kaplin believes in a symbiotic relationship between twelve-step recovery and other forms of addiction treatment. He told me that the medications we have for addiction now—drugs like buprenorphine, that target specific neurotransmitters—are incredibly useful, but they're still just "knocking on the door of the mechanism." When he described his "big picture" dream for addiction medicine, a drug that could recondition the mechanisms of dependence itself, I asked if this would render recovery obsolete. Was it just another way of knocking on the door? Would it eventually, *ideally*, be unnecessary, if we could rejigger the mechanism itself?

"You can give someone as much methadone as you want," he told me. "But they will still need a social network."

Writing about Berryman's drinking, Lewis Hyde described "the thirst of the self to feel that it is part of something larger" as something comparable to the "body's need for salt." That thirst is Jackson craving the street full of strangers, or Duras dreaming the ones who never sang for her. "An animal who has found salt in the forest," Hyde wrote, "will return time and time again to the spot."

The Big Book of AA was initially called *The Way Out*. Out of what? Not just drinking, but the claustrophobic crawl space of the self. When he comes off heroin in *Blueschild Baby*, dope-sick and despairing, George Cain finds glimpses of hope in moments of self-escape: listening to jazz at a smoky club on 116th — "Feel myself outside myself as we follow the music, shattered into a million tiny fragments chasing the sound, all outside ourselves" — or sleeping with a woman, for the first time, clean, sweating and shaking: "naked and defenseless....another device to get outside yourself." Critic Alfred Kazin, in a review of William Burroughs's novel *The Wild Boys*, described the addict-author as someone struggling to escape an "infatuation with the storeroom of his own mind."

Writing could be part of this escape, Kazin argued, but only if it looked outward: "All stream of consciousness writing, in order to rise above the terrible fascination with itself, has to find something other than itself to love." David Foster Wallace, too, believed that great art came from "having the discipline to talk out of the part of yourself that can love instead of the part that just wants to be loved." He knew what it meant to consider yourself just 1/500,000th. "You're special — it's OK," he wrote to a friend, "but so's the guy across the table who's raising two kids sober and rebuilding a '73 Mustang. It's a magical thing with 4,000,000,000 forms. It kind of takes your breath away."

The way out: the salt in the forest, the street full of strangers. The hunger to escape myself had always manifested in physical ways: I'd tried to bleed it out when I cut, to whittle myself to nothing but bones when I starved. Drinking myself senseless had been another way of getting rid of myself for a while. When I was hungover, I tried to sweat out my insides by running — booze trickling out of my pores.

Meetings were another way out entirely. They were one of the first places I could ever fully sit still in my own body. Listening to other people speak was an alternative to bleeding, and an alternative to the scale in the closet, with its glowing red verdict. It was an alternative to the closet full of gin in my novel. It was another type of escape hatch, into another type of relief.

It's hard to write this way, full-throated and shameless, with such crude awe at what recovery came to mean in my life. But it's the only language that feels accurate, holding recovery the way a sail holds the air—not made of wind, only moved by it.

W hat's a meeting? It's just one life after another: an anthology held together by earnestness. It might begin with an ordinary woman at an old fishing hostel in Maryland. Her name is Gwen, and she's an alcoholic.

During the days of her drinking, Gwen worked as a social worker and served as the social-ministry chair at her church. She helped poor families who had gotten moved to public housing. She wasn't supposed to be the one with a problem. At church, she won Citizen of the Year. At home, she poured Kool-Aid for her son's Boy Scout troop with her own vodka and Kool-Aid perched on the fridge above their reach. She tried to keep her drinking hidden, but it was impossible to keep people from noticing what happened when she got drunk. One day a stranger knocked on her door and said he'd found a little girl, just a toddler, wandering outside. Did the little girl belong to her? She did. Tiffany was three.

When Gwen's son came home from school one day and told her he never knew if he'd find her "sad, mad, bad, or glad," she slapped him across the face. Another day she told her kids that if they finished their homework she'd take them over to Leesburg, Virginia, on White's Ferry. "But we went last week," they told her. "You took us last week." And she had, in a blackout—put her kids in the station wagon and taken them across the river. She couldn't remember it at all.

For her son's birthday one year, Gwen took him and his friends to a baseball game. It was a party she was proud of planning: He'd get an autographed ball, a free cake, and his name in lights at the stadium. But as she was drinking beer out there in the sun, kicking the empty paper cups, he turned and said: "I wish we'd left you at home."

Back at home she'd started pouring vodka into empty white vinegar bottles—her husband never cooked, her kids would never try to drink it—so she could secretly refill her martinis. That way it never looked like she was having more than one a night. When she went out, she tucked plastic formula bottles full of booze into her purse, so she could drink from them in secret, in bathrooms. From reading Lillian Roth's memoir, *I'll Cry Tomorrow*, she'd learned that glass bottles in a purse would make too much noise. She was putting a little vodka in her Kool-Aid, and eventually a little Kool-Aid in her vodka. At home one afternoon, she woke up groggy—passed out from booze, now coming back—to find her toddler daughter standing over her with a wet washcloth, saying: "Tiffany make it all better."

What's a meeting? It takes you from one life to another—easy as that, with a raised hand, no segue or apology necessary.

His name is Marcus, and he's an alcoholic and an addict—born in D.C. in 1949, a black man in a divided city. He never saw his parents drunk. *Can't put that on them*, he thinks now. He got a scholarship to play basketball at Cleveland State, where the whole team got drunk, then went down to the gym and played until dawn. They drank Mad Dog 20/20, which was nearly forty proof but tasted like candy. They felt immortal.

When Marcus joined the Peace Corps after college, he was sent to a city called Buchanan on the Liberian coast. He taught English and coached basketball. He was thousands of miles from home and—he believed—any possible consequences. In Buchanan he drank palm wine with the locals. In Monrovia he drank with the other Peace Corps volunteers at a place on Gurley Street, where one guy liked cane juice, white lightning, but when Marcus tried it, it made him sick as a dog. He stuck to the national favorite, Club Beer. They liked to say it stood for "Come Let Us Booze, Be Ever Ready." That pretty much summed up Marcus's time in Liberia, where you could get a liter of Club for seventy-five cents. Marcus had too much time, too much freedom, too much room to do whatever he pleased—which meant drinking as much as he wanted. He started to learn how much ex-pats loved to drink: They were often restless, and rarely wanted to stay inside the mistakes they'd made.

For six more years, Marcus stayed abroad, working for Saudi Arabian Airlines, based in Jeddah, during the heart of the Saudi oil boom. Oil money was everywhere, and the mayor was investing in sculptures: a car perched on a flying carpet in the middle of a traffic island, a bronze man raising his stump arms to the blue desert sky. Marcus was flying all over the world. In Bangkok he drank with Vietnam vets who couldn't bring themselves to go home. In Bombay he drank with Europeans hunting for spiritual enlightenment in ashrams. He went to Addis Ababa with a crew of guys who worked for Saudi Air, and they took over an entire hotel floor—met girls in clubs and brought them back, paid no attention to the curfew. This was 1977, under Mengistu, and there was martial law: no one allowed out between midnight and six in the morning. They disobeyed that. They did what they pleased. On the train to Mogadishu, they got fucked up and made noise.

The first time Marcus ever freebased was 1980, on a vacation back in the States. He'd flown all the way around the world, and he ended up hanging out with a friend's ex-wife up in White Plains. She called it "baseball." He put down three hundred dollars and liked it so much he put down another three hundred right away.

All that drinking, being an asshole all over the world, none of that had felt like trouble. But crack felt like trouble. It was too sweet.

Thirty-five years later, when Marcus told me about smoking for the first time, he said it three times in a row: "It was too sweet. It was too sweet. It was too sweet."

It wasn't until Marcus moved back to D.C., a few years later, that his crack habit spiraled fully out of control. He tried to start a business driving limousines but he couldn't balance his expenses. He lost fifty pounds in six months. He was six foot five and down to 149. After his business failed, he started working for his uncle, who owned a trash company. Marcus had been living on top of the world — flying everywhere, money everywhere — and now he was underweight and handling other people's garbage. He described those six months after he got back to the States as an express train to zero. Once he got there, he called a hotline and someone on the other end suggested Seneca House.

Marcus didn't arrive till evening, too late to check in, and had to spend the night with a Seneca alum — a man who worked nearby as a farmhand, taking care of the horses — sleeping on his couch, above the barn. At Seneca the next day, Marcus was wearing one of his nicest suits, though it was falling apart. He could pay only part of the deposit for a twenty-eight-day stay. He was thirty-four years old, and he felt like a dressed-up garbage can.

Decades later, he would work as a counselor at a 102-bed program for federal prisoners with substance-abuse problems. He'd tell them to look at the buildings outside their windows, and ask, "What's on this compound?," trying to show them where they might end up. They pointed at the jail and the hospital. He pointed at the cemetery. In a group session Marcus led, one man asked another, "How did you negotiate that anger?" And the second man said, "Oh, I started to speak."

Her name is Shirley, and she's an alcoholic. When she was nine, she found an open bottle of wine in her living room. The warmth in her throat, then her gut, helped her understand why her father got so drunk it left him retching at the toilet in the middle of the night. Shirley didn't become alcoholic by accident; she wanted it. She romanticized geniuses like Robert Burns and Edgar Allan Poe, but she was disgusted by drunks who'd failed at their drinking, who had nothing to show for it — like her 250-pound uncle, lumbering and frightening in his cups. That kind of drinking repulsed her.

During college, she worked for a small-town Oregon paper, keeping tabs on how many crummies full of loggers got sent into the mountains to fight each forest fire. The first time her boss took her to the Portland Press Club, she was hooked on booze and reporting at once, intertwined: all these hard-core reporters getting blitzed from stashes in their private liquor lockers. She had her first highball there, bourbon and ginger ale, and ended that night throwing up in the ladies' room. The attendant stood by, saying, "Must've been something you ate." They both knew it wasn't. For her twenty-first birthday, a friend baked her a cake that said BALLOTS OR BOOZE!

During J-school in Minneapolis, Shirley lived in an apartment above a tea shop and ate one meal a day, at noon: a thirty-five-cent hamburger. She sold her blood for extra cash. She drank only on dates, when a guy was paying. She dated a lot. When she heard she'd gotten a junior reporter job at *Life* magazine, she screamed so loud she wondered if her screams had embedded themselves permanently in the tea shop walls. She moved to New York in June 1953, the same summer the Rosenbergs were executed. *Life* kept booze in the office, especially on Saturdays, when the magazine closed. One week Marlene Dietrich had a case of champagne delivered to the office with a note: *It's 4 PM! Love Marlene.* But Shirley mainly drank alone in her apartment. She felt perpetually out of place—as a woman, without an Ivy League degree, it seemed impossible she'd ever rise through the ranks.

She decided to take a job at a small paper in Montana, near the Judith Mountains, where she lived above the Gold Bar Saloon, drank gin upstairs while she listened to the jukebox and the cowboy brawls below. She wrote a piece about a wild-horse roundup; she fried eggs on the sidewalk for a story about the heat; she snapped shots of a forest fire from a two-seater plane. After they closed the paper around ten each night, her boss took her across the street to the Burke Hotel for highballs. The bartender was a guy named Frank, ten years sober, who used to tell them, "You guys are the lost generation." They loved to hear it. A grocery clerk gave her tango lessons in an abandoned bakery—dipping between the old mixers and dusty countertops—and when they performed their tangos at a roadhouse called Bar 19, they got rounds of free bourbon in return.

One day Shirley got a fan letter from a man named Lou, a reporter in Pennsylvania, who'd read her cowboy-roundup piece and loved it. They started writing to each other. Less than a year later, on Valentine's Day, they got married. It turned out Lou was knee-deep in gambling debts; he'd even written bum checks to the priest and the organ player for their wedding. They lived on Christopher Street in the West Village, in New York, and drank whatever they could, whenever they could afford it. Lou worked for a Jersey paper but hated it. He wanted something better. They bought a suit for his job interviews and then they threw his suit a little party, hung it up in the window and toasted it with wine: "To the suit!"

Over the course of the next decade, Shirley devoted herself fully to Lou's career—helping him come up with pitches, putting her own career on the back burner, moving for his newspaper jobs in Harrisburg, Tulsa, Oregon, Maine, and eventually Beirut, where he worked for the *Daily Star* and got paid in cash. They lived in a high-rise overlooking the bay and rode taxis all over town: old Mercedes with watermelon rinds littering the floors, blasting music as they drove past shawarma shops fluttering with flies. People asked why they didn't have kids, and Lou wanted them badly, but Shirley was secretly relieved she hadn't gotten pregnant. She thought becoming a mother would mean she'd have to give up her career for good, and she'd already sacrificed so much for her husband's. Maybe sometimes, *sometimes*, she had a drink. When the local *New York Times* correspondent threw a big party for Henry Luce's arrival in town, with belly dancers and buckets of booze, Shirley got so drunk she collapsed in the bathroom. They had to kick in the door to get her out. "You need to take her home," her husband was told. "It must have been something she ate." Déjà vu.

Back in the States, they adopted a baby girl named Laura. When they stopped for formula on the way home from the adoption office, Lou ran into the store while Shirley stayed in the car and whispered to the baby: "I don't want you. I don't want you. I don't want you." A few years later, unexpectedly, they had their own biological child—a daughter they named Sonia. Staying at home with the two kids drove Shirley crazy, but it also let her drink as much as she wanted during the day. She lost her temper easily, raging at Laura for spilling the cat food. Lou kept them moving for his work and traveled constantly. One night, right after they'd moved to a new town, Shirley wanted a drink so badly she took both kids in the car with her and they went out searching. She told them to look out for signs that spelled L-I-Q-U-O-R.

It was after Lou made a comment about a shelf that hadn't been properly dusted that Shirley started picking up pieces of her mother-in-law's crystal and hurling them one by one against the dining room wall. "I'm going mad!" she yelled. "I'm going mad!" Not long after that, the kids came downstairs late one night and saw her making peanut butter sandwiches for their school lunches. She'd been throwing up and her hair was stringy with vomit. She promised them she'd get help, and she did.

Decades after Shirley had stopped drinking, one of her children—now an adult, and newly sober—called her from the hospital after a suicide attempt, and Shirley read from the Big Book over the phone: *Remember that we deal with alcohol—cunning, baffling, powerful! Without help it is too much for us.*

Six months into my second sobriety, I took a trip down to Memphis with my friend Emily—glamorous in tortoiseshell sunglasses, sober since twenty-two. In college, we'd eaten tacos at three in the morning to soak up the vodka in our stomachs. She'd drunk until she reached the place she called the *fuck-it* point, where she just didn't care. She'd spent a summer drinking her way across Nicaragua on a freelance writing gig—lush days that landed her in a Managua hospital with dengue fever. Now that she was sober, Emily's life had a certain thickness. She salvaged furniture and finished it herself. She'd once taken me to a North Carolina gas station for boiled peanuts and hush puppies in a plastic basket, spotting their paper with grease, then shown me the Beaufort cemetery at night, the graves of bootleggers and pirates. Her sobriety was contagious. The world vibrated under her gaze.

In Memphis, she took me to watch the Peabody Hotel ducks, marching on a red carpet from the lobby fountain to a glass elevator. We went to an old converted bordello with claw-foot bathtubs, where we drank Coke from plastic cups and she told me about the upstairs bartender, a man who'd been sober for decades. I loved thinking that the world had been full of sober people all this time, hidden in plain sight. Emily told me about the first few months after she'd quit drinking, those long nights spent baking elaborate cakes and watching endless TV, and I remembered pacing the tofu factory, watching that miniseries about Manchester—panicking when I reached the last episode, that last scene on a railway platform, because I was scared of the silence.

We drove around Memphis looking at the Big Empties: huge buildings the city couldn't afford to tear down. They stood thirty, forty stories high, with cracked windows and boarded doors, walls moldering with asbestos. We went to an old cemetery shrine with a secret grotto of quartz inside a concrete tree stump, with jittery music fluted from interior speakers. I needed that, something twinkling inside. I needed the world to tell me there was more out there, waiting.

"What you really want," Berryman wrote, "is to stay just who you are *and* not drink. That's not possible, of course. Jack-Who-Drinks has got to alter into Jack-Who-Does-*Not*-Drink-*And*-Likes-It." Who was that Jack in me, the Jack who didn't like to drink? And what did she like instead? I'd always associated drinking with falling in love and driving to New Orleans; dancing on wooden bars, between foam-crusted beers; taking swigs from a bottle of cheap red in a graveyard—wriggling out of the tight swaddling of self-awareness.

But in sobriety, it was getting easier to take myself less seriously. At the bakery, during morning production, Jamie liked to tease me by putting on a playlist she called the Wounded Mix, full of my favorite songs. Mazzy Star crooned, "I want to hold the hand inside you," while I tried and failed to properly ice a cake. During my first year at the bakery, I'd made the mistake of telling Jamie that my mom and I had sometimes made collages together when I was young, and whenever I came to work in a bad mood she immediately asked if I needed to take some time to collage about it.

Jamie was a funny, generous, candid woman whom I hadn't been able to see fully—at first—because I felt muted and intimidated by her. Now she was teaching me alternatives to taking a long warm bath in your own pain, like waking up and getting shit done. *EFD* was our catchphrase for necessary daily commitments: *Every Fucking Day.* Whenever Jamie needed me to draw her out, she'd say, "Take me to your emo igloo," and one time when we were talking over coffee she started crying, describing the exhaustion of her days—her kids, the bakery—how she sank into a black zone after bedtime. It was strange to see her cry, this brash no-bullshit woman. But this was something that kept happening in sobriety, understanding that everyone—your boss, your bank teller, your baker, even your partner—was waking up every fucking day and dealing with shit you couldn't even imagine.

That last summer in Iowa, I befriended a woman who was newly sober and struggling. Her pain seemed expansive and unyielding, beyond speech, and I was often not sure what to say to her. Sometimes I told her how obsessed I had been with drinking, and that seemed to help. I wanted to give her some version of the sparkling grotto I'd seen in Memphis—proof of the world as interesting, infinite, still unknown—and so I decided to take her to the raptor center just outside town, a refuge for wounded birds of prey: spooky owls with swivel heads; a pair of mated hawks who barely tolerated each other's feathered bodies on the same tree branch. Almost past saving, these birds had been given a new home. I didn't care how obvious it was.

I got lost, though. I couldn't find the raptor center. We found a picnic bench and smoked there instead. It wasn't what I'd bargained for. If I helped this woman, I was supposed to get a fucking raptor center! She was supposed to get a raptor center. But we didn't. We just got a picnic bench. We got each other's company for a while.

— XII —

SALVAGE

When Dave and I moved back to New Haven after two years in Iowa, I envisioned it as our second chance. We would return to our doctoral program to write our dissertations, and we'd live a thousand miles away from that second-floor apartment that held the ghosts of all our arguments—far from the gazebo where I'd fled our party, drunk; far from the streets I'd walked in the hours before dawn, sober and fuming.

New Haven was the city where our relationship had begun. The air was crisp. Our shared life felt possible. The trees broke out in cherry blossoms like hives every spring. I gathered the materials of our new neighborhood as talismans: the sullen boy selling chocolate milk at the farmers' market with his mom; the curly-haired tutor who was always running everywhere, backpack bouncing; the Italian grocery store with veal hearts for sale, with *osso buco* and homemade bologna and a Ten Commandments mural painted on the wall by the exit, to strike guilt in the hearts of would-be shoplifters. These particulars helped me write the story of our love's recovery. *We didn't know whether we'd make it or not, but then we moved to that place in Wooster Square and that was when we really pulled it together.*

But the city almost immediately saturated me with nostalgia for the ways I used to drink. I knew there were meetings in New Haven, like a secret city happening underneath the city I lived in. But I wasn't sure I wanted to visit them. If I never followed another set of darkened stairs into another church basement, maybe I could be someone who didn't need to. Sometimes, walking home from campus after teaching, I took the long way up State Street, past the bar with peanut shells where I'd gotten drunk with Peter years earlier. Its sidewalk still gave me chills: *This* sidewalk, by *this* tree, had been full of the taste of vodka, just about to happen.

The firm belief that I could probably start drinking again arrived about three weeks after the last meeting I attended—back in Iowa City, before the move—like a train pulling into the station on schedule. It was mild-mannered and persuasive, this faith in my own ability to drink. It knocked very politely. It anticipated my skepticism. *I'm not saying you can DEFINITELY drink*, it said. *It would just be an experiment.* The shimmering alternate world had grown close once more, its long nights wondrous, its floors covered in peanut shells. It lay just beyond the drudge work of recanting: *I know I said I was an alcoholic and then took it back and said I wasn't really and then took that back and said I actually was but the thing is I'm really not, I promise.* Then I'd be back in the sweet autumnal swirl of red wine and hard cider, the chilled salt slide of dirty martinis. It would be like finally crawling back under the covers on a cold morning—back into the swell, as Rhys would have it, letting the river become an ocean again.

"I'm thinking about drinking again," I told Dave calmly over dinner. "I really think I could do it better."

At that point I was nine months sober, after seven months back out, after seven months sober, after two tries before that. I kept my voice measured and upbeat, like I was talking to a cop who'd pulled me over for speeding and I didn't want him to find the pot in my glove compartment.

Dave didn't tell me I shouldn't drink. "Go to a meeting," he said. "See how you feel after that."

I went to a church the next night and tried a door. It was locked. *Thank God.* I walked back to my car; at least I could say I'd tried. But something in my gut wasn't right—something in me knew that trying wasn't enough—so I turned back and circled around the church. There they were, farther back, the telltale signs: lit basement windows, a brick propping open the door, the stranger in a camo jacket ashing his cigarette outside.

During that meeting, as others were speaking, I tried to figure out how to spin my drinking so I could leave the meeting and eventually drink again. Instead I raised my hand and said exactly what I was thinking: "I'm trying to figure out how to spin my drinking so I can eventually do it again." When I opened my mouth to speak, it was like a valve releasing a toxic, pressurized gas.

After the meeting, a young woman — maybe twenty years old, with a shiny curtain of blond hair, skinny jeans and heels, straight from some sorority pledge class — came up to me and started crying. "I can't stop trying to convince myself that I don't have to be here," she told me. "Even though I need to be here."

I was about to tell her that she should probably talk to someone better at sobriety — someone who hadn't just spent three weeks avoiding meetings — but then I realized she'd come up to me because I'd just announced that I'd spent three weeks avoiding meetings. She connected to that part of me, and to the part of me that had come back anyway. We were both in that room for a reason. She said she'd never gotten drunk in the mornings until she heard someone in a meeting confess that he used to get drunk in the mornings.

"That's fucked up, right?" she asked me. It seemed like half of her wanted me to tell her she was beyond hope, and half of her wanted me to tell her there was hope for her. But maybe she was just a Quinnipiac sorority girl who drank too much — and who was I to tell her anything?

That's when she pulled up her bubblegum-pink baby tee to show me her colostomy bag — a beige pouch tucked against the salon-tanned concavity of her abdomen. "I'm making myself sick," she said. Nothing before or since has dissolved my self-absorption faster than the sight of that colostomy bag. She told me she knew she was supposed to drink less, now that she had it, but she couldn't moderate. She'd just changed what she drank — no more beer, since it bloated the bag.

Looking down at the ground, mumbling, she asked if she could have my number. I said of course she could, though it seemed absurd to think that I could help her. *And you, you ridiculous people, you expect me to help you.* It turned out I needed her help, too.

A few weeks after my first meeting in New Haven, I started reading David Foster Wallace's *Infinite Jest.* I'd been surprised to hear it was a novel about recovery, because I'd always thought of it as ego-inflated—a blue brick of a book by a smart guy who'd wanted to buoy his ego by writing it, beloved by other smart guys who wanted to buoy their egos by reading it. But once I started reading *Infinite Jest,* it seemed like much more than virtuosity for its own sake. The core of the book—for me, at least—was Ennet House Alcohol and Drug Recovery House ("Redundancy *sic*"), where a massive and genuinely decent man named Don Gately is recovering from his Dilaudid addiction and helping other people get better *one day at a time.* The novel seemed self-aware about the trite sheen of these slogans, their simplicity and handled polish, but unapologetically committed to their messages anyway.

Infinite Jest wasn't *just* about recovery, of course. It was also about a tennis academy right up the hill from Ennet House—and three brothers living there, a punter, a prodigy, and a "stunted and complexly deformed" boy barely taller than a fire hydrant, all grieving a father who'd stuck his head in a microwave. It was also about the lethal film their father had made before he died, and the Québécois separatist wheelchair assassins hell-bent on finding the film and deploying it as a weapon. This film was the engine at the center of the whole story, so engrossing that no one who watched it wanted to do anything but watch it forever. That's how it killed you.

I approached my reading like a recovery program, by reading fifty pages a day—showing up for them whether I wanted to or not. At the top of each page, I took note of what had happened: *He is weeping from desperation, but detached even from his own weeping.* Or: *Millicent makes a move.* Or: *Lyle licks the sweat.* These notes were a way of taking my own attendance, a way of saying *I've been here.*

It wasn't that *Infinite Jest* took me back to meetings. It was the persistent desire to drink that took me back to meetings. But *Infinite Jest* helped me understand why I needed them. More specifically, it helped me understand that certain things about meetings could drive me crazy, and I could *still* need them. The novel had metabolized recovery with so much rigor it had already asked all of my questions and weathered all my intellectual discomforts. It documented what it called the "grudging move toward maybe acknowledging that this unromantic, unhip, clichéd AA thing—so unlikely and unpromising...this goofy slapdash anarchic system of low-rent gatherings and corny slogans and saccharine grins and hideous coffee" might actually offer something, in its simplicity and its slogans, in its church-basement coffee and its effusion of anonymous and unqualified love. The novel offered an encounter with recovery charged by double consciousness: both interrogating and affirming it, investigating its labor, its oddness, and its sublimity. The novel was questioning the recitations of recovery but still alive to its miracles, and not afraid to say so.

Recovery is hope in *Infinite Jest*, but it's also absurd. It's grown men crawling across cheap carpeting with teddy bears tucked into the crooks of their arms. It's guys killing alley cats to get a sense of "resolution." It's old-timer crocodiles and their emphysema-addled voices of prophecy. It's the soul-swollen, heartbroken, chain-smoking world of Boston AA in all its "unromantic, unhip" wonder. "Serious AAs look like these weird combinations of Gandhi and Mr. Rogers," the novel observes, "with tattoos and enlarged livers and no teeth." *Infinite Jest* gets at something truthful and astonishing about how all of these people gather together seeming so "humble, kind, helpful, tactful," how they actually *are* these things, not because anyone is forcing them, but simply because it's the way they survive. The novel conjures the strange foods of recovery: meatloaf covered in cornflakes, pasta doused with cream-of-something soup, ordinary things I'd also eaten—in the company of other ordinary people and their ordinary drinking memories.

If I'd read *The Lost Weekend* rooting for Don Birnam to get drunk again, I read *Infinite Jest* rooting for Don Gately to stay sober. I was grateful to direct my narrative desires toward recovery rather than relapse, glad to know it was possible for a book to make me thrill toward wellness. If Berryman had imagined *Recovery* as Twelfth Step work, then I was Twelfth-Stepped by Wallace. The novel was my old-timer just when I needed one. Gately describes the newly sober as "so desperate to escape their own interior" that they want "to lay responsibility for themselves at the feet of something as seductive and consuming as their former friend the Substance." I wanted to lay myself at the feet of the book that told me that.

Wallace himself went to a Boston rehab called Granada House in late 1989, seven years before *Infinite Jest* was published. "It's a rough crowd," he wrote to a friend. "Sometimes I'm scared or feel superior or both." Years later, he described his experiences at Granada House in an anonymous online testimonial:

> They listened because, in the last analysis, they really understood me: they had been on the fence of both wanting to get sober and not, of loving the very thing that was killing you, of being able to imagine life neither with drugs and alcohol nor without them. They also recognized bullshit, and manipulation, and meaningless intellectualization as a way of evading terrible truths—and on many days the most helpful thing they did was to laugh at me and make fun of my dodges (which were, I realize now, pathetically easy for a fellow addict to spot), and to advise me just not to use chemicals today because tomorrow might very well look different. Advice like this sounds too simplistic to be helpful, but it was crucial.

In his biography of Wallace, D. T. Max argues that he quickly understood the ways that recovery was also a "literary opportunity." Wallace was learning a new world; he was glimpsing hundreds of exposed interior lives. He kept a list called "Heard in Meetings" that still remains in his archives, written on ordinary yellow lined paper:

> "The happiness of being among people. Just a person among people."
> "They say it's good for the soul, but I don't feel nothing inside you could call a soul."
> "I shit myself every day for years."
> "I came in to save my ass and found my soul was attached."
> "'No' is also an answer to my prayers, as well."
> "It hurts."

But recovery was far from just a source of material for Wallace. Max argues recovery was part of his growing commitment to "single-entendre writing, writing that meant what it said." Recovery shifted Wallace's whole notion of what writing could do, what purpose it might serve—made him want to dramatize the saving alchemy of community, the transformative force of outward-facing attention, the possibilities of simplicity as an alternative to the clever alibis of complexity: *meaningless intellectualization as a way of evading terrible truths.*

In *Infinite Jest*, Wallace describes irony and recovery as oil and water: "An ironist in a Boston AA meeting is a witch in church." The novel believes in the sincere wisdom an ironist might scoff at, the kind you might find on a tear-off calendar or a daily prayer book. It doesn't believe in bromides as revelations, but it believes in what they seek—the possibility of common ground.

After Hurricane Irene, our first August back in New Haven, the world was raw and wet and dazed. The Occupy movement filled

Zuccotti Park, and then our own downtown green: a cluster of tarps and tents that sheltered protesters alongside people who had already been homeless. Years before, I might have dismissed a movement without a clear agenda as something without purpose, but collectivity itself had started to seem purposeful — the construction of a horizontal society right there on the grass, behind the downtown churches that held our meetings in their basements.

Dave and I lived in a brick loft whose walls were literally crumbling, leaving little piles of brick dust in the corners. From a huge circular window in our living room, we could see the old converted corset factory where we'd gotten drunk that night Peter first found out about us, back when our love still felt reckless and destined, an animal with an incontestable will of its own.

In this current chapter of our love, three years later — in which I was sober, and we were struggling to find our pulse — we had friends over to a breakfast-for-dinner party one night: eggs scrambled with melted ribbons of cheese, bacon and fried potatoes that filled the apartment with salty humidity. We ate syrup-soggy pancakes while dusk fell over the smokestacks by the railroad tracks. Other people drank mimosas and I drank orange juice and it was okay, though it was an okay where I still had to remind myself, *This is okay.* While we were washing dishes at the end of the night, I went into the bathroom and willed myself to remember that a year before I would have been yelling at Dave right now, or fuming, or flinching at his touch. And I wasn't.

But it didn't make everything right. After everyone left, on that night and others, I watched Dave physically drain out — almost like he was deflating. We could still put on the show of ourselves for other people, but on our own we were becoming shells. There was something tender and forced about our jokes, saturated with effort. I'd been sober nine months, and I was going to meetings five times a week, sometimes seven. After that first New Haven meeting, I'd flung myself into them fully, and I'd also started working with a new sponsor, Susan, a lawyer in her sixties who wore big chunky beaded necklaces and drank her lattes with a straw. The first time I ever heard her speak, she talked about packing a magnum bottle of wine to take with her to rehab. That made more sense to me than someone saying, "You never have to drink again." It made me think of the calligraphy poster in *Infinite Jest*, hanging in the Ennet House bathroom: EVERYTHING I'VE EVER LET GO OF HAD CLAW MARKS ON IT.

Susan was warm and sarcastic and real about what hurt; she held me accountable to every rule I wanted to be an exception to. She had ended her marriage just a few months after getting back from rehab, which program wisdom didn't recommend. You were supposed to wait a year before you made any big life choices. But Susan's divorce had also opened up the next era of her life: a move away from the Connecticut suburb where she'd lived for decades, to a downtown studio with a piano in the corner and gauzy afternoon light. She drove women to meetings four or five days a week. Sobriety had granted her enough clarity to see that the life she'd spent decades creating wasn't the one she wanted to stay inside of—which was a gift, but not a gift anyone wants. I didn't think I was living Susan's story—the story of sobriety as rupture—but I was oddly compelled by it: the idea that happiness might look like the end of love, rather than its repair.

During that first year of recovery, I felt so liberated from one type of dependence, that bodily thirst, that I started to push back against the idea of dependence itself. It was hard to distinguish between the kinds of desire that might compose me and those that would diminish me. In many ways, AA was all about embracing need: resisting self-sufficiency, seeking humility, granting help and receiving it. But as I grew comfortable inside the system of validated need AA provided, I grew less comfortable with the more diffuse, nebulous, cluttered needs that defined my relationship with Dave. With him, I started to cauterize every need like an open wound. I stopped asking him for anything. Meetings were easier than love because there was a simple pattern: *Do* x, *do* y, *do* z. You knew you were doing what you were supposed to. Love was more like: *Do* x, *or else do* y, *hope for* z, *and pray something works, and maybe it will, and probably it won't.*

Many evenings I was away from our apartment, at AA meetings or with my sponsor, and often left in the morning, sometimes before Dave woke, to walk to an early meeting downtown. On a Saturday afternoon Dave suggested we spend together, I told him I was going to an apple orchard with two girls from the program and I could see a flicker of hurt, or disappointment. There was beauty in my life that day—wind-rustled apple trees, soft soil, the mush of fallen fruit— but it was a beauty I inhabited without him. I never imagined he'd feel excluded, though—only thought he'd be relieved I wanted less.

That fall, I lived in a different version of New Haven than I'd lived in the first time around. This new version of the city was less cloistered by the university, more populated by everyone who lived beyond its borders. At meetings, I ended up in homeless shelters and retirement homes, swapping numbers with women after they'd gotten their court-order slips signed. I was moving between the worlds of graduate school and recovery, straddling the powerful rifts between their conflicting imperatives: *Think harder. Don't overthink it. Say something new. You can't say anything new. Interrogate simplicity. Keep it simple. Be loved because you're smart. Be loved because you are.* My dissertation was reckoning with a question I hoped might bridge these worlds, examining authors who'd tried to get sober and exploring how recovery had become part of their creative lives. It wasn't criticism as autobiography, exactly, so much as speculative autobiography—trying to find a map for what my own sober creativity might look like.

Once a week, I led an undergraduate discussion section for a lecture course on Faulkner, Fitzgerald, and Hemingway: the old, mythic drunks. In one of our classes, we talked about "Babylon Revisited," Fitzgerald's short story about an alcoholic named Charlie who comes back to Paris—the city where he used to live, where his wife died—

and finds that he can no longer stand his old life of debauchery. He just wants to become a better father. At the end of the story, he loses custody of his daughter but manages to limit himself to just one drink. I asked my students if they thought the story reached any resolution. Would things turn around for Charlie? I knew this wasn't how we were supposed to teach, acting as if Charlie was a real guy — someone I'd met at a meeting, say — and we were just speculating about his fate; acting as if he were another number on a Narco Farm intake slip (Prognosis guarded). But I was seeking company in pretty much every story I encountered. So I asked my students if they thought Charlie would ever manage to stay sober, and kept calling on people until finally someone said yes, he thought he would.

I don't want to sound melodramatic here," Raymond Carver wrote to his editor Gordon Lish in 1980, protesting a drastic round of edits, "but I've come back from the grave to start writing stories once more." By *the grave*, Carver meant the drinking that had almost killed him, and by *stories* he meant the stories in *What We Talk About When We Talk About Love*, the ones he'd been writing since getting sober, in 1977. Lish's radical edits threatened Carver's faith in his newfound sober creativity from many directions at once. "I'm serious," Carver wrote, insisting the stories were "intimately hooked up with my getting well, recovering, gaining back some little self-esteem and feeling of worth as a writer and a human being."

Although Carver's early sobriety stories were full of desperation, they were also shot through with unexpected veins of hope and surprising moments of connection — the residue of recovery. But Lish had always been attracted to Carver's "bleakness." When Lish edited the early sobriety stories, it wasn't just that he explicitly downplayed references to drinking and AA, he also pushed back against what he understood as the lurking threat of sentimentality — places where he felt the prose reaching for too much sappy affinity or ham-handed redemption. Carver's original versions, written during the days when he was first finding respite in AA's community of strangers, often landed on moments when strangers connected in odd or surprising ways: feeding each other, identifying with each other, praying for each other. But Lish's edited endings usually landed on moments of disdain or unintentional cruelty instead, strangers resenting or abusing each other. Poet Tess Gallagher, Carver's partner at the time, recalled:

> I remember [Ray's] bafflement at one particular suggestion: that he remove all the references to drinking from the stories. I remember responding that his editor must not realize what Ray had been through, that he had nearly died from alcoholism and that alcohol was practically a character in the stories. This was to be Ray's first book since he had become sober. He was telling the truth about physical and emotional damage and what it was like to come back from the dead.

Near the end of his drinking, Carver hadn't been anything like the rogue I'd once imagined. He was bloated and overweight. He lived like a hermit, and often called his students to cancel class because he was too sick to teach. When he invited three of them to dinner one night, they ate Hamburger Helper and shared a single fork. When he came back to Iowa City to give a reading before his first book came out, it should have been like the return of a conquering hero—but he was so drunk the audience could barely understand a word he said. This wasn't reckless debauchery or existential knowledge plucked from the dark maw of some universal psychic void; this was just a human body pushed to the edge of its own poisoning.

Carver finally stopped drinking on June 2, 1977. "If you want the truth," he said in one interview, "I'm prouder of that, that I've quit drinking, than I am of anything in my life."

❖

The stories Carver wrote in early sobriety weren't just full of the chaos of drinking but also the possibilities of recovery. They were full of guys who'd drunk too much and were trying to patch things up with their wives. Full of gin ghosts and AA commitments. Full of guys learning to fish and to pray; a sober man sneaking out of his house in the middle of the night to kill slugs; a sober man lying about knowing famous astronauts; a drunk man stealing his estranged wife's holiday pies. One man listens to his wife remembering how he carried her to the bathroom when she was pregnant—"no one else could ever love me in that way, that much," she says—while he obsesses about the half-pint of whiskey hidden under her couch cushion: "I began to hope she might soon have to get up."

These sobriety stories carry the pulse of the booze not just in the obvious places, in the whiskey shots and the morning doses of champagne and the clever one-liners about drinking ("Booze takes a lot of time and effort if you're going to do a good job with it"), but in those quiet moments when characters have fallen away from each other and don't know how to come together again. These silences are the hollow spaces that booze wants to fill.

When Carver first saw Lish's versions, not just whittled but spiritually rearranged, he couldn't stomach the thought of their publication. At this point, the two men had known each other for nearly a decade. Lish had given Carver his big break when he acquired one of his stories for *Esquire* in 1971, and he'd been editing him ever since. This time he'd removed more than half his prose, and under the guise of renovating Carver's style, he smuggled in a different vision of human nature—less prone to care, concern, and empathetic imagination; and more inclined to rupture, resentment, and disconnect. In his 1981 review of the collection, critic Michael Wood lamented the "unkindness and condescension of some of these stories," the same stories about which Carver had written to Lish: "I don't want to lose track, lose touch with the little human connections."

It's not clear why Carver allowed his stories to be published with the edits he resisted so vehemently, but it's quite possible his consent was a product of the same fragility that had made him worry about the edits in the first place: He was eager for the affirmation of a book, hated the idea of disappointing anyone, and wanted to believe in the future of his sober writing. But the book that came into the world wasn't the same book Carver had written.

In the story eventually published as "The Bath," the most famous in the collection—a story Lish cut to less than a third of its original length—a boy named Scotty is struck by a car on the morning of his birthday. While he's lying in a coma in the hospital, his parents start getting calls from a menacing stranger who turns out to be the baker who made Scotty's birthday cake, growing increasingly irritated that nobody ever came to pick it up. When the boy's mother picks up the phone, asking—utterly desperate—if it's someone calling for news of her son, the baker says: "It is about Scotty. It has to do with Scotty, yes." In Lish's version, the story ends on that baker's *yes*, his voice over the phone, that closing beat of irony and unwitting brutality. We don't find out if the boy lives or dies. This version of the story is about senseless tragedy and the human fissures it illuminates; about the ways distance can verge into malice.

But Carver's original version, "A Small, Good Thing," eventually published years later, doesn't close with the phone call. Scotty's parents end up visiting the baker in his shop and explaining their loss—in this version, their son has died. After they tell him what happened, the baker feeds them "warm cinnamon rolls just out of the oven, the icing still runny," and a loaf of fresh dark bread, telling them about his own weary days: "They listened to him. They ate what they could. They swallowed the dark bread. It was like daylight under the fluorescent trays of light."

The baker offers the minor solace of tangible pleasure—the kind of "small, good thing" my own days in a hot Iowa kitchen had taught me something about—and this broken bread ultimately catalyzes another type of communion: "They talked on into the early morning, the high pale cast of light in the windows, and they did not think of leaving."

Carver's original ending offers neither utter despair nor unequivocal redemption. It's more like chiaroscuro, light and dark: The parents are granted temporary respite from their grief, and the baker isn't entirely defined by callousness. The couple's son is gone, but the world isn't an utterly irredeemable and indifferent place. However small its doses, grace comes with stealth and arrives from unexpected corners—incomplete, imperfect, important.

In the story Lish called "After the Denim," an elderly sober man finds himself enraged by a young hippie couple he spots cheating at bingo. Underneath this rage, he's in anguish over the return of his wife's cancer, and the story ends with his grief expressed as anger—with the man picking up his needlework and "stab[bing] at the eye with a length of blue silk thread." But the original version of the story, which Carver had called "If It Please You," ends not with anger—a man stabbing at his needlework, powerless to change fate, furious with those whom fate has treated better—but with the inexplicable alchemy of anger turning into something more forgiving. "He and the hippie were in the same boat," the old man thinks, and senses "something stir inside him again, but it was not anger this time." The story closes with this "something" stirring:

> This time he was able to include the girl and the hippie in his prayers. Let them have it, yes, drive vans and be arrogant and laugh and wear rings, even cheat if they wanted. Meanwhile, prayers were needed. They could use them too, even his, especially his, in fact. "If it please you," he said in the new prayers for all of them, the living and the dead.

This act of prayer, not simply praying for a stranger but for a stranger he loathes, is actually a specific part of AA teaching: *If you have a resentment you want to be free of, if you will pray for the person or thing that you resent, you will be free.*

Lish's edits may have been fighting prose Lish understood as sentimental, but if sentimentality indulges in false emotion that turns away from the world ("the wet eyes of the sentimentalist betray his aversion to experience...his arid heart," as James Baldwin put it), then Carver never turns away from the complexity of experience. The old man's prayer is an ending that allows for multiple layers of emotion—grace alongside fury—rather than settling into a simpler and more predictable vein of unmediated disdain. Carver's solace is vexed and hard-won, but his endings have faith in the communion of dark bread—in small, good things exchanged in the deep night.

A few years after this fraught round of edits, Carver insisted to Lish that his next story collection couldn't go through the same process: "Gordon, God's truth, and I may as well say it out now, I can't undergo the kind of surgical amputation and transplant that might make them someway fit into the carton so the lid will close. There may have to be limbs and heads of hair sticking out. My heart won't take it otherwise. It will simply burst, and I mean that." Carver was willing to risk melodrama (*It will simply burst*) to stand behind the writing of his recovery—writing that was messier, full of grit and swell, ragged intimacies and inexplicable attachments. He wanted to stand behind stories that didn't end on irony, stories awkward and grasping enough to hold the longings of sobriety, with its strange permissions and unexpected bonds.

That first fall back in New Haven, I started going to a meeting downtown at seven-thirty every morning. Walking on Chapel Street just past seven—during early winter, when it stayed dark late—took me through the quieter city that got swallowed up each morning once the familiar one awoke. Lights flicked into sharp fluorescence at the tire shop; commuter trains deposited plaid-scarfed businessmen on the State Street platform; the dollar store showed a window full of kids' backpacks and discount rolling suitcases through its chain-metal grating.

The seven-thirty meeting was held in a stately stone building downtown. About half its crowd had come straight from one of the city's homeless shelters, which asked clients to leave at seven. Some people came for the meeting, and others came for the coffee—bitter and scalding, served with a handful of creamers on a table in the back—and many probably came for both. It wasn't always clear what someone had come for, and it was probably rarely only one thing anyway. The meeting was full of old-timers, some sober for decades, who sustained a fierce and opaque ecosystem of ancient feuds and intimacies. An elderly black man named Theo was the unofficial spiritual leader of the group. You could tell he'd been through a lot of shit but wasn't putting it in your face, and he showed up every morning—just like he'd showed up every morning for decades.

At that meeting, I was painfully aware of how much I had, and how much I hadn't lost. I was wary of how anything I shared might come across to others in the room, people who were struggling with so much more: the woman fighting for custody of her kids; the guy who'd been in and out of shelters for almost a year, but had finally gotten a job at a pizza parlor in town. How could comparing my addiction to theirs seem like anything but a misunderstanding of what they'd suffered? I didn't want to suggest *I've been through that too*, with my very presence—when of course I hadn't. My story was contoured by desire more than loss.

But I was surprised by the ways other people sought commonality, and at a certain point I realized I was the one projecting difference by assuming others felt it. Believing in what we shared didn't have to make me blind to what we didn't. Resonance wasn't the same as conflation. It didn't mean pretending we'd all lived the same thing. It just meant listening. People had gotten punched in the face for different reasons, but drinking had made all our bodies vulnerable. We weren't there to assume or insist on perfect correspondence; we were there to open ourselves to the possibility of company.

I liked how often people at that meeting said: "I just can't get a fucking break." How often they got angry at other people, at their own lives. One day a man stood up and shouted at another man across the room: "When are you gonna give me back that twenty bucks?" The guy called back: "Why don't you go *suck* someone for twenty bucks?" It was liberating to hear voices break from the sacrosanct script of chanting the steps, from the promises or the preamble: "a fellowship of men and women who share their experience, strength, and hope with each other that they may solve their common problem." And also, honestly, so they could get something straight about money that was owed, or how so-and-so was fucking *wrong*. People were putting their lives back together after many losses and many relapses. Desire and regret still glowed fiercely in that room, still hot to the touch.

Infinite Jest is honest about the weirdness of depersonalized good-will in recovery—what it feels like to be loved indiscriminately, not for your qualities but just *stam*, "because because." The book understands the discomfort of hearing the program promise, *Let us love you until you learn to love yourself,* and the aggressive insistence of being hugged by strangers. After a meeting, one character asks a stranger: "You gone risk vulnerability and discomfort and hug my ass, or do I gone fucking rip your head off and *shit* down your neck?"

Don Gately was unlike any literary hero I'd ever encountered: a sober felon with a big square head, his meaty tattooed hands often carrying the cakes he bakes for other people's sobriety birthdays. In meetings, he talks about "fucking up in sobriety," and he gets irritated at sober drunks all the time. When someone complains too much, he uses his pinkie finger to mime the world's smallest viola playing the theme from *The Sorrow and the Pity*. Gately's no saint. That's why he made salvation seem possible. That's what I loved about sobriety in the book—it wasn't stolid, or pedantic; it was palpable and crackling and absurd. It was so brutally alive on every page.

After Gately protects an asshole rehab resident in a gunfight and ends up getting shot, he spends his hospital days refusing morphine. "No one single instant of it was unendurable," he thinks. "What was undealable-with was the thought of all the instants all lined up and stretching ahead, glittering." It reminded me of how I'd imagined sobriety: one dull evening after another, a mountain of dried-up tea bags—no single night impossible, their infinite horizon unthinkable. *We're all drama queens, even in our sobriety:* My dry nights were gunshot wounds.

But even when Gately is enduring "emergency-type pain, like scream-and-yank-your-charred-hand-off-the-stove-type pain," he still spends most of his time—somewhat grudgingly—listening to other people unload their woes: "Gately wanted to tell Tiny Ewell that he could totally fucking I.D. with Ewell's feelings, and that if he, Tiny, could just hang in and tote that bale and put one little well-shined shoe in front of the other everything would end up all right." In the hospital, Gately becomes a huge mute confessional booth, like Luther holding court at Seneca, silent and smoking at the kitchen table while everyone else talked.

Infinite Jest was full of people like me, people who were trying to outsmart recovery but still sought affirmation from its rituals—like one businessman in a Boston AA meeting, who has "the sort of professional background where he's used to trying to impress gatherings of persons." Lying in his hospital bed, Gately imagines himself standing "at a lavish Commitment podium, like at an AA convention, offhandedly saying something that got an enormous laugh." Gately isn't taking morphine, sure, but he's also fantasizing about how he'll tell the story of that heroism in a meeting someday. Gately shared my desperate desire to get the loudest applause, to tell a story that wouldn't make a man call out "This is boring!" ever again. The book could *totally fucking I.D.* with the ways my ego intruded on my recovery. It knew the ordinariness of that intrusion. It understood my wariness about recovery culture. It got my embarrassment and my worship. It showed me that my disdain for unoriginal clichés was entirely unoriginal. It gave me hope because its hope was so unvarnished.

I read *Infinite Jest* like a desperate old man running his metal detector over the sand, waiting for every ding that signified buried wisdom—even though I worried that Wallace was too smart to be read with this type of greed. I felt indicted by critics like Christian Lorentzen, who wrote disdainfully of "readers who look to novels and novelists for instruction on how to lead their lives," who were drawn to Wallace's "bromides about brains beating like hearts, literature as a salve for loneliness, and novels comforting the afflicted and afflicting the comfortable, etc." But I was bromide-dependent. The most important things I'd ever endured or believed probably lived in Lorentzen's *etc.*, covering their faces in shame. I read Wallace with my psychic highlighter always at the ready. Perhaps that made me simplify him, as I sucked on lozenges of truth—"sometimes human beings have to just sit in one place and, like, *hurt*"—but his novel had gotten me through plenty of moments of just sitting there and, like, hurting. It pursued what Berryman called "wisdom-work."

In my PhD program, other grad students talked about their undergraduate students with fond condescension, how they were always looking for *the moral of the story*, or *the lesson to learn*. But fuck that easy dismissal. Fuck that charge of reduction, and that snickering at bromides. Because sometimes I just needed to sit there and remember that *Infinite Jest* said sometimes I just needed to sit there and, like, hurt. Sometimes I needed the single-entendre truth. Sometimes I needed the cherry blossoms, the abundant meat aisle, the cold sunlight, the new life. "Too simple?" Wallace wrote in the margin of one of his self-help books. "Or just that simple?"

I'd been so afraid of sobriety as a flatline, as Jackson had been afraid of sobriety as a flatline, as Berryman and Stephen King and Denis Johnson and the older waitress sitting at the Tuesday-morning meeting had been afraid of sobriety as a flatline. I'd been afraid that meetings were basically lobotomies served alongside coffee-flavored water and Chips Ahoy!; afraid that even if sobriety could offer stability and sincerity and maybe even salvation, it could never be a story. But *Infinite Jest* knew better. It wasn't that the novel's brilliance had survived the deadening force of sobriety. Its brilliance depended on what sobriety had wrought.

On his first sobriety birthday, Wallace received a copy of a 1987 play called "Bill W. and Dr. Bob" as a gift from his sponsor. The cover was inscribed "To David, Congratulations on Year 1" and featured an illustration that suggested fellowship: two men in suits, their faces out of frame, one holding a mug of coffee with a wisp of steam curling out of it. Wallace marked only one passage, a piece of dialogue:

> DR. BOB (*Inching his chair closer*): If I don't drink, I'm a monster. I need it to function, to be a doctor, husband, father. Without it, I'm so afraid, I can't function at all. Booze is the glue holding me together, the one thing I can count on.

Next to that, Wallace wrote just three words: "How I Feel."

It's easy to feel good about resonance. It's actually quite addictive, the nodding rhythm of communion — *Yes, I know how you feel.* This presumed empathy tastes righteous and expansive on the tongue. During my early days of sobriety, I started seeing resonance everywhere, like a primary color I'd never noticed. One afternoon I sat at an oak desk tucked in the silent hallways of the library, and noticed what a stranger had carved in the wood: *I am a virgin*. Then others had written around that: *Me too. So am I. So am I! So am I!*

But the flip side of communion's humility, being willing to say *I'm not the only one*, is the danger of assumption or conflation: *I've felt what you've felt*. It's so satisfying to acknowledge what's shared that it can become its own temptation — to insist on commonality everywhere.

Partway through his book about working with skid-row addicts, clinician Gabor Maté brings himself into the frame: "Hello, my name is Gabor, and I am a compulsive classical music shopper." After the portraits that have come before — crack and heroin addicts who are homeless or turning tricks, losing limbs to infections at their injection sites — Maté's confession reads at first like a joke, then like a provocation, asking us to accept a continuity he suspects we will initially resist. Describing the thousands of dollars he has compulsively spent on classical music, the way he plays it loud to drown out his family, Maté acknowledges that his addiction wears "dainty white gloves," but he also insists on a single "addiction process" that manifests across a continuum of behaviors: "the frantic self-soothing of overeaters or shopaholics; the obsessions of gamblers, sexaholics, and compulsive Internet users; or the socially acceptable and even admired behaviors of the workaholic." It's what Eve Kosofsky Sedgwick calls "addiction attribution," the ways we try to understand everything as addiction: shopping, email, even exercise, the mascot of willpower. Addiction attribution can become an addiction in its own right. The satisfaction of an expansive rubric offers its own intoxication: *We're all in this together!* If addiction is a continuum, then we all get to live on its axis somewhere, blasting Beethoven to drown out the voices of our children, or gorging on chocolate after we get fired.

But I'm wary of attributing addiction so broadly it ceases to mean anything besides compulsively desiring something capable of causing harm. I don't want to ignore the particular physical mechanisms of addiction by mining it too easily for universal truths: *We all crave. We all compensate. We all seek relief.* Because we don't all seek in the same ways, and the seeking doesn't always punish the seeker. It's important to acknowledge the specific damage wrought by certain cravings: what they can do to a brain, what they can do to a life.

When the American Psychiatric Association released the fifth edition of its Diagnostic and Statistical Manual of Mental Disorders, in 2013, and officially changed its definition of "substance use disorder" from a category to a spectrum, many scientists were afraid that its broadened criteria for addiction would effectively produce too many addicts—that it would, in essence, make *everyone* who had ever drunk recklessly an addict, and destroy a vital distinction between dysfunction and disease.

What do I think? That it's important not to lose our grip on the notion of disease or its physical mechanisms by defining it too broadly, but it's also true that everyone has longed for something that harms her. I wish we could invoke that universality not to render the boundaries of addiction utterly porous, but to humanize those under its thrall.

When I asked my own diary, drunk, *Am I an alcoholic?* I was trying to answer a question about desire: When does ordinary craving become pathology? Now I think: When it becomes tyrannical enough to summon shame. When it stops constituting the self, and begins to construe it as lack. When you want to stop, and can't; and try again, and can't; and try again, and can't. "It is not till many fixes pass that your desire is need," George Cain wrote. "It was what I'd been born for, waiting for all my life."

When I asked my own diary, drunk, *Am I an alcoholic?* I was looking for a category that might tell me whether my pain was real—as if drinking more would make it incontestable. Of course my pain was real, just like everyone's. Of course it wasn't quite like anyone's, just like everyone's.

As culprit and cause, drinking offered a convenient vessel for certain difficulties I found harder to pin down precisely. When I was first getting sober, I wrote myself a story about my relationship with Dave in which I was the source of our troubles, my insecurity and distrust, and booze was the source of *my* troubles—and so, by getting rid of the booze, I'd start to fix them. But we were less broken than that, or more broken than that, and back in New Haven an odd, eerie quiet settled over our joint life: days in libraries; stew bubbling in the slow cooker; old coffee grounds in the French press, then the trash can. This calm didn't feel like relief from fighting; it was more distant than that. In some strange, corrosive way, our fights had been intimate and binding: toxic but saturating, impossible to turn away from. Fighting meant we were both fully present. Back in New Haven we were kinder with each other, gentler, but also robotic somehow; when we came back home to each other at the end of the day, it was as if we were both reaching for bodies that weren't quite there.

That fall we went to another wedding—our tenth or twelfth or hundredth, who could count—and pitched our tent in a meadow. The wedding was full of people who had been in various a cappella groups with the groom, and every so often a cluster of strangers would break into song beside me, like a spontaneous brush fire. "I promise to enjoy spirituality with you," the bride told the groom during their vows. "I promise to enjoy nature with you," he replied. That night it rained until dawn and I woke up tangled in a corner of our tent, muddy ground slippery beneath the thin vinyl floor—my body fully out of our sleeping bag, as if I'd been trying to roll as far away from Dave as possible. He took a photo of me that morning, standing in my long underwear outside the tent, with the meadow and hills behind, and once the photo had been glossed with the right cell phone filter, it made our campsite look like a magical elfin land. "Gorgeous!" said everyone on Facebook. But I knew I'd actually been irritated and tired, dispirited by the happiness of others.

The night before, the reception had been a *supra*, a traditional Georgian feast that revolved around an elaborate and dizzyingly comprehensive series of toasts—to God, to the dead, to the living, to our tents—with the bride and groom drinking red wine from a silver-lipped, animal-furred drinking horn. With each new round of toasts, a different stranger looked at me and frowned.

"Don't you know?" one finally said. "It's horrible luck to toast with water."

Back home, I'd started to smell something strange in our bedroom: a barn smell, like soggy hay or damp fur, something wet and animal. The prior tenants had told us they'd had a squirrel infestation, and I wondered if they were still nesting behind our brick walls, their little burrows soaked with urine and packed with nuts, squirming with hairless babies—helpless, grotesque creatures wriggling all around us.

When we started spotting mice, it was almost a relief. There *was* something wrong, and we would get rid of it. We set up snap traps under our cupboards and smeared them carefully with gobs of peanut butter. At first the mice managed to steal the peanut butter without setting them off, licking the yellow plastic paddles absolutely clean, like tiny superheroes with one specially honed skill. I sat on the couch and watched one mouse move so gracefully—with so little weight on its claws, and such a barely present tongue—that it managed to get everything it wanted without dying.

We set up glue traps next, and woke in the night to hear one mouse squealing as he struggled: still horribly, painfully alive. We lay beside each other, listening. It was impossible to sleep. Finally, Dave got up and smacked the mouse against the floor. A mercy kill. The apartment grew quiet again.

When I confessed to Susan that I'd begun to fantasize about breaking up with Dave, just imagining what it might be like, she reminded me that the program suggested against making any major changes in the first year of sobriety, and that included ending a relationship. I wanted to say, *You ended yours.* She had an apartment of her own, a life alone that seemed—somehow—deeply generative.

In recovery meetings, I was surrounded by the stories of people who were living in the clean, empty aftermaths of new beginnings: leaving old relationships, old homes, old cities, and beginning again at rehab, in meetings, with the steps. In truth, plenty of people were simply getting sober inside the lives they'd always lived—with the same jobs, the same marriages, the same children—but I kept seeing the story of rebirth because it was the story I wanted to see: people who were starting again, who were lonely and free. When I looked at Dave, I felt exhausted, as if our relationship was a messy room I had to clean up. Part of me craved the relief of a clean beginning—a pure loss, then rebuilding on my own.

Seneca House compelled me because it had been the threshold of a new beginning, for thousands of addicts, or at least its promise. I wanted to see the place for myself. But by the time I visited Seneca Creek in 2015, the house itself was just a ghost: a bare patch of grassy land tucked between the water and the woods. The building had been torn down after the rehab shut its doors in 1992, after an unsuccessful merger with a larger treatment center. I'd driven out with Sawyer the Lawyer, who now suffered from a degenerative muscle disease that kept him largely immobilized; so we'd taken a special van outfitted to accommodate his wheelchair.

Over the phone, Sawyer had referred to the disease as his "affliction" in a wry tone that suggested scare quotes. After decades spent in a community whose currency was shared pain, Sawyer knew the various tones in which suffering could be articulated. He knew what it sounded like when people milked their lives for drama, and he was choosing another tone of voice: matter-of-fact, calling out the temptation to dramatize rather than indulging it. He also had cancer in his prostate, and in one of his ribs. These maladies were mentioned as afterthoughts.

When I visited Sawyer at his home in Maryland, just a half hour from Seneca Creek, it was a July day so hot and bright it threatened to close his morning glories by noon. His fridge was cluttered with the faces of his grandkids, a granddaughter's carefully typed babysitting ad: *I am serious and dependable.* Getting Sawyer settled in his van required two motorized wheelchairs, a walker, and one motorized chairlift. I secured his motorized wheelchair to the interior of his van with four straps, harnessed to latches on the floor, and—terrified he'd come unstuck—drove at a steady twenty miles per hour, my sweaty palms locked on the steering wheel. From the back of the van, Sawyer pointed out the old clapboard general store down the road from Seneca, built and opened in 1901, where Seneca guests had walked to buy the cigarettes they weren't supposed to smoke indoors. He pointed out the golf course that the guests had walked across during Hurricane Agnes, to stay in a cheap hotel when the house itself flooded.

Back at home, Sawyer hadn't wanted to give me his drunkalog: the stories of Chinatown rotgut and his kids eating by candlelight. He'd wanted to talk instead about self-improvement and his success in sobriety: as an attorney, as a real estate developer in Delaware, as a recovery diplomat in his parents' homeland, where he'd once been called, he said, the Bill Wilson of Lithuania. He'd visited alcohol wards all over the country in 1991, just after it declared its independence from the Soviet Union, and left behind a copy of the Big Book translated into Lithuanian.

This work in Lithuania was a crucial part of the story Sawyer wanted to tell about himself—in which the upward mobility of his sobriety had been the culmination of a life committed to self-supporting labor: guarding produce stands overnight, as a boy, or working in a steel mill where molten steel poured like quicksilver over the flames. Sobriety allowed Sawyer to keep following the narrative arc he knew he'd been destined for: the story of a maid's son who'd done right by his mother's dreams, a story that began when his mother took him to the 1933 Century of Progress Exposition in Chicago and he saw the highways of the future, their impossible swirl and swoop. That day he felt awe—wanted to become someone who built things, someone with power, someone who changed the world.

The sobriety story Sawyer told me was the story he'd constructed for himself to live inside of, like a house by the banks of a creek: a story in which he'd worked hard and been rewarded for that hard work, in which that work functioned as penance for drinking away the money his mother had saved for his education, or the money his family had needed for the gas bill. In his narrative, industry was the theater of his recovery. Good intentions turned into profit, and sobriety made the alchemy possible.

It wasn't until we were parked by the old Seneca site, with the engine killed, that Sawyer told me about the arrests, or the girl he'd fallen for in Baltimore ("the one who got away") before he was married, and how he ruined his chances by getting drunk before their first date. It was as if the creek itself—or the memory of the house—had opened something in him, as if we were having our own meeting, right there by the water, surrounded by the ghost walls of a home he'd helped build. We faced the lock house on the canal, with its white-washed bricks. Summer campers in life jackets gathered by the water in pockets of rustling neon orange.

When he wrote poems, Sawyer said, they weren't about his drinking. They were about his sober awe. He was still a boy wondering at the impossible highways of the future, still a man who was shown a bend in a creek, a dirty old fishing hostel, and thought, *Sure, a bunch of drunks could stay here for a while.* Decades after it got torn down, he found himself buckled into a motorized wheelchair by the same creek, telling a stranger *what it was like*—a stranger fifty-five years younger, who fifty-five years after Sawyer got sober gave her own version of the same moist-eyed apologies for the same stubborn thirst.

W"e tell ourselves stories in order to live," Joan Didion wrote, and at first I took her words as gospel: *Stories help us survive!* But eventually I realized they were more like an admonition — a suggestion that there was something compromised and shameful about our dependence on their false coherence. When Didion wrote, "I began to doubt the premises of all the stories I had ever told myself," understood her skepticism as an accusation: trusting stories was naive, a refusal to confront actuality in all its senselessness.

But in recovery, I started to believe again that stories could do all the things Didion had taught me to distrust, that they could lend meaningful arcs of cohesion; that they could save us from our lives by letting us construct ourselves. I'd always had faith in doubt — in questioning and undermining, looking for fissures, splitting the seams of tidy resolution to find the complexity teeming underneath — but I started to wonder if sometimes doubt was just an easy alibi, a way to avoid the more precarious state of affirmation, making yourself vulnerable by standing behind something that could be criticized, disproven, or ridiculed. Maybe it was just as much a crutch to doubt stories as to stand behind them. It was so easy to point out gaps without filling them, to duck into the foxhole of ambivalence. Maybe sometimes you just had to accept that the story of your life was a crafted thing — selected, curated, skewed in service of things you could name and probably other things you couldn't. Maybe you could accept all that, and still believe it might do you, or someone else, some good.

Recovery reminded me that storytelling was ultimately about community, not self-deception. Recovery didn't say: *We tell ourselves stories in order to live*. It said: *We tell others our stories in order to help them live, too*.

When I went looking for the tales of Seneca House, I found that every sobriety story had its own particular veins of redemption. Sawyer crafted the story of his sobriety as a story of accountability — learning to be a responsible father — and manifest destiny. That's why he needed to tell me about how much money he made. Gwen told her story as a tale of necessary humbling; Marcus told his story as a myth of hubris punished; and Shirley narrated sobriety as self-reclamation, finally putting herself first.

If Sawyer told a sobriety story about upward mobility, then Gwen—the mother who'd driven her kids over the Potomac River in a blackout—told one whose first chapter hinged on failure. For the first sixteen months after she started going to meetings, Gwen kept getting nostalgic and picking up again. She saw a Schlitz ad with a woman at the prow of a sailboat, in a long flowing white dress—"You only go around once in life," the voice-over said; "go for all the gusto you can"—and kept trying to figure out if there was a way she could still live on that sailboat, with her white dress billowing in the wind.

Eventually, Gwen got so fed up with AA that she drafted a letter of resignation. The only problem was, she didn't know where to send it. She asked her sponsor, who had been around for a while, and she said: "Why don't you just give it to me?"

Not long afterward, Gwen heard at a meeting that the old wooden fishing hostel—the one across the creek from her house—was getting turned into a rehab. She could see its creaky old sign from her living room window. She thought, *Holy Toledo!* She had to stay sober now, or else she'd be reminded of her failure every time she watched TV. Her last drink was a single shot of warm vodka at two o'clock on a Sunday afternoon. She and her husband had been entertaining all weekend and she'd been so *good*, hadn't drunk a thing, and then once everyone left she went down to the basement bar and poured herself what she'd been denying herself for forty-eight hours straight.

Forty-four years after her last shot, on March 7, 1971, I spent the day with Gwen at her retirement community in Maryland, where she told me about hitting bottom while we stood in the cafeteria line for Tuscan flounder: disappointing her kids, filling the vinegar bottle. When she finally showed up at Seneca, it was to offer her services as a counselor—she was a trained social worker, after all—but Craig the manager wasn't having it. He knew her from AA, and knew she kept relapsing. He said she couldn't be a counselor until she'd been on Antabuse for a year. But she could volunteer if she wanted. So that's how Gwen became the Hobby Lady: teaching residents how to make moccasins, belts, wallets. She came across the bridge every morning with her Gordon setter, Misty.

She spent that year on Antabuse terrified of relapsing. One time she accidentally swallowed crème de menthe that had been poured on a sundae; she tasted it as the ice cream melted over her tongue. After that, she carried the suspicion that even the pleasures still available to her, even hot fudge sundaes, might get her in trouble. But she also wasn't sure what was left of her without drinking. "If you carve me out," she wondered, "will there be enough here to be a person?"

What came after all that humbling? After serving her time as Hobby Lady, Gwen became a counselor at Seneca, and eventually director. She started working there seven days a week, often ten hours a day. By this point, at home, her marriage was in trouble. Her husband just wanted to get back the little girl he'd married, he said. But Gwen told him that little girl had never existed. They eventually divorced, and Gwen threw herself into Seneca House work—a new marriage to replace the old one.

After five years sober, Gwen reread her own letter of resignation from AA. The woman she'd given it to had kept it for years, just so she could give it back. Gwen had effectively sent her resignation letter to a future version of herself, who was living a sobriety she couldn't have imagined.

Four decades later, Gwen told me she was grateful for her grandchildren, who had offered her a second chance to do the things she hadn't done with her own kids. She'd gotten down on the floor to play with them. She'd given them that.

Marcus told his sobriety story as a version of the Icarus legend: He'd flown too close to the sun, in a hundred Saudi airplanes, and then smoked himself skeletal. If drinking and drugging were all about restlessness—flying all over the world, making money, feeling special—then recovery was about giving up the delusion of his own exceptionality. During his first days at Seneca, Marcus could identify with the other residents' cravings but not with their experiences. He'd lived more. But no one believed he'd traveled Bombay to Bangkok to Manila to Honolulu to San Francisco in a month. They'd heard so much bullshit from so many addicts.

Marcus's breakthrough happened in a session with a Seneca counselor named Bart, an older black man with a steady government job. These were things Marcus wanted: a decent salary, a résumé that demanded respect. Marcus was doing a halfhearted First Step in front of the group and Bart said, "Why don't you get real?" That's when something snapped in Marcus. He got so mad he threw his chair across the room and started to see how much anger he had: at his country—at its racism, its hypocrisy—and at himself, too, though he couldn't quite see that yet. He sat on a front-porch bench with the house dog, a beagle named Snoopy, thinking, *I made such a mess*. His family hadn't been a family where you talked about your feelings. He hadn't talked about his feelings much on the train to Mogadishu, or playing baseball with a crack pipe in White Plains, or in those bleary Bangkok bars. But decades later, by the time I met him at a café near Dupont Circle, he'd been talking for years. He'd just come back from a stint working as an election observer in Haiti, where he'd gone to AA meetings in Port-au-Prince, whose slogans were in Creole though the message was the same: *Yon sèl jou nan yon moman* ("One day at a time"). He'd ended up committing much of his professional life to giving other men—the prisoners in his federal rehabilitation program—the tools they needed to speak.

Shirley's sobriety story was about reclamation. For much of her adult life, she'd put herself in servitude—to her husband, to their home, to her children — and drank to make it tolerable. Getting sober was about waking up and saying she needed something for herself. At first she didn't think she'd be able to do twenty-eight days at Seneca, because who would take care of her kids? But one of the Seneca counselors, Madeline, said that Shirley needed to put her sobriety before everything else — kids, marriage, career. Couldn't her husband take care of their children for once?

When Shirley showed up at Seneca, in 1973, she was its 269th guest. She spent her first lunch weeping at a long wooden table, eating a cheeseburger while "Keep On Loving You" played on the stereo. A gruff old man brought her a carton of milk and told her everyone cried when they arrived and everyone cried again when they left. Shirley was happier doing housework at Seneca than she had been doing it at home, because it was more reciprocal — everyone else had chores too — and less like indentured servitude. She cooked for forty people when the cook relapsed and went AWOL. One time she put Tide in the dishwasher instead of Cascade, then spent the next few hours trying to sweep up all the suds as foam crept all the way into the living room.

Shirley was such a good listener that another resident gave her a tourniquet for her bleeding heart. But in group sessions, Madeline pushed her to get honest. "Let's talk about your mother-in-law's crystal," she said, and on Shirley's last day at Seneca, Madeline put her through a marathon session. She got ten counselors in a room and locked the doors, then said, "Let's see how truthful you can be." When Shirley asked what would happen if she needed to go to the bathroom, Madeline said: "You will not piss away your emotions!"

Shirley adored Madeline, who eventually became her sponsor: fierce, but fully present. "I'm right here, love," she'd say.

Before Madeline had become an exhibitionist drunk, running naked in the snow with her husband chasing after her, she'd been a child without parents. She'd grown up in India, orphaned at the age of ten when her stepfather shot her mother and her mother's lover in a

Delhi hotel. Her stepfather had tried to molest Madeline years before that. One day at Seneca when Madeline and Shirley were walking by the creek, Madeline picked up a branch that had been hit by lightning and pointed to its charred core. "You see that blackness?" she told Shirley. "That's how I felt when things happened to me."

To celebrate three years together, our first October back in New Haven, Dave and I went out for dinner at the pizza joint with vinyl booths behind our apartment. We ate clams on a white pie and toasted with white birch beer. House special. "I know it's basically the length of a bathroom break in the scale of your relationship," I wrote to a friend who'd been with his wife for a decade, "but for me three years is forever. I'm proud of us."

We signed up to collect weekly installments of produce from a farm in Woodbridge, a half hour northwest of us: torpedo onions, parsley and collards, bok choy, tatsoi, greens I'd never heard of and had no idea what to do with. Signing up for these weekly bundles was like putting a down payment on the life I wanted to be living but wasn't, quite—a life in which we happily drank seltzer and followed the recipes that came over email from the farm: tangy glazed carrots with cranberries, browned butter pasta with tatsoi, chocolate beet cake. Mostly, the greens wilted in our crisper and left little puddles of brown juice at the corners of the plastic drawer.

Back in Iowa, Dave and his distances—or the ways I projected these distances onto him—had kept our relationship charged by longing. The fact that I could never fully have him meant I always wanted him. Now that he was more available, I was often gone, leaving our apartment many nights to write at a diner outside of town that stayed open twenty-four hours a day. It was called the Athenian, with big glass windows and stone siding, and at two in the morning it was pretty much empty—just a few cops and a tired graveyard-shift waitress. I got curly fries or apple pie and worked on the proposal for my dissertation about writers who had gotten sober. I liked the adrenaline I got from going to the diner late at night, surrounded by desolate strangers. It made sobriety surge with electricity, with late-night caffeine spikes of bitter coffee, and it was often easier to be away from home, away from Dave—as if I were proving something about independence, proving what I didn't need from him any longer.

When I started visiting the archives of writers who had gotten drunk and gotten sober, I was looking for the underbelly of the whiskey-and-ink mythology—for the blood and sweat and vomit of what their drinking had been, and also for what their sobriety had made possible. Finding their voices in the archives reminded me of being at a meeting: all those savage losses lurking under the ways strangers composed themselves.

Every archive had its own rituals: Leave your bags here. Sign your name there. Get your key over here. Use these folders. Use this code. Use this room for your conspiracy research. Wear these headphones for the scratchy recording of the old Creole songs. Buy this postcard of a beat-up kitchen table. Write to this widow for permission. Everything depends upon this pencil stub.

Every archive held the same imperative of careful touch. Every archive was a shrine to the futile task of preserving a life. Every archive was a siren song coaxing the same intimate, deluded ventriloquism—wanting to speak the truth of someone who couldn't speak. Every archive breathed quietly against the shameless volumes of the past, the lost noise of everything broken and breaking, all that violence crackling under fragile yellowed pages.

In a pristine room at Dartmouth, full of cold New Hampshire sunlight, I wanted to refute Charles Jackson's fear of becoming a sapped soul like the other AA folks, *not very bright or interesting or anything*. But when I went looking for the fruits of his sober creativity, I found a manuscript that bored me. When I went looking for the promise that I wasn't losing myself in recovery, I didn't find the resolution of my fears but their reflection—lurking with its gleaming eyes, waiting me out.

Jackson may have told an AA meeting that writing *The Lost Weekend* didn't help him stay sober, but it did console him in the wake of one devastating relapse: "It was absolutely honest, syllable for syllable," he wrote to a friend. "It was a writer really on the beam, telling nothing but universal truth." In his archives, his scribbled handwriting on a cardboard box holding the first typescript evokes his conflicted view of the book: "Original MS of The Lost Weekend Not Valuable but Please Save."

When I read Jackson's letters, I stared down the glowing comet trails of my impossible counterfactual desires: What if he'd treated his wife better, fought his ego better, stayed sober longer? My desires lived in an awkward tense—an impossible past perfect—and at night I went back to the room I was renting in the hills of Vermont from a lesbian couple who lived with their daughters in a bright farmhouse with a Finnish wood-burning stove. Their duck pond was frozen for the season but their chickens were still laying, and they scrambled fresh eggs for breakfast every morning. The residue of their home, its warmth, lingered with me in the archives as I sifted through letters from Jackson's wife, Rhoda, and imagined the marriage she'd never had. "I keep dreaming of what a good and happy marriage could have meant to me," she wrote to her brother-in-law. "How different it would be with love." Years later she told her daughter that Charles was the best thing that had ever happened to her. This was the trick of living, that both feelings could be true at once.

At the Center of Alcohol Studies at Rutgers, where Rhoda worked for decades while her husband kept relapsing, early AA newsletters listed loner meetings with only one member: Waldo in Caracas, Alessandro in Colombia, Mildred at the Taj Mahal Hotel in Delhi. One flyer announced a "30th Anniversary Celebration" where Bill W. would make a live appearance: "In person! In person! In person!"

By the time I got to Stepping Stones, Wilson's home in Westchester, New York—a brown barn-style colonial revival, hobbit-quaint but oddly large—it had become a pilgrimage site. "We always say it's not a successful tour," the director once said, "unless at least one person cries." People cried at the big wooden bed where Wilson and his wife, Lois, read recovery literature to each other every morning. They cried at the artifacts of their daily lives—the can of hair spray, the single bobby pin—and at the kitchen table where Wilson drank gin and pineapple juice while Ebby talked to him about sobriety and Wilson told himself that his gin would last longer than his friend's preaching. They cried at the little silver stove-top coffeepot perched beneath a wall of mugs, the same pot that had brewed coffee for hundreds of newly sober addicts. (My own eyes welled up.) But if this place was a house of worship, Bill Wilson wasn't its god. The god was communion itself: the cups of coffee, the possibility of penetrating the ordinary loneliness of being a drunk.

In Wilson's archives, on an early manuscript of the Big Book, I saw a line he had crossed out from another man's testimony: At "no time did I ever find a place where I could not get liquor ~~when I wanted it~~." *When I wanted it.* Had there been a time when he didn't? The words were already implied. Something in me rose to salute Wilson's strike-through. It was like nodding at a meeting: *Amen.*

The evening I left Berryman's archives for the last time—after days spent poring over AA step work covered with coffee stains and cigarette burns—my Uber driver was a man named Kyle who'd recently come back to Minnesota from the West Coast, where he had been working graveyard shifts as a poker dealer in a speakeasy. He had come back to get away from a life that had grown toxic, he told me—too much drinking, a full-fledged gambling addiction—and because he wanted to reconnect to his core passion: Christian rap. In his teens he'd been unstoppable, playing churches all over the Midwest, and when things had gotten bad back in California, all Kyle had wanted was to write raps again. But now that he was back—no longer gambling, and drinking less—he had writer's block.

Just that afternoon, I'd been reading the note from Berryman's analyst (*your creative skills are not so intertwined with your emotional problems*) and I asked Kyle if he thought he wrote better from crisis or stability. Kyle thought for a while, then said he wrote from both, though the raps turned out differently. But if he had to choose, he'd choose stability in a heartbeat—even if it meant he never wrote again. For a simple reason: Stability was when he felt closest to God.

J ust before Halloween, I asked Dave if he thought Iowa had broken something between us that couldn't be fixed. It was easier to construct the sentence like that: Iowa had done it.

"It's like something has gone numb," I told him. "Can't you sense that?"

"Yes," he said simply. "I can."

I'd been ready to convince him, but it was horrible when he agreed immediately. He told me he'd been trying to explain to a friend what it felt like to hug me when we got home at the end of the day: how stiff, how empty. This made me flinch, imagining all the times we'd hugged and he'd been thinking, *This is empty*. I'd wanted to believe in *intention, intention, intention*—going through the motions, showing up for commitments, all that program language that had given me a rudder when my own instincts seemed totally fucked—but apparently sometimes going through the motions could be just that, nothing saving, only hollow. Like hugging a corpse.

Whatever was broken, I told him, I wasn't sure we could fix it. When I said that, Dave started crying. This was something I'd never seen him do. A flurry of snow fell beyond our giant picture window, sifting a layer of powdered white onto the bricks of the old corset factory where we'd been drunk, falling in love, three years earlier. It was the beginning of the massive early nor'easter they'd call Snowtober.

Not for the first time, I accused Dave of thrilling toward my strength and pulling away from my weakness, from those times I'd been needy, or dull, or low. But for the first time, he agreed.

"I know that coldness," he said, after a long silence. "I'm ashamed of it."

In three years, he'd never really owned this—and I felt a sudden wash of relief, like an exhalation, that I hadn't been crazy all this time.

But it was never because he only wanted the good parts of me, he explained. It was never that he didn't want my sadness. That was just the story I'd written. He hadn't been pulling away from my fear, only the ways I'd blamed him for it.

"I didn't blame you—" I started to say, then thought of all the times I'd cried *at* him, like a weapon.

"What I gave was never enough," he continued. "It was exhausting." He said there was an ice that ran through him sometimes—a sense of shutting down—and he wanted to fight it. But he'd never been repulsed by my need, only tired of the ways I constantly forgot how much he'd given me.

That first time I'd seen the coldness on his face? The night before my surgery, when I said I was scared? Had it ever occurred to me, he asked, that he might have been scared, too?

And honestly, it never had.

Had it ever occurred to me, he asked, that the day after we'd first kissed, down in Newport News, canvassing for Obama, that the whole time I'd been waiting for a sign from him, he'd been waiting for a sign from me?

It sounds ridiculous, but it stunned me. I'd always assumed his assurance.

I'd never seen him like this before, pleading. Could we try? Could we keep trying? We agreed that we could, we would. This was sobriety, I thought—not the clean break, the clear-cut-and-burn-it-down approach, but something else. This was staying inside the mess and seeing it through. Coming down from all our crying that night, Dave and I watched *Blade Runner* and I cried some more. Nobody believed the replicant could feel anything, but it turned out he'd been moved by so much: attack ships on fire off the shoulder of Orion, C-beams glittering in the dark.

In the morality play I'd written, things had been simple: I suffered and Dave recoiled from my suffering. So many times, I'd told Dave that he hated being around me when I was sad, but I was starting to see that he'd just hated how I'd accused him of hating being around me when I was sad. I'd convinced myself that the problem between us was about Dave's aversion to my needs—that he was the embodiment of not-needing itself, an absence in human form—but perhaps the problem was that I'd translated need so immediately into accusation, *your stone face*, when in truth his face was many things: often kind, often listening, often curious. I just feared the stone face so much I'd started to expect it, to feel him retracting, to feel my own inadequacy as cause, to feel, feel, feel. Emotion was my compulsion and obsession, the organ through which I processed the world— turning it to praise and harm like the liver turns ethyl alcohol to acetaldehyde and acid. I could do better.

That evening, we decided to make food for the Occupy protesters camped downtown. This would be the thing we did instead of breaking up, a sign of hope and possibility. We baked sugar cookies that filled our loft with their sweet heat. I imagined how they'd be received—with surprise and gratitude.

It was dark by the time we arrived at the green. After someone directed us to the food tent, we set our plate of cookies on a table crowded with brownies, lemon squares dusted with sugar, a blueberry pie with a plastic cover, and a ring Danish from the grocery store. As we left, I heard someone say, "Why does everyone bring *cookies*? We've got so much fucking dessert here."

Contract logic justifies all kinds of labor, and makes all kinds of promises—*If I do* x, *I'll get* y—but anyone who lives by contract logic for long enough is eventually betrayed by it. The people in the

Occupy tent don't always say what you want them to say. The sober writer doesn't always write a sober epic. The sober writer doesn't always even stay sober. Charles Jackson eventually decided AA had "flatten[ed] him out," and that it worked best "for the mindless"—that it had doomed him to "years of a kind of grey, bleak, empty well-being" that made true creative work impossible, consigning him to "apathy, spiritlessness, blank sobriety, and a vegetable health." Jackson decided he believed in the Faustian bargain after all, believed in the choice between sobriety and genius. "Should I say the hell with it and return to my former indulgence," he wondered, "and thus be freed from my healthy prison, free once more from fear, able to function as a writer again?" After years of Möbius-strip sobriety—in and out, on and off—Jackson finally committed suicide by overdosing on Seconal in 1968.

If my obsession with authors who had gotten sober was another version of contract logic, played out with whatever god I was tentatively praying to (*If I get sober, you'll show me writers whose sobriety inspired them*), it was an obsession that delivered a humbling and partial hope. Which isn't to say I didn't find writers who wrote beautifully from recovery—Wallace, Johnson, Carver—but that the universe responded to my demands the way it often does: unpredictably, on its own schedule, without the grand drama of either boundless manna or unequivocal refusal. I wanted every recovery story to wear its sobriety like a shimmering, supernatural gown. But sometimes a story is just a thing someone needed to say, or a way someone needed to fail.

Contract logic involved its own tyrannical authorial impulse—*I will write the script, and God will make it come true*—but sobriety didn't dutifully deliver on its end of the contracts I'd written. It did the opposite: offered relief from my own plotline.

The sobriety stories I heard from Seneca House often hinged on overturned scripts and thwarted expectations. Marcus thought he was destined for a reckless expat life abroad, but ended up petting a beagle on a soggy creek-side porch. Gwen had been Citizen of the Year before she spent time as the Hobby Lady. Shirley thought she had one life mapped out for herself—a career in journalism and marriage to another journalist—but sobriety delivered something else entirely: a divorce, a cross-country move, years as a single parent. Sobriety wasn't instantaneous wish fulfillment; it was more like tearing off a bandage and reckoning directly with everything she'd been drinking to survive.

Shirley almost committed suicide the first time she ever did a Fourth Step. Her inventory was ninety-six single-spaced typed pages long, full of all her resentments at her husband and all her ambivalence about being a mother. She was planning to kill herself with carbon monoxide in the Pinto in her garage, and she'd gotten as far as turning the ignition when she thought about her kids coming home from school and finding her body there. So she killed the engine and went inside to call her shrink instead. She ended up in a locked ward for thirty days, on suicide watch. That was the real end of her marriage, she told me: her stay at a psychiatric hospital. Lou's pride couldn't stomach it.

After they divorced, Shirley moved back to Portland—with two kids, no husband, and no job. Her first AA meeting was in a smoky room full of strict old-timers: "We don't hold hands," they said, "and we don't say hi." She attempted suicide once more, after the move to Portland—slit her wrists—but survived.

So much unfolded after Shirley didn't die: two more cross-country moves, two children coming of age, one child's gender transition, six AA love affairs, two bouts of cancer. She got a job teaching journalism in Louisiana, spent decades in activism—protesting the Keystone Pipeline, marching with Black Lives Matter—and growing a robust flock of Portland pigeons, other sober women she sponsored. At meetings, she was always the one arguing that you never threw out a newcomer, no matter how drunk he was. You had to find a way to let him stay in the room.

Forty years after she got sober, Shirley showed me her Portland: not backyard beehives and artisanal gelato shops, but the hospital where she'd gotten her mastectomy, the bend in the Willamette River that reminded her of a suicide attempt. She showed me the partially deflated balloons from her most recent sobriety milestones—thirty-five years, then forty—dangling from her apartment ceiling like hanging plants; and a poster on her office wall, a blow-up of a feature called "Cheap-n-Chic" from her daughter Laura's college newspaper, that showed Laura wearing clothes she'd gotten from secondhand stores, sassy pedal pushers and a plush green velvet hat. That "Cheap-n-Chic" spread meant something to Shirley, in part because it was a validation of her sober mothering, when she'd encouraged her children to learn how to shop for themselves.

During my Seneca visits—with Sawyer, Gwen, Marcus, and Shirley—the ghosts of old dramas set up shop in the banality of the present, in living rooms and coffee shops: memories of hair stringy with vomit, nights in jail, crack in White Plains, white lightning in Monrovia, children driven over bridges during blackouts. After Gwen told me about her suicide attempt, we held out our plates of Tuscan flounder for scoops of rice pilaf. Recovery works like this: You bring old traumas into the buffet line. You dump the old coffee grounds and listen to the story of a suicide attempt. It's no diminishment of what was painful, and no romanticizing of it either, only an awareness of everything giving way to something else: this chicken and dumplings, this salad bar.

Certain stories might carry the easy lilt of practiced narrative grooves: Madeline's blackened branch and Gwen's moccasin making. Marcus throwing a chair across the room in anger. Sawyer touring drunk wards in Lithuania. Shirley dancing tango in an empty bakery. But just because a story has been crafted for survival—sculpted by memory, polished by repetition, whittled into artifact—doesn't mean it doesn't also hold truth.

Years after her second suicide attempt, Shirley met a man in the Portland recovery scene, a guy who rowed supplies out to the oil rigs, who had slit his wrists too. Whenever he and Shirley ran into each other at meetings, they bumped their wrists together and touched suicide scars.

In recovery, certain kinds of difficulty are harder to confess than others. The hardest stories for Shirley to tell—early on—were about her marriage. It wasn't hard to talk about how much she resented her husband, his rages and his self-absorption, but it was hard to talk about how much she'd relished being his "sacrificing helpmeet." Shirley had a certain narrative about their life together, about how she'd hated her role in it, and it was harder to admit this other part: the thrill of martyrdom and sacrifice. It took her an even longer time to share what she'd whispered to Laura, her infant daughter, the day of her adoption: *I don't want you, I don't want you, I don't want you.*

Sometimes the hardest things to confess are the difficulties of sobriety. The story of Shirley's parenting wasn't a simple conversion narrative: that she had been a terrible parent drunk and a better one sober. Her sobriety was hard on her kids, too. They missed her when she was away at rehab. When Shirley asked her daughter to speak at her fourteenth sobriety anniversary, Laura talked about how she felt Shirley had abandoned her for sobriety. As a girl, Laura had once asked Shirley's sponsor, Madeline: "Why doesn't my mother love me?" And Madeline told her: "Your mother can't love anyone right now."

At a 1970 AA convention in Miami, one speaker lamented that an AA member might believe "that he must tell an unqualified success story or not speak," that he might think he should "not speak about his fear of people, his inability to work or understand all aspects of the program, or the fact that he may frequently behave badly, or that he is unhappy and depressed, even when all these things may be true."

But in meetings, I found these weren't the experiences you were expected to excise from sobriety; they *were* sobriety — the bad behavior and grumpiness, as much as the wonder. Sawyer had a piece of framed calligraphy hanging on the wall of his basement: *Alcoholics Anonymous is not a history of our personal success stories. It is, rather, a history of our colossal human failures.*

At one point, Sawyer told me that Gwen had gone through a burnout when she was director of Seneca House. "Let her tell you this, not me," he said, "but we had to send her away to a rehab that they have for burned-out treatment people. They had an intervention on her."

When I finally worked up the nerve to ask Gwen about it, we were sitting in the Blue Note, the bar at her retirement home — in the middle of the afternoon, when it was utterly empty — and she said the intervention had happened during an incredibly stressful time. She'd been organizing her son's wedding and pulling together the paperwork for Seneca House to get the accreditation it needed for third-party reimbursement from insurance companies. She'd broken down crying. *Once*, she said. Then she'd shown up at Seneca to find a circle intervention waiting for her. "Which of course," she told me, "I used to teach people how to do."

At her staff's request, Gwen ended up at a specialized treatment center in Palm Springs, California. It was recovery for people who had wrung themselves dry trying to recover others. Gwen knew all their exercises. They hung purses and pillows from her outstretched arms. "They burdened you until you could hardly stand up," she said. "And then said, 'How do you feel?' I thought, 'Eh. I know what you want me to say.'"

It was clear there were certain kinds of vulnerability that Gwen had readily admitted into her narrative — her fallibility as a mother, her early lapses in sobriety, the necessary humbling of becoming the Hobby Lady, staying on Antabuse until she'd been sober a year — and other kinds of vulnerability her story hadn't fully metabolized: the day when she was the focus of the circle rather than its leader, the day she stood accused of being overwhelmed.

But the most useful sobriety stories are the ones that acknowledge how sobriety can bottom out, because they also acknowledge its surprise and depth, that sobriety is fundamentally full of unpredictability: miraculous, harrowing. For me, it wasn't just moving but useful to know that Gwen had hit a wall one day and started crying.

Recovery means giving what you need yourself, not what you already possess. Your own fragility isn't a liability but a gift. You bump suicide scars with a stranger. You don't kick the drunk out of a meeting. You find a way to let him stay in the room.

For much of that first autumn back in New Haven, I clung to what my sponsor told me—*No big changes in the first year*—and stayed in my relationship with Dave. But by clinging to that prohibition, I'd also flipped it into possibility: Once a year had passed, I would have permission. And when I hit a year of continuous sobriety in early December, I told Dave I couldn't do it anymore.

Everything between us felt exhausted, brittle, depleted. The hot magma of conflict—with all its heat and surge—had cooled into hardened ridges of resentment, a quieter lunar landscape. The realizations I'd had about what had broken between us had come too late to resuscitate what had already bled out. It was hard to explain the *almost* in our love—to myself or anyone—how consuming it was, that sense of being almost able to make it work. His mind was the mind I most wanted to ask every question. He'd spread a picnic across the marble of a train station at midnight. He'd told me I should take vitamins so my bones didn't break when he fucked me. He'd read Berryman to me in a humid August kitchen. He was fully alive without drinking. When we were up, we were so fully together in that state of upness, but when I came low, I always believed that I'd betrayed the person he wanted me to be. I loathed this version of myself so much I couldn't believe he didn't loathe her as well.

When I told him that I thought we were done, Dave looked so pained. He asked me to take some time to think about it. It seemed cruel—to both of us, somehow—that the thing that made him reach for me was the idea I might finally pull away.

I went to stay for a few days with a friend in Brooklyn, in her tiny studio on Ninth Street, where we binge-watched Rihanna videos: She was falling in love! She was sad in a bathtub! She was smoking eight cigarettes at once! I cried over greasy hamburgers at the dive joint on her block. While I was there, I got a note from Dave saying he'd found my Big Book lying on our bed. When he confessed he'd started looking through it, reading notes I'd scribbled in the margins, I felt the sad gratification of symmetry: his desire to know those parts of me that didn't involve him. "You've been examining yourself so fearlessly," he wrote, "in this quiet way I haven't ever really asked about." He quoted a passage in the Big Book that I'd underlined—*Fear is an evil and corroding thread*—and wrote: "I think I feel now something like what you must have felt so often in Iowa." It wasn't just that he was afraid I'd leave him, it was that he had begun to understand the ways fear could rearrange you, could fill you with disarming and overwhelming kinds of longing—to know another person, to gather all their pieces, to read their secret thoughts.

When I came back to our apartment, I saw three empty nips of liquor in our recycling bin, the kind you'd find in a hotel minibar. He'd been drinking, he said. This was what it looked like when he drank: three little bottles. I knew that I wanted him to be happy but worried that I resented him too much to make him happy. I looked at those three empty nips and told him, "I can't."

When we had sex that afternoon, it was familiar and domestic— pulling socks off each other's feet, peeling away long underwear. All the leaves had fallen from the trees and couldn't block the sun any longer. He bent my leg so that my knee jutted in front of the window, winter light gleaming behind. It felt possible to reach for him without reservation now that I knew I was losing him. I watched our limbs tangled, thinking, *I can't believe this is ending.* I'd told myself I was learning to live without drinking so I could become a stronger version of myself, someone who could build a life with him without rotting it with fear. I'd told myself that I was giving up drinking to make our love possible. Now I was sending myself into another life without either one.

—XIII—

RECKONING

At the back of the composition book filled with notes for *Recovery*, his unfinished novel, Berryman left behind a fairy tale called "The Hunter in the Forest." He wrote it with his daughter Martha, and most of it was transcribed in her effortful child's print. In the story, a hunter gets lost in a forest where two bears live, both named Hungry "because they were always hungry, every single second." They steal the hunter's food, put his gun in a squirrel hole, and take off his pants. ("That was a very angry hunter!") Then they put him in a cage and lock the door. Though the story never frames it this way, these are the dilemmas of addiction: The bears are hungry every single second. The hunter is lost. The hunter is in a cage. Berryman and his daughter wrote four different endings, three of them in Berryman's cursive:

He fixed the lock, got out of the cage, and conquered all the animals.

And they said "There! That's what you do to us. You're lucky we didn't kill you!" Moral: Be kind to animals and they will be kind to you.

He awakened and they fed him nothing but hay.

One ending offered victory: The hunter triumphs over the animals. Another one offered a moral: If you are good to the world, it will be good to you. A third offered disappointment: nothing but hay. Martha wrote the fourth ending in her serious childish scrawl. She labeled it "Real Ending": "The hunter awakened and said, 'Well?'"

This final ending, the *real* ending, offered the true anticlimax of salvation: The hunter doesn't know what to make of the world he has woken into. *Well?* After waking up, there is always the question of what comes next — what life might lie beyond the life you've left behind.

After Dave and I moved out of our apartment, I rented a brick studio near the gray flank of I-91. It was one long sunlit room directly above a middle-aged couple who filled their hallway with bulk boxes of mason jars. They were jammers. She had a long braid down her back and he had staples on his scalp from an unmentioned procedure. Just after moving in, I gave them a plate of gingerbread cookies I'd made with a new set of cookie cutters shaped like forest animals — moose, squirrel, fox — purchased to signify the beginning of a new era of unwilled generosity and outward focus, in which I would always be doing little things for others. *Oh, that?* I'd say. *That was nothing.* I imagined the casual voice I'd use, the self-effacing tone of someone who wasn't doing anything for karmic credit. *No biggie, just baked you some foxes.* I lived in that apartment for eighteen months, and used my cookie cutters once.

The sharp, stinging thrill of my aloneness was like diving into an unheated pool. I told myself *You'll adjust, you'll adjust, you'll adjust.* All our furniture had been Dave's, so he let me keep the battered chairs we'd bought together from an Iowa thrift store, upholstered with vinyl roses — we'd been so excited to spot them on the thrift-store sidewalk, so excited to buy something together. Now they sat on a hardwood floor in a room still waiting for a bed, a bookshelf, a table, anything. I was low on cash. Our landlady had kept our security deposit because we'd broken our lease. She said that maybe next time we'd think a little harder about living with somebody if we were going to break the lease after just six months.

At my new place on Lyon Street, I started spotting signs of

mice—little droppings like BB pellets by the fridge—but didn't want to kill them, so I tried to banish them with mint extract, which I'd been told they hated. But they stuck around, savaging my foil pouches of cocoa mix into little shreds of tinsel. One died under my stove, something I realized only once I started to smell his rotting body under the unforgiving peppermint odor that had settled like a blanket over my whole life.

Each morning at dawn I sat on my kitchen counter and watched the cars surge north up I-91. The absence of booze tingled like a ghost limb. The specter of another life felt like someone breathing heavily nearby, another version of this breakup in which I drank myself sense-less each night, weeping and blowing my nose into toilet paper, drunk-dialing Dave after midnight to ask: *Who are you with right now?* I knew I wasn't supposed to want that other life—unseemly, falling apart—but some part of me longed for it. In that life, I would make a fool of myself, and that foolishness would tell him how much I missed him, better than anything else could. Instead I was just pushing my yogurt around, dry-eyed. Every few weeks a new jam—blackberry, rhubarb, red currant—showed up outside my door, sealed so tightly I could never open it. I ran the jars under water and smacked them against counters, then lied to my neighbors weekly about how much I loved their various jams on my morning toast.

I started chairing the seven-thirty meeting every Wednesday morning, trudging to that warm room through the bitter January cold. Whenever the court-order folks came up to me afterward to get their cards signed, my first impulse was to direct them somewhere else—not because I didn't want to sign their cards, but because I didn't think I was qualified. *You should get someone more official,* I wanted to say, but then realized I was as official as anyone.

I still loved that early-morning meeting. The voices of others still made me want to drop down on my knees in front of them—to thank them for letting me lose myself for a moment by listening to them—and there was also this guy in a maroon tracksuit who'd started looking at me from across the room. My psyche was hungry for suste-nance, my outfits carefully chosen. "I don't care why you newcomers are here," said Theo, the group's anchoring old-timer. "You come because you want to get sober or you come because you want the free coffee or you come because you want to get laid, I don't fucking care. Just keep coming."

The man across the room, whose name was Luke, told me that every morning before the meeting he walked his dog to the top of East Rock, a huge hill on the edge of town, to watch the sunrise. Did I want to join them sometime? I did. He texted twenty minutes before he picked me up—at five-thirty the next morning—to ask if I wanted milk or sugar in the coffee he was bringing me. We walked uphill, with snow on the ground, and flirted in the early cold, watch-ing dawn spread like a murky juice over the industrial buildings of New Haven. I'd always wondered what sober dating would be like, and here it was—nothing like dipping into the sweet buzz of wine over candlelight. It was walking uphill on a sludgy winter morning, with chapped lips and a mouth sour with the aftertaste of plain black coffee—raw and unknown, thrilling.

In those days, acquaintances who wondered if they had a problem with their drinking often got drunk and pulled me aside to tell me about it. I was like a sober version of them, a hypothetical self they felt accountable to. One night, as I was leaving the Anchor—a dive bar that I still loved for its vinyl and fries—a woman rushed after me onto the sidewalk, holding a can of Sea Hag. She was a friend-of-a-friend from grad school, often drunk at parties, and she told me she was get-ting scared by her blackouts. Had I gotten blackouts? Was that why I didn't drink? She'd noticed I didn't drink. And how had I stopped? And what was it like? I wrote her the next day: *A lot of what you said about drinking made sense to me. If you ever want to come to a meeting...* And then, ashamed of proselytizing: *No pressure at all.*

Ha! she wrote back. *I don't even remember saying any of that!*

Through meetings, I became friends with a woman who'd been in the nurse-anesthetist program at Yale New Haven Hospital. She'd been stealing opiates from work and she'd accidentally overdosed in a hospital bathroom and gone into cardiac arrest. "If you're going to go into cardiac arrest, a hospital bathroom isn't a bad place to do it," she told me over lunch one day. "Just don't lock the door." When she described her stubborn desire to court that sweet blackness, I didn't feel pity or disgust. Part of me just craved the surrender.

We finished our lentil soup—our green smoothies, our tiny bread loaves, icons of our wholesomeness—and then I went home and Googled "What does Dilaudid feel like?" and found a user-forum thread called "What's all the hype about?" A user called SWIM talked about trying Dilaudid and counting to ten. At seven seconds, it hit him like a wave—better than anything he'd ever experienced. But in the very next post, SWIM said he couldn't understand why anyone would choose Dilaudid over heroin. What was the deal with SWIM? He kept changing his mind. He seemed to have six different minds. Then I realized: *Someone Who Isn't Me.* It was the name everyone used. One SWIM said the Dillie rush could literally knock you down. Another put a blotter under his tongue so he could save the rest of his saliva for later. Maybe someone who wasn't him could get a little high from what was left. Another SWIM loved his first fentanyl high so much he decided to write about it on the Dilaudid thread. He posted the play-by-play of his second time: *SWIM is starting to feel more and more stoned. Unfortunately his whole body doesn't feel like it's glowing of warmth like it felt with the previous experience with fentanyl…SWIM is feeling more happy and contend, but not enough in his opinion.* I imagined someone who wasn't me sitting there one night, all alone with her computer and her disappointing high, faithfully narrating it for a world of strangers.

When Amy Winehouse was getting high or drunk, the paparazzi photos always tried to zoom in as close as possible on her cuts and bruises, the residue of her benders. These little wounds were like openings in the tent flaps of her privacy. It was as if the photos were trying to get inside the wounds themselves, the closest thing to fucking her that the camera could possibly manage.

After she died, one journalist reflected that her death forced the public to "choke a bit on the rock mythology that's been crammed down our collective throats.... The tortured genius, the hellion libertine, the martyr dying for the noble cause of nihilism." It was unending, our collective fascination with the self-inflicted pain of a beautiful woman. It was another incarnation of Elizabeth Hardwick's awe at Billie Holiday's "luminous self-destruction," though it was Holiday who'd said, "If you think dope is for kicks and for thrills, you're out of your mind."

If only that were true. But I've always perked up at drunkalogs. The night Amy Winehouse won five Grammys, she told her friend Jules: "This is so boring without drugs." The answer on the Narco Farm intake form had stated it so simply. *Reason for addiction: To avoid monotony of living.* My dad had always been irritated by the ways my high school Human Development class seemed to whitewash the truth. "How can they keep you from getting into trouble with drugs," he said, "if they aren't honest about how *good* they feel?" He always told me that one of the most dangerous things about drugs was the fact that they were illegal—this from a man born in 1943, the same year as George Cain, who never did time for the drugs he did, but knew that others had.

It's not that there aren't thrills. It's just a question of aftermath. Holiday might have continued: If you think dope is for kicks, then think of a woman spreading foundation on the sores across her face, asking her bodyguard why she's not getting her period, as Winehouse did after years of boozing and bulimia—when she was utterly cloistered by her fame and by her using, her body battered. She wasn't just a legend but also a woman who couldn't walk straight, a woman on a bed who wasn't sleeping but gone. When she died, her blood alcohol content was 0.4 percent, a level well above deadly. The coroner ruled it "death by misadventure."

"Dope never helped anyone sing any better," Holiday insisted, though it's true that if Winehouse had gone to rehab that first time, we might never have gotten *Back to Black*, the album that made her famous. I wonder what we would have gotten instead. "She had the complete gift," said her idol Tony Bennett. "If she had lived, I would have said, *Life teaches you, really, how to live it, if you live long enough.*"

I would have loved to hear Amy Winehouse sing sober. Not just two weeks sober, but three years sober, twenty years sober. I never lived her life and she never lived mine, but I know that when I was twenty-seven I stopped and when she was twenty-seven she died. I know that when I watch a video of her onstage in Belgrade—drunk out of her mind, like she's been air-dropped into a moment she can't possibly fathom—I think of coming out of a blackout into the strange new world of a Mexican bathroom stall, or a dirt basement in Cambridge, or a breezeless bedroom in Nicaragua where it was easier to let a man finish fucking me than to stop him.

When she lurches across that Belgrade stage and finally squats there—still and quiet, smiling—just waiting for something to happen or for something to stop happening, it's less that I know what's happening in her, and more that her eyes know something that happened in me. I hate that she didn't have years of ordinary coffee dates and people saying, *I get that*, that she stayed doomed to her singularity and her vodka-thinned blood and her drunken stumbling under the broken tower of her beehive, her body barely holding up the weight—until it wasn't, until it couldn't any longer.

Alone in my new apartment, I was constantly imagining Dave in his new apartment across town. I'd ended things because I was sick of obsessing about the exhausting question of whether we should be together—but now that we weren't together, I only obsessed about us more. It was a familiar vein of disappointment. I'd stopped drinking so that I wouldn't think about drinking, but after I stopped, I thought about it constantly, without respite or relief.

Plenty of nights, I wanted to text Dave drunk. But I didn't drink anymore, so I couldn't. Instead I texted him sober. We texted to say nothing, and by saying nothing we also said: *I am still here.* Some nights we said more. "I still feel like you're my real life," I told him. "Nothing else feels like my real life."

I'd picked up a second job—adjunct teaching at a college forty minutes upstate—to pay back the credit card debt on a room's worth of Ikea furniture, and to distract myself from my quiet nights with more essays to grade. My students wrote about varsity swim team politics and the acid residue of overbearing mothers, and I marked up their work with my own agendas: *Gratuitous cynicism,* I wrote, or *Irony without a point?*

With colleagues at this job, I had slipped into a strange set of white lies: after referring to "my partner" once in conversation, as if I still had one, I'd kept up the lie. It was as if I'd created a parallel universe in which Dave and I had made it work.

In class, I started our discussion of Denis Johnson's *Jesus' Son* by asking my students if they had a favorite story from the collection. "Don't worry," I said. "There's no right answer." But I was lying. There was a right answer. Their favorite story was supposed to be *my* favorite story, which was now "Beverly Home," the only one about recovery. Johnson's narrator, Fuckhead, is working at a rehabilitation center for the elderly and disabled. He spends his evenings going to Narcotics Anonymous meetings where sober addicts sit "around collapsible tables looking very much like people stuck in a swamp." It's no postcard vision of salvation. Meetings make Fuckhead feel like a swamp creature. He's a caregiver in a rehab center full of despair. He sleeps with a woman he meets in NA who has black-widow bad luck. The men she loves all die—from trains or car crashes or overdoses—and when Fuckhead hears about them he is filled with "a sweet pity...sad that they would never live again, drunk with sadness." He thinks, "I couldn't get enough of it." The same way he'd responded to a grieving woman's scream, how he'd gone "looking for that feeling everywhere." Fuckhead spends his days walking the *O*-shaped circuit of the rehab center with the deformed and the desperate: "All these weirdos, and me getting a little better every day right in the midst of them," he says. "I had never known, never even imagined for a heartbeat, that there might be a place for people like us."

I read that line, the closing line of the story, aloud to my students. I read it—once, twice, three times—while they quietly swept up crumbs from the doughnuts I'd brought to class to bribe them into loving me. On the first day of class, I'd shown up with two dozen doughnuts and a cardboard box of coffee, and then I kept bringing them each week—along with a stack of paper cups, sweeteners and creamers, plastic swizzle sticks, an anxious bouquet—afraid that if I stopped bringing them, the students would be disappointed. It was going to cost four hundred dollars over the course of the semester, more than half a month's rent, just to stave off the possibility that they'd stop liking me.

There might be a place for people like us. Every voice I'd ever heard in meetings was somehow part of that closing line. Maybe some of my students found it sappy or maudlin, that sense of belonging, but my heart swelled righteously against their imagined accusations. I told myself that the students who liked the early stories best, the ones full of drugs and fever-dream escapades, were still caught up in deluded fantasies of meaningful wreckage. Who knew what drugs they were doing after the end of our Friday-afternoon class? One told me he'd recently discovered his totem animal during a shamanic ritual. But the students who liked "Beverly Home" best, they were the ones who *got it*. That story believed in something besides the self-immolating antics of dysfunction—their flickering, intoxicating glow. It was gazing somewhere beyond the horizon, past the blaze.

❖

One of Johnson's early drafts of "Beverly Home" began like this:

> I had sobered up just in time to have a nervous breakdown.
> I had no ide
> I had
> I was a wi a whimpering dog inside. nothing more than that.

Johnson first tried to dry out in 1978, in his parents' home in Tucson, where he was living with his "eccentric" grandmother Mimi, but he didn't get sober for good until the early 1980s. "I was addicted to everything," he told an interviewer decades later. "Now I just drink a lot of coffee."

Johnson was "concerned about getting sober," and knew this was "typical of people who feel artistic," but he'd written only two stories and a handful of poems in ten years (while he was actively using) so he figured he didn't have much to lose. In the decade after he got sober, he produced four novels, one collection of poetry, a collection of stories, and a screenplay. His was the arc I'd been looking for: the possibility of sobriety as jet fuel. He dedicated two of his novels to H.P., which I never would have recognized, years earlier, as shorthand for a Higher Power. He wrote the whimpering dog inside, without apology or instant redemption—and every once in a while, he wrote about the consolations this dog might find. "Approval was something I craved more than drugs or alcohol," he wrote in an early draft of "Beverly Home." "I hadn't been able to get it in the bars, but it seemed attainable in the rooms." He meant the rooms of recovery.

Are we really all that tormented? Jackson had wondered. *Or is it something we hang onto, foster, even cherish?* In 1996, a younger writer wrote to Johnson: "I want to thank you for your unfailing support and friendship in helping me get acquainted with my alcoholism. It seems there are two kinds of American writers. Those who drink, and those who used to. You introduced me to the latter. Thanks, brother."

A t one Thursday-night meeting, I met a woman who was beautiful but fidgety — maybe mid-twenties, a few years younger than
me, olive-skinned, with tight jeans, a shimmery blouse, and hair in a
wispy brown bun. She moved as if she were breaking a rule by inhabiting her own skin, and didn't want to get caught. Her eyes had dark
hollows beneath them; she kept tucking back stray wisps of hair
behind her ear. At a party in Iowa, I might have been threatened by
her — might have watched how she talked to men, or to Dave — but
in that church basement I recognized her discomfort so immediately
and strongly that it made me fidget in my seat.

Shifting in her plastic chair, she spoke during the meeting about
how hard it was to be in her first week, her tone clipped and uncertain. Afterward, I went up to her and introduced myself. "I really connected to what you said," I told her, which was less about her words
than the way she'd said them.

"I didn't know what to say," she said.

"That's part of what I connected to," I said. "And the part about
drinking alone."

She nodded and looked down. She seemed pleased. "Could I," she
started. "I mean, if it's not strange…" I knew those pauses well, or at
least my own version of them: *Am I basically hurling myself on this
stranger, right here in this basement?*

"Exchange numbers?" I smiled. "I was just about to suggest it."

Her name was Monica, and she was the first woman I ever sponsored. When she initially asked, I almost said, *You might want a sponsor with a different drinking history. You might want a sponsor who knows
the program better than I do.* But what did I know about what she
wanted? Maybe she drank like I drank; maybe she needed to hear
from me that your drinking could be boring and still pretty fucking
demoralizing. Maybe she needed to hear about the program from
someone who was still learning it.

The first time we got together, I sat on a bar stool in Monica's kitchen—in a brick apartment complex in the suburbs, with a view of a parking lot—and she told me about coming home from work and getting quietly drunk on her futon. The ghosts of those nights whispered around us, stirring her scarves, passed out on her sequined throw pillows. I wanted to help her, and I could see how much she wanted help—how much she wanted to give herself to recovery— which only made me nervous. *What future can I give this woman?* I wondered, as if her future were mine to give. *What's the right thing to say next?* So I grasped at the ladder rungs of what other people had said to me before: my own sponsors, the people I'd heard at meetings. I told her my story, *what it was like,* and then she told me hers. We followed the script. And honestly, it's hard to say what she would have gotten if I'd tried to reinvent it.

The obsession I'd described was exactly what she'd felt, Monica said. It was what a million other people had felt, too. It wasn't anything original, our yearning—and our conversation wasn't original either. I could have been anyone, and she could have been anyone. But there we were, on our stools, in that particular Connecticut apartment, in that particular twilight. It wasn't new, our talk. It was just new for us.

During those early days of sponsoring Monica—while both of us found solace in the simple fact of communion—a group of incarcerated female addicts was working a chain gang in the Arizona desert. Their guards made them chant: "We are the chain gang, the only female chain gang." They wore T-shirts that said I WAS A DRUG ADDICT. Or: CLEAN(ING) AND SOBER. They lived in Tent City, a cluster of sweltering tents full of scorpions on the ground and mice in the trash heaps. Temperatures in the tents often hit 140 degrees. "If I had to design a system that was intended to keep people addicted," clinician Gabor Maté told a journalist, "I'd design exactly the system we have right now." João Goulão, the architect of Portugal's drug decriminalization, believes the "terroristic" approach pioneered by Harry Anslinger—dealing with addiction "by chaining, by humiliating"—is "the best way to make [addicts] wish to keep using drugs."

But Anslinger's legacy has endured. Tent City was the brainchild of one of his protégés, Joe Arpaio, who was hired by the Bureau of Narcotics in 1957 and served as sheriff of Maricopa County for twenty-four years, from 1993 through 2016. When journalist Johann Hari interviewed Arpaio for his 2015 book, *Chasing the Scream*—a dizzying account of the lineage and devastating legacy of drug criminalization—Arpaio proudly showed Anslinger's signature framed and hanging on his office wall. "You got a good guy there," Arpaio said. With Tent City, Arpaio had finally—literally—made good on the dreams of the Los Angeles police officer whom Anslinger had quoted years earlier: "These people are in the same category as lepers, and...the only defense society has against them is segregation and isolation whenever possible."

In 2009, at a prison twenty-two miles west of Tent City, one prisoner—Number 109416—was literally cooked alive in a cage in the middle of the desert, a bare outdoor holding cell with nothing more than a chain-link roof shielding her from the sun. She'd been sent there as punishment for a minor disciplinary infraction. Prisoner 109416 was serving time for solicitation, but her prostitution had been supporting her meth habit for years. Her addiction got her incarcerated, and it ultimately got her killed. Her body was discovered with blisters and burns all over her skin. According to one witness, her eyeballs were "as dry as parchment." Her temperature was recorded at 108 degrees before she died. That was as high as the paramedics' thermometers went.

Before she died in a holding cell, Prisoner 109416 lived as Marcia Powell. In *Chasing the Scream*, Hari excavates the human particulars of her life from the dehumanizing tragedy of her death. She was a teenage runaway in California, sleeping on the beach sand for warmth and washing in McDonald's bathrooms. She was generous and drawn to bodies of water. She loved panning for gold in the lakes of Arizona. She cooked a full breakfast for her boyfriend's dog each morning: eggs and sausages.

Marcia Powell died in 2009, the same year I got sober for the first time. While she was in a cage in the middle of the desert, I was getting welcomed into church basements, handed poker chips, bombarded with phone numbers. I was walking into meetings where my body was treated as valuable simply because it was in the room, simply because it *was*. I didn't have to march in a chain gang picking up trash tossed by commuters who'd voted for the sheriff who was making me wear a T-shirt that said I WAS A DRUG ADDICT. What luck. What luck not to wake up in a cage, or a 140-degree tent in the Arizona desert; not to serve time for the thrall that had already corroded me.

Marcia Powell's death in the desert is another glitch in the song of my pain as private. It had been possible for that song to play seamlessly in Iowa City, where I ordered my whiskey shots in the company of mythic poets—white men serving the brutal god of their white logic. But in the world where Marcia Powell died in the desert, where Melanie Green faced a grand jury for being a pregnant addict, where Jennifer Johnson was initially convicted of delivering a controlled substance to her own child, where George Cain got a gun pulled on him in a doctor's office, where Billie Holiday died handcuffed to a hospital bed—in *this* world, the story of my drinking is not a private story. I used to think it was, or that it only involved me, and maybe also the men I'd been fucked by and fought with, the man who hit me on the street, the men with my last name, who drank before I was born.

But the story of my sadness was never just mine. It has always included strangers: not just the strangers I met in meetings, but the strangers whose dependence had taken them to highway chain gangs rather than church basements, the strangers who weren't stopping at the Stop & Shop to pick up off-brand coffee for old-timers. My story included the woman who died in a cage in a desert, or her story included me; not just because of my guilt—the guilt of my privilege, or my survival—but because we both put things inside our bodies to change how we felt.

It's easy to forget that Prisoner 109416 and I are part of the same story, because we have been granted the right to tell very different tales about our pain. According to the scripts of our culture, one of us is a victim, and the other a prisoner. But keeping our stories apart, understanding them as unrelated, would ratify the logic that let our fates diverge in the first place: the desert cage, the basement chorus. Our stories are both stories about coming to depend on a substance— to crave it, seek it, use it—and I no longer want to live by the traditions that keep them apart.

When I finally visited the Narcotic Farm in 2014—eight decades after it opened and fifteen years after it had been converted to a full-fledged prison—I found its soaring brick buildings enclosed by tangled loops of silver barbed wire. Its aspirational architecture, cloisters and courtyards and magisterial art deco facades, seemed sinister beneath these ragged, gleaming coils and their brute reminder of prison's purpose: keeping punished bodies quarantined.

My guide, who was in charge of media relations, used the language of rehabilitation, but it was often just as chilling as the language of punishment. "Maybe he's had a couple of infractions, made a couple bad choices," he said, describing a typical prisoner deemed eligible for minimum security, "but we still believe he's programmable." *Programmable:* the troubling descendant of an older faith in the ways an institution could "rearrange" someone.

Since the Lexington facility had been converted to a prison, it was no longer exclusively dedicated to treating addicts, but it still had one major program committed to addiction: a nine-month residential drug abuse program, known as RDAP and housed in something called the Veritas Wing. Posters invited participants to become

"Navigators" or "Expeditors," to follow in the footsteps of cartoon men who fixed things or assisted others. The program preached the dangers of eight major "thinking errors," including indolence, entitlement, and sentimentality, which it defined as the impulse to invoke self-serving emotional excuses for one's crimes. In the community room, a converted bowling alley, I sensed the ghosts of old attempts at rehabilitation: 8,842 hours of bowling logged in 1937. Now inmates gathered in this room to give each other push-ups (compliments) and pull-ups (suggestions). The cell blocks were named after virtues—like Humility Alley, a self-contained set piece of irony that seemed to insist that the disempowerment of incarceration would grant access to virtue. *Do you still know everything?* the drug-court judge had asked an addict. *Willing to LISTEN now?*

My PR guide was proud to show me all the prison's vocational facilities: the Braille workshop, where inmates designed Braille books for blind kids in pre-K, and the bare wooden frame of a house, in the central open-air courtyard, that got built and rebuilt by various carpentry classes, its roof beams covered with pigeon shit. It seemed strange that the birds could come and go as they pleased, while the men remained. My guide proudly pointed out their Very Pluralist Religious Architecture: the Native American sweat lodge, the Wicca fire pit, the Asatru fire pit—this last one referred to with a smugly casual air, as if I would say, *Yes, of course, the Asatru fire pit*, but when I asked how many Asatru inmates they'd had I got no solid answer.

"Every inmate is a walking testimonial to a victim," one of the wardens told me, which I knew wasn't true, at least not as he meant it, and seemed a sentimental thinking error of its own. The warden translated the tattoo on my arm perfectly from Latin ("I am human, nothing human is alien to me"), then said: "Not sure it's true, though." He assured me there were prisoners who were alien to me, people who had done things so bad I couldn't possibly understand them. But I didn't believe in the same categorical divide he believed in, and I agreed with what he said only insofar as it insisted on the limits of my knowledge. I knew there was plenty I couldn't understand about the men incarcerated here, plenty I couldn't see behind the barbed wire and the scenic inmate-built gazebo, past the welding simulators and the A-frame caked in bird shit, the sweat lodge and the fire pits, past the actual and straw-men victims who stood behind the fully human inmates all around me, men to whom I was not allowed to speak.

I asked the education warden what he knew about the prison-hospital this place had been, and he told me he knew all about it. It had been an experiment in rehabilitation, he said, and it failed.

Instead of a cage in the desert, or a cell on Humility Alley, I got fellowship. I got to hear people describe their *first drink*, always so specifically conjured. It usually came out tender and liberated, like a eulogy for a bully, and carried the whiff of unfinished business in its particulars: the gleam of a whiskey bottle, the nauseating sweetness of cooking sherry, the walnut shelves or squeaky metal trolley. I was humbled, almost scared, by how sharply I remembered my own first drink, at my brother's graduation party: the upholstery grain of the couch; the jutting stone fireplace; the flinty crackle of champagne. How could I remember it so well if some part of me didn't still crave it?

If memory and longing were two radio dials tuned to the same frequency, then others were listening as well. A woman with multiple sclerosis named Petra said, "It was all day, every day." She talked about drinking to forget the fact of living in her ill body, and the embarrassment of knocking her wheelchair into chairs and tables, but there was also something in her voice, almost wistful, that missed the escape. A woman named Lorrie—obese and impeccably made up, crying so hard she shook—came to a meeting drunk and said she'd once gotten drunk with her rapist after he raped her. Just this morning, she'd gotten up at six-thirty so she'd have time to buy liquor before the seven-thirty meeting. I took her out to a diner afterward, where she got an Oreo milk shake and I drank so much black coffee I thought I was going to pee for hours. She told me she tried to hit a meeting during every available spot of free time because she was afraid she might drink otherwise, and I thought: *I want to help you. I don't know how.* I told her about getting drunk and letting a guy finish fucking me because it was easier than stopping him. She said, "Exactly." I don't think she meant it was exactly what had happened to her, because it wasn't what had happened to her. I think she meant there was a place drinking can take you where you forget that your body even matters, and we'd both spent time there.

I started giving rides to Wendy, twenty years old, the girl with a colostomy bag I'd met in a church basement across town. One morning when I came to pick her up, she was clearly drunk, holding a huge Styrofoam cup full of 7-Eleven coffee from the night before that she'd microwaved that morning, she explained in a slurred voice, because she didn't want to be wasteful. It was as if she wanted to compensate for being drunk by explaining some small thing she'd done right. I didn't know what to do. I couldn't just leave her in her driveway. Or could I? The story I'd told myself about her recovery went something like this: *This cool older woman started giving me rides, and showed me that sobriety could be something I actually WANTED.* But her sobriety story wasn't mine to write. I drove her to the meeting anyway.

If I understood anything that winter, I understood how difficult it could be to let go of what you loved, even if you'd decided it wasn't what you needed. It was the claw marks all over again. A few months after breaking up, Dave and I met one night at a swanky hotel on his block downtown. It was the kind of get-together where you'd say, "Let's get drinks," except we both knew I'd get a seltzer and cranberry with lime. We sat on low leather couches, in the dim light, and ordered dessert to give ourselves a reason to stay: doughnuts dusted in cinnamon sugar, served alongside a ramekin of hot vanilla cream. It reminded me of the first night we'd ever kissed—how we'd stood by the kitchen sink of our friend's house for hours, refilling our cups of water, just so we could keep talking. We stayed at the hotel bar until it closed, sometime past midnight, like strangers who'd just met, like people without a history. It was recklessness without the alibi of drunkenness, running on the fuel of club soda and juice. I woke up in his bed the next morning, baked with late-winter light—in his home that was not my home, under his sheets that were not my sheets.

Everything that happened next happened without booze as pretext or excuse: I saw Dave sober. I slept with him sober. We ate late-night cookies from the cookie shop on his block, sober. But it didn't exactly feel sober. Before our early-morning meetings, I was still going on hikes with Luke. When it got warm enough, another man I'd met in meetings took me sailing on the Long Island Sound, where I lay on the canvas mesh stretched across the bow, glazed by sun, and loved the uncluttered sense of possibility that lived in the company of someone with whom I carried no baggage, no resentment, no mistakes. When I went on early-morning hikes with Luke, I kept our flirtation at a certain distance: far enough away that it wouldn't become an actual relationship, close enough to sense its glow. These times with other men were not against the rules—in those months of purgatory, Dave and I had none—but they felt selfish anyway, a way of hoarding affirmation so I wouldn't ask for more of it from Dave. I no longer believed I deserved it from him. Because I wasn't in a relationship with Dave any longer, I no longer expected as much from him—which reminded me, in an uncomfortable way, of giving up drinking: how *possible* it felt to drink, once I wasn't drinking, how it shimmered in the rearview mirror.

That winter Susan and I started meeting at a downtown bistro for our sponsor meetings. The restaurant was always empty, the flagging business of a friend she was trying to support. The long tally of my second Fifth Step was bound up with the hush of that room in the late afternoons, the light thick and milky as cappuccino foam, the paired tastes of sweet milky coffee and french fries. So much of sobriety was full of oddly twined tastes: mint gum and cream-filled vanilla cookies at meetings; onion rings and milk shakes and omelets on post-meeting diner runs, with everyone on different sleeping schedules, swapping bites off one another's plates.

I didn't talk to Susan about the fact that I'd started seeing Dave again. It seemed messy and inexplicable and maybe unwise, what we were doing, and I didn't know how to put it in the context of my sober narrative. It was the blemish of a ragged plotline. One day Susan told me—with real pain in her voice—that she could feel me pulling away from her. It was hard to make a date with me and then I kept postponing them. At first I wanted to protest: *I did everything I was supposed to! I filled out everything on my inventory!* But it felt good to tell Susan the truth—that I hadn't told her about things with Dave because they seemed too messy to fit inside our conversations or my step work.

"That's exactly your problem," Susan told me. "You don't know how to say anything when it's still a mess inside you. You need to have everything figured out before you say it out loud."

Berryman started *Recovery* as an ode to fellowship, but the novel wasn't an account of his recovery so much as a projected vision of the recovery he never fully experienced. It was an exhortation to himself to recover better, but Berryman couldn't stay sober the whole time he was writing it. A friend of mine once observed that writing about yourself is "like trying to make a bed while you're still in it," and in *Recovery* the lump under the sheets is palpable. Even the chapter titles expose the novel as a document of maddening repetition rather than progressive redemption: "The First Step" is followed by "The Last Two First Steps," which is followed by "Dry Drunk." After the *first* First Step, there's another First Step, and then *another* First Step, and after all that Severance is somehow *still* a dry drunk.

Berryman's marginal notes on an early draft of the novel, when he's listing the "symptoms" of an alcoholic, suggest that he's still reckoning with self-diagnosis ("drinking in the morning — drinking on the job — These are not the marks of a social drinker") and they testify to his relapses: "infinite resolutions — periods on the wagon — terrible remorse." As Severance confesses on the eighth page of *Recovery*, "'Sincerity' was nothing in this game." A hundred and sixty pages later he says: "I have lately given up the words 'sincerely' and 'honestly' as mere con-words designed by my diseased brain to support its lying products." He has given up on sincerity *again*, more than a hundred pages after he gave up on it the first time. One character accidentally writes his Third Step prayer, *May I Do Thy Will Always*, as *May I Do My Will Always*.

In life, Berryman was frustrated by his relapses, but kept trying to surrender again anyway. On a slip labeled "1st Step, Sat night," he wrote:

> I doubt if this will be an acceptable first step; and I don't care. I doubt if any man can actually "take" the 1st step; maybe some can, but I know I tried hard and failed. Last spring I wrote...a comprehensive account of 23 years of alcoholic chaos, lost wives, public disgrace, a lost job, injuries + hospitalization, a blacked out call to a girl student threatening to kill her; involuntary defecation in a public place, DTs, convulsions once, etc, and it was completely sincere...and a month later I had a slip, 4 or 5 over the next two months, two months sobriety, five days drinking, and here I am again — in spite of dead seriousness, never missing either an AA meeting or St. Mary's encounter group, and all sorts of other help, including daily prayer + the 24-hr-book. So screw <u>that</u> first step. This is only a short true account of my present thinking on the subject.

But even as he said *screw that*, he turned the paper over and scribbled a message to himself on the back: "As you comb yr hair + beard in the morning, say to the mirror: 'Berryman...God is interested in you, and conscious of yr struggle + yr services. Good luck.'" He kept trying to redirect himself from crisis to purpose: *yr struggle + yr services.* His inventories kept circling back to the same futilities and frustrations: *Do I feel I'm unstoppable? (Y) Do I ever "go on the wagon" to prove I can quit? (Y)* He didn't even mark *Y* or *N* for *Do I ever get drunk?*—as if it were a question too obvious to bear answering. His whole life had already answered it.

If the novel was an attempt to write himself into recovery, Berryman's handwritten edits on the early draft betray his unresolved questions. One rehab patient looking at Severance "with real interest" became "with the appearance of real interest." Another handwritten insertion insists that each rehab patient returns to "his own world" after reciting the Serenity Prayer in unison. At one point, Severance knows "he felt—depressed." But he can't even connect to what makes him cry. "I don't know what the hell I was crying about," he says. He "felt—nowhere." Disappointment lurks on the other side of each dash, after the held breath of each pause.

In a group-therapy session near the end of the novel, Severance confesses that he has a son from whom he has been estranged for years. He's not even precisely sure of his age. ("Thirteen. I think.") As Severance acknowledges "miserably," he doesn't know his son well, though he's not yet ready to take full responsibility for it. "His letters are very childish," Severance complains. "I can't find out anything about him."

Berryman had an estranged son of his own, and his archives hold letters that express—as clearly as anything—the unspoken white margins of distance between them:

> Dear Dad,
>   I've done well in school this quarter with a 91% average. I have enclosed a copy of my report card. I hope you like it.

I've been accepted at South Kent School. This has been the only acceptance I've received so far so I don't know if I'll be going there.
Say hello to Kate and Martha for me.

Much love,
Paul Berryman.

His letters are very childish. I can't find out anything about him. A few weeks later, Paul Berryman sent a copy of his acceptance letter from Phillips Academy—with that full name in his signature, again, as if writing to a stranger. At that point, it had been several years since he and his father had seen each other.

But Berryman wanted to share the fruits of his recovery with Paul; he wanted recovery to be something that brought them closer together. Just before his birthday one year, Berryman wrote his son a letter:

FOR MY SON: On the eve of my 56th birthday, after struggles, I think I have learned this: To give an honest (sincere) account of anything is the second hardest task man can set himself. . . . The only harder task, in my opinion at the moment, is to try to love and know the Lord, in impenetrable silence.

It's hardly surprising that Berryman's letter to his estranged son is all about longing for a stronger sense of connection to an estranged God, another absent father turned divine. It's also unsurprising that it's all about Berryman and his own quest. Recovery can make you self-absorbed, even as you're trying to learn otherwise—trying to reach out to neglected children, or wounded spouses, or an impenetrable God.

By fall 1971, Berryman had given up on *Recovery* entirely. He left the novel unfinished, and it wasn't published until after his death. He only left yellow notecards suggesting the possible endings he'd imagined.

"END OF NOVEL," he wrote on one. "TURN THIS CARD OVER." On the back, he wrote: "He might, certainly, at any time drink again. But it didn't seem likely. He felt—calm." There it was again, that dash.

Berryman was trying to imagine an ongoing state of serenity, but he could summon it only in abstract terms. On a separate notecard he wrote an alternative "LAST PAGE OF BOOK": "On Pike's Peak, coming down. He was perfectly ready. No regrets. He was happier than he had ever been in his life before. Lucky, and he didn't deserve it. He was very, very lucky. Bless everybody. He felt—fine."

Berryman was clutching at the possibility of stability beyond the dash: *He felt—calm. He felt—fine.* But it's hard to trust these feelings, not only because they exist on notecards that never got used, but also because they are haunted by the dashes that came before them in the book: *He felt—depressed. He felt—nowhere.*

Berryman kept his *Recovery* notebook even after he gave up on the novel, but his final entries, from December 1971, are full of despair. "Just try," he told himself. "Happy a little, grateful prayers." It got bad anyway: "terrible continual thoughts of suicide—cowardly, cruel, wicked—beating them off. Don't *believe* gun or knife; *won't.*"

In the unfinished novel, Severance begins his final stretch of sobriety by saying: "If I don't make it this time, I'll just relax and drink myself to death." In a motel room in Hartford, Berryman wrote: "It's *enough!* I can't BEAR ANY MORE / *Let this be it. I've had it.* I can't wait."

On January 8, 1972, Berryman jumped off the Washington Avenue Bridge at the University of Minnesota, where he'd taught for almost twenty years, and landed on the riverbank below, dead on impact. He'd relapsed just days before jumping—after eleven months of sobriety, his longest stretch.

I can't bear much more of my hideous life," Jean Rhys once wrote to a friend. "It revolts me quite simply." No surprise, then, that Rhys found herself wanting to write away from the "I" of personal experience, the shame of thinly veiled autobiography, and into "another I who is everybody." Like Jackson, she wanted to get outside herself. This was harder when other people were around. "Jean could not listen!" said Selma Vaz Dias. "She does not seem to connect."

It was fiction where Rhys grew closest to the consciousness of others, where she wanted to dissolve the barriers between "I" and "everybody," and *Wide Sargasso Sea*—her fifth novel, the one that made her famous—was her fullest expression of this desire. Rhys's first four novels had been rooted in the landscapes of her own life, dingy hotel rooms and bleak boardinghouses in Paris and London, but this last one found her core wounds, alienation and abandonment, in the imagined life of someone else: Mr. Rochester's first wife from *Jane Eyre*, the madwoman in the attic. Rhys reimagined this opaque character as Antoinette, a woman exiled from her country and spurned by a man: a life rediscovered in the wreckage, a character reclaimed from mad villainy. (No resemblance to Rhys at all.)

It took Rhys nearly twenty years to write the novel—two decades full of poverty, binge drinking, itinerant living, and trying (often failing) to care for her increasingly ill husband, Max. She burned one draft of the novel to a crisp in her kitchen grate during a bout of drunken fury. Once she had finally completed the manuscript, she wrote to her editor, Diana Athill: "I've dreamt several times that I was going to have a baby then I woke—with relief. Finally I dreamt that I was looking at the baby in the cradle—such a pussy weak thing. So the book must be finished." As it happened, Max died just as she was finishing it. Athill wrote to say she'd visit as soon as she could: "I'll come armed with a bottle!"

The "pussy weak" story of *Wide Sargasso Sea* explores the unhappy marriage of Antoinette, a Dominican girl raised on a crumbling plantation, to a British second son seeking an inheritance: the young man who would become Brontë's Mr. Rochester. *Wide Sargasso Sea* grants a full consciousness to Antoinette—the character who appears only as a dangerous madwoman in Brontë's masterpiece — and dramatizes her destruction at the hands of a husband who doesn't love her, but brings her to England anyway and shuts her in his attic. Rhys conjures their heartache of a honeymoon as days of dislocation and estrangement spent at a crumbling old island estate: rain puddles in the red earth, steam rising off the greenery, firelight flickering across the veranda, moths dying in the candle flames. The ripe land is cruel. It deepens the sting of the couple's distance with its beauty. If the mind can make a hell of heaven, then a loveless honeymoon can make it even worse.

Antoinette tries everything she can to make her husband love her more, but he can't fathom the abandonments that have whittled her need for love to such a sharp blade. After Antoinette fails at using the obeah magic of her childhood nurse to secure his affection — a pile of chicken feathers in the corner, some doctored wine — she takes refuge in the rum in the veranda sideboard.

"Don't drink any more," her husband tells her.

"What right have you to tell me what I'm to do?" she replies, and keeps drinking. The rum, we understand, is little more than a poor substitute for an older magic. It grants some diluted version of the relief her nurse's obeah once offered. Her core desire is for love. Booze is just meager consolation, a sham form of sustenance.

In *Wide Sargasso Sea*, Rhys found two vessels for empathy. She recovered the character of Mrs. Rochester, but she also imagined the psyche of the man who spurned her. The novel doesn't wonder only what it was like to be a woman imprisoned, but what it was like to be the man who'd imprisoned her. The middle section of the novel is told from Rochester's perspective, and its third portion allows his childhood governess, Mrs. Eff, to speak on his behalf: "I knew him as a young man. He was gentle, generous, brave." Mrs. Eff's insistence that it would be a mistake to see Rochester simply as a devil echoes Rhys's self-critiques in her imagined trial. *I do not know others*, she had confessed. *I see them as trees walking.*

By granting Rochester a voice in the novel, Rhys allows him to emerge as something more than just another glimpsed tree, something more than a hook upon which she could once again hang her poison coat. Rochester is a symbol of abandonment turned human again: multiple and contradictory. "I am not used to characters taking the bit between their teeth and rushing away," Rhys had written to a friend as she was writing *Wide Sargasso Sea*. In Rochester, she imagined a man who looked like a devil but had once been a boy; and through him, she began to imagine the possibility of a "gentle, generous" boy in every man who'd ever looked like a devil to her. When Rochester tells Antoinette that he was forced as a young man to keep his emotions hidden, Antoinette begins to understand that almost every villain has also been a victim.

If the novel reimagines villainy as the fruition of victimhood, then its ending reframes an act of destruction—Antoinette burning down Rochester's manor—as an expression of pain. In *Jane Eyre*, the fire is opaque and wholly threatening, the revenge of a "mad lady, who was as cunning as a witch." But Rhys gives the "mad lady" an intricate psychology, and exposes pain at the root of what seems like senseless self-destruction, or blind malice. The fire becomes an articulate conflagration. It resurrects the manuscript from ashes in the grate, where Rhys drunkenly burned it. "Now at last I know why I was brought here," Antoinette says, when she picks up the candle. "And what I have to do."

For the last thirteen years of her life, between the publication of *Wide Sargasso Sea* and her death in 1979, at the age of eighty-eight, Rhys lived in a Devon village called Cheriton Fitzpaine, in a block of cottages called Landboat Bungalows. She was landlocked and thirsty. It was stunning that she drank as much as she drank and lived as long as she did. She told a friend that ghost stories and whiskey were the only things that brought her comfort, but technically that wasn't true. Her bills from the liquor store JT Davies and Sons show that in addition to whiskey (Jameson Black Barrel and Teacher's), Rhys was drinking plenty of Gordon's Gin, Smirnoff, Martini Bianco, and Beaujolais. Her monthly booze bill sometimes rivaled all her other household expenses combined.

By the end of her life, Rhys was unable to live without assistance. In a red composition book bound with twine, her friend Diana Melly wrote a list of instructions for her various caregivers:

1. Avoid argumentative subjects like politics
2. Never discourage her from things she wants to do with her looks etc (i.e. like buy a red wig)
3. Don't discuss age and related subjects like grandmothers
4. Try and change the subject when things get emotional but do it slowly

Most of Melly's instructions, however, had to do with managing Rhys's daily drinking:

12:00. Drink. Only when she asks for it and in a small wine glass. Lots of ice, little gin, and fill with martini [vermouth]. It's always the same drink — morning and evening. Don't offer another drink <u>unless</u> she asks for it. (EVER)

1:00. Lunch. Pudding. (Nearly always there is an ice cream in the deep freeze.) Wine —if possible not more than two glasses. Only if she asks.

Melly crossed out those words as if admitting that any attempt to curtail might be futile. Elsewhere, she says: "NEVER drink anything different like whiskey in front of her or she will want it too." If Rhys demanded it, Melly suggested "tiny ones with masses of ice." Rhys almost always wanted them at twilight. "I stay with her then until 7-o-clock," Melly wrote, "as it is the time when she is most likely to get sad." Melly understood her friend's sadness as a type of clock-work, arriving with the dusk. It called for a drink, but what it really wanted was company. The drinking was past argument. It was less like a disease to be cured and more like a creature in the room, a wild animal that could be cajoled—with open ears, careful tongue, masses of ice—into a less ferocious version of itself.

But Rhys was wise to these tricks. During a visit with her friend David Plante, near the end of her life, she complained that other peo-ple were always filling her drinks with too much ice. "All of writing is a huge lake," she explained to him, her metaphors getting more fluid as she got drunker. "There are great rivers that feed the lake, like Tol-stoy and Dostoevsky. And there are trickles, like Jean Rhys." As Plante rose to leave, she asked, "Give me another drink, will you, honey? And put only one cube in it."

During that purgatory spring—after Dave and I had broken up, and then started seeing each other again—I asked him if he wanted to come hear me tell my story at a meeting. He seemed pleased and said yes. So on a chilled night in March, I picked him up in my tiny black Toyota, heat blasting as he came down to the lobby of his building (still strange to say that, *his*) in a plaid scarf and dark peacoat.

When I thanked him for coming, he looked me straight in the eye and told me it meant a lot to him that I'd asked.

We drove to a church at the edge of town, halfway to the Dairy Queen in Hamden, a black steeple against the sky, with only its base-ment glowing underneath, as if a little bit of yolky light had spilled under the church and gathered into a puddle. This was the Morse code signal for a meeting: dark church, lit basement. It was strange to bring Dave into that basement, where I'd cried about the end of our relationship. It made me feel like a fraud, or a fool. But he sat comfortably—near the back, with his messenger bag leaning against the metal legs of his folding chair. Seeing him alongside people I knew from recovery was like a dream in which all the corners of your life collide: There's your grandma clinking Coronas with the fencer you used to make out with junior year. Now Dave was chatting with a middle-aged woman sitting in the row behind him, laughing about something. And when I told the room, partway through my story, "Drinking made me selfish," I was really telling him.

We both knew it was more complicated than that, anyway. My selfishness was preexisting condition as well as consequence, and who isn't selfish, anyway? Maybe telling myself—or the room, or Dave—that drinking made me selfish was just a pragmatic way of holding myself accountable: *You've got no excuse to be selfish now.*

On one of the first warm days of spring, we took a boat ride through the Thimble Islands, off the Connecticut coast—salt wind off the Sound, both our mouths full of my flapping hair, cobalt water sparkling with hard flashes of sunlight like scattered glass. I imagined a possible future for us on every island, where our children could read in their lawn chairs, demanding pancakes. Dave had once written in a poem, the same one that had me drinking alone behind our house:

and now you're gone—
with wet hair and all our unborn children.
As I sit here giving them indelicate names
they crowd around the edge of the porch
raising their hands to be called on, rain
streaming down their arms, then through them.

These orphan children in the rain felt palpable, actual, as if we'd summoned them into being by loving each other so much, and then abandoned them by breaking up. So they had to stay outside the house—every house, on every thimble island—raising their hands, waiting to get called on, melting into the margins of *What if.*

It was like falling in love again, that spring — the giddiness, the wondering, the fantasizing — except that all these feelings were happening on top of an entire compost heap of other ones rotting into mulch: expectations, righteousness, anger. Our breakup had seemed final: the broken lease, our tearful conversations with each other and with everyone we knew; and this resuming held an eager secrecy, a sense of feverish urgency. Everything was tea leaves — the pattern of light, or the time Dave happened to call, a sign telling me, *This might work*, or else saying, *Give it up*. Every text message was a tarot card, auguring.

That summer, Dave went back to Iowa City — where many of our friends were still living — to teach. Over the distance I felt him disappearing into its patchwork of bar talks and whiskey nights on porches. It was like an old lover had found him in the phone book. I tried not to resent it, tried not to keep tallies — how much he'd been in touch, how much I'd been in touch — tried not to resent his distances, tried to tell myself I was ridiculous, I'd broken up with him, couldn't I give him this freedom? What did I think I was entitled to?

"I keep trying to fight myself to be a person who can be with D," I wrote to the same friend who'd hosted me in her tiny apartment as we were breaking up, feeding me Rihanna videos like pain medication. Fighting myself to be a person who could be with Dave reminded me of fighting myself to be a person who could drink. It wasn't that either Dave or booze was necessarily destructive — Dave wasn't toxic, just human; and plenty of people could drink just fine — it was that I kept trying to rearrange myself to make it work with both, kept telling myself I ruined things by needing them too much.

For Dave's birthday in August, after he got back from Iowa, I pooled money with some of our friends to rent a house in a town in the Catskills called Fleischmanns, a yeast baron's summer paradise full of Orthodox Jews from the city. The main bridge had been blown out by Hurricane Irene, and had a handwritten note tacked on its railing: WAYNE, PLEASE FIX THIS BRIDGE. The world was full of requests.

As a birthday present, I'd spent months gathering letters and photographs from everyone in Dave's life: friends, former teachers, his parents, his brothers. It was my attempt to resist the notion of love as a finite economy, where his love for others meant he had less of it for me. On that trip, I believed in us again. Our years together were not lost. My sobriety would save us. I hadn't been to a meeting in weeks. It had been getting harder and harder to share in meetings, because I'd shared so much about our breakup. Now I didn't know how to tell the story of our getting back together.

On our drive home from the Catskills, we stopped to play paintball. We were thirty going on thirteen, in rented coveralls, pelting each other with adrenaline. I'd been told the pellets might hurt, but they just felt like hail. The only one that really stung, that left a bruise, was the one that hit my neck and wouldn't break when it was supposed to.

That fall, I presented my dissertation topic for the first time, sitting at a polished conference table in a looming Gothic tower, talking to a group of graduate students and faculty. I'd been worried about sounding like a prude, making my unsexy case for the relationship between sobriety and creativity, and so I was wearing darker lipstick than usual, hoping to suggest—with MAC's diva-red Ruby Woo—that I still had a grip on things like risk and extremity. My Diet Coke stayed in my purse.

"But what about the relationship between *addiction* and creativity?" one professor asked. "Don't certain obsessions also produce experiment and variation?"

The eyes of the room flicked back and forth between us. I dutifully copied his question in my notebook. *Addiction = variation?*

"The generative aspects of obsession," he continued. "Now *that's* interesting to me."

I recognized his loaded *that*. It was standard academic protocol, pointing out hypothetical interest in a different question as a way of suggesting that the one you were asking wasn't interesting at all. It was as if this professor had said: *Tell yourself whatever you want, but nothing will ever yield as much as brokenness.*

"I think that—" I paused, stuttered. "I think addiction often feels like the opposite of variation."

What I wanted to say: *Addiction is just the same fucking thing over and over again. Thinking of addiction in terms of generative variation is the luxury of someone who hasn't spent years telling the same lies to liquor-store clerks.*

But I couldn't entirely dismiss what he'd said. Addiction wasn't simply creative gasoline, but it wasn't just blunt-force trauma either. I'd been so eager to dismiss the myths of whiskey and ink that it took me a while to stomach their truths: that yearning is our most power-ful narrative engine, and addiction is one of its dialects; that addiction is a primal and compelling story, structured by irony and hinged by betrayal, the fantasy of escape colliding with the body in ruin. "Pain comes from the darkness and we call it wisdom. It is pain," Randall Jarrell had written, but even his lines admitted their own deception: They were wisdom, and they'd come from pain.

The possibility of writing from addiction was more than an allur-ing lie; it was also genuine alchemy. When I went looking for the end of a mythology, I'd found strategies of exportation: Raymond Carver brought his drunk days into his sober stories. Amy Winehouse spent a sober week at her producer's condo in Miami, scribbling lyrics about booze that became the soundtrack to a million lives—a heartbroken professional, professionalizing her heartbreak. It was almost like measurements in a recipe: The right amount of pain could fuel the job without getting in the way of its execution. The lie wasn't that addic-tion could yield truth; it was that addiction had a monopoly on it.

In James Baldwin's story "Sonny's Blues," a jazz pianist tells his brother why he needs heroin: "It's not so much to *play*," Sonny tells him. "It's to *stand* it." But later Sonny recants his own assertion: "I don't want you to think it had anything to do with me being a musician. It's more than that. Or maybe less than that." His theory is most useful in its declaration of uncertainty: *Or maybe.* The hinge of that "or" refuses the easy argument that addiction makes him an artist, but it also confesses that he can't entirely dismiss the relationship either. The same pain drove him to find relief in both.

For me, recovery wasn't creative death; but it wasn't instant propulsion. It didn't deliver the New Creativity like a telegram. It was more like a series of generative formal constraints: finding stories in the world and trying to map their contours.

That year—when I lived alone, trying to wrestle my dissertation into a proposal—I went to Texas to try to write another reported piece. I spent four days interviewing people who believed they had a strange disease that made inexplicable fibers, threads, crystals, and fluff emerge from under their skin. Most doctors didn't believe them. At their annual conference, these patients used a microscope as large as an MRI scanner to search for fibers, traded stories of skeptical doctors, and swapped treatment tips: borax and root beer and antifungal creams. Their predicament didn't seem inexplicable to me, but utterly intuitive: They knew there was something wrong with them, but it didn't seem to be something anyone else could see. Everyone thought they were doing it to themselves. It made sense that they'd seek community as a way of understanding whatever was wrong with them, or fighting it.

When I talked to these patients, standing with my little silver tape recorder in the dry Texas heat; or when I ate vending-machine potato chips in a West Virginia prison; or sat on a picnic bench with weary long-distance runners; or strolled past community gardens in Harlem and asked a woman about relearning how to walk, I got to listen to voices that weren't mine. During those days of pitched tents and gray rain and power bars and bugle taps, withered tomato plants and late frost by the Hudson, it was sobriety on a different stage: showing up and paying attention.

Eventually I let myself give up on the Sandinista novel—understood that I was simply flinging myself against the wall of its ambitions, the literal wall of my office—and started seeking what the novel had been seeking all along: lives that weren't my own. The essays I started writing manifested a version of Jackson's ethos, *out of myself,* though they often held my own life as well: still a voice in the room, but not the only one. It was writing that was literally beyond me, insofar as it was often beyond my control: I couldn't shape what people said, or how they said it. This made the world feel infinite, as if it had suddenly arrived—when of course it had been there the whole time.

When Hurricane Sandy struck in late October, Dave and I holed up together in his sixth-floor apartment on Chapel Street as the wind wheezed and railed against his corner windows. After the storm was over, we wandered the quiet streets—cloaked by an eerie, dampened stillness—and found a huge oak tree uprooted in the downtown green, its roots exposed to the sky. By fall, we'd moved from the adrenaline rush of getting back together, the hotel bars and island orphans of our early renewal, back into the daily patterns of a relationship, irritated about who'd forgotten to buy toilet paper. Dave was making extra money by renting out his apartment on Airbnb and spending nights at my place. Our relationship had become a compromised version of itself, like a manuscript we were carrying around as loose-leaf papers in a shopping bag. When we fought, it was like both of us were more concerned with proving we were right—*I'm right to need these kinds of daily commitment! I'm right to need these kinds of freedom!*—than with figuring out how we might make it better.

During a walk in Wooster Square, Dave told me that one of his friends had called me emotionally abusive. We were in our old neighborhood, near our old apartment, trees full of leaves the same rust-orange and scarlet they'd been when we saw them from our living room the previous fall. It caught me off guard, *emotionally abusive,* but

I had to admit—looking at everything objectively—I couldn't say it was wrong. All of our messy reversals felt like a function of how hard I'd wanted to *try*, proof of the fact that something in me couldn't give up on us. But from the outside, or maybe even the inside, it just looked crazy and selfish.

One night that fall I nearly fainted at a restaurant downtown, while I was having dinner with a friend. Everything went dark near the counter full of cakes. When I sank to the floor and put my head in my hands, my closed eyes were playing shooting streaks of light. As my friend took me to the health center, she kept calling Dave, and he kept not picking up. When he finally arrived at the doorway to my hospital examining room—hours later, explaining that his phone had died—there was a look on his face that wasn't frustration, but it wasn't exactly love. Years later, my friend told me that she'd known we were done, or hoped we were done, when she saw the look on his face that night. She said it didn't look like someone who wanted to care for me. I knew he did, and that he had—but I also knew we were both tired.

I started to fantasize about relapsing, putting a case of wine in the backseat of my Toyota and driving up I-91, just like the cars I watched each morning from my apartment window, to drink myself into oblivion in some Hartford hotel room. Sometimes the relapse fantasy involved sleeping with strangers, or smoking crack, even though I hadn't been the kind of drunk (usually) who'd take home a stranger from a club, and I wouldn't have the first idea how to get my hands on crack. Sometimes the fantasy involved calling Dave in the middle of the night to come rescue me, even though he didn't have a car. Would he take the train? Would he have to *transfer* trains? It became an absurdly convoluted Cinderella complex. But I loved the cinematic melodrama of that screenshot: him bursting through a hotel door, telling me he'd do anything to help me get better. When in reality, I knew if I relapsed in a hotel room, I would probably just drink enough to splurge recklessly on pay-per-view and pass out halfway through the movie, or buy vending-machine chocolate bars and then get drunk enough to shove them into my mouth without guilt.

I'd spent much of my first round of sobriety telling other people in recovery that maybe I had to binge on harder drugs just to get bad enough to never drink or use again. "That sounds like a great plan," one woman said. Another shrugged, smiling, and said: "That sounds like something an addict would say."

Hartford seemed like the right landscape for these daydreams because of its grim skyscrapers and its unglamorous insurance companies, its resistance to redemption arcs. In online images, the downtown Hilton had a teal pool gleaming like a fruit lozenge—like something you could suck on, something my neighbors could turn into Technicolor jam—but it seemed too corporate and varnished, an imposing gray skyscraper. The Flamingo Inn was better, surrounded by yellow grass covered in dirty patches of snow, where a politician's son would die of a fentanyl overdose a few years later. Even when the sky was blue and full of puffy clouds, this place looked like it was getting rained on. It was perfect.

Relapse would be my revenge against sobriety, which hadn't inoculated me against disappointment—especially, most recently, my sinking realization that this second relationship with Dave was falling into the same tense patterns as our first one. If I were going to relapse, I certainly wouldn't do it on a single cocktail, like last time, trying to drink "better." This time, I wanted to give myself license to drink endlessly.

It's enough! Berryman had written, in his own Hartford motel room. *I can't BEAR ANY MORE.* It wasn't suicide I wanted but another bottom, an explosion whose rubble I could emerge from, ash-dusted and glittering with shards of glass. The fantasy of crisis—or explosion—was an alternative to the hard, ordinary work of living through uncertainty; and sobriety had given me fewer explosions to recover from.

That fall, Dave and I told each other we either needed to get married or break up for good. Those seemed like our only choices. When one of my best friends told me about another woman's relationship—"She says they either need to get married or break up, and you know those relationships are in trouble"—I just nodded, mute. *Yep.* But our day-to-day felt like purgatory, and I craved an impossible certainty; as if a relationship were ever anything besides waking up each morning and doing the best you could, not knowing where it would go next.

It had always been easier to imagine a future with Dave—on one of the Thimble Islands, maybe—than to live inside our present tense. We lived well in the cinematic epic mode, and not so well in the mundane realities of daily life. It was like jamming a jigsaw piece somewhere it wouldn't fit. I kept telling myself that I'd been wrong two years before, two weeks before—that I'd been trying the piece from the wrong angle. It would work now. In meetings, I'd heard: *Insanity is doing the same thing over and over again and expecting different results.*

At a meeting that fall, at a sober house in the suburbs, a woman spoke about wanting to be willing to stand with both her hands empty until something came to fill them. I wanted to be brave enough to do that, to let my hands stay empty for a while—and worried that perhaps I'd tried again with Dave because I hadn't been willing to stand with empty hands. But the truth was that I hadn't known how to stand with empty hands when I was with him, either. "Things don't always get better," someone had once told me at an Iowa meeting, "but they always get different."

Dave and I finally broke up the second time, for good, in a meatball restaurant in January, seven months after we'd gotten back together. We had to end twice, just like the drinking did; and like the end of the drinking, it was less like an explosion than plain depletion. We didn't have anything left. We had one last cigarette on his fire escape.

Walking away from his building, I remembered a woman I'd known in my early twenties, petite and dark-haired and beautiful as a witch, describing the aftermath of a difficult breakup: sitting on her bare hardwood floor and drinking red wine and listening to records. But that night, my despair was nothing glamorous. It was a late-night cookie as large as my palm, and chocolate smeared on my lips. Once I was home, I noticed a dead leaf stuck to the wool of my leg warmers, from a walk I'd taken with Dave a few days earlier, and I turned to the trash can, ready to throw it away—then took it off carefully and put it in a drawer instead. There was something in Dave I'd never find in anyone else. I might get other things, things I couldn't even imagine, but I would never get him. That felt unbearable.

—XIV—

HOMECOMING

I've had two different lives," Raymond Carver once said, meaning he'd lived one drunk, the other sober. "The past really *is* a foreign country, and they do do things differently there." His first life was spent largely with his first wife, Maryann, whom he'd met as a teenager when she was working behind the counter of a Spudnut Shop. She got pregnant at seventeen. They both had big dreams. They both drank. "Eventually," Carver wrote later, "we realized that hard work and dreams were not enough." Maryann packed fruit and waited tables to give her husband time to write. He drank himself bloated and silly. At a cocktail party in 1975, he hit her over the head with a wine bottle after she flirted with another man, severing an artery near her ear and almost killing her. Still, they loved each other deeply. Even after their marriage ended both said that repeatedly. But their life was "chaotic," he wrote, "without much light showing through."

Carver spent most of his second life, the decade after he got sober, with the poet Tess Gallagher, living in a town called Port Angeles—on the Olympic Peninsula in Washington, overlooking the Pacific—fishing in the ocean and in strong clear rivers. In the early years of his sobriety, he was writing so much he decided to buy himself a new typewriter to better handle his output. It was a Smith Corona Coronamatic 2500. "It sounds like a cigar," he told friends, "but it's my first electric typewriter." At one party he hid in the bushes because he was afraid of getting drunk. He looked back on the drama of his first life and understood his writing as something that had happened despite this chaos, rather than something fueled by it. "I was trying to learn my craft as a writer," he said, "how to be as subtle as a river current when very little else in my life was subtle."

This was manna to me: the idea that Carver's creativity had struggled *against* the chaos of his drinking years. I replaced my vision of Drunk Carver, delirious and darkness-facing at the Foxhead, with Sober Carver, pounding his typewriter at home and facing the wind in his sailboat, in the Strait of Juan de Fuca, catching big fish under bigger skies.

Sober Carver was a far cry from the drunk rogues of the white logic. He lived on Fiddle Faddle, a kind of candy-coated popcorn. At a teaching job in Vermont, he stole brownies and doughnuts from the cafeteria and stashed them in the desk drawers of his twin-bed dorm room. When he got flown to Zurich for a speaking gig, he sent back postcards saying he was "mainlining" chocolate and wanted to return to Zurich as the "Tobler Chocolate Chair in Short Fiction." Carver wasn't alone: In *Infinite Jest,* Wallace describes the "pastry-dependence" of sobriety, and I pictured my own early days as a towering stack of pink bakery boxes—full of blueberry muffins and smeared petits fours that never tasted like vodka, no matter how many I ate.

Sober Carver wanted sugar and affirmation. When his first collection came out, he carried around all the positive reviews in a briefcase and pulled them out to read aloud to friends. He also crafted bits of his own sober legend. Eight years into his sobriety, he wrote to a man who'd just quit drinking:

> *It took me at least six months— more— after I stopped drinking before I could attempt to do any more than write a few letters. Mainly I was so grateful to have my health back, and my life back, that it didn't really matter to me in one large way if I ever wrote anything again, or not…I tell you, and it's true, I wasn't worrying about it. I was just very happy, very happy to be alive.*

But the Carver of 1986 may have misrepresented the Carver of 1978. Maryann insisted that he started trying to write almost immediately after he stopped drinking, in a cabin they shared together during that first sober summer, where they celebrated their twentieth wedding anniversary with apple juice, smoked salmon, and fresh oysters. In his letter, Carver was pushing back against one myth (you had to surrender your creativity in sobriety) with another (getting sober meant you wouldn't care about your creativity anymore), presenting his life in ways he thought might be useful to a newly sober man.

If good fiction brings "the news from one world to another," as Carver once said, then his stories brought the news of what it had been like to get drunk and what it was like afterward. As his biographer Carol Sklenicka put it, "Bad Ray" from the alcoholic past sent dispatches that were diligently transcribed by "Good Ray" in the sober present. There was nothing dull or passionless about this transcription. "Each day without drinking had a glow and a fervor," Gallagher wrote. "The leopard of his imagination pulled down the feathers and blooded flesh of stories." Sober Carver's writing was virile and bold. He wrote poems like he caught fish. "I'm not into catch and release," he said. "I just start clubbing them into submission when I get them near my boat." The part of the Pacific coast that Carver called home was salt-charged and sea-swollen, its rivers cold and clear and surging. He was waking up at five each day to write, replacing chaotic fury with discipline. Jay McInerney, a friend and student, had always considered writers "luminous madmen who drank too much and drove too fast and scattered brilliant pages along their doomed trajectories." But Carver showed him "you had to survive, find some quiet, and work hard every day."

Carver treated his characters as he treated his fellows at an AA meeting—with curiosity and compassion, without condescension. "Ray respects his characters," Gallagher wrote, "even when they can't respect themselves," an echo of one AA slogan: *Let us love you until you can learn to love yourself.* Carver was surprised when reviewers remarked about how pathetic his characters were, because he thought of them as simply ordinary. He was saved from condescension by a sense of interchangeability. When a drunk ran in front of his car once, he said: "There but for the grace of God go I."

"Where I'm Calling From," one of his most famous stories, is set at Frank Martin's, a fictional "drying-out" place based on Duffy's, the Calistoga rehab where Carver himself had gone. The story evokes the dazed disorientation of early rehab—cigarettes smoked on the front porch, horror stories over eggs and toast—along with the ragged desperation that made it necessary: an exploded marriage, and then a car ride to detox with a new girlfriend, a bucket of fried chicken, and an open bottle of champagne. "Part of me wanted help," the narrator says. "But there was another part."

At rehab, the narrator finds solace in listening to a chimney sweeper named J.P. "Keep talking, J.P." he says. "Don't stop now, J.P." The narrator loves J.P.'s story, which ends up taking up more space on the page than his own, because, as he explains: "It's taking me away from my own situation." J.P.'s story didn't have to be interesting—"I would have listened if he'd been going on about how one day he'd decided to start pitching horseshoes"—it just had to belong to someone else.

The poetry Carver wrote during his final decade—those years on the Olympic Peninsula, fishing and writing—is electrified by gratitude and open-nerved beholding. "I have a thing / for this cold swift water," he wrote. "Just looking at it makes my blood run / and my skin tingle." The physical world isn't just pretty; it's a rush along his skin and in his blood. Gallagher called his poetry "as clear as glass and as sustaining as oxygen."

When he wrote about the water, his voice was always thankful. "It pleases me, loving rivers…Loving them all the way back / To their source. / Loving everything that increases me." The writer Olivia Laing finds a "boiled-down, idiosyncratic version" of the Third Step in this moment: *Made a decision to turn our lives over to the care of God as we understood God.* For Carver, loving rivers back to their source was a way of surrendering himself to something larger than he could properly understand—the palpable splendor and awe of the world itself. And I loved Carver back to his sources as well, reaching for the myths of sobriety once I got sober, just as I'd reached for the myths of drinking when I drank. I turned Sober Carver into another Higher Power, with surging rivers for veins, casting lines to hook the blooded flesh of his stories. But ultimately his work moved me largely because it had little time for myths. It preferred oxygen.

Gallagher says that Carver's sober poetry forges a "bond of mutuality" with the reader by creating a "circuitry of strong emotional moments in which we join the events at a place beyond invitation." The truest thing I can say of Carver's sober poetry is that I've joined it there: *A house where no one / was home, no one coming back, / and all I could drink.* Those lines resonated so much they felt like a meeting, as if I were sitting on a folding chair in some church basement— listening to Carver's voice deliver the news that it might be possible, someday, to want more than that.

In Carver's poems, sobriety isn't pious or humorless. It's wry and playful and it's often hungry. Sobriety means staring at the vast Pacific and eating buttery popcorn. *Loving everything that increases me.* Carver is increased by popcorn—also by the heavy sea churning, and the distant fireflies of strangers' homes lit up against the night. He insists he'll "smoke all the cigarettes I want, / where I want. Make biscuits and eat them / with jam and fat bacon." His sobriety is no Boy Scout. It wants to loaf around and smoke all day and hang out with its posse. "My boat is being made to order," Carver writes. "It's going to have plenty of room on it for all my friends." His boat will have fried chicken and piles of fruit. "No one will be denied anything."

Carver's sobriety isn't ascetic, it's just trying to imagine desire in new terms: a yacht of bounty, biscuits with jam and bacon. His speakers acknowledge temptation without lapsing into bitterness. One dreams about raising a bottle of whiskey to his lips, but then wakes up the next morning to see an old man shoveling snow, a reminder of daily persistence: "He nods and grips his shovel. / Goes on, yes. Goes on." That *yes.* As if Carver is talking to someone, or to himself— saying, *This is how the world continues.* If you talk to enough recovering alcoholics in cold climates, I can promise you will hear someone compare his sobriety to shoveling snow.

Of his drinking past, Carver once said: "That life is simply gone now, and I can't regret its passing." But it haunted his poems, that other life with the first woman he loved—the one with whom he wasn't sharing his sober years. "He'd known for a long time / they would die in separate lives and far from each other," he wrote, "despite oaths exchanged when they were young." Inside his second life, far from Maryann, Carver was still writing poems about his regret: "A problem with alcohol, always alcohol...What you've really done / and to someone else, the one / you meant to love from the start."

During the months after Dave and I broke up for good, New Haven had three huge blizzards. There were stretches of days when I didn't see anyone. One afternoon I tried to dig out my car, to free it before the plows arrived and blocked it in. (If you talk to enough recovering alcoholics in cold climates...) A couple were digging out beside me and by the time they were done with their car, I was done with one tire. The guy helped me dig out the other three. "You look like Amy Adams," he said, and his girlfriend said, "Not really." I'd never heard of Amy Adams, but I went home and Googled her face and ate an entire box of Swedish Fish and didn't talk to another person for three days. I wrote in my journal: *My soul is an endless mouth.*

That spring, I started volunteering at a writing group at the Connecticut Mental Health Center, a massive outpatient facility near the hospital. There were about five or six of us each week, gathered around a small table in a room that always smelled like clean gauzy bandages and wet clay. It was full of little plastic watercolor trays and stiff spiky brushes in plastic cups; it did double duty for art therapy. The group already had a leader, a paid staff member, and though I'd been enthusiastically welcomed as someone who could help facilitate, in practice I was more like just another participant, trying to find a good metaphor for my depression.

One week a man imagined what he would do with his last day of sight, and his piece included looking at a traffic jam: scuffed metal hubcaps and pissed-off New Englanders leaning on their horns. It seemed weirdly accurate, that you'd want to hold on to even the ugly stuff. Another week, a woman wrote a fairy tale about a butterfly looking for a queen bee. At the end, it turned out the queen had been looking for *her*. This was an old and good fantasy: the possibility that what you thought was beyond your grasp had actually been seeking you the whole time.

In the bitter middle of February, a university flew me out to Las Vegas to give a reading. No one had ever flown me anywhere to give a reading. Afterward we went out to the Strip, and sat in a bar that was supposed to look like the inside of a chandelier. I drank a mocktail with salt around the rim and felt entirely, exquisitely alive. Past midnight, one of my hosts asked if there was anything else I wanted to do, and I told him I wanted to buy a onesie for my friend's new baby—ideally something incredibly tacky. "Shouldn't be too hard," he said, and we drove to the biggest souvenir shop in town. Closed. We drove to the convenience stores near the wedding chapels. Closed. "This isn't done," the man said. We kept looking.

I loved him for that, for saying our night wasn't over. For me, it meant *nights* weren't over. He showed me the sharks in the aquarium at the Golden Nugget, gliding serenely around the glass tube of a waterslide. We eventually found my onesie on Fremont Street, under a giant dome of plasma screens, in a shop full of witty shot glasses. This was sobriety: three in the morning in Vegas, shopping for someone else's baby.

I went to meetings everywhere. I went to a meeting at the Riviera, at the north end of the Strip, spilling coffee onto the frayed carpet. I went to a meeting at a monastery in California—on a porch above a murmuring creek, our faces lit by oil lamps — led by a monk in robes. I went to meetings at a café in Los Angeles, full of recycled velour movie seats and women with birdlike faces and huge sunglasses who surprised me, time and again, with the earnest effort in their voices: *My name is…My name is…*I could sense their faith like a creature breathing — calling the names, one by one.

I officiated a friend's wedding and gulped ice water at the reception. Dave's ghost was everywhere: eating pea-shoot risotto, talking to the woman behind the bar. I was even nostalgic for the things I hadn't been able to stand. I left early and stopped at a gas station on the Merritt Parkway, smoked a cigarette outside the convenience store while rain came down in the dark. You can reclaim some things once you're ready; they've been waiting for you patiently. But some things are just lost for good.

That spring, I met Monica for fruit salad and coffee once a week. Part of our sponsoring relationship involved going over her answers to the same twelve-step worksheets I'd filled out with my own sponsor. *Did you ever get drunk even when you swore you wouldn't?* I told her about drinking with a Holter monitor dangling around my neck, wires hooked up to my pulse and cords hanging down my shirt, passing out drunk and waking up the next morning with a small metal box grinding into my ribs. She smiled and said I didn't look like the kind of person who'd drink with a little metal box around my neck, and I said: "Wouldn't you?"

Maybe she could have been anyone, and I could have been anyone; maybe those coffee dates only meant something because we wanted them to. But her trust, her belief that talking to me might help her get better, meant everything to me. What does that mean, *everything?* It means I was drawing on every part of my life that had come before, every blindfolded night and sour-mouthed morning. And it means that every moment of the rest of my sober life has held those ordinary coffee dates, that cut fruit under chilly spring sunlight. It was a life I would have dreaded, our lines of bubble letters carefully scripted across worksheets, our days full of iced tea and everything we were afraid of. This wasn't about epiphanies of the lightning-strike variety. This was more like *What was your answer for 12A?*

One evening, when Monica was driving me to a meeting, I saw a photo of her mother—who'd died when she was young—tucked under the passenger-side visor of her sensible midsize sedan. It took my breath away, imagining what had been waiting for Monica in every bottle of wine. We went to meetings at a senior center in East Haven with notes on the jigsaws: *Do not work on puzzles! Not fair to day patients.* I'd heard about the sober glow, the gradual radiance that came from being at ease in your own skin. I'd never seen it in myself, but I could see it in Monica. I would arrive at meetings to find her listening to the story of someone's day, or bringing him a cookie.

Berryman's *Recovery* knew how good it felt to feel so much for someone else. It was more than altruism. It felt righteous. That didn't make it false.

When I moved away from New Haven, Monica moved into my apartment, the first place I'd ever lived on my own without booze— where I'd watched the highway on crystalline early mornings, where the winter sun laid hot stripes across my knees while I whispered prayers to a God I wasn't sure I believed in. My sobriety lived there alone for a while, and then it lived there with hers.

On a bright November day, a year after I'd left New Haven, I drove out to Port Angeles from Seattle. I wanted to see the land where Carver had spent his second life—the years he didn't think he'd get—to find the rivers he had been increased by and the land where he was buried, in a cemetery high above the Strait of Juan de Fuca, overlooking the regal, bracing beauty of the Pacific. I wanted to see the poem fragment carved on his headstone like a catechism: *And did you get what / you wanted from this life, even so...And what did you want? / To call myself beloved, to feel myself / beloved on the earth.* I knew there was a notebook tucked in a black metal box beside his grave, and I wanted to see it, too—full of handwritten messages left by people who'd made the pilgrimage, people who'd been inspired by his work: sober people and relapsed people and still-drinking people who wanted to be not-drinking people; and maybe some people who had a nonalcoholic relationship to Carver, just like it was apparently possible to have a nonalcoholic relationship to booze itself.

In other accounts of visiting his grave, I'd seen quotes from the notebook: *R.C.—I traveled across the country to find myself at your grave…I come here from Japan to tell you the truth…Spending is an escape just like alcohol. We are all trying to fill that empty hole.* I imagined the notebook as the holy grail of my quest to make sobriety the best story of all: a swelling crescendo, the crowd-sourced "Amen." Thank God you wrote from sobriety, RC! Here's what it meant to us.

The Olympic Peninsula stunned me, all shimmering blue water at the Agate Pass and jagged white-capped mountains, layered spruces and lavender fields. It was easy to see how this land could make the high ritual cadences of a second life seem apt, as true as goose bumps on your arm in the generous fall light. It seemed saturated by sobriety, abundant and alive. I rolled down the windows and drove between forests of dappled evergreens, past the sun-sluiced water of a sudden cove and an old railway car turned into an ice cream shop; past brown hills shaggy from logging and pocked with apologies: FORESTERS PLANT SEEDS, said staggered signs, FOR THE FORESTS TO BE. At every vista I was struck by the expansive, anonymous beauty of it all, a beauty that didn't care if you found it beautiful or not, that just unfurled across the miles.

Hours earlier, on the ferry out to Bainbridge Island—surrounded by the outrageous splendor of the water, in the theater of Carver's self-mythologized rebirth—I'd read letters Rhys had written near the end of her life, about her squalid cottage and her nightly whiskey.

In the open spaces of Carver's recovery, I thought of the barred windows of the Narco Farm, and how the fishing trawler offered Billy Burroughs Jr. something that a prison never could, though neither was enough to save him. He died of cirrhosis at the age of thirty-three, after even a liver transplant couldn't keep him from drinking.

When I arrived in Port Angeles, it wasn't as quaint as I'd been picturing—and it was better that way. Rust-pocked cranes and lumberyards full of piled tree trunks flanked crane-shadowed commercial docks and marinas full of boats with names like *Tinker Toy* and *Mermaid's Song*. One writer had called the town "pretty and hard, like a beautician in a Carver story." A church marquee spread the word about a local 5K run called Hope Against Heroin, and a group of picketers across the street was picketing against hopelessness. NO MORE METH, said their signs. TAKE BACK OUR TOWN. Little neon crabs lit up the motel awnings. The farmers' market sold magenta-throated collard greens and ribbed yellow squash. A shop called Necessities and Temptations sold egg timers and crockpots and not one single ounce of cannabis, which was for sale up the hill, next to a place hawking salmon jerky and ocean-frozen albacore.

I had a Dungeness crab omelet at the Cornerhouse, the downtown diner where Carver and Gallagher had been regulars. I'd been told Gallagher still got what she called the Cyclops: an egg on a pancake. Every Tuesday night was still all-you-can-eat spaghetti. I wanted to find diner waitresses who would remind me of Carver's diner waitresses, with twin pulses of cynicism and hope running through the varicose veins beneath their panty hose. My waitress was mainly kind. It was her birthday. I felt guilty for not getting up and serving her a crab omelet instead. She would be celebrating that afternoon by babysitting her granddaughter. The walls were full of old photos: loggers leaning against felled trees with diameters twice the men's height. Grinning, all of them.

Stuffed, I tried to leave the final third of my omelet on my plate, but my waitress refused to let me off the hook. "We don't throw away

Dungeness crab in this diner," she said, no question mark in sight, and how could I disobey or disappoint her? I arrived at the graveyard full of crab. Carver had written that no one would be denied anything, on his boat. It was only right to arrive at his grave with a full stomach.

His gravestone was near the ridge, high above the water: a black granite slab beside one set aside for Gallagher. On the marble bench beside his grave, I sat between curves of bird shit. There was a black metal box under the bench, like a mailbox for the dead, with a Ziploc baggie tucked inside. My heart started beating fast as I opened it, palms damp with sweat. The notebook was red and fat and marked with a price tag from Bay Variety, a general store I'd seen downtown, and I flipped through its pages with a lump in my throat, ready for the silent chorus of a hundred different voices.

As it turned out, it was nearly blank. Gallagher had put a fresh notebook in the box the month before. This was the wounded owls all over again, never there when I needed them—the raptor center I'd tried to give a girl in early sobriety and hadn't been able to find. Knowing somewhere, *somewhere*, the maimed turkey vultures were living out their soap operas in cages among the trees. Now I was here with a blank book, neatly tucked between parentheses of shit.

I briefly, wildly imagined heading back downhill into town, driving to a bar or a meeting to rouse a few world-weary fishermen or loggers to write something in the notebook so I could quote them. *Make it brutal,* I'd say. Or perhaps the teacher in me would nudge, *Make it specific.* But it was just me and the dead, and Gallagher's note on the first page, left for everyone else who might write, and addressed to Ray himself: *There was a stubbed out cigarette on the bench and I brushed it away. I didn't get the message. An eagle is crying. A red tailed hawk flew up to us as we approached the bench. Life is still amazing and you are my precious cargo.* It gave me the goose bumps I'd imagined.

On the next page, one message from a stranger said: *When we pass we go where we believe.* A few pages later, a North Carolina musician had written that his first time reading Carver was his first time in the presence of true art. He'd tucked one of his CDs into a plastic shopping bag and put it in the mailbox too. If Carver had believed in an afterlife of boom boxes, perhaps he was already listening to it. The most recent note was from someone visiting from South Korea: *I walk my walk you have your rest. Thanks for what you have done and what you left for us.*

Nothing else. No eagle cried for me. I felt the old ghost of contract logic sitting beside me on the bench: If I make this pilgrimage, I'll get the words. If I care about this sober girl, we'll get the raptors. If I get sober while I'm with this man, we'll make a life together that sticks. I'd found an empty book where I was looking for a full one, and almost brushed it away. I didn't get the message. But the program Carver believed in wasn't really about what you took so much as what you gave. So I flipped to the first empty page and wrote simply, *Thank you.*

In Iowa, I found a librarian and a biker and a single mother standing in an alley behind a church. We said: *Hello. What's your name? Here's my damage.* In Kentucky, I sat beneath the gems of Christmas lights and listened to a man describe the burial ceremony he'd given his last bottle of whiskey. In Amsterdam, I put two euros in a porcelain clog and listened to a woman describe why her daughter wouldn't speak to her. In Los Angeles, I listened to an old man weep when he said his cat had died.

In Wyoming, in a room thick with Marlboro smoke, a twenty-year-old with a two-year-old said she wanted to become a geologist. In Boston, on Thanksgiving, a woman said she'd tried to kill herself, three years ago that day, and it hadn't worked, and here she was. In Portland, an activist and an oil rigger bumped the scars on their wrists. *It didn't work, and here we are.*

In Iowa, in Kentucky, in Wyoming. In Los Angeles, in Boston, in Portland. I could say I wrote this book for all of them—for all of us—or I could say they wrote this book for me.

In Minneapolis, a man shrank himself into the margins of his reading, becoming *1/500,000th*. In a little brown notebook, a woman put herself on trial. In the open country of Texas, a man worried God could see him too clearly. In a Manhattan hospital, a dying woman was handcuffed. Beside a river in Washington, a man was increased. Beside a river in Minnesota, a man was dead. Behind a church in Iowa, a biker in leather said the journey was just beginning, and a single mother said she couldn't imagine it continuing, and I heard them both, and the door was locked, and it did not stop us.

AUTHOR'S NOTE

This book devotes much of its attention to Alcoholics Anonymous, a singularly valuable grassroots organization that has become an important part of sobriety for many people. But twelve-step recovery isn't the only approach to substance dependence, and it's certainly not sufficient, or even helpful, for everyone. The problem isn't twelve-step recovery in its own right—though every few years, as if by clock-work, a mainstream magazine runs a polemical think-piece arguing just that—it's allowing twelve-step recovery to have a monopoly on our understanding of care. Any ethically responsible vision of treatment needs to include a much broader array of options, including medications like buprenorphine and methadone, as well as therapeutic approaches including cognitive-behavioral and motivational-enhancement therapy.

For much of the second half of the twentieth century, many rehabs steeped in twelve-step recovery believed that medication-assisted treatment compromised sobriety. It's as if medication became a sign of moral failure, a sign that someone was effectively still using—rather than confirming an understanding of addiction as a disease. But as journalist Lucas Mann writes in his essay "Trying to Get Right," an article about the regulations and often-great risks that thwart doctors who want to prescribe buprenorphine in communities facing addiction crises, medication is importantly different from *still using*, which isn't a moral failure anyway. Buprenorphine, for example, works as a partial agonist, binding to opiate receptors in a way that blocks other opiates from binding, but stimulating them to a ceiling of only 47 percent—so patients experience a limited (often nonexistent) high. Its antagonist component blocks overdose even when it's being "abused." And it's one of the most effective treatments we have, helping heroin addicts as they stabilize and rebuild their lives.

Every single clinician I consulted as I was writing this book stressed the importance of twelve-step recovery *and* medication-assisted treatment, all of them articulating a desire for more open communication between the twelve-step and the medical communities. As Dr. Greg Hobelmann put it, "There are a hundred ways to skin a cat," and over the course of writing this book I came to believe—quite firmly—in a pluralistic approach to recovery. For those interested in reading more about medication-assisted treatment and harm reduction, I'd suggest Mann's essay "Trying to Get Right" (published in *Guernica* magazine); Sarah Resnick's essay "H." (published in *n +1* magazine); Gabor Maté's *In the Realm of Hungry Ghosts: Close Encounters with Addiction*; and Maia Szalavitz's *Unbroken Brain: A Revolutionary New Way of Understanding Addiction*, an extraordinarily lucid book that reframes addiction as a learning disorder. If addiction is defined by its persistence in the face of negative consequences, Szalavitz argues, how can punishment ever be the most effective solution?

The stories we tell about addiction have always had a deep impact on legal policy and social opinion. (The War on Drugs is only the most radical demonstration of this.) And when it comes to narratives of addiction, it can be tempting to focus on a single kind of happy ending—enduring abstinence. But abstinence is a limited definition of healing that threatens to ignore the necessary work of harm reduction: clean-needle programs, supervised injection sites, over-the-counter distribution of Narcan (a life-saving overdose medication), and medical care for addicts. Accepting other story lines besides abstinence means accepting the fact that not every addiction story is going to follow the same arc, and pursuing policy measures that don't act as if abstinence is the only outcome we can imagine seeking.

When I spoke about the process of writing this book with Lucas Mann—who happens to be a personal friend, in addition to being a journalist who has written extensively about addiction—he told me that I probably had a lot more faith in twelve-step recovery than he did. He'd seen firsthand the damage it could do. He told me he knew a guy who'd gotten kicked out of a methadone-maintenance program for having dirty urine. Was that treatment? To Lucas, it seemed like the draconian outgrowth of an abstinence-only culture that could not make room for the messier story of relapse. The man died of an over-dose six weeks after getting kicked out of the program. Lucas was talking about his brother.

Every addict is someone's brother, or someone's son, or someone's lover, or someone's father, or all of the above—or none of the above, and all alone—but always, still, someone in the midst of a valuable human life.

We don't always like the messy parts of sobriety stories, the epi-logues and footnotes and afterwords: Bill Wilson's experiments with acid; Charles Jackson's returns to Seconal and booze; John Berry-man's relapses; Sober Carver smoking dope and snorting coke. But sometimes the story of getting better isn't a story about absolute abstinence. Sometimes it's a story about reducing danger and restor-ing health. As Gabor Maté told Sarah Resnick: "Abstinence is just not a model you can force on everybody. There's nothing wrong with it for those for whom it works. But when it comes to drug treatment there's an assumption that one size fits all. And if you're going to wash your hands of people who can't go the abstinence route, then you're giving up."

Supporting harm reduction involves acknowledging that sobriety might not come immediately, or even eventually, for everyone—that it might not be the triumphant concluding chapter at the end of every addiction story. (And even when it is, it's never a conclusion, and it's never easy.) When we resist the tyranny of abstinence—the notion that abstinence has a monopoly on meaningful healing—we allow ourselves to recognize that there are still lives that can be saved, still sick people who can be brought to better health.

On the level of policy, this book has already made its argument for shifting our national paradigm away from incarceration and toward decriminalization. But in this closing note, I'll just say that there are inspiring precedents to follow in this vein: Portugal's and Ireland's drug decriminalization programs, as well as successful supervised injection clinics in Switzerland and Canada, and efforts to set up similar clinics in America—in Ithaca, New York, for example, under the mayoral leadership of Svante Myrick. Drug decriminalization is only one part of the work we need to do to tackle the epidemic of substance abuse in America, and only part of the work we need to do to tackle the moral stain of mass incarceration, but it's the necessary legal infrastructure in which treatment can happen most effectively.

It's not just a question of policy, but a question of radically restructuring the way we think about addicts as villains—and, for that matter, criminals as villains—worthy only of punishment. It's not just about compassion, but pragmatism: What will help people get better? It's about adjusting our vision. Johnny Perez, a formerly incarcerated man now working as a criminal justice reformer, puts it like this: "If we see people as people, then we'll treat people as people. Period."

ACKNOWLEDGMENTS

The story of this book is the story of its sources. Because I wanted to write a book that worked like a meeting, I knew I needed to include the stories of others alongside my own. But one of my highest priorities in writing about recovery was preserving the anonymity of many of the people I was writing about. To this end, the people in recovery whose stories appear most extensively here—Sawyer, Gwen, Marcus, and Shirley—are all people I approached as a journalist, and their names have been changed. They agreed to have their lives become part of this project, and I am deeply grateful to them for their time, their honesty, their memories, and their insights. Their stories are based on telephone and in-person interviews conducted over the course of 2015.

I have also changed the name of almost every contemporary person in recovery who appears in this book—except when they requested I didn't—and, in certain cases, identifying details such as geographic location or gender. Whenever possible, I have secured the consent of everyone who appears as a figure in these pages, and if they are part of my narrative, I have given them the opportunity to read through the pages in which they appear. I'm grateful for their generosity and their openness.

In order to preserve their anonymity, I have not written extensively about many of the people who were most important to my recovery. But my gratitude to them runs deep. Thank you to everyone—the unnamed, anonymous, glorious everyone—whose sobriety has become part of my own.

In researching this book, I spent time at a number of archives, and I'm grateful to everyone who helped me navigate them: the Charles R. Jackson Papers at the Rauner Special Collections Library at Dartmouth College, Hanover, New Hampshire; the John Berryman Papers at the University of Minnesota, Minneapolis; the Jean Rhys Archive at the McFarlin Library at the University of Tulsa, Oklahoma; the Narcotic Farm Records at the National Archives in College Park, Maryland; the Stepping Stones Foundation Archive in Katonah, New York; the Center of Alcohol Studies Library at Rutgers University, New Brunswick, New Jersey; the David Foster Wallace Papers and the Denis Johnson Papers at the Harry Ransom Center at the University of Texas at Austin; and the William S. Burroughs Papers at Columbia University, New York City.

I consulted three clinicians and researchers for their perspectives on the science and treatment of addiction: Meg Chisolm, Adam Kaplin, and Greg Hobelmann, all practicing clinicians at (or affiliated with) Johns Hopkins University Hospital. I also found several conversations with writer Lucas Mann tremendously valuable in thinking about the relationship between twelve-step recovery and medication-assisted treatment. Carlton Erickson's *Science of Addiction*, Carl Hart's *High Price*, and Maia Szalavitz's *Unbroken Brain: A Revolutionary New Way of Understanding Addiction* all clarified and reshaped my sense of the physiological and psychological complexities of addiction—as well as the ways addiction research has been skewed to tell particular stories.

The literary and biographical analysis in these pages owes a tremendous amount to the work of literary biographers. I'm particularly indebted to Blake Bailey for his enchanting and impeccably researched biography of Charles Jackson, *Farther and Wilder*, and for his always convivial company, on the page and off. Blake's feedback on my own work about Jackson went above and beyond the call of duty.

Acknowledgments

We do not always agree, but my work is always strengthened by our disputes. I consulted D. T. Max's thoughtful biography of David Foster Wallace, *Every Love Story Is a Ghost Story*, as well as his reported work on Malcolm Lowry and Raymond Carver, and he was kind enough to provide insightful and generous feedback on several sections of this book. A number of other biographies were invaluable: Douglas Day's *Malcolm Lowry*; Carol Sklenicka's *Raymond Carver: A Writer's Life*; Carole Angier's *Jean Rhys: Life and Work*; Lilian Pizzichini's *The Blue Hour: A Life of Jean Rhys*; John Haffenden's *Life of John Berryman*; John Szwed's *Billie Holiday: The Musician and the Myth*; and Julia Blackburn's *With Billie: A New Look at the Unforgettable Lady Day*, as well as Billie Holiday's *Lady Sings the Blues*. I'm also grateful to George Cain's family—especially Jo Pool and Malik Cain—for sharing memories of his life.

In my literary analysis, I was in conversation with a number of deeply insightful critics and scholars who helped shaped my understanding of the complicated links between addiction, recovery, and creativity: John Crowley's *White Logic: Alcoholism and Gender in American Modernist Fiction* and Olivia Laing's *Trip to Echo Spring: On Writers and Drinking*, as well as Elaine Blair's *New York Review of Books* essay on David Foster Wallace ("A New Brilliant Start"), are all works of literary criticism that examine with humanity and insight the relationship between addiction, recovery, and creativity. Crowley's book was especially formative and helpful in its illuminating treatment of the rivalry between Jackson and Lowry, and the ways in which *The Lost Weekend* and *Under the Volcano* offer contrasting visions of alcoholism.

As I tried to figure out the larger social context for how addiction has been narrated in twentieth-century America, I found tremendous—and necessarily horrifying—insight and illumination in Michelle Alexander's *The New Jim Crow: Mass Incarceration in the Age of Colorblindness*, Drew Humphries's *Crack Mothers: Pregnancy, Drugs, and the Media*, Johann Hari's *Chasing the Scream: The First and Last*

Days of the War on Drugs, and Doris Marie Provine's *Unequal Under Law: Race in the War on Drugs.* Avital Ronell's *Crack Wars: Literature Addiction Mania* and Eve Kosofsky Sedgwick's "Epidemics of the Will" helped structure my thinking about how the social imagination has absorbed and produced various, often contradictory, notions of addiction. Gabor Maté's *In the Realm of Hungry Ghosts: Close Encounters with Addiction* helped me think about addiction, harm reduction, and decriminalization in new ways. Nancy Campbell, J. P. Olsen, and Luke Walden's *The Narcotic Farm* was a vital resource on the cure at Lexington. I also consulted the literary accounts of the Narcotic Farm offered in Clarence Cooper's *Farm,* William Burroughs's *Junkie,* Billy Burroughs Jr.'s *Kentucky Ham,* and Helen MacGill Hughes's *Fantastic Lodge: The Autobiography of a Girl Drug.*

I'm grateful to all the clinicians, social workers, and caregiving professionals aiding vulnerable populations struggling with substance dependence who shared their insights and wisdom with me along the way. Substantial portions of the advance from this book have gone to support two nonprofit organizations devoted to aiding vulnerable populations affected by substance dependence: the Bridge, a New York City transitional housing facility; and Marian House, a Baltimore transitional housing facility that serves women emerging from incarceration, homelessness, and inpatient treatment programs.

Much of the research for this book was drawn from the dissertation I wrote for my doctoral program at Yale University, and I'm grateful to my advisers there: Wai Chee Dimock, Amy Hungerford, and Caleb Smith. All three of them supported me with hard questions and keen insights, again and again, over the course of many years. Caleb offered me the provocation I needed, even—often—when I didn't know I needed it. My once-teacher and forever-friend Charles D'Ambrosio is one of the most extraordinary people I've ever met. His words are with me every time I sit down to write.

The Lannan Foundation generously gave me a residency in Marfa, Texas, for the month of April 2015, and it's not hyperbole to say that this month allowed the book to come to life: I spread an outline across the floor of my office, worked twelve hours a day, and finally believed that it could actually *be*.

I've been lucky enough to work with extraordinary editors near and far, especially Max Porter at Granta, Karsten Kredel at Hanser Berlin, Svante Weyler at Weyler Förlag, Robbert Ammerlaan and Diana Gvozden at Hollands Diep, Sophie de Closets and Leonello Brandolini at Fayard, and — of course, always — Jeff Shotts and Fiona McCrae at Graywolf, and the inimitable Amber Qureshi, all friends and allies and kindred spirits for life, as well as Michael Taeckens, who holds a special place in my heart. Thank you to Trinity Ray and Kevin Mills at the Tuesday Agency, who make hitting the road possible. Thank you to my inspiring colleagues at Columbia University, a community I'm perpetually grateful to be part of; and to all my students past and present — at Columbia, Yale, Wesleyan, and Southern New Hampshire University — who have challenged, surprised, and inspired me. Sean Lavery spent almost a year fact-checking this book, setting me straight about *Real World*, the War on Drugs, and everything in between.

I've been working with the Wylie Agency for more than a decade, and I consider myself absurdly lucky to have landed with Andrew Wylie, who believed in me from the beginning, and the unstoppable Jin Auh, a force of nature who has been my ally, confidante, fierce advocate, and cherished friend for years. A particular thanks also to Jessica Friedman, savior and wunderkind, and to the folks at Wylie UK, especially Luke Ingram and Sarah Chalfant.

Thank you to everyone at Little, Brown: Reagan Arthur, for believing, and Michael Pietsch, for inviting me into a legacy I admire so deeply. Thank you to Allison Warner, for designing such a beautiful jacket; to Pamela Marshall, Deborah P. Jacobs, and David Coen, for making sure everything was right inside; and to Craig Young, Lauren Velasquez, Sabrina Callahan, and Liz Garriga, for helping to bring it to the world. Thank you to Cheryl Smith and Charles

McCrorey, for welcoming me into their enchanted audio cave; to Sarah Haugen and Cynthia Saad; and of course to Paul Boccardi, for coming to that first meeting. Last but not least, my deep gratitude to the fiercely intelligent and deeply passionate Ben George. I believed you were the editor for this book from the very beginning, but working on it with you was more intense, and more rewarding, than I ever could have imagined. Thank you for your humanity, your relentless belief, and your soulful eye. You do the work right.

I am lucky to count so many extraordinary writers and thinkers as the deep and lasting friends of my life. They listened to me talk about this book for eight years, and I'm grateful for it, particularly to the ones who read portions of this book (Jeremy Reff and Greg Pardlo) and the ones who—miraculously—read the whole damn thing: Harriet Clark, Colleen Kinder, Greg Jackson, Nam Le, Emily Matchar, Kyle McCarthy, Jacob Rubin, and Robin Wasserman. I'm also grateful for the grace of their company and wisdom, along with countless others, especially Rachel Fagnant, Abby Wild, Aria Sloss, Katie Parry, Bri Hopper, Tara Menon, Alexis Chema, Casey Cep, Miranda Featherstone, Ben Nugent, Kiki Petrosino, Max Nicholas, Jim Weatherall, Nina Siegel, Bridget Talone, Emma Borges-Scott, Margot Kaminski, Jenny Zhang, Michelle Huneven, Micah Fitzerman-Blue, Taryn Schwilling, Ali Mariana, Susan Szmyt, Staci Perelman, the ladies of DeLuxe—especially Jamie Powers and Mary Simmons—and the Lunch Bunch from way back when: Eve Peters, Amalia McGibbon, Caitlin Pilla, and Meg Swertlow.

I owe a particular note of thanks to David Gorin, who read drafts of this book not once but twice, and offered his heart and singular mind to the task of making it truer. DG: Thank you for our years together, and for the care, intelligence, insight, and grace you brought to this project.

Thank you to my entire extended family, who fill my life with anchoring and inspiration: Jim, Phyllis, Ben, Georgia, Genevieve, Ian, Cathie, Kerry, Colin, and all their next generations; Grandpa

Acknowledgments

Jack (at one hundred years old!); and especially my aunts Kay and Kathleen, as well as my stepparents, Mei and Walter. Gratitude to my brothers, Julian and Eliot, worshipped from the very beginning, and their beautiful families; to my father, Dean, whom I love so much it makes my heart swell; and to my singular, beloved mother, Joanne Leslie, for whom there will never be enough words, or enough gratitude, only the knowledge that nothing I do would be possible without her love.

Thank you to Lily: beautiful human, dervish tornado, firecracker and delight.

Thank you to Ione Bird, who breaks me open with love each day. Everything is still ahead.

Finally, thank you to my husband, Charles Bock, who read this book first, and helped me see what it could become; then read it again, a year later, and helped me take it the rest of the way. I'm grateful for your intelligence, your own beautiful writing, and—most of all—your love. You make me laugh like no one else. Thank you for making every day of life better than the script I could have written for it.

NOTES

I. WONDER

7   It has always been a hazard for me to speak at an AA meeting...I think I got tired of being my own hero...I've written a book that's been called the definitive portrait of the alcoholic...Charles Jackson, speech, Alcoholics Anonymous, Cleveland, Ohio, 1959.

17   The myths of Iowa City drinking ran like subterranean rivers beneath the drinking we were doing....For more on John Cheever in Iowa, see Blake Bailey's biography *Cheever: A Life* (New York: Knopf, 2009). For more on Ray Carver in Iowa, see Carol Sklenicka's biography *Raymond Carver: A Writer's Life* (New York: Scribner, 2009); and for a vivid and incisive account of their friendship, see also Olivia Laing's *The Trip to Echo Spring: On Writers and Drinking* (New York: Picador, 2014). For more on Berryman in Iowa, see John Haffenden's biography *The Life of John Berryman* (London: Methuen & Co., 1984).

17   *just a poor mortal human*...Denis Johnson, "Where the Failed Gods Are Drinking," *The Throne of the Third Heaven of the Nations Millennium General Assembly: Poems Collected and New* (New York: Harper Perennial, 1995).

17   When Cheever showed up to teach in Iowa, he was grateful for the glen...For more on Carver and Cheever's friendship, see Sklenicka, *Raymond Carver: A Writer's Life*, 253, 258. For Yates and Dubus, see Blake Bailey's biography of Yates, *A Tragic Honesty: The Life and Work of Richard Yates* (New York: Picador, 2003).

18   He and I did nothing *but* drink...Carver, qtd. in Sklenicka, *Raymond Carver: A Writer's Life*, 253.

18   blue mice and pink elephants...the pitiless, spectral syllogisms of the white logic...Jack London, *John Barleycorn* (New York: The Century Company, 1913), 7–8.

18   bitten numbly by numb maggots...sees through all illusions...God is bad, truth is a cheat, and life is a joke...Ibid., 14. In certain versions, the text is quoted as "Good is bad, truth is a cheat, and life is a joke" (for example, a serialized version of London's novel in the *Saturday Evening Post* 185, no. 7, March 15, 1913).

19   cosmic sadness...Ibid., 309.

19 **so bad it was like somebody was sticking wires**...Raymond Carver, "Vitamins," *Collected Stories*, ed. William Stull and Maureen Carroll (New York: Library of America, 2009), 427.

19 **You can't tell a bunch of writers not to smoke...Now we are going to tell each other our life stories**...Carver, qtd. in Sklenicka, *Raymond Carver: A Writer's Life*, 270.

20 **Ray was our designated Dylan Thomas, I think—our contact with the courage**...Sklenicka, *Raymond Carver: A Writer's Life*, 265.

20 **It was really difficult even to look at him, the booze and the cigarettes were so much there**...Ibid., 269.

20 **Of course there's a mythology**...Raymond Carver interview, Mona Simpson and Lewis Buzbee, *Paris Review* (Summer 1983).

20 ***invisible* forces**...Sklenicka, *Raymond Carver: A Writer's Life*, 269. See Sklenicka for a fuller account of Carver's attachment to *John Barleycorn*.

22 **like a hummingbird over a blossom**...Denis Johnson, *Jesus' Son* (New York: Picador, 2009), 53.

22 **McInnes isn't feeling too good today**...Ibid., 37.

23 **The sky was torn away**...Ibid., 66.

23 **When Johnson arrived in Iowa City as a college freshman in the fall of 1967**...These details about Johnson's freshman year are from a letter he wrote to his parents, Vera Childress and Alfred Johnson, September 20, 1967, Denis Johnson Papers, Harry Ransom Center, University of Texas at Austin.

23 **Boy, I tried all day to get you out of jail**...Peg [last name unknown.] Greeting card to Denis Johnson, November 1967, Denis Johnson Papers, Harry Ransom Center, University of Texas at Austin.

23 **I kissed her fully**...Johnson, *Jesus' Son*, 93.

24 **diamonds were being incinerated in there**...Ibid., 9.

24 **And you, you ridiculous people**...Ibid., 10.

24 **Because we all believed we were tragic**...Ibid., 32.

26 **Whisky and ink...These are the fluids John Berryman needs**...Jane Howard, "Whisky and Ink, Whisky and Ink," *Life Magazine*, July 21, 1967, 68.

27 **I am, outside**...John Berryman, "Dream Song 46," *The Dream Songs* (New York: Farrar, Straus and Giroux, 1969).

27 **Are you radioactive, pal?**...John Berryman, "Dream Song 51," *The Dream Songs*.

27 **Hey, out there!—assistant professors, full, / associates,—instructors—others**...John Berryman, "Dream Song 35," *The Dream Songs*.

27 **whole fucking life out in the weather**...Deneen Peckinpah to John Berryman, July 8, 1970, John Berryman Papers, University of Minnesota.

27 **At present, the figure is mountainous**...James Shea to John Berryman, September 1954, John Berryman Papers, University of Minnesota.

27 **The day Berryman showed up in Iowa, he fell down a flight of stairs**...See Laing, *The Trip to Echo Spring: On Writers and Drinking*, 225.

27 **Mr. Berryman often called me**...Bette Schissel, qtd. in Haffenden, *The Life of John Berryman*, 283.

28 **Hunger was constitutional with him**...John Berryman, "Dream Song 311," *The Dream Songs*.

28 **I, who longed for her love**...Jill Berryman to John Berryman, qtd. in Haffenden, *The Life of John Berryman*, 9.

28 **I have the authority of suffering**...Haffenden, *The Life of John Berryman*, 149.

28 **in violent temper & razor sensibility**...Ibid., 154–55.

28 **I would not worry...about an analogy to Rilke**...James Shea to John Berryman, January 19, 1954, John Berryman Papers, University of Minnesota.

28 **Inspiration contained a death threat**...Saul Bellow, "Introduction," John Berryman, *Recovery* (New York: Farrar, Straus and Giroux, 1973), xii.

29 **With your work...I often have the feeling that yr poems are the light...** Deneen Peckinpah to John Berryman, July 8, 1970, John Berryman Papers, University of Minnesota.

29 **Something can (has) been said for sobriety**...John Berryman, "Dream Song 57," *The Dream Songs*.

29 **nihilistic and sentimental idea of 'the interesting'**...Susan Sontag, *Illness as Metaphor* (1978; repr., New York: Picador, 2001), 31, 26, 28.

30 **see the truth, the simplicity, and the primitive emotions once more**...Patricia Highsmith qtd. in Olivia Laing, "'Every hour a glass of wine' — The Female Writers Who Drank," *The Guardian*, June 13, 2014.

31 **A woman could not know the perils**...Malcolm Lowry, *Under the Volcano* (New York: Reynal and Hitchcock, 1945), 108.

31 **I will *not* drink**...Elizabeth Bishop, *One Art: Letters*, ed. Robert Giroux (New York: Farrar, Straus and Giroux, 1995), 210–11.

31 ***Please* just don't...scold me**...Ibid., 600.

31 **Maybe Jane Bowles understood something**...Negar Azimi, "The Madness of Queen Jane," *The New Yorker*, June 12, 2014.

31 **Maybe Marguerite Duras understood something**...These pieces of Duras's story are from Edmund White's "In Love with Duras," *New York Review of Books*, June 26, 2008. As White writes, "Then [Duras and her companion Yann Andréa] would start uncorking cheap Bordeaux and she'd drink two glasses, vomit, then continue on till she'd drunk as many as nine liters and would pass out." Nine liters translates to twelve bottles, and is well over the amount generally considered lethal, so it's most likely that White is offering a tall-tale version of Duras and her drinking — but regardless, she was drinking enough to incapacitate herself daily.

31 **When a woman drinks**...Marguerite Duras, *Practicalities* (London: William Collins Sons, 1990), 17.

32 **Intoxication in a woman was thought to signal a failure of control**...Sherry H. Stewart, Dubravka Gavric, and Pamela Collins, "Women, Girls, and Alcohol," *Women and Addiction: A Comprehensive Handbook* (New York: The Guilford Press, 2009), 342.

32 **I've escaped...A door has opened and let me out into the sun**...Jean Rhys, *Smile Please: An Unfinished Autobiography* (New York: Harper & Row, 1979), 142.

32 **Even though they were young and poor...** Details about Rhys's life in Paris in late 1919 from Carole Angier's *Jean Rhys: Life and Work* (New York: Little, Brown, 1991), 107–13.

32 **Paris tells you to forget, forget, let yourself go...** Jean Rhys, *After Leaving Mr. Mackenzie,* in *The Complete Novels* (New York: W. W. Norton, 1985), 91.

32 **I was never a good mother...** Angier, *Jean Rhys: Life and Work,* 113.

32 **This damned baby, poor thing, has gone a strange colour...** Qtd. in ibid., 112.

32 **He was dying...** Jean Rhys, *Smile Please,* 119.

33 **I know about myself...** Jean Rhys, *Good Morning, Midnight,* in *The Complete Novels* (New York: W. W. Norton, 1985). Qtd. in Angier, *Jean Rhys: Life and Work,* 378.

33 **struggle with life...the way a sleeper struggles...** Mary Cantwell, "Conversation with Jean Rhys, 'the Best Living English Novelist,'" *Mademoiselle,* October 1974.

33 **It was astonishing how significant...** Jean Rhys, *Quartet,* in *The Complete Novels* (New York: W. W. Norton, 1985), 130.

34 **When you were drunk...you could imagine that it was the sea...** Rhys, *After Leaving Mr. Mackenzie,* in *The Complete Novels,* 241.

34 **I must get drunk tonight...** Rhys, *Quartet,* in *The Complete Novels,* 217.

34 **the bright idea of drinking myself to death...** Jean Rhys, *Good Morning, Midnight,* in *The Complete Novels,* 369.

34 **Sometimes I'm just as unhappy as you are...** Ibid., 347.

34 **You said that if you drink too much you cry...** Ibid., 449.

35 **It was bad policy to say that you were lonely...** Rhys, *Smile Please,* 94.

35 **I could deny myself...Then I could make them love me and be kind to me...** Jean Rhys, Black Exercise Book, Jean Rhys Archive, University of Tulsa.

35 **Now I have had enough to drink...** Rhys, *Good Morning, Midnight,* in *The Complete Novels,* 393.

II. ABANDON

43 **I had two longings and one was fighting the other...** Jean Rhys, Green Exercise Book, Jean Rhys Archive, University of Tulsa.

43 **I searched for a big stone...** Jean Rhys, *Smile Please: An Unfinished Autobiography* (New York: Harper & Row, 1979), 31. All details of Rhys's Dominica days come from her unfinished memoir, unless otherwise noted as coming from Carole Angier's *Jean Rhys: Life and Work* (New York: Little, Brown, 1991).

43 **I wanted to identify myself with it...** *Smile Please,* 66.

43 **the sound of cocktail-making...** Ibid., 17.

43 **Hanging above the family silver...** Rhys, *Smile Please,* 17

43 **Rhys's writing could never fully reckon with the suffering closer at hand, and larger than herself: the long shadow of slavery...** Rhys's family had owned and run the Geneva plantation (acquired by her great-grandfather, James Potter Lockhart, in 1824; his ledgers record that he owned twelve hundred acres and 258 slaves) until it was destroyed in the so-called Census Riots (also called La Guerre

Negre, which followed Emancipation in 1844). See Lillian Pizzichini, *The Blue Hour: A Life of Jean Rhys* (New York: W. W. Norton and Company, 2009), 12.

44 **When she was twelve**...Rhys's age when she was abused by Mr. Howard varies in different versions of the story that she wrote down (from twelve to fourteen). See Angier, *Jean Rhys: Life and Work* (27) for a fuller account, as well as Rhys's Black Exercise Book.

44 **Would you like to belong to me?**...Rhys, Black Exercise Book, Jean Rhys Archive, University of Tulsa.

44 **It was then that it began**...Rhys, Black Exercise Book, 64, Jean Rhys Archive, University of Tulsa.

44 **I've made a complete wreck of myself**...Ibid., 72.

44 **I wish I could get it clearer this pain that has gone through all my life**...Ibid.

44 **You've no idea darling**...Ibid.

45 **she kept the receipt from his burial for the rest of her life**...Angier, *Jean Rhys: Life and Work*, 113.

45 **You're much too early**...Ibid., 235. See Angier for a fuller account of Rhys's relationship with her daughter Maryvonne.

45 **My mother tries to be an artist**...Ibid., 285.

48 **As legend had it, he'd painted the mouth of a cave onto a wall in the emperor's palace**...For a fuller version of the legend of the Wu Tao-tzu legend, see Herbert Allen Giles's *Introduction to the History of Chinese Pictorial Art* (London: Bernard Quaritch, 1918), 47–48.

52 **I'm finding out what a useful thing drink is**...Ibid., 74.

52 **Kitten...you make my heart ache sometimes**...Lancelot Grey Hugh Smith's letters qtd. in ibid., 68.

52 **And then it became part of me**...Rhys, *Smile Please*, 97.

52 **The whole earth had become inhospitable to her**...Francis Wyndham qtd. in Angier, *Jean Rhys: Life and Work*, 71.

53 **You see I like emotion**...Jean Rhys to Peggy Kirkaldy, July 3, 1946, in *Jean Rhys Letters, 1931–1966*, ed. Francis Wyndham and Diana Melly (London: Andre Deutsch, 1984), 45.

53 **"Why We Drink"**...Angier, *Jean Rhys: Life and Work*, 53.

53 **On an extended canvas...one becomes more than ever conscious**...Review from *The New Statesman* qtd. in ibid., 234.

53 **the subject of her first manuscript, *Voyage in the Dark***...*Voyage in the Dark* was the first novel Rhys wrote, though it was not the first novel she published. It was drafted in 1911–1913 but published in 1934, after both *Quartet* and *After Leaving Mr. Mackenzie*. See Lillian Pizzichini, *The Blue Hour*.

53 **I'm not miserable**...Jean Rhys, *Voyage in the Dark*, in *The Complete Novels* (New York: W. W. Norton, 1985), 68.

54 **Oh no...not a party exactly**...Rhys, *Smile Please*, 101.

III. BLAME

61 **Someone carrying crack gets five years in prison**...Michelle Alexander, *The New Jim Crow: Mass Incarceration in the Age of Colorblindness* (New York: The New

Press, 2010), 206–7. For statistics on the number of alcohol-related driving fatalities per year, see the CDC report at https://www.cdc.gov/motorvehiclesafety /impaired_driving/impaired-drv_factsheet.html. The report states that "10,265 people died in alcohol-impaired driving crashes" in 2015, as opposed to just under 7,000 cocaine-related deaths. (See National Institute on Drug Abuse, https://www .drugabuse.gov/related-topics/trends-statistics/overdose-death-rates.)

61 **who is viewed as disposable—someone to be purged from the body politic**...Alexander, *The New Jim Crow*, 206.

61 **the drug-scare narrative**...See Drew Humphries's fuller and astute discussion of the phenomenon of the "Drug Scare Narrative" in *Crack Mothers: Pregnancy, Drugs, and the Media* (Columbus: Ohio State University Press, 1999).

62 **the most malignant, addictive drug known to mankind**...Physician Michael Abrams qtd. in Dirk Johnson, "Good People Go Bad in Iowa, and a Drug Is Being Blamed," *New York Times*, February 22, 1996.

62 **But by the time a 2005 *Newsweek* cover story called meth**...Jacob Sullum, "Hyperbole Hurts: The Surprising Truth about Methamphetamine," *Forbes*, February 20, 2014, referring to "The Meth Epidemic—Inside America's New Drug Crisis," *Newsweek*, July 31, 2005.

62 **not particularly exciting nonaddiction story that never gets told**...Carl Hart, *High Price: A Neuroscientist's Journey of Self-Discovery That Challenges Everything You Know About Drugs and Society* (New York: Harper, 2013), 122, 19, 188–91. Statistics demonstrate that most people who use drugs don't become addicts. Even with heroin, the drug (apart from tobacco) with the highest "capture rate," only 13 percent of users develop an addiction. Other studies put the number a bit higher, reporting that heroin's "capture rate" is around 23 percent; that is, around 23 percent of those who use will become dependent, which still means that the majority do not. See this report from the UK National Addiction Centre, http://www.nta.nhs.uk/uploads/ dangerousnessofdrugsdh_4086293.pdf.

63 **Anslinger effectively channeled the punitive impulse that had fueled Prohibition**...Doris Marie Provine called prohibition and drug criminalization "sister movements." *Unequal Under Law: Race in the War on Drugs* (Chicago: University of Chicago Press, 2007), 89.

63 **But during the decades that followed, the American legal system would polarize alcohol and drug addictions into separate categories in the public imagination: the former a disease, the latter a crime**...One of the most common questions I received while working on this book—and before that, while I was working on this book as a dissertation—was whether I was writing about alcoholism or drug addiction, as if it was somehow strange to think about them together. In truth, I think it's more strange to think of them apart—or at least, to draw a dividing line between alcohol and everything else. It's only the legal system and the popular imagination that have categorized nicotine and alcohol on one side of a categorical divide, and "illicit" drugs on the other. Physiologically, it's an arbitrary border. Not because there aren't differences between substances—the kinds of dependence they produce, and how likely they are to produce it—but because every substance works differently, and alcohol is just one substance among many. In *The Science of Addic-*

tion: From Neurobiology to Treatment (New York: W. W. Norton, 2007), Carlton Erickson recommends more specific language around addiction—specifically, recommends replacing the catch-all term of "addiction" with more specific categories of "abuse" (using with negative consequences) and "chemical dependence" (unable to stop without help) and offers a chart of "dependence liability" (25–26) that ranks heroin highest, then cocaine, then nicotine—with alcohol close behind. The British medical journal *The Lancet* released a chart that attempted to measure the respective "dependence potentials" of a variety of substances—calculated from the amount of pleasure they offer, their potential to create physical dependence, and their potential to create psychological dependence—and ranked them in the following order: heroin, cocaine, tobacco, barbiturates, alcohol, benzodiazepines, amphetamine, cannabis, ecstasy. (David Nutt et al., "Development of a rational scale to assess the harm of drugs of potential misuse," *The Lancet* 369, no. 9566 [2007]: 1047–53.) But all this research suggests a new paradigm that replaces binary categories (cigarettes and alcohol on one side, "illicit" drugs on the other) with a way of seeing that understands each substance as its own particular confluence of probabilities and effects.

63 **Before the Harrison Narcotics Tax Act of 1914...** The next two decades witnessed a sea change in the way Americans thought about drugs and the figure of the addict, and how the American legal system treated them. More comprehensive criminalization measures followed in the wake of the regulatory Harrison Act: the Jones-Miller Act of 1922, the Anti-Heroin Act of 1924, and the Uniform State Narcotic Drug Act of 1934.

63 **psychopaths...created by infectious contact with persons already drug-conditioned...** Harry Anslinger and William Tompkins, *The Traffic in Narcotics* (New York: Funk and Wagnalls, 1953), 223.

63 **loathsome and contagious diseases...** Anslinger qtd. in Johann Hari's *Chasing the Scream* (New York: Bloomsbury, 2015), 14, citing Larry Sloman, *Reefer Madness* (New York: St. Martin's Press, 1998), 36. Even though alcohol has been our go-to "legal" drug, alcoholism has inspired its own fraught history of cognitive dissonance. Officially categorized as a disease in 1956 by the American Medical Association—four years before E. Morton Jellinek, a Yale physiology professor, released his seminal study *The Disease Concept of Alcoholism*—alcoholism was also deemed "willful misconduct" by a 1988 Supreme Court Decision (*Traynor v. Turnage*) that held a pair of alcoholic veterans legally accountable for their alcoholism. The veterans' petition for an extension of the ten-year time limit on their G.I. Bill benefits, on the grounds that they had been disabled by alcoholism during that decade, was denied. For more on *Traynor v. Turnage*, see Durwood Ruegger, "Primary Alcoholism Due to 'Willful Misconduct': Supreme Court Upholds VA Regulation," *Journal of Health and Human Resources Administration* 13, no. 1 (Summer 1990): 112–23. In George Cain's 1970 novel, *Blueschild Baby* (New York: McGraw Hill, 1970), about a black heroin addict in Harlem in the 1960s, heroin and alcohol are paralleled in terms of physical dependence. Alcoholics are described as "[w]inos shivering in a doorway beg[ging] the needed pennies for their medicine" and the narrator says, "There is no longer anything

dramatic or pleasurable about junk, it is only medicine, a restorative to enable me to function" (19, 5).

63 **wearing shiny suits and ties printed with Chinese pagodas**...Julia Blackburn, *With Billie: A New Look at the Unforgettable Lady Day* (New York: Pantheon, 2005), 53.

64 **more than one administrator worried that it would be mistaken for a facility that actually grew opium**..."U.S. Not Raising Drugs at Its Narcotic Farm," *New York Herald*, January 24, 1934. RG 511—Alcohol, Drug Abuse, and Mental Health Administration, National Institute of Mental Health, National Archives, College Park, Maryland.

64 **roughly two-thirds of the fifteen hundred "patients" at Lexington were prisoners**...Nancy D. Campbell, J. P. Olsen, and Luke Walden, *The Narcotic Farm* (New York: Abrams, 2010), 62.

64 **By the time the Narco Farm opened, in 1935**...The Narco Farm was opened twenty years after the Harrison Act of 1914 ushered in an era of escalating federal anti-narcotic legislation, but twenty years before the harsh punitive measures Anslinger would eventually promote with the Boggs Act (passed by Congress in 1951), and the Daniel Act of 1956, also known as the Narcotic Control Act of 1956.

64 **I feel that these people are in the same category as lepers**...Anonymous Los Angeles Police Department officer qtd. in Anslinger and Tompkins, *The Traffic in Narcotics*, 272.

65 **He spent the rest of the thirties creating a reason for his agency to matter by drumming up public anxiety about drugs**...Hari, *Chasing the Scream*, 12–13.

65 **he gave the House Committee on Appropriations a speech about "colored students" partying with white coeds "and getting their sympathy with stories of racial persecution. Result: pregnancy"**...Ibid., 15, 17.

65 **the majority of drug users have always been white**...John Helmer and Thomas Vietorisz, *Drug Use, the Labor Market and Class Conflict* (Washington: Drug Abuse Council, 1974), unpaged.

65 **NEGRO COCAINE "FIENDS" NEW SOUTHERN MENACE**...The article written by Edward Huntington Williams, M.D., appeared in the *New York Times*, February 8, 1914. See fuller accounts of paranoid racist portraits of the black cocaine addict in Doris Provine, *Unequal Under Law*, 76–78. One account projected almost superhuman powers onto the African-American drug addict ("You could fill him with bullets and he still wouldn't fall..."). See also Hari, *Chasing the Scream*, 26.

65 **most of the attacks upon white women of the South are the direct result of a cocaine-crazed Negro brain**...*Literary Digest* (1914), 687. Qtd. in Provine, *Unequal Under Law*, 76–77.

66 **at the bottom of something**...James Baldwin, "Sonny's Blues," *Going to Meet the Man* (New York: Dial Press, 1965).

66 **the first book to treat with authority the horrifying national problem of drug addiction...not to satisfy a desire for morbid sensationalism**...Anslinger and Tompkins, *The Traffic in Narcotics*, flap copy.

66 **guide and implement the national desire**...Ibid.

66 **to buy wine and reefers**...Anslinger and Tompkins, *The Traffic in Narcotics*, 22–25.

66   **while under marihuana intoxication**...Ibid., 296.

67   **normal people...usual emotional plane**...Ibid., 251, 249–50.

67   **the face of "evil" is always the face of total need**...William Burroughs, *Deposition: Testimony Concerning a Sickness* (1960), reprinted in *Naked Lunch* (New York: Grove Press, 1962).

67   **His concept of illness was selective and self-serving**...Anslinger and Tompkins, *The Traffic in Narcotics*, 223, 226.

67   **Live things, frogs and insects kick in the liquid coming out**...Cain, *Blueschild Baby*, 148.

67   **A doctor won't help**...Ibid., 149.

68   **He's a sick man. You're a doctor**...Ibid., 150.

68   **denied the privilege of freely yielding**...Margo Jefferson, *Negroland* (New York: Pantheon, 2015), 171. Understanding the public narratives that permitted my private suffering was another moment of waking from what Ta-Nehisi Coates has called "The Dream," the white American aspirational fantasy that depends on the ongoing injustices of systemic racism to sustain its thrall. The different narratives that attach to various substances—often racially coded—are yet another iteration of the Dream. In *Between the World and Me* (New York: Spiegel & Grau, 2015), Coates writes about witnessing the Dreamers in action on West Broadway, in lower Manhattan, where "white people spilled out of wine bars with sloshing glasses and without police" (89).

73   **In 1944, a novel came along that rejected the white logic entirely**...John Crowley's critical account of alcoholism in American literature, *The White Logic: Alcoholism and Gender in America* (Amherst: University of Massachusetts Press, 1994), was essential in offering me a context for understanding the significance of Jackson's *The Lost Weekend* (New York: Farrar and Rinehart, 1944)—particularly its account of how Jackson broke from an American literary tradition that conflated alcoholism and metaphysical profundity.

74   **the most compelling gift to the literature of addiction since De Quincey**...Philip Wylie, "Review of *The Lost Weekend*," by Charles Jackson, *New York Times Book Review*, January 30, 1944.

74   **should have definite clinical value**...Dr. Sherman qtd. in Blake Bailey's definitive biography of Jackson, *Farther and Wilder: The Lost Weekends and Literary Dreams of Charles Jackson* (New York: Vintage, 2013).

74   **If he were able to write fast enough**...Jackson, *The Lost Weekend*, 16–17.

75   **"Don Birnam: A Hero Without a Novel" or "I Don't Know Why I'm Telling You All This"**...Ibid., 46.

75   **Who would ever want to read a novel about a punk and a drunk**...Ibid.

75   **Melodrama! In all his life**...Ibid., 237.

75   **It wasn't even decently dramatic**...Ibid., 216.

80   **They say you're arrested for crime, narcotics, prostitution, robbery, murder**...Cain, *Blueschild Baby*, 56.

81   **Did we know we were lying about the drugs?**...John Ehrlichman interview with Dan Baum, "Legalize It All: How to Win the War on Drugs," *Harper's*, April 2016. Ehrlichman's family has denied the posthumous account of his comments. In a

statement issued to CNN, his children said, "The 1994 alleged 'quote' we saw repeated in social media for the first time today does not square with what we know of our father. And collectively, that spans over 185 years of time with him. We do not subscribe to the alleged racist point of view that this writer now implies 22 years following the so-called interview of John and 16 years following our father's death, when dad can no longer respond." But journalist Dan Baum recorded the comment during an interview for his 1996 book *Smoke and Mirrors* and likens Ehrlichman's account to the stories of traumatized war veterans, recounting events years after the fact: "I think Ehrlichman was waiting for someone to come and ask him," Baum told CNN. "I think he felt bad about it. I think he had a lot to feel bad about." See: http://www.cnn.com/2016/03/23/politics/john-ehrlichman-richard-nixon-drug-war-blacks-hippie/index.html.

81 **haunted huddle...nodding, stinking, burning, high...gaunt and hollow...skin strapped tight around the skull...there's not enough junk in the world to quench his need...** Cain, *Blueschild Baby*, 114–15.

81 **Drug use was actually declining in 1982...** See Alexander, *The New Jim Crow*, 49.

81 **the addict violator...** Anslinger and Tompkins, *The Traffic in Narcotics*, 297.

81 **ideological fig leaf...** Reinarman and Levine qtd. in Provine, *Unequal Under Law*, 105.

82 **The argument began, police say...** Jacob Lamar, "The House Is On Fire," *Time*, August 4, 1986.

82 **Crack it up, crack it up...** Ibid.

82 **imagining crack as a predatory "epidemic" spread by black addicts who were morally responsible for what they carried...** In 1990, the Ku Klux Klan declared that it would "join the battle against illegal drugs" by acting as "the eyes and ears of the police." "Ku Klux Klan Says It Will Fight Drugs," *Toledo Journal*, January 3–9, 1990. Cited in Alexander, *The New Jim Crow*, 55.

82 **Crack was the hottest combat reporting story...** Robert Stutman qtd. in Alexander, *The New Jim Crow*, 52.

83 **They were allowed to confiscate the cash, cars, and homes of everyone arrested in drug busts...** See Alexander's *The New Jim Crow* for a more comprehensive account of the militarization of local police forces during the War on Drugs. Police departments got to keep the spoils from their drug busts, Alexander writes, not only by confiscating drugs but also by taking "the cash, cars, and homes of people suspected of drug use or sales." The cultural narratives that legitimated these confiscations found their authority in a much deeper narrative about addiction and guilt: the belief that addicts were *guilty*, and deserved to have their possessions taken from them (79).

83 **equivalent to crack...** Qtd. in Provine, *Unequal Under Law*, 112. As early as 1991, a report from the U.S. Sentencing Commission found that most judges found mandatory minimums "manifestly unjust." See Eric E. Sterling, "Drug Laws and Snitching: A Primer," *Frontline*, http://www.pbs.org/wgbh/pages/frontline/shows/snitch/primer/.

83 **One San Francisco judge wept on the bench...** See Provine, *Unequal Under Law*, 10.

83 **Between 1980 and 2014, the number of incarcerated drug offenders increased from just over 40,000 to almost 490,000, and the majority of those incarcerated were people of color...** The number of people in prisons and jails for drug offenses was 40,900 in 1980, and 488,400 in 2014. These statistics are taken from The Sentencing Project's report "Trends in U.S. Corrections," last updated December 2015, drawn from the Bureau of Justice Statistics. Prisoners are classified according to the offense for which they are serving the longest sentence, so these prisoners are either serving only a sentence for drugs, or else for drugs and another crime—so long as the drug-related crime is the one for which they are serving the longest sentence. Many other people convicted of drug offenses are currently incarcerated, but are not listed as such as long as it's another conviction for which they are serving the longest sentence.

Whether the War on Drugs is the primary driver of American mass incarceration has been the subject of recent debates. Michelle Alexander laid out the argument bluntly in *The New Jim Crow*: "Nothing has contributed more to the systematic mass incarceration of people of color in the United States than the War on Drugs" (60). It's important to make some distinctions here: this doesn't mean that the majority of incarcerated people in America are "nonviolent drug offenders"—a phrase that has become a comfortable compound subject in the mainstream liberal critique of mass incarceration in America, especially since Alexander's book. But in his recent book *Locked In: The True Causes of Mass Incarceration, and How to Achieve Real Reform* (New York: Basic Books, 2017), David Pfaff argues that the narrative of the War on Drugs as the primary driver of mass incarceration in America misunderstands the problem—that it's really the discretion of prosecutors (taking more cases to court) that has driven up incarceration rates—and that even if we freed all nonviolent drug offenders from prison, it would only make a dent in the problem of mass incarceration: America would still incarcerate more people, per capita, than any other country in the world. But it's also true that while nonviolent drug offenders make up only a fifth of the incarcerated population, a large number of those offenders incarcerated for violent offenses owe their incarceration to the War on Drugs—which creates the conditions under which the drug trade has become and remains so violent. All that said, it's important to recognize the War on Drugs and its racialized punitive project as one part of a much broader systemic injustice, rather than the entirety of the problem.

For hard data on these questions, see annual reports from the U.S. Department of Justice, for example, "Prisoners in 2015," https://www.bjs.gov/content/pub/pdf/p15.pdf. Additional resources include Jennifer Broxmeyer, "Prisoners of Their Own War: Can Policymakers Look Beyond the 'War on Drugs' to Drug Treatment Courts?" *Yale Law Journal* 118 (2008–9). For a fuller account of the War on Drugs and its legacy of incarceration, see also Marc Mauer and Ryan S. King, *The Sentencing Project, a 25-Year Quagmire: The War on Drugs and Its Impact on American Society* 2 (2007), available at http://www.sentencingproject.org/Admin%5CDocuments%5Cpublications%5Cdp_25yearquagmire.pdf. See also Alexander, *The New Jim Crow*,

6, 20. More than 31 million people have been arrested for drug offenses since the War on Drugs began.

83 **A 1993 study found that only 19 percent of drug dealers were African American, but they made up 64 percent of arrests**...Hari, *Chasing the Scream*, 93.

83 **By waging a war on drug users and dealers, Reagan made good on his promise**...Alexander, *The New Jim Crow*, 49.

83 **The drug problem reflects bad decisions by individuals with free wills**... George H. W. Bush, "National Drug Control Strategy," 1992, qtd. in Jennifer Broxmeyer, "Prisoners of Their Own War: Can Policymakers Look Beyond the 'War on Drugs' to Drug Treatment Courts?" *Yale Law Journal*, June 30, 2008.

83 **Would you close your eyes for a second, envision a drug user, and describe that person to me**...Betty Watson Burston, Dionne Jones, and Pat Robertson-Saunders, "Drug Use and African Americans: Myth Versus Reality," *Journal of Alcohol and Drug Abuse* 40 (Winter 1995): 19, qtd. in Alexander, *The New Jim Crow*, 106.

84 **I enjoy it much more, because I don't go to bars**...Berryman qtd. in Haffenden, *The Life of John Berryman*, 287.

87 **A fellow patient at the sanitarium**...The memory of Jackson's footprint in wine is from Bailey, *Farther and Wilder.*

87 **Jackson first stopped drinking at the age of thirty-three, using something called the Peabody Method**...The Peabody Method was based on Richard Peabody's *The Common Sense of Drinking* (Boston: Little, Brown, 1931). I have drawn my account of Jackson's time using the Peabody Method from the longer account in Bailey, *Farther and Wilder*, 103–4.

87 **It was an approach grounded in pragmatism**...See Peabody's *The Common Sense of Drinking.*

88 **We regulate our lives in orderly and profitable fashion**...Jackson to Bud Wister, December 19, 1936, Charles Jackson Papers, Rauner Special Collections Library, Dartmouth College.

88 **Why don't you write me a letter about it?**...Jackson, *The Lost Weekend*, 149–50. While Jackson himself was also an avid Fitzgerald fan, he didn't have the same respect for other scribes of alcoholism. In an undated letter to Robert Nathan, in the Jackson archives at Dartmouth, Jackson wrote that he couldn't find the "pathos of *The Sun Also Rises*...it's bathetic, merely." He thought alcoholism deserved to be represented as something more than tragic farce.

89 **the books begun and dropped**...Jackson, *The Lost Weekend*, 17.

89 **It had long since ceased to matter Why**...Ibid., 221–22.

89 **I am not saying that the critics could have cured Berryman of his disease**...Lewis Hyde, "Alcohol and Poetry: John Berryman and the Booze Talking," *American Poetry Review*, October 1975; repr. Dallas: The Dallas Institute of Humanities and Culture, 1986.

90 **It is my thesis here...that [a] war, between alcohol and Berryman's creative powers**...Ibid., 17.

90 **an alcoholic poet on his pity pot**...Ibid., 14.

90 **We can hear the booze talking**...Ibid., 17.

90 **It would not have been easy**...Ibid., 18.

91 **he confesses that for two years he worked as an orderly**...Ibid., 2.

92 **luminous self-destruction**...Elizabeth Hardwick, "Billie Holiday," *New York Review of Books*, March 4, 1976.

92 **very attractive customer**...George White qtd. in Blackburn's *With Billie*, 219.

92 **I got a habit and I know it's no good**...Holiday interview with Eugene Callender qtd. in Hari's *Chasing the Scream*, 21.

92 **shyness so vast**...John Chilton qtd. in Blackburn's *With Billie*, 63. Blackburn's book is a tremendous compilation of oral histories about Holiday's life and career. The context of Blackburn's book is an interestingly haunted one: Its oral histories were assembled from taped interviews left by Linda Kuehl, the biographer who committed suicide before she could finish her biography of Holiday.

92 **She was told nobody could sing the word "hunger" like she sang it**...Holiday, *Lady Sings the Blues*, with William Dufty (New York: Doubleday, 1956), 195.

92 **She sang the clubs on West Fifty-second**...These details from Blackburn, *With Billie*, 94.

92 **sheer enormity of her vices...For the grand destruction one must be worthy**...Hardwick, "Billie Holiday."

93 **Anslinger assigned several agents to Holiday's case during the late 1940s, and they busted her on multiple occasions, including the 1947 conviction that sent her to Alderson Federal Prison Camp, in West Virginia, for almost a year**...Johann Hari offers an excellent account of Anslinger's fixation with Holiday in his 2015 *Chasing the Scream*, and Julia Blackburn gives the perspectives of the two agents assigned to her case, Jimmy Fletcher and George White, in *With Billie*. For my account of the legal dimensions of Holiday's addiction, her persecution at the hands of the law, and the racial inflections of this persecution, I have drawn from Holiday's own autobiography, *Lady Sings the Blues*, as well as Hari's history and Blackburn's assembled testimonies. In *Lady Sings the Blues*, Holiday describes the media attention surrounding her drug busts, including one January 1949 headline that made her particularly indignant because it seemed to be gloating in her perpetual trouble with the law: "Billie Holiday Arrested on Narcotics Charges."

93 **At Alderson, Holiday got Christmas cards**...These details from Holiday's time at Alderson are from *Lady Sings the Blues*.

93 **When you form some sort of friendship with anybody**...Jimmy Fletcher, qtd. in Blackburn, *With Billie*, 215.

93 **in July 1986, ABC News introduced the American public to Jane**...Information about ABC report (July 11, 1986) and NBC report (October 24 and 25, 1988) from Drew Humphries's *Crack Mothers: Pregnancy, Drugs, and the Media*, 29–30.

94 **As criminologist Drew Humphries argues, the media effectively created the "crack mother"**...In her urgent and revelatory survey of the "crack mother" phenomenon, *Crack Mothers*, criminologist Drew Humphries surveys news programs that covered women and cocaine between 1983 and 1994—84 in total, largely drawn from ABC, CBS, and NBC evening news—with a swell during the peak of the crack panic in 1989 (19–20).

94 **although the majority of pregnant addicts were white**...Ibid., 128.

94 **the public outrage around crack mothers effectively redirected public notions of addiction away from disease and back to vice** . . . One of the central ironies of America's brief and passionate obsession with the figure of the "crack mother"—an obsession driven by pity for her misconstrued child and contempt for her misconstrued villainy—was that it somehow turned an essentially vulnerable group of women into a powerful public scapegoat. As Humphries puts it: "How . . . did an unusually powerless group of women emerge as a threatening symbol of disorder? The unenviable enemy in the domestic war on drugs?" (15).

94 **Dr. Ira Chasnoff, whose early reports on the effects of cocaine in utero had fueled the press frenzy** . . . In a 1992 article in the *New England Journal of Medicine*, Chasnoff presented a follow-up study that disproved media conclusions based on his prior work. He publicly chastised the "rush to judgment" on the part of the press, based on his preliminary research, and said he had "never seen a 'crack kid'" and doubted he ever would. See Humphries, *Crack Mothers*, 62; and Ira Chasnoff, "Missing Pieces of the Puzzle," *Neurotoxicology and Teratology* 15 (1993): 287–88, qtd. in Craig Reinarman and Harry Levine, *Crack in the Rear-View Mirror: Deconstructing Drug War Mythology* (Berkeley: University of California Press, 2007). Based on sensational extrapolations of early scientific findings, the media had predicted that the surging population of "crack babies" would become a doomed underclass: a vast fleet of struggling preemies and little "possessed" Arthurs. The July 30, 1989, column in the *Washington Post* by the singularly horrific Charles Krauthammer offered an infamous version of the doomsday prophecy: "The inner-city crack epidemic is now giving birth to the newest horror: a bio-underclass, a generation of physically damaged cocaine babies whose biological inferiority is stamped at birth." Krauthammer pronounced their futures "closed to them from day one. Theirs will be a life of certain suffering, of probable deviance, of permanent inferiority. At best, a menial life of severe deprivation." He wondered if "the dead babies may be the lucky ones." It's now medical consensus that "crack babies" weren't doomed at all, and that the whole notion of a "crack baby" was impossible to isolate anyway. These babies had been influenced by such an array of intertwined variables—not only other drugs but also environmental factors like poverty, violence, short-term foster placements, and homelessness—that it was impossible to identify what damage crack itself had done (Humphries, *Crack Mothers*, 62.)

94 **If you give drugs to your child because you can't help it** . . . Qtd. in ibid., 2.

94 **Instead of showing shame, Tracy was defiant** . . . Ibid., 52.

95 **when white pregnant drug addicts were covered in the media** . . . Ibid.

95 **Now they weren't just part of the "undeserving" poor, welfare junkies who were corroding the civic body** . . . It was stereotypes like the crack mother that fueled the New Right's campaign to diminish social services in the late 1980s. See Jimmie L. Reeves and Richard Campbell, *Cracked Coverage: Television News, the Anti-Cocaine Crusade, and the Reagan Legacy* (Durham, NC: Duke University Press, 1994).

95 **Unlike most addicts, they entered the criminal justice system through the hospital** . . . Humphries, *Crack Mothers*, 6.

95 **Prosecutors twisted familiar laws in new ways** . . . See full description of Melanie

Green and Jennifer Johnson's cases in ibid., 72–73 and 75–79. Jennifer Johnson's conviction was eventually overturned.

95 **I had concerns about an unborn helpless child to be...**Judge Peter Wolf, qtd. in ibid., 35. Now that it's medical consensus that "crack babies" weren't doomed at all, or if they were doomed, they were doomed by the social conditions that their government wasn't doing enough to address, it seems apparent that this "concern" for unborn children should have been translating into expanded social services rather than the vilification of crack mothers themselves.

96 **If you think dope is for kicks and for thrills...**Holiday, *Lady Sings the Blues*, 212–13.

96 **Holiday's coauthor, journalist William Dufty, thought addiction would be a good "gimmick"...**I've drawn this from John Szwed's account of the publication history of *Lady Sings the Blues* in his biography *Billie Holiday: The Musician and the Myth* (New York: Viking, 2015), 20. Even though *Lady Sings the Blues* warned against the dangers of addiction, its sales also ended up financially supporting Holiday's habit. The idea to publish an autobiography was certainly driven by financial necessity: Holiday owed money to the IRS and couldn't play most nightclubs in New York because her felony conviction meant she'd lost her cabaret license. She was looking for positive publicity that might help her get it back. But the same drug record that had taken away Holiday's cabaret card also made it possible for her to earn money by selling her "sensational" story to glossy magazines, in articles called "How I Blew a Million Dollars," "Can a Dope Addict Come Back," and (trumpeting the tinny optimism she would ultimately disavow) a piece called "I'm Cured for Good." One issue of *Tan* magazine featured a cover photo of Holiday in an emerald gown with white gardenias on her breast and her two white Chihuahuas in her arms. Account of the financial imperatives behind the autobiography's publication is from Szwed, *Billie Holiday*, 12. "How I Blew a Million Dollars" ran in *Our World*, March 1953; "Can a Dope Addict Come Back" ran in *Tan*, February 1953; and "I'm Cured for Good" ran in *Ebony*, in July 1949.

96 **I've been on and I've been off...**Holiday, *Lady Sings the Blues*, 218.

96 **No Guts Holiday...**Hari, *Chasing the Scream*, 23.

96 **A habit is no damn private hell...**Holiday, *Lady Sings the Blues*, 218.

96 **Dope never helped anybody sing better...**Ibid., 214.

96 **Carl...don't you ever use this shit!...**Carl Drinkard qtd. in Blackburn, *With Billie*, 230.

96 **I want you to know you stand convicted as a wrongdoer...**Holiday, *Lady Sings the Blues*, 151.

96 **Would he treat a diabetic like a criminal?...**Ibid., 153.

96 **She was born just a month after the Harrison Act came into effect...**The Harrison Act was passed in December 1914 and became effective in March 1915. Holiday was born in April 1915.

97 **for the sake of young kids whose whole life will be ruined...***Lady Sings the Blues*, 212.

97 **William Burroughs's *Junkie*, subtitled *Confessions of an Unredeemed Drug Addict*, was published in 1953...same year as Anslinger's *Traffic in Narcotics*,** and three

years before the Narcotic Control Act. Part of a "Two Books in One" package from Ace Books, *Junkie* was sold for thirty-five cents and bound with *Narcotic Agent*, a memoir by a former undercover agent named Maurice Helbrant. In a picaresque of stings and busts and deceptions, Helbrant tells his story as an opposite narrative: the *pursuit* of the unredeemed junkie. But it emerges as a parallel tale instead, another account of addiction—a parade of vignettes in which a maniacal crusader is camped out with whiskey bottles in seedy motel rooms. Helbrant is obsessed with heroin: how to use it, how to fake using it, how to spot someone who is using it. His fixation on punishing the obsession of the addict became an obsession all its own. The moral indignation becomes another kind of drug, the crusade another kind of bender.

97 **Given cooperation**...William Burroughs, *Junkie*, 99.

97 **an addict with "no pleading need to quit"**...Hardwick, "Billie Holiday."

97 **With cold anger**...Ibid.

98 **Why do they keep putting her on stage? Surely they know she has a problem**...Both newscasters qtd. in *Amy* (dir. Asif Kapadia, 2015).

IV. LACK

111 **the surplus of mystical properties**...Eve Kosofsky Sedgwick, "Epidemics of the Will," *Tendencies* (Durham, NC: Duke University Press, 1993), 132.

111 **Ever to confess you're bored**...John Berryman, "Dream Song 14," *The Dream Songs*.

112 **narrowing of repertoire**...Meg Chisolm interview with the author, August 11, 2016.

112 **through the turnstile**...Adam Kaplin interview with the author, October 13, 2016.

112 **the unmistakable feeling of coming home**...Ibid.

112 **Scientists describe addiction as a dysregulation**...For a fuller account of the scientific mechanisms underlying addiction, see Carlton Erickson's *The Science of Addiction: From Neurobiology to Treatment* (New York: W. W. Norton, 2007). In chapter 3 Erickson outlines the basic mechanisms of chemical dependence, while in chapters 5, 6, and 7 he reviews the specific mechanisms of various substances.

112 **pathological usurpation**...Ibid., 64.

113 **FACTUAL GAIN AND LOSS CHART ON UN-CONTROLLED DRINKING**...Factual Gain and Loss Chart on Un-Controlled Drinking, Archives at the Center for Alcohol Studies, Rutgers University, New Brunswick, New Jersey.

113 **spiraling distress/addiction cycle**...G. F. Koob and M. Le Moal, "Drug Abuse: Hedonic Homeostatic Dysregulation," *Science* 278 (1997): 52–58.

113 **the chart explaining the spiraling distress/addiction cycle looks like a tornado**...Erickson, *The Science of Addiction*, 59.

113 **When I look back at a night with a stranger in Nicaragua, I can say the GABA receptors in my neurons were activated by the rum in my veins**...For a summary of several accounts of the mechanisms of alcohol on neurotransmitter systems, see Erickson, *The Science of Addiction*, 69. See also *Neurochem Int.* 37, no. 4 (October 2000): 369–76. "Alcohol enhances characteristic releases of dopamine

and serotonin in the central nucleus of the amygdala." Yoshimoto et al. "Alcohol and Neurotransmitter Interactions." C. Fernando Valenzuela. NIAAA, http://pubs. niaaa.nih.gov/publications/arh21-2/144.pdf.

114 **When I'm drunk it's all right**...Jean Rhys, *After Leaving Mr. Mackenzie*, in *The Complete Novels* (New York: W. W. Norton, 1985), 262.

118 **We're all dependent people**...John Berryman, *Recovery* (New York: Farrar, Straus and Giroux, 1973), 154.

118 **densely affected by alcoholism**...NIAA, "Collaborative Studies on Genetics of Alcoholism (COGA) Study," https://www.niaaa.nih.gov/research/major-initiatives/ collaborative-studies-genetics-alcoholism-coga-study.

119 **In so much of your writing...there are so many hooks to hang the pain on, but no explanation of where the poison coat came from**...David Gorin, manuscript notes. August 2016.

119 **The sky was bright red; everything was red**...Elizabeth Bishop, "A Drunkard," *Georgia Review* (1992). The fire that Bishop remembers witnessing was the Great Salem Fire of 1914. See Claudia Roth Pierpont, "Elizabeth Bishop's 'Art of Losing,'" *The New Yorker*, March 6, 2017, http://www.newyorker.com/magazine/2017/03/06/ elizabeth-bishops-art-of-losing.

120 **half-hearted disclaimer**...Brett C. Millier, "The Prodigal: Elizabeth Bishop and Alcohol," *Contemporary Literature* 39, no. 1 (Spring 1998): 54–76.

120 **Why do you drink?...(Don't really answer)**...John Berryman, handwritten note, John Berryman Papers, University of Minnesota.

121 **I told him I drank a lot**...Marguerite Duras, "The Voice in Navire Night," *Practicalities* (London: William Collins Sons, 1990).

121 **The question of *why* stopped mattering**...Charles Jackson, *The Lost Weekend* (New York: Farrar and Rinehart, 1944), 221–22.

121 **In *Junkie*, Burroughs anticipates the questions**...William Burroughs, *Junkie: Confessions of an Unredeemed Drug Addict* (New York: Ace Books, 1953), 5.

122 ***bottle as breast***...Adam Kaplin interview with the author, October 13, 2016.

V. SHAME

134 **WHETHER WICKEDNESS WAS SOLUBLE IN ART**...John Berryman, from a prefatory sonnet he wrote in 1966, qtd. in John Haffenden, *The Life of John Berryman* (London: Methuen & Co., 1984), 183.

134 **You licking your own old hurt...What the world to Henry**...John Berryman, "Dream Song 74," *The Dream Songs* (New York: Farrar, Straus and Giroux, 1969).

134 **I am the little man who smokes & smokes**...John Berryman, "Dream Song 22," *The Dream Songs.*

135 **in the mood / to be a tulip**...John Berryman, "Dream Song 92" ("Room 231: the forth week"), *The Dream Songs.*

135 ***all* regret, swallowing his own vomit**...John Berryman, "Dream Song 310," *The Dream Songs.*

135 **the anger of anyone who has been close to an active alcoholic and gotten hurt**...Lewis Hyde, "Berryman Revisited," in *Recovering Berryman*, ed. Richard Kelly and Alan Lathrop (Ann Arbor: University of Michigan Press, 1993).

Notes

136 **Diet: *poor*...**John Berryman, handwritten note, John Berryman Papers, University of Minnesota.

138 **half crabbed, half generous...**Malcolm Lowry, *Under the Volcano* (New York: Reynal and Hitchcock, 1945), 43.

139 **Who's been putting pineapple juice in my pineapple juice...**Anecdote cited in John Berryman, *Recovery* (New York: Farrar, Straus and Giroux, 1973), 107.

141 **the fire of the tequila run down his spine...**Lowry, *Under the Volcano,* 278.

143 **his greatest weakness...into his greatest strength...**Malcolm Lowry, *Dark as the Grave Wherein My Friend Is Laid* (London: Jonathan Cape, 1969), 41.

143 **when Jackson published *The Lost Weekend,* in 1944, Lowry was devastated and indignant...**For a wonderfully astute account of the Lowry-Jackson rivalry, see John Crowley's *The White Logic: Alcoholism and Gender in America* (Amherst: University of Massachusetts Press, 1994).

143 **swift leathery perfumed alcoholic dusk...**Lowry, *Under the Volcano,* 55.

144 **were taking an eternal sacrament...**Ibid., 50.

144 **Do you realize that while you're battling against death...**Ibid., 281.

144 **The will of man is unconquerable...**Ibid., 118.

144 **suddenly overwhelmed by sentiment...**Ibid., 168.

145 **cantina in the early morning...How, unless you drink as I do, can you hope to understand the beauty...**Ibid., 62–63.

145 **Ah none but he knew how beautiful...**Ibid., 115.

145 **a great book about missing grandeur...**Michael Wood, "The Passionate Egoist," *New York Review of Books,* April 17, 2008.

145 **Vague images of grief and tragedy...**Lowry, *Under the Volcano,* 111.

145 **Success may be the worst possible thing...**Malcolm Lowry letter qtd. in D. T. Max, "Day of the Dead." *The New Yorker,* December 17, 2007.

146 **He is the original Consul in the book...**Dawn Powell qtd. in D. T. Max, "Day of the Dead."

146 **His delirium tremens got so bad...**Ibid.

146 **A little self-knowledge is a dangerous thing...**Lowry, *Under the Volcano,* 232.

147 **He had lost the sun...**Ibid., 264.

153 **creatures with scrawny necks, small mouths, emaciated limbs...**Gabor Maté, *In the Realm of Hungry Ghosts: Close Encounters with Addiction* (Toronto: Knopf Canada, 2008), 1–2.

153 **They have much in common with the society that ostracizes them...**Ibid.

153 **From the late sixties to the late eighties, the scientific studies that got the most press...**John P. Morgan and Lynn Zimmer, "The Social Pharmacology of Smokeable Cocaine: Not All It's Cracked Up to Be," in *Crack in America: Demon Drugs and Social Justice,* ed. Craig Reinarman and Harry Levine (Berkeley: University of California Press, 2007), 36.

153 **the definition of a drug was any substance...**Ibid.

154 **"Cocaine Rat" was the title of a 1988 PSA video...**Partnership for a Drug-Free America, "Cocaine Rat," 1988. The pellets in the video are also misleading: most rats were surgically outfitted with a "permanent injection apparatus" in their backs. They were literally *built* for addiction, as well as being trapped in conditions that primed them for it.

154 In the early eighties, these scientists designed "Rat Park"...Bruce Alexander, "Addiction: The View from Rat Park," 2010. The original results from Rat Park were published in B. K. Alexander et al., "Effect of Early and Later Colony Housing on Oral Ingestion of Morphine in Rats," *Pharmacology Biochemistry and Behavior* 15, no. 4 (1981): 571–76. Carl Hart also gives an account of the "Rat Park" experiment in *High Price: A Neuroscientist's Journey of Self-Discovery That Challenges Everything You Know About Drugs and Society* (New York: Harper, 2013).

    The results from the original Rat Park experiment have also been replicated. See S. Schenk et al., *Neuroscience Letters* 81 (1987): 227–31; and M. Solinas et al., *Neuropsychopharmacology* 34 (2009): 1102–11. For a graphic account of Rat Park, see Stuart McMillen's "Rat Park."

154 What was it that did in reality make me an opium eater?...Thomas De Quincey, "Confessions of an English Opium-Eater," *London Magazine*, 1821.

155 the interior jigsaw's missing piece...David Foster Wallace, *Infinite Jest* (New York: Little, Brown, 1996), 350.

156 The Collaborative Studies on Genetics of Alcoholism is an ongoing research project...The National Institute on Alcohol Abuse and Alcoholism defines the mission and method of COGA as follows: "To learn more about how our genes affect vulnerability to alcoholism, NIAAA has funded the Collaborative Studies on Genetics of Alcoholism (COGA) since 1989. Our goal is to identify the specific genes that can influence a person's likelihood of developing alcoholism. COGA investigators have collected data on more than 2,255 extended families in which many members are affected by alcoholism. The researchers collected extensive clinical, neuropsychological, electrophysiological, biochemical, and genetic data on the more than 17,702 individuals who are represented in the database. The researchers also have established a repository of cell lines from these individuals to serve as a permanent source of DNA for genetic studies" (https://www.niaaa.nih .gov/research/major-initiatives/collaborative-studies-genetics-alcoholism-coga-study). More information about COGA, along with a fuller account of its findings, can be found in Laura Jean Bierut et al., "Defining Alcohol-Related Phenotypes in Humans: The Collaborative Study on the Genetics of Alcoholism," National Institute on Alcohol Abuse and Alcoholism, June 2003, https://pubs.niaaa.nih.gov/publications/ arh26-3/208-213.html.

    What contributes to being at greater risk for alcoholism? Traits associated with physiology (metabolism and organ sensitivity), with psychopharmacology (structures of reward and aversion in the brain), with personality (impulsivity and sensation-seeking), and with psychopathology (depression and anxiety). Carol A. Prescott, "What Twin Studies Teach Us about the Causes of Alcoholism," paper for Samuel B. Guze Symposium on Alcoholism, Washington University School of Medicine, 2004, http://digitalcommons.wustl.edu/guzepresentation2004/4. The "alcohol dependence" phenotype was measured according to DSM and WHO classifications.

156 The evidence supporting a genetic basis for alcoholism is pretty much indisputable...One study examining alcohol abuse in twins showed a 76% concordance rate in monozygotic twins, and a 61% concordance rate in dizygotic twins. For more information, see Roy Pickens et al., "Heterogeneity in the Inheritance of Alcoholism: A Study of Male and Female Twins," *Archives of General Psychiatry* 48, no. 1 (1981): 19–28. See also Erickson, *The Science of Addiction: From Neurobiology to Treatment* (New York: W. W. Norton, 2007), 84–85.

170 **For shame is its own veil**...Denis Johnson, "Where the Failed Gods Are Drinking," *The Throne of the Third Heaven of the Nations Millennium General Assembly: Poems Collected and New* (New York: Harper Perennial, 1995).

170 **The novel takes place in Manhattan during the summer of the 1967 Newark riots, evoking New York as an orchestra of noise and need and possibility**...Cain summons the glamour and grit of Harlem at once, the "big shiny cars caught in neon sparkle like jewels" and the way these cars look "dull with dew and exhaustion in the morning," as he watches from a diner at dawn, drinking coffee, and watching the fluorescence bring out the wrinkles of hungover revelers. When he visits the West Side housing projects where he was born, he describes Lincoln Center ("marble bathroom, carpeted halls, chandeliers"), which is right across the street but a world away—"I ain't never been anywhere like that," one woman explains, "wouldn't know how to act, got nobody to go with." One of the defining features of Cain's experience has been feeling like a mascot of upward mobility—a carrier of collective dreams, and an ambassador between worlds: "Did not think of myself as black or white," he says, "but marginal man, existing somewhere in time and space on the edge of both." He feels anger at having been expected to carry this burden of upward mobility in the first place, and shame about the ways he has failed. George Cain, *Blueschild Baby* (New York: McGraw Hill, 1970), 50, 69, 115, 177.

171 **a strange moon hung in the sky...calm, terribly sudden and infinite**...Ibid., 197–99.

171 **a character who is smart and full of yearning, but often acts aggressively, even callously**...The character of George Cain is adamantly—purposefully—objectionable. Much of his aggression directs itself at white characters, and the novel refuses to apologize for it or condemn it—it simply dramatizes this aggression, and never forgets its context. Cain forces himself on a white teenage girl, neglects his daughter's (white) mother, and fantasizes about killing a white man. Instead of papering over his character's anger in deference to respectability politics, Cain allows this anger to live on the page, alongside depictions of all the social realities that lie beneath it.

171 **bones scraping against one another inside**...Ibid., 200.

171 **to live life unhindered**...Ibid., 7.

171 **nodding junkies...victims of the Newark rebellion...no longer [as] the chosen driven to destruction by their awareness and frustration, but only lost victims, too weak to fight**...Ibid., 129.

172 **I knew better**...Quotes from Jo Lynne Pool and almost all of the biographical information about George Cain in this section, from the interview conducted on March 30, 2016.

172 **he had the makings of a book**...Jo Lynne Pool interview with the author, March 30, 2016. Cain also had the makings of a book jacket bio. The first edition from McGraw-Hill is careful to disclaim its author's bio as one Cain himself wrote. "The

author writes: 'George Cain was born Scorpio, 1943, in Harlem Hospital, New York City. Attended public and private schools in the city, and entered Iona College on scholarship. Left in his junior year to travel, spending time in California, Mexico, Texas, and prisons.'"

172 **the most important work of fiction by an Afro-American**... Addison Gayle Jr., review of *Blueschild Baby*, by George Cain, *New York Times*, January 17, 1971, 3.

173 **George Cain, former addict, emerges phoenix-like**... Ibid.

173 **A few days after getting his first royalty check, he ran into one of his friend's little brothers on the street and took him to a record store nearby**... Rasheed Ali, "Tribute to a 'Ghetto Genius,'" *The Black American Muslim*, http://www.the blackamericanmuslim.com/george-cain/.

174 **What were you like when you were doing well?**... Adam Kaplin interview with the author, October 13, 2016.

174 **Drugs dashed these hopes**... William Grimes, "George Cain, Writer of 'Blueschild Baby,' Dies at 66," *New York Times*, October 29, 2010.

177 **The book was subtitled** *A Love Story*... Caroline Knapp, *Drinking: A Love Story* (New York: The Dial Press, 1996).

178 **Last year our drunken quarrels had no explanation**... Robert Lowell, "Summer Tides," *New Selected Poems*, ed. Katie Peterson (New York: Farrar, Straus and Giroux), 2017.

180 *Dear Sir: This is a funny letter*... Ervin Cornell letter to the US Bureau of Narcotics, June 26, 1939. RG 511—Alcohol, Drug Abuse, and Mental Health Administration, National Institute of Mental Health, National Archives, College Park, Maryland.

180 **nearly three thousand people showed up each year requesting entry**... Nancy D. Campbell, J. P. Olsen, and Luke Walden, *The Narcotic Farm* (New York: Abrams, 2010), 63.

181 **If theres any way in the world to be cured I wont to try it**... J. S. Northcutt to Federal Bureau of Narcotics, National Archives, College Park, Maryland.

181 *I have been smoking marijuana cigarettes for six years*... Milton Moses to Federal Bureau of Narcotics, May 8, 1938, RG 511, National Archives, College Park, Maryland.

181 *Dear Sir, I would like very much*... Paul Youngman to Federal Bureau of Narcotics, December 1, 1945. RG 511, National Archives, College Park, Maryland.

181 PLEASE SEND APPLICATION FORMS... Chester Socar telegraph to "Bureau of Narcotics," September 6, 1941. RG 511, National Archives, College Park, Maryland.

182 **The press called the Narco Farm a "New Deal for Addicts"**... Campbell et al., *The Narcotic Farm*, 12.

182 **a Lexington newspaper ran a contest to get suggestions from local residents**... Ibid., 36–37.

182 **In truth, the prison-hospital-Big-Shot-Dream-Castle was still figuring out** *what* **it was**... In addition to "rehabilitating" addicts—or ostensibly in service of the rehabilitation of addicts everywhere—the Narco Farm also used its residents as test subjects in a series of ongoing experiments (ostensibly in service of the rehabilitation of addicts everywhere). Many of these experiments were questioned by ethical boards decades later, during the 1950s. The Narco Farm's Addiction Research

Center was conducting groundbreaking but deeply controversial experiments into the mechanisms of withdrawal and the possibilities of a non-addictive opiate pain-killer, and was one of the first places that ever tested methadone treatments. For more information, see Campbell et al., *The Narcotic Farm*.

182 **courteous treatment that we discovered at the farm**...Ibid., 83. The other details of life at Lexington in this paragraph are also taken from this history, including the particulars of labor and recreation: tomatoes and dentistry and dairy farming.

182 **a magician named Lippincott performed at the Narco Farm**..."Magician to Appear at Hospital Tonight," *Lexington Leader*, November 15, 1948. RG 511, National Archives, College Park, Maryland.

183 **In 1937, the hospital logged 4,473 collective patient hours of horseshoe toss-ing and 8,842 hours of bowling**... Campbell et al., *The Narcotic Farm*, 142.

183 **banana-smoking epidemic**...William Burroughs Jr., *Kentucky Ham* (New York: E. P. Dutton, 1973), 100.

183 **So many musicians...at Lexington**...Campbell et al., *The Narcotic Farm*, 152.

183 **The treatment is, for the most part, a skillful rearrangement**...Robert Casey, "Destiny of Man 'Traded In' at Kentucky Laboratory," *Chicago Daily News*, August 23, 1938. RG 511, National Archives, College Park, Maryland. A front-page story in the *Atlanta Georgian* ran under a cartoon showing a long line of addicts marching toward the soaring towers of the Narco Farm with a blinding sun captioned as "Public Enlightenment." The story's message was earnest: Every state should have a Narco Farm because it was a necessary humanitarian reform. But the Narco Farm was uneasily perched between grand rhetoric and de facto punishment, and much of its rhetoric of rehabilitation rang hollow in practice. Many addicts had come to their addictions to escape the trap of their lives, then found themselves trapped again, inside the habit itself, and so they'd sought the promised liberty of another contain-ment—the Narco Farm itself.

184 **"Not very much" / "You mean Not Very Well"**...Clarence Cooper Jr., *The Farm* (New York: Crown, 1967), 27.

184 **Name: Robert Burnes**..."Report on Non-Medical Addict," October 24, 1944. RG 511, National Archives, College Park, Maryland.

VI. SURRENDER

195 **It meant you didn't have to build the rituals of fellowship from scratch**...The feeling of being liberated by the constraints of ritual is nothing singular: it's part of nearly every religious tradition—but Leon Wieseltier expresses it with particular precision when he describes how the mourning ritual of Kaddish saved him from hav-ing to improvise his grief: "I see again that the kaddish is my good fortune. It looks after the externalities, and so it saves me from the task of improvising the rituals of my bereavement, which is a lot to ask." From *Kaddish* (New York: Vintage, 2000), 39.

197 **this was the answer—self-knowledge**...All these quotes are from "Bill's Story," chapter one of *Alcoholics Anonymous*, more commonly called the "Big Book."

198 **I felt lifted up, as though the great clean wind of a mountain top**...Also quoted from "Bill's Story," *Alcoholics Anonymous*. Bill Wilson's hospital epiphany

story bore a strong resemblance to a conversation narrative he'd grown up hearing from his own grandfather, Grandpa Willy: the story of Willy's liberation from "demon rum," which happened when he encountered God on the top of Mount Aeolus, in Vermont. This echo doesn't make the story false, it only testifies to the way we craft our salvation narratives from whatever materials we have at hand—the stories we've inherited, the ones we find ourselves needing most. For fuller accounts of Wilson's grandfather's conversion story, see Susan Cheever's *My Name Is Bill: Bill Wilson—His Life and the Creation of Alcoholics Anonymous* (New York: Washington Square Press, 2005); or Don Lattin, *Distilled Spirits: Getting High, Then Sober, with a Famous Writer, a Forgotten Philosopher, and a Hopeless Drunk* (Berkeley: University of California Press, 2012).

200 **his autobiography confessed a few more binges after this visit**...Bill Wilson always expressed aversion to writing an autobiography, but eventually—in order to preempt inaccuracies in the biographies he sensed would be written—he recorded his life in a series of taped conversations in 1954 that were eventually published in 2000 as *Bill W.: My First Forty Years* (Center City, MN: Hazelden, 2000).

200 **rather than pinning sobriety on the type of intense spiritual experience that some people might never have**...When Wilson experimented with LSD, years later, these experiments were largely driven by the hope that perhaps everyone could have intense spiritual experiences like the one he had at Charles B. Towns Hospital—visionary and overpowering—and that, if they could have these experiences, it might be easier for them to stick with sobriety.

201 **play the foundations... down**...Wilson, *Bill W.: My First Forty Years*.

201 **number-one man**...This quote from Bill Wilson appears in the 2012 documentary made about his life: *Bill W.* (dir. Kevin Hanlon). This feature-length documentary about Wilson explores his conflicted feelings about the intense veneration that accompanied his status as AA's founder. He found himself the "number-one man" in a sphere where he didn't want his story to be more important than anyone else's.

201 **I am like you...I, too, am fallible**...Bill Wilson remarks ("Every Reason to Hope") at closing session, AA Conference, Prince George Hotel, April 27, 1958, Stepping Stones Archives, WGW 103, Bx. 31, F. 6. Access to Stepping Stones Archives and use of excerpts from its materials does not imply that the author's views or conclusions in this publication have been reviewed or are endorsed by Stepping Stones. The conclusions expressed herein, and the research on which they are based, are the sole responsibility of the author. All excerpts in this work from Stepping Stones Archives are used with permission of Stepping Stones—Historic Home of Bill & Lois Wilson, Katonah, NY, 10536, steppingstones.org, (914) 232-4822.

201 **He wrote a letter to an AA member named Barbara**...This letter to Barbara is quoted in the documentary *Bill W.* Responding to a note in which a woman named Barbara had accused him of "disappointing" her, Wilson explains that an impossible perch had been constructed for him, an "illusory pedestal no fallible man could occupy." He didn't want his story to be regarded as sacred artifact.

201 **I have always been intensely averse**...Wilson, *Bill W.: My First Forty Years*, 2.

202 **Ed and I just had a good laugh about the Wall Street days**...Ibid., 80.

202 **behaved like a bunch of actors sent out by some Broadway casting agency**...Jack Alexander, "Alcoholics Anonymous: Freed Slaves of Drink, Now They Free Others," *Saturday Evening Post*, March 1, 1941.

203 **spends many of her nights sitting on hysterical women drinkers**...Ibid.

203 **For many a day you will be the toast of AA**...Bill Wilson to Jack Alexander, January 6, 1941, Alcoholics Anonymous, Digital Archives.

203 **By the end of 1941, the program had more than 8,000 members**...Statistics for 1941 membership from the foreword to the second edition of the Big Book, http://www.aa.org/assets/en_US/en_bigbook_forewordsecondedition.pdf.

　　Statistics for 2015 from AA General Service Office, http://www.aa.org/assets/en_US/smf-53_en.pdf.

204 **French philosopher Catherine Malabou proposes three different models of recovery, attaching each one to an animal: the phoenix, the spider, and the salamander**...Catherine Malabou, "The Phoenix, the Spider, and the Salamander," *Changing Difference*, trans. Carolyn Shread (Cambridge: Polity Press, 2011), 74–75.

204 **covered with marks, nicks, scratches**...Ibid., 76–77.

204 **There is no scar, but there is a difference**...Ibid., 82.

205 **witness authority**...Meg Chisolm interview with the author, August 11, 2016.

205 **You'd be doing heroin, too, Doctor**...Adam Kaplin interview with the author, October 13, 2016.

205 **contingency management and community reinforcement**...In addition to recognizing the effectiveness of twelve-step treatment itself in supporting addiction recovery, The National Institute on Drug Abuse (NIDA) recognizes four major types of behavioral treatment that have proven effective: cognitive-behavioral therapy, contingency management, community reinforcement, and motivational enhancement therapy. (Some of these are supplied by twelve-step groups, like community reinforcement and contingency management, though these groups are not the only means by which they can be found or sustained.) One study found that three kinds of therapeutic treatment (cognitive behavior, motivational enhancement, and twelve-step facilitation) achieved roughly equal levels of abstinence after a year, with twelve-step facilitation achieving higher levels of abstinence among patients with low psychiatric severity. See "Matching Alcoholism Treatments to Client Heterogeneity: Project MATCH Posttreatment Drinking Outcome," *Journal of Studies on Alcohol and Drugs* 58, no. 1 (January 1997): 7–29.

205 **people who need to hear themselves confessing**...Adam Kaplin interview with the author, October 13, 2016.

206 **You're really smart**...Meg Chisolm interview with the author, August 11, 2016.

206 **mystical blah blah**...Jackson qtd. in Blake Bailey, *Farther and Wilder: The Lost Weekends and Literary Dreams of Charles Jackson* (New York: Vintage, 2013), 144.

206 **You S.O.B.! If you don't think**...Ibid., 147.

206 **solution [is] offered, so to speak, and then taken away, not used**...Charles Jackson to Stanley Rinehart, 1943, Charles Jackson Papers, Dartmouth College.

207 **care to learn or hear of the real, the uncomfortable**...Jackson, *The Lost Weekend*, 113.

207 **I couldn't get outside myself**...Charles Jackson, speech, Cleveland, Ohio, May 7, 1959.

207 **I tell you, boy, there is much, much more to AA**...Charles Jackson to Charles Brackett, September 14, 1954, Charles Jackson Papers, Dartmouth College.

207 **But at a Hartford AA chapter**...See Bailey, *Farther and Wilder*, for a fuller account of Jackson's visit to the Hartford AA meeting (145).

207 **These people *knew* about me**...Charles Jackson qtd. in ibid., 310.

208 **I am thinking solely of the responsibility that is yours**...C. Dudley Saul qtd. in ibid., 308–9.

208 **intellectual equals**...Charles Jackson qtd. in ibid., 308.

208 **When he called one AA chapter in Montpelier**...Incident described in ibid., 312.

208 **Through his sponsor, he grew increasingly enamored with a quote from G. K. Chesterton**...Chesterton quote (and Jackson's affection for it) cited in ibid., 337.

213 **It's all so easy and natural and no posing or anything**...Rhoda Jackson to Frederick Storier Jackson (nicknamed "Boom"), November 24, 1953, Charles Jackson Papers, Dartmouth College.

213 **vegetable health**...Charles Jackson, "The Sleeping Brain," unpublished manuscript, Charles Jackson Papers, Dartmouth College.

213 **Please don't squirm at this**...Charles Jackson to Walter and Merriman Modell, January 9, 1954, Charles Jackson Papers, Dartmouth College.

213 **like visiting a birth control clinic**...Richard Lamparski qtd. in Bailey, *Farther and Wilder*, 347.

214 **the members simply wouldn't let him go**...Jackson qtd. in Bailey, *Farther and Wilder*, 339.

214 **star pupil**...**new addiction**...Ibid., 341, 346.

214 ***My dear Charlie, Thanks for your thoughtfulness***...Bill Wilson to Charles Jackson. April 24, 1961, Stepping Stones Foundation Archives. WGW 102.2 Bx. 15, F. 1-9.

214 **Jackson landed a commission with *Life* to write a two-part article about AA**...See account of Jackson's *Life* commission in Bailey, *Farther and Wilder*, 320.

218 **What luck, I thought**...Raymond Carver, "Luck," *All of Us: The Collected Poems* (New York: Knopf, 1998), 5.

218 **Alcoholics get to a point in the program where they need a spiritual experience**...Wilson qtd. in Lattin, *Distilled Spirits*, 198. For a more complete account of Bill Wilson's experiments with LSD, see *Distilled Spirits*. See also Alcoholics Anonymous, *'Pass It On': The Story of Bill Wilson and How the AA Message Reached the World* (New York: Alcoholics Anonymous World Service Inc., 1984).

219 **Describing that first trip to a friend, Wilson compared it to his early visions of AA as a "chain of drunks around the world, all helping each other"**...Osmond qtd. in Lattin, *Distilled Spirits*, 195.

219 **helped him eliminate many barriers erected by the self, or ego, that stand in the way of one's direct experiences of the cosmos and of god**...Ibid., 206.

219 **cynical alcoholics**...Lattin, *Distilled Spirits*, from an interview with Will Forthman. No surprise that Bill Wilson's acid trip echoed the vision he'd had at Towns, where he had been given a hallucinogen called belladonna. Describing the "residue" of his early acid trips, Wilson extolled the virtues of his "heightened" appreciation of "the livingness of all things and a sense of their beauty." Wilson to Sidney Cohen, Stepping Stones Foundation Archives, qtd. in *Distilled Spirits*, 198. Wilson didn't imagine that acid would replace the program's emphasis on listening and humility. "I consider LSD to be of some value to some people," he once remarked, "[but it] will never take the place of any of the existing means by which we can reduce the ego, and keep it reduced" (Alcoholics Anonymous, *'Pass It On,'* 370).

219 **Most AAs were violently opposed to his experimenting with a mind-altering substance**... Alcoholics Anonymous, *'Pass It On,'* 372.

219 **spook sessions**... Nell Wing qtd. in Lattin, *Distilled Spirits*, 194.

219 **One turned up the other day calling himself Boniface**... Wilson to Ed Dowling, July 17, 1952, from Bill Wilson and Ed Dowling, *The Soul of Sponsorship: The Friendship of Fr. Ed Dowling and Bill Wilson in Letters* (Center City, MN: Hazelden, 1995).

220 **first things *first*... take it easy**... Bill Wilson, handwritten notes, Stepping Stones Foundation Archives, Katonah, New York. WGW 101.7, Bx. 7, F. 6.

220 **Are you going to stop smoking**... Bill Wilson, handwritten note, Stepping Stones Foundation Archives, Katonah, New York. WGW 101.7, Bx. 7, F. 6.

221 **Suggested that at this point "John" speak extemporaneously**... General Service Headquarters of AA, "Pattern-Script for Radio and Television," February 1957, 2. This 1957 "pattern script" was actually an update to an existing "pattern script." Collection at the Center of Alcohol Studies, Rutgers University.

224 **when a clinician described the classic addict temperament as stubbornly focused on the present moment**... Adam Kaplin interview with the author, October 13, 2016.

VII. THIRST

232 **like hungry men who can talk about nothing but food**... William Burroughs, *Junkie: Confessions of an Unredeemed Drug Addict* (New York: Ace Books, 1953), 63.

232 **There's just nothing to do, nothing — except talk about junk**... Helen MacGill Hughes, ed., *The Fantastic Lodge: The Autobiography of a Girl Drug Addict* (New York: Fawcett, 1961), 214. *The Fantastic Lodge* was marketed as a "case study": the life story of a pseudonymous female heroin addict based on tape-recorded interviews conducted and edited, respectively, by sociologists Howard Becker and Helen MacGill Hughes. It illuminates the particular experience of being a woman suffering from a largely male addiction, and offers a vision of an addict's story constructed and articulated for sociological (rather than strictly literary) purposes.

232 **She had come to put great hope in getting this book published**... Ibid., 266.

233 **Cured, prognosis good (3) / Cured, prognosis guarded (27) / Cured, prognosis poor (10)**... "The Annual Report, Fiscal Year Ending June 30, 1945, U.S. Public Service Hospital, Lexington, Kentucky," submitted to the Surgeon General by J. D. Reichard, Medical Director USPHS, Medical Officer in Charge — August 11, 1945. RG 511, National Archives, College Park, Maryland.

235 **Everyone's cute after twelve cocktails**... For a fuller account of Trishelle, Steven, and Frank — the one I knew my editor would make me cut — see http://www.mtv.com/news/2339854/real-world-las-vegas-hookups/.

236 **Here's to five miserable months on the wagon**... *The Shining* (dir. Stanley Kubrick, 1980), screenplay by Stanley Kubrick and Diane Johnson.

236 **Would he ever have an hour**...Stephen King, *The Shining* (New York: Doubleday, 1977), 25.

237 **clenched tightly in his lap, working against each other, sweating**...Ibid. See references to clenched or sweaty hands on 7, 53, 186, 269, 394.

237 **If a man reforms**...Ibid., 346–47.

237 **One for every month I've been on the wagon**...Ibid., 350.

237 **The floor of the Wagon**...Ibid., 354.

238 **looking at him expectantly, silently**...Ibid., 508–9.

238 **Jack brought the drink to his mouth**...Ibid., 509.

238 **What was he doing in a bar with a drink in his hand?**...Ibid., 507.

238 **It was just before the curtain of Act II**...Ibid., 356.

238 **You had to make him drink the Bad Stuff. That's the only way you could get him**...Ibid., 632.

239 **almost guiltily, as if he had been drinking secretly**...Ibid., 242.

239 **he gets the same sensation he usually felt**...Ibid., 267.

239 **The party was over**...Ibid., 641.

239 **without even realizing...that I was writing about myself**...Stephen King, *On Writing: A Memoir of the Craft* (New York: Scribner, 2000), 95. King wrote denial into Jack while he was still deep in denial himself, projecting onto his character not only his addiction but also the delusion of its absence. "He hadn't believed he was an alcoholic," King wrote about Jack. He always told himself, "Not me, I can stop anytime" (*The Shining*, 55).

239 **I was afraid that I wouldn't be able to work anymore**...King, *On Writing*, 98. Even when Stephen King wasn't fully facing his addiction, he writes, "the deep part of me that knew I was an alcoholic...began to scream for help in the only way it knew how, through my fiction and through my monsters" (96). King has described three of his novels — *The Shining, Misery,* and *Tommyknockers* — as attempts to articulate his problem to himself: *Tommyknockers* was about "alien creatures that got into your head and just started...well, tommyknocking around in there. What you got was energy and a kind of superficial intelligence" (97). It wasn't a subtle sublimation: *Energy + superficial intelligence = cocaine*. He wrote the book in 1986, when he wasn't just metaphorizing coke but madly metabolizing it, "often working until midnight with my heart running at a hundred and thirty beats a minute and cotton swabs stuck up my nose to stem the coke-induced bleeding" (96). He bled all over that story, but it was *Misery* — the story of a deranged nurse named Annie and her terrorized patient, the writer she holds hostage — that finally got him to quit: "Annie was coke," he wrote, "Annie was booze, and I decided I was tired of being Annie's pet writer" (98).

240 **The fantasy of every alcoholic**... *The Oxford Handbook of Philosophy and Psychiatry*, ed. by K. W. M. Fulford et al. (Oxford: Oxford University Press, 2013), 872.

242 **You are walking along a road peacefully**...Rhys, *Good Morning, Midnight*, in *The Complete Novels* (New York: W. W. Norton, 1985), 450.

242 **Rumors spread that she'd died at a sanitarium**...Carole Angier, *Jean Rhys: Life and Work* (New York: Little, Brown, 1991), 437.

242 **the late Jean Rhys**...Hunter Davies, "Rip van Rhys," *Sunday Times*, November 6, 1966, 6.

242 **Will anyone knowing her whereabouts**...Selma Vaz Dias, personal advertisement, *The New Statesman*, November 1949. Jean Rhys Archive, University of Tulsa.

242 **MRS. HAMER AGITATED**...*Beckenham and Penge Advertiser* qtd. in Angier, *Jean Rhys: Life and Work*, 451.

242 **But who was JEAN RHYS and WHERE WAS SHE?**...After receiving Rhys's reply to her advertisement, Vaz Dias went to visit her "in a daze of excitement." Rhys answered the door wearing a "long pink housecoat," and to Vaz Dias she seemed like a woman lost to the world: "I immediately knew that for her there was little distinction between night and day." Rhys was "parched for a drink" when they met, so Vaz Dias walked "miles in cold stark Beckenham to find a pub, and succeeded after some effort in buying some doubtful sherry." Selma Vaz Dias, "It's Easy to Disappear," manuscript draft, 3. Jean Rhys Archive, University of Tulsa.

242 **Jean's life...really did seem to be the same few scenes**...Angier, *Jean Rhys: Life and Work*, 455.

242 *Magna est veritas et praevalet*...Truth is great and it prevails...Ibid., 362.

243 **NO teas—NO water—NO lavatory**...Jean Rhys, qtd. in ibid., 475. It was while living in Cheriton Fitzpaine, in need of money, that Rhys made an ill-advised deal with Vaz Dias: Rhys signed away half the profits to any adaptation of her work, a mistake she would later call "The Adventure of the Drunken Signature." See a fuller account of this "adventure" in Angier's biography, which is the source for much of the information in this book about Rhys's life in Cheriton Fitzpaine.

243 **I'm struggling with a new thing**...Rhys to Eliot Bliss, June 28, 1957, Jean Rhys Archive, University of Tulsa.

244 **I am drunk every morning, almost, at Yaddo**...Patricia Highsmith qtd. in Joan Schenkar, *The Talented Miss Highsmith: The Secret Life and Serious Art of Patricia Highsmith* (New York: St. Martin's Press, 2009), 255.

VIII. RETURN

253 **there were *four* things [he] did every day**...Lee Stringer, *Grand Central Winter* (New York: Seven Stories Press, 1998), 17.

253 **in the pipe**...Ibid., 111.

253 **yeasty anticipation...caramel-and-ammonia smoke...yellow-orange glow [that] blossoms, wavers, recedes**...Ibid., 220.

253 **clinging to the idea of finishing**...Ibid., 247.

254 **As soon as I am not able to be _personal_**...Charles Jackson to Mary McCarthy, November 24, 1953, Charles Jackson Papers, Dartmouth College.

255 **consolation, repose, beauty, or energy...beauty delusively attributed to the magical element**...Eve Kosofsky Sedgwick, "Epidemics of the Will," *Tendencies* (Durham, NC: Duke UP, 1993), 132.

255 **My God I'll never take another drink**...John Berryman, *Recovery* (New York: Farrar, Straus and Giroux, 1973), 83.

257 **a killer and a fighter**...Qtd. in Carole Angier, *Jean Rhys: Life and Work* (New York: Little, Brown, 1991), 442.

257 **going over and over miseries of one sort and another**...Diana Melly qtd. in ibid., 649.

257 **has proved herself to be enamoured of gloom**...Rebecca West, "The Pursuit of Misery in Some of the New Novels," *The Daily Telegraph*, January 30, 1931. Jean Rhys Archive, University of Tulsa.

257 **"Fated to Be Sad"**...Hannah Carer, "Fated to Be Sad: Jean Rhys Talks to Hannah Carter," *Guardian*, August 8, 1968, 5.

257 **pre-destined role, the role of victim**...Rhys qtd. in Angier, *Jean Rhys: Life and Work*, 588.

257 **End of moan in minor**...Jean Rhys to Peggy Kirkaldy, July 8, 1948, *Jean Rhys Letters, 1931–1966*, ed. Francis Wyndham and Diana Melly (London: Andre Deutsch, 1984), 47. "The nuns used to say that there were only two sins, Presumption and Despair," Rhys wrote in an undated handwritten fragment. "I don't know which mine is" (Jean Rhys Archive, University of Tulsa).

257 **Everyone saw the characters in her books as victims**...Jean Rhys, interview. "Every Day Is a New Day," *Radio Times*, November 21, 1974, 6. Jean Rhys Archive, University of Tulsa.

257 **I'm a person at a masked ball without a mask**...Mary Cantwell, "Conversation with Jean Rhys, 'the Best Living English Novelist,'" *Mademoiselle*, October 1974, 170. Jean Rhys Archive, University of Tulsa.

257 **I am not an ardent Women's Libber**...Rhys qtd. in Angier, *Jean Rhys: Life and Work*, 631.

258 **I see an angry woman who had good reason to be angry**...Lillian Pizzichini, *The Blue Hour: A Life of Jean Rhys* (New York: W. W. Norton and Company, 2009), 308.

258 **tortured and tormented mask**...Jean Rhys, *Good Morning, Midnight*, in *The Complete Novels* (New York: W. W. Norton, 1985), 369–70. Rhys was constantly dissecting self-pity by pulling apart the threads of its alibis and its promises, punishing herself with the hair shirts of her unflattering literary avatars. One of her male characters, regarding one of her heroines, thinks: "Surely even she must see that she was trying to make a tragedy out of a situation that was fundamentally comical" (Rhys, *After Leaving Mr. Mackenzie*, in *The Complete Novels*, 251). This boomerang perspective allows Rhys to do so much more than simply *inhabit* a state of self-pity: She conjures how it must look from the outside, and how absurd it must seem. In *Voyage in the Dark*, she conjures Anna's vulnerability in precise and unsettling terms: "I was so nervous about how I looked that three-quarters of me was in a prison," Anna thinks, "wandering round and round in a circle." A woman "three-quarters" in prison is far more specific—and much more interesting—than a woman simply *imprisoned*. A woman "three-quarters" in prison is also hovering outside herself, her remaining quarter measuring the terms and severity of her incarceration—poking fun at what it means to parse the difference between two-thirds and three-fourths jailed (*Voyage in the Dark*, in *The Complete Novels*, 47).

258 **a tall hat with a green feather**...Rhys, *Good Morning, Midnight*, in *The Complete Novels*, 370.

260 **fall into the hands of someone whom it would help**...John Lloyd qtd. in Blake Bailey, *Farther and Wilder: The Lost Weekends and Literary Dreams of Charles Jackson* (New York: Vintage, 2013), 168.

260 **to solve psychiatric problems**...Charles Jackson qtd. in May R. Marion, "CJ Speaks at Hartford AA," *AA Grapevine*, January 1945. Bailey, *Farther and Wilder*, 168.

260 **What do you know, I'm drinking again**...Charles Jackson to Rhoda Jackson, qtd. in Bailey, *Farther and Wilder*, 226.

260 **Nothing could make me take another drink**...Charles Jackson, in a 1948 promotional brochure released by Rinehart and Company, called *The Lost Novelist*, qtd. in Bailey, *Farther and Wilder*, 238.

260 **AUTHOR OF LOST WEEKEND LOSES ONE HIMSELF**...Ibid., 283. The results of Jackson's head-on car crash were surprisingly minor. As Bailey reports, the passengers of the other car suffered only minor injuries, and Jackson himself emerged seemingly unharmed.

260 **I realized yesterday...how he managed to stop drinking**...Rhoda Jackson to Frederick Storrier Jackson, July 3, 1947, Charles Jackson Papers, Dartmouth College.

261 **No telling what might happen next time but why worry about that?**...Charles Jackson, *The Lost Weekend* (New York: Farrar and Rinehart, 1944), 244.

261 **Chas. & Billy based their movie version far less on the book**...Charles Jackson to Robert Nathan, February 19, 1945, Charles Jackson Papers, Dartmouth College.

263 **You watch, baby**...See accounts of Billie Holiday's death in John Szwed, *Billie Holiday: The Musician and the Myth* (New York: Viking, 2015); and Johann Hari, *Chasing the Scream* (New York: Bloomsbury, 2015). See also the obituary in the *New York Times*: "Billie Holiday Dies Here at 44; Jazz Singer Had Wide Influence," July 18, 1959.

264 **an open wound...vocal cords flayed**...Michael Brooks qtd. in Szwed, *Billie Holiday: The Musician and the Myth*, 194.

264 **Now I'm going to eat breakfast!**...Qtd. in Julia Blackburn, *With Billie: A New Look at the Unforgettable Lady Day* (New York: Pantheon, 2005), 171.

264 **I had seen pictures of her ten years before**...Ellis qtd. in ibid., 269.

264 **other customers were also crying in their beer and shot glasses**...Studs Terkel qtd. in Szwed, *Billie Holiday: The Musician and the Myth*, 105.

265 **She tried to breast-feed her godson from breasts that didn't have milk**...Much of this information is drawn from Szwed, *Billie Holiday: The Musician and the Myth*, 44–45.

265 **Everyone and I stopped breathing**...Frank O'Hara, "The Day Lady Died," *The Collected Poems of Frank O'Hara*, ed. Donald Allen (Berkeley: University of California Press, 1995).

IX. CONFESSION

273 **Why do you deserve another chance**...This exchange is excerpted from a transcription of a drug-court trial included in an ethnographic account of drug courts. Stacy Lee Burns and Mark Peyrot, "Tough Love: Nurturing and Coercing Responsibility and Recovery in California Drug Courts," *Social Problems* 50, no. 3 (August 2003): 433.

The first drug court was established in Miami in 1989, and by June 2015 there were more than 3,142 operating in the United States (National Institute of Justice, "Drug Courts," http://www.nij.gov/topics/courts/drug-courts/pages/welcome

.aspx). New York, Maryland, Kansas, and Washington were some of the first states to pass legislation like California's Proposition 36 (2000), which essentially made drug courts the mandatory default for all low-level offenders. Scott Ehlers and Jason Ziedenberg, "Proposition 36: Five Years Later," Justice Policy Institute (April 2006).

As sociologists Burns and Peyrot put it, drug court is about "demonstrating the recovering self" ("Tough Love," 430)—the new self that is strong enough to resist addiction. Defendants are required to follow an individualized treatment plan mandated by a drug court judge. These plans typically include AA/NA meetings, counseling sessions, vocational training, in- or out-patient rehab, and urine tests. There is often a graduation ceremony at the end of the program, complete with applause and chocolate cake, cap and gown, and T-shirts that say "Refuse to Abuse" or "Hooked on Recovery" (433).

274 **tongue lashings..."I'm tired of your excuses!"..."I'm through with you!"...** Terance D. Miethe, Hong Lu, and Erin Reese, "Reintegrative Shaming and Recidivism Risks in Drug Court: Explanations for Some Unexpected Findings," *Crime and Delinquency* 46 (2000): 522, 536–37. Drug courts depend on a theory of "reintegrative shaming," the idea that being publicly shamed can bring an offender back into the folds of the community. Reintegrative shaming is predicated on the idea that the shame is directed away from the person and toward the act itself, though drug courts in practice often dissolve this distinction.

274 **salvageable...irremediably deficient...** Burns and Peyrot, "Tough Love," 428–29.

274 **There isn't a soul on this earth who can say for sure that their fight with dope is over until they're dead...** Billie Holiday, *Lady Sings the Blues*, 220.

275 **Yes, Nic relapsed...** David Sheff, "Afterword," *Beautiful Boy* (New York: Houghton Mifflin Harcourt, 2008), 323–24.

276 **stopping-drinking and...enormous interest in AA...a lot to do with this new attitude...** Charles Jackson to Walter and Merriman Modell, January 9, 1954, Charles Jackson Papers, Dartmouth College.

276 **At that point, Jackson was working on the book he imagined would become his magnum opus: an epic novel called *What Happened*...** *What Happened* wasn't meant to be explicitly about recovery, and in this way it was distinct from *The Working Out*, Jackson's hypothetical sequel to *The Lost Weekend*, committed to how Don "got out of it." But for a time Jackson wrote the early pages of *What Happened* under the influence, as it were, of the recovery ethos he'd found in AA.

277 **novel of affirmation and acceptance of life...** Charles Jackson to Stanley Rinehart et al., February 27, 1948, Charles Jackson Papers, Dartmouth College.

277 **would be host to the gathering...** Charles Jackson to Stanley Rinehart, March 8, 1945, Charles Jackson Papers, Dartmouth College.

277 **working on every conceivable thing...** Blake Bailey, *Farther and Wilder: The Lost Weekends and Literary Dreams of Charles Jackson* (New York: Vintage, 2013), 346.

277 **it's far & away the best thing I've done, simpler, more honest...** Charles Jackson to Walter and Merriman Modell, January 9, 1954, Charles Jackson Papers, Dartmouth College.

Notes

277 **I can put it best by saying the story <u>happens</u>**...Charles Jackson to Roger Straus, December 30, 1953, Charles Jackson Papers, Dartmouth College.

278 **It is really wonderful, simple, plain, human, life itself—nothing in the dazzling intellectual class**...Charles Jackson to Roger Straus, January 8, 1954, Charles Jackson Papers, Dartmouth College.

278 **can do just about what it pleases...<u>I</u> please to make it plain, like everyday people**...Ibid.

278 **life unfolding moment by moment...careless and rambling...total lack of originality**...Charles Jackson to Dorothea Straus, qtd. in Bailey, *Farther and Wilder*, 318.

278 **all of it <u>outside</u> of myself—outside!**...Charles Jackson to "Angel," January 8, 1954, Charles Jackson Papers, Dartmouth College.

279 **loyalty to my wife, helped at times by extreme drunkenness**..."Bill's Story," *Alcoholics Anonymous*, 3.

282 **What has bothered me most about myself all my life?**...John Berryman, "Fourth Step Inventory Guide," undated, c. 1970–71, John Berryman Papers, University of Minnesota.

283 **inviting the prisoners to have dinner at his house**...See John Haffenden, *The Life of John Berryman* (London: Methuen & Co., 1984), 408.

283 *Hurts oneself. Always for the unchangeable*...John Berryman, handwritten note, undated, c. 1970–71, John Berryman Papers, University of Minnesota.

283 **the so-called Minnesota Model**...The "Minnesota Model," what we now think of as "rehab," was developed in the mid-fifties at a place called Willmar State Hospital, an "inebriate asylum" in Willmar, Minnesota, which had been practicing custodial care for late-stage alcoholics for decades. (It was originally called the Willmar Hospital Farm for Inebriates when it opened in 1912.) Their more holistic program model, officially launched in 1954, was based on AA principles but designed for residential patients, and it believed in the possibility of recovery: They unlocked the doors to the inebriate ward, started giving lectures to the patients, and hired sober alcoholic counselors to work with them. Creating positions officially designated for alcoholic counselors met with resistance from many corners. Governor Clyde Elmer Anderson was "laughed at" when he first advocated for the position of an "alcoholic counselor" in the civil service system, and AA members were worried about members getting paid for the "twelve-step" work that was a crucial part of their program. But Willmar had a close and collaborative relationship with AA, and with another treatment facility nearby: a farmhouse called Hazelden that would eventually become one of the most famous rehabs in America. Hazelden started small in 1949 (only two years after Holiday was incarcerated for her addiction) with just four patients in residence at a time. On its first Christmas, there were only two patients; one cooked Christmas dinner for the other. The only medication they handed out was a placebo pill given to newcomers who said they didn't feel good, but they did start handing out personalized coffee cups to every resident. The Minnesota Model of treatment, which rose from these early facilities, focused on community bonding and shifted attention away from a psychoanalytic approach to alcoholism (finding

its *cause*), instead stressing the idea that structured daily living practices could produce sobriety. The Minnesota Model expanded rapidly over the sixties, seventies, and eighties (someone described Hazelden in 1968, with 1,420 patients, as "Grand Central Station at Rush Hour") and eventually it came to be known simply as "rehab." (Its origins in Minnesota were also part of how the Land of Ten Thousand Lakes earned its other nickname, the "Land of Ten Thousand Treatment Centers.") Information on the development of the Minnesota Model and the early days of Hazelden comes from William White's *Slaying the Dragon: The History of Addiction Treatment and Recovery in America* (Bloomington, IL: Chestnut Health Systems, 1998).

283 **Wife left me after 11 yrs of marriage bec. of drinking**...John Berryman, handwritten note, 1970, John Berryman Papers, University of Minnesota.

284 **a list of his "Responsibilities"**...John Berryman, handwritten fourth step, November 8 (1970 or 1971), John Berryman Papers, University of Minnesota.

284 **When Berryman started to consider writing a novel about recovery**...The shift in genre (from poetry to novel) was also significant for Berryman. The form of the novel allowed for narrative progression, or its explicit disruption or repudiation, rather than lyric moments existing in temporal isolation. The shift from one genre to another also facilitated other structural shifts: away from experiments in voice and image and toward a psychological portrait rendered through scenic interactions.

284 **useful 12th step work**...John Berryman, handwritten note, undated, John Berryman Papers, University of Minnesota.

284 **He thought of calling the novel *Korsakov's Syndrome on the Grave* but found he preferred *I Am an Alcoholic*...Give half my royalties to—who? Not AA—they won't take it...** Ibid.

285 **This summary & deluded account of the beginning of my recovery**...John Berryman, typewritten draft fragment of *Recovery*, John Berryman Papers, University of Minnesota.

285 **The Post-Novel: Fiction as Wisdom-Work**...Haffenden, *The Life of John Berryman*, 396. Malcolm Lowry's *Under the Volcano* was on Berryman's syllabus.

285 **Good, evil, love, hate, life, death, beauty, ugliness**...All quotations from "The Trial of Jean Rhys" are from an unpublished handwritten notebook entry that can be found in the 1952 diary known as the "Ropemakers' Diary," so-called because Rhys kept it while staying at an inn called the Ropemakers Arms in 1951–52. Jean Rhys Archive, University of Tulsa.

285 **I do not know others. I see them as trees walking**...In this moment in "The Trial of Jean Rhys," Rhys is most likely alluding to the Gospel of Mark, verses 22–25, when a blind man is brought to Jesus to be healed. The first time Jesus heals him, the man's sight is only partially restored. He looks up and says, "I see men, for I see them like trees, walking around." Then Jesus lays his hands on the blind man again, and his sight is fully restored: he "began to see everything clearly." It's a vexed moment of flawed and partial salvation (the man's sight is not fully restored the first time around), and Rhys's invocation is a painful one: she does not seem to be imagining this fullness of vision as possible for herself.

287 *If I can do this book, it won't matter so much will it?*...Rhys's hunger for redemption—the idea that writing well enough could help her "earn death"—evokes the ghost of her mother, stirring guava jam in the pot and reading *The Sorrows of Satan*, the story of Satan's desire for a redemption he couldn't ever achieve. If Rhys was going to fail at loving others, she wanted to redeem her failures by writing them brilliantly.

287 **powerful argument against biography itself**...A. Alvarez, "Down and Out in Paris and London," *New York Review of Books*, October 10, 1991.

287 **Write 8 or 9–1 pm in study**...John Berryman, handwritten note, John Berryman Papers, University of Minnesota.

288 **We worked like I never did at Lexington**...William Burroughs Jr. *Kentucky Ham* (New York: E. P. Dutton, 1973), 155.

288 **You know what work does?**...Ibid., 174.

X. HUMBLING

295 **It's purely a clinical study...it's only a small part of yours...achieving something that was unique**...Lowry, *Dark as the Grave Wherein My Friend Is Laid* (London: Jonathan Cape, 1969), 24–25. For my discussion of Lowry's anxieties about publishing *Under the Volcano* after it had already been "scooped" by Jackson's *The Lost Weekend*, I drew on John Crowley's *The White Logic* and its wonderful account of the rivalry between Jackson and Lowry. In Lowry's unpublished novel *Dark as the Grave*, Sigbjørn's disappointment is sharpened by his sense that his alcoholism was the thing that would finally let him break "new ground," that it would finally release him from the "suspicion that he would never write anything original." Like Rhys, he'd hoped that his work would be the thing that redeemed his ruined life: *If I can do this book, it won't matter so much, will it?*

295 **a long regurgitation [that] can only be recommended as an anthology held together by earnestness**...Jacques Barzun, *Harper's Magazine*, "Moralists for Your Muddles," April 1947.

295 **PS: Anthology held together by earnestness—brrrrr!**...Malcolm Lowry to *Harper's Magazine*, May 6, 1947. Lowry struggles with how to end the letter, and thinks better of dismissing Barzun completely: "So if, instead of ending this letter 'may Christ send you sorrow and a serious illness,' I were to end it by saying instead that I would be tremendously grateful if one day you would throw your gown out of the window and address some remarks in this direction upon the reading of history, and even in regard to the question of writing and the world in general, I hope you won't take it amiss."

   The complete letter is available at http://harpers.org/blog/2008/08/may-christ-send-you-sorrow-and-a-serious-illness/.

296 **What would have happened to Danny's troubled father**...Stephen King, *Doctor Sleep* (New York: Gallery Books, 2013), 529.

296 **The women in the doorway had gone back to the kitchen**...Ibid., 517.

297 **I want a poem I can grow old in**...Eavan Boland, "A Woman Painted on a Leaf," *In a Time of Violence: Poems* (New York: W. W. Norton, 1995), 69.

297 I can only write the human, meanderingly...Jackson letter to Dorothea Straus, qtd. in Blake Bailey, *Farther and Wilder: The Lost Weekends and Literary Dreams of Charles Jackson* (New York: Vintage, 2013), 319.

297 What life means, it came to him...Ibid. The whole passage is even more "meandering" and redundant in its entirety: "What life means, it came to him (or he seemed to overhear it), it means *all* the time, not just at isolated dramatic moments that never happened. If life means anything at all, it means whatever it means every hour, every minute, through any episode big or small, if only one has the awareness to sense it...Some day, perhaps, existence might gather itself and reveal its full meaning to him in the kind of moment he had, till now, been romantically expecting...but he doubted it. For now he knew (he had just been told so) that what life means it means now, this instant, and yesterday, and tomorrow, and ten years ago, and twenty years hence—each step, the dramatic and the humdrum alike—every fleeting second of the way..." Unpublished manuscript, 204, Charles Jackson Papers, Dartmouth College.

298 with scarcely any "plot" but much character...Jackson to Walter and Merriman Modell, January 9, 1954, Charles Jackson Papers, Dartmouth College.

298 what he called the "alcoholocaust" of his life...D. T. Max, "Day of the Dead." *The New Yorker*, December 17, 2007.

299 just about as tedious as anything I'd ever read...Albert Erskine to biographer Gordon Bowker, qtd. in ibid.

299 Rambling...Seems like a dissertation on alcohol. Nothing useful here... Margerie Lowry qtd. in ibid.

299 He had the impulse to pull the car over...Jackson, *Farther and Wilder*. Unpublished manuscript, 36, Charles Jackson Papers, Dartmouth College.

303 I used to think you had to believe to pray. Now I know I had it assbackwards...David Foster Wallace, handwritten notes, undated, David Foster Wallace Papers, University of Texas at Austin.

304 was most of all impressed by the sense that, in spite of the hero's utter selfabsorption...Charles Jackson to Warren Ambrose, March 1, 1954, Charles Jackson Papers, Dartmouth College.

305 So long as I considered myself as merely the medium...John Berryman, handwritten note, August 1971, qtd. in John Haffenden, *The Life of John Berryman* (London: Methuen & Co., 1984), 414. The relationship between addiction and creativity was under discussion in many spheres. In the 1970 *Playboy* roundtable discussion mentioned in an earlier note, literary critic Leslie Fiedler insisted that "literature has always been drug-ridden," and "many American writers always thought of alcohol as representing or even being their muse." But it was Burroughs himself, the great heroin sage, who disagreed: "It has been my impression that any sedative drug that decreases awareness—the narcotics, barbiturates, excessive alcohol and so forth—also decreases the author's ability to create." "Playboy Panel: The Drug Revolution," *Playboy* 17, no. 2 (February 1970), 53–74.

306 Are we really all that tormented?...Charles Jackson, "We Were Led to Hope for More," review of *Selected Letters of Malcolm Lowry*, ed. Harvey Breit and Margerie Bonner Lowry, *New York Times*, December 12, 1965.

306 **if by some supreme effort, some mystical or psychological shifting-of-gears**...Ibid. Although Jackson's review lamented Lowry's "hyper preoccupation with self," it eventually became—by acrobatic critical contortions, and seemingly without a trace of self-awareness—almost entirely about Jackson himself. "I must perforce inject a strictly personal note, it cannot be avoided," he wrote, and this "personal note" consumed most of the rest of the review, offering an account of Lowry's fears that *The Lost Weekend* had preempted his own alcoholic epic. It was an ouroboros of authorial egos: Jackson obsessing about Lowry obsessing about Jackson.

306 **Instead of drinking coffee when I woke up**...Marguerite Duras, *Practicalities* (London: William Collins Sons, 1990), 130.

306 **Drunkenness doesn't create anything**...Ibid., 17.

307 **three brutal "disintoxication" treatments**...See Edmund White, "In Love with Duras," *New York Review of Books*, June 26, 2008.

307 **exactly ten thousand tortoises...The sound of singing, solo and in chorus**...Duras, *Practicalities*, 137–38.

307 **take up, outside your blocked selves, some small thing**...Berryman, "Death Ballad," *Love and Fame* (New York: Farrar, Straus and Giroux, 1970). See Haffenden, *The Life of John Berryman* (363) for more information about Berryman's relationship to Tyson and Jo.

308 *To listen...1 / 500,000th*...Berryman, handwritten marginalia, *AA Grapevine* 28, no. 4 (September 1971). John Berryman Papers, University of Minnesota.

308 *My groups*...Berryman, handwritten note, March 25, 1971, John Berryman Papers, University of Minnesota.

309 **Towers above the trees across the river reminded him**...Berryman, *Recovery* (New York: Farrar, Straus and Giroux, 1973), 63.

309 **His own hope was to forget about himself**...Ibid., 148.

309 **You don't remember a time when you didn't have it?**...Ibid., 208. Severance's expertise in immunology gives Berryman a new way to consider the relationship between the self and everything outside it. As Severance frames it, immunology is committed to the "question of how the body recognizes some substances as 'self' and others as 'not self.'" And in his journal, Severance applies this to sobriety: "The point is to learn to recognize whiskey as *not* my 'self'—alien, in fact" (22). Whiskey was the wrong kind of *not-self*, what Sedgwick might call the "external supplement," but recovery offers a better kind of *not-self* in its place: the selves of everyone else. After learning about a young woman's abortion, Severance "yearned toward her," and when she finally articulates the anger she's kept bottled up for years, he is "beside himself with pride and love" (193–94). The idea of being *beside himself* is key: he is somehow liberated, like Bill Wilson channeling spirits, or Charles Jackson getting *outside himself*.

309 **In hospitals he found his society. About these passioning countrymen he did not need to be ironical**...Bellow continues: "Here his heart was open, submitting democratically and eagerly to the criticisms of truckers, graceful under the correction of plumbers and mentally disturbed housewives." Bellow's tone betrays both awe and amusement, offering a bit of irony to compensate for all the "ironical" reac-

tions that Berryman's open heart rejected. Bellow implies that for Berryman rehab implied a kind of class humbling: truckers and plumbers become the professor's tutors. Saul Bellow, "Foreword," *Recovery*, by John Berryman (New York: Farrar, Straus and Giroux, 1973), xi.

310 **Cheers from everybody, general exultation**...Berryman, *Recovery*, 31.

310 **There was more, but Severance**...Ibid., 30. It's also possible that Severance's empathy for a man seeking his dead father's approval was also, at least in part, about himself, as Berryman had lost his own father when he was young.

310 **his rich, practiced, lecturer's voice**...Ibid., 12.

310 **he couldn't ever be wholehearted about belonging with the rest of us**...Betty Peddie qtd. in Haffenden, *The Life of John Berryman*, 374.

310 **just another addiction memoir**...Some examples of the "just another addiction memoir" phenomenon: Matt Medley, "Interview with Bill Clegg," *The National Post*, July 9, 2010; Nan Talese talking about James Frey's memoir in Pauline Millard, "James Frey Chronicles His Former Addiction," Associated Press, May 8, 2003; Stefanie Wilder-Taylor, blurb for *Drunk Mom* (2014), by Jowita Bydlowska. *The Hampton Sheet* lists Joshua Lyon's *Pillhead* as its Best-After-the-Afterparty-Read: "Five pages into *Pillhead*, and you'll stop accusing Lyon of writing just another addiction memoir" (July/August 2009).

311 **Frey's editor, Nan Talese, said she'd almost passed on his manuscript because—as one account put it—it seemed like (yes) "just another addiction memoir"**...Pauline Millard, "James Frey Chronicles His Former Addiction," Associated Press, May 8, 2003.

311 **A social worker who'd recommended the book to her clients**...Evgenia Peretz, "James Frey's 'Morning After,'" *Vanity Fair*, April 28, 2008. Random House offered a refund to any reader who sent back page 163 (Motoko Rich, "James Frey and His Publisher Settle Suit over Lies," *New York Times*, September 7, 2006).

311 **Frey's distortions became a stand-in for the "truthiness" of his times**...In a *New York Times* op-ed, Maureen Dowd connected Frey's distortions to deceptions on the national scale: "It was a huge relief, after our long national slide into untruth and no consequences, into Swift boating and swift bucks, into W.'s delusion and denial, to see the Empress of Empathy icily hold someone accountable for lying and conning" ("Oprah's Bunk Club," *New York Times*, January 28, 2006). Journalist and former addict—and future author of his own addiction memoir—David Carr wrote another *New York Times* article called "How Oprahness Trumped Truthiness" (January 30, 2006). Calvin Trillin even published a poem in *The Nation* called "I Dreamt That George W. Bush Adopted James Frey's 3-Step Program—Denial, Larry King, and Oprah—to Get to the Truth about the War in Iraq" (February 2, 2006).

311 **My mistake was writing about the person**..."Frey's Note to the Reader" appeared in the February 1, 2006, *New York Times*, and was subsequently included in reprints of *A Million Little Pieces*.

312 **Exceptional case, my ass!**...Helen MacGill Hughes, ed., *The Fantastic Lodge: The Autobiography of a Girl Drug Addict* (New York: Fawcett, 1961), 224.

312 **The man pulling radishes / pointed my way / with a radish**...Kobayashi Issa, "The Man Pulling Radishes," eighteenth-century poem.

313　**Half measures will avail you nothing**...*The Book That Started It All: The Original Working Manuscript of Alcoholics Anonymous* (Center City, MN: Hazelden, 2010).

313　**Do You Think You're Different?**...Alcoholics Anonymous World Services, "Do You Think You're Different?" (1976). Center of Alcohol Studies, Rutgers University, 19

314　**What's the first memory you have of drinking?**...Karen Casey. *My Story to Yours: A Guided Memoir for Writing Your Recovery Journey* (Center City, MN: Hazelden, 2011), 60, 115.

314　**You might have some fond memories of the drinking days**...Ibid., 60.

314　**Do you believe in destiny?**...Ibid., 127.

315　**Why is the truth usually not just un- but *anti*-interesting?**...David Foster Wallace, *Infinite Jest* (Boston: Little, Brown, 1996), 358.

XI. CHORUS

319　**We started with all volunteer help in a little ramshackle hostel**...E-mail to the author from "Sawyer," January 11, 2015. The history of Seneca House has been compiled from interviews with Sawyer (January 21, 2015, telephone, and July 31, 2015, in person) and a document sent by Sawyer (January 20, 2015) as well as interviews with "Gwen" (January 22, 2015, telephone, and March 10, 2015, in person); "Marcus" (July 28, 2015, telephone, and November 3, 2015, in person); "Shirley" (March 6, 2015, telephone, March 20, 2015, telephone, and August 10, 11, 12, 2015, in person); and "Raquel" (December 4, 2015). All of their names have been changed to protect their anonymity. I also used extensive replies from Shirley to questions I sent by e-mail (March 5, 15, and 20, 2015).

320　**Hmmm...it would be a tougher sell here**...Charlie Homans e-mail to the author, January 30, 2015.

320　*It is really wonderful, simple, plain, human, life itself*...Charles Jackson to Roger Straus, January 8, 1954, Charles Jackson Papers, Dartmouth College.

320　**His name is Sawyer, and he's an alcoholic**...The material about Sawyer's life was gathered during interviews conducted on January 21, 2015 (telephone) and July 31, 2015 (in person).

323　**When it first opened, Seneca charged six hundred dollars for a twenty-eight-day stay**...Early history of Seneca from conversations with Sawyer (January 21, 2015, telephone, and July 31, 2015, in person); conversations with Gwen (January 22, 2015, telephone, and March 10, 2015, in person); conversations with Shirley (March 6 and 20, 2015, telephone, and August 10, 11, 12, 2015, in person); written document from Sawyer, January 20, 2015; and pseudonymous article by Shirley.

323　**We all have to be on the vomit line**...From an article that Shirley wrote, under another pseudonym, about her experience at Seneca House: Barbara Lenmark, "An Alcoholic Housewife: What Happened to Her in 28 Days," *Baltimore Sun*, November 18, 1973.

323　**This was 1971, the same year Bill Wilson died and Nixon launched his War on Drugs**...Nixon called for $155 million to fight the war on drugs, but his administration also spent more money on treatment than law enforcement, the first and only administration to do so. His successor, Gerald Ford, cut treatment funding and made it fifty-fifty. After he left office, Ford's wife went public with her own addiction and started the Betty Ford Clinic, which became one of the most famous treatment centers in the country. Reagan cut funding even further, dismantling the program for heroin addicts. We're paying for these choices now—America's punitive relationship to addiction, and its inadequate relationship to treatment—with the worst opiate epidemic our country has ever seen. Nixon put two-thirds of his drug war funding into cutting off demand (treatment), and one-third into cutting off supply (law enforcement). For Nixon and his war on drugs: Emily Dufton, "The War on Drugs: How President Nixon Tied Addiction to Crime," *The Atlantic*, March 26, 2012; and Richard Nixon's "Special Message to the Congress on Drug Abuse Prevention and Control," delivered on June 17, 1971, http://www.presidency.ucsb.edu/ws/?pid=3048.

In his "Special Message," Nixon divided the field into bad guys and their marks: "I will ask for additional funds to increase our enforcement efforts to further tighten the noose around the necks of drug peddlers, and thereby loosen the noose around the necks of drug users." The $155 million and $105 million amounts are also quoted in that speech.

323　WE HAVE MET THE ENEMY AND IT IS US...Lenmark, "An Alcoholic Housewife."

324　**You don't ever go into a convenience store**...Sawyer interview with the author, January 21, 2015.

324　**Seneca residents were often assigned contracts**...Information on Seneca House contracts from interviews with Gwen (January 22, 2015, telephone, and March 10, 2015, in person) and photocopies of Seneca House programming, provided courtesy of Gwen.

325　**Once you are Real you can't be ugly**...Margery Williams, *The Velveteen Rabbit* (New York: Grosset & Dunlap, 1987).

325　**Lips Lackowitz—sober front man of the band Tough Luck**..."Obituary: Mark Hurwitz, Blues Musician," *Washington Post*, August 4, 2002. From interview with Gwen, March 10, 2015.

327　**AA skeptics often assume that its members insist on it as the only answer**...Examples of this skepticism, and in particular the claim that AA members promote it as the only solution, include Lance Dodes and Zachary Dodes, *The Sober Truth: Debunking the Bad Science Behind 12-Step Programs and the Rehab Industry* (Boston: Beacon Press, 2014); and Gabrielle Glaser, "The Irrationality of Alcoholics Anonymous," *The Atlantic*, April 2015.

328　**There are a hundred ways to skin a cat**...Greg Hobelmann interview with the author, August 30, 2016.

328　**Many addiction researchers predict that we'll eventually be able to track the impact of meetings on the brain itself**...See Carlton Erickson, *The Science of Addiction: From Neurobiology to Treatment* (New York: W. W. Norton, 2007), 155.

328　**knocking on the door of the mechanism...You can give someone as much methadone as you want**...Adam Kaplin interview with the author, October 13, 2016.

328　**the thirst of the self to feel that it is part of something larger...An animal who has found salt in the forest**...Lewis Hyde, "Alcohol and Poetry: John Berryman and the Booze Talking," *American Poetry Review*, October 1975. Rpt. Dallas: The Dallas Institute of Humanities and Culture, 1986, 3.

328 **The Big Book of AA was initially called *The Way Out*...** The founders of AA decided to change the title of the Big Book to *Alcoholics Anonymous* once they realized that too many other books were already called *The Way Out*, which is one of the recurring lessons of sobriety anyway: Whatever you want to say, it's probably already been said.

329 **Feel myself outside myself as we follow the music...** Cain, *Blueschild Baby* (New York: McGraw Hill, 1970),133.

329 **naked and defenseless...another device to get outside yourself...** Ibid., 135.

329 **infatuation with the storeroom of his own mind...All stream of consciousness writing...** Alfred Kazin, "The Wild Boys," *New York Times Book Review*, December 12, 1971.

329 **having the discipline to talk out of the part of yourself that can love...** Larry McCaffery, "A Conversation with David Foster Wallace," *The Review of Contemporary Fiction* 13, no. 2 (Summer 1993).

329 **You're special—it's OK...** Wallace letter to Evan Wright, qtd. in D. T. Max, "D.F.W.'s Favorite Grammarian," *The New Yorker*, December 11, 2013, 285.

330 **Her name is Gwen, and she's an alcoholic...** This section based on interviews conducted with Gwen, January 22, 2015, telephone, and March 10, 2015, in person.

331 **His name is Marcus, and he's an alcoholic and an addict...** Material in this section drawn from interviews with Marcus conducted July 28, 2015, telephone, and November 3, 2015, in person.

333 **How did you negotiate that anger?...** National Public Radio, "Program Targets Rehab Help for Federal Inmates," *Morning Edition*, September 27, 2006.

333 **Her name is Shirley, and she's an alcoholic...** Material in this section drawn from interviews conducted March 6, 2015, telephone; March 20, 2015, telephone; and August 10, 11, 12, in person.

336 *Remember that we deal with alcohol—cunning, baffling, powerful!...Alcoholics Anonymous*, 58.

337 **What you really want is to stay just who you are *and* not drink...** John Berryman, *Recovery* (New York: Farrar, Straus and Giroux, 1973), 141.

XII. SALVAGE

346 **stunted and complexly deformed...** David Foster Wallace, *Infinite Jest* (New York: Little, Brown, 1996), 744.

347 **grudging move toward maybe acknowledging...** Ibid., 350.

347 **Serious AAs look like these weird combinations...** Ibid., 357.

347 **humble, kind, helpful, tactful...** Ibid. An addict in *Infinite Jest* named Poor Tony rides the Gray Line in the thick of withdrawal, shitting himself as invisible ants crawl up and down his arms. He wears red high-heels and old eyeliner, weeping in shame, with ghost ants catching his tears. At the top of that page, I wrote: *The humane quality of this novel is that it makes us bear witness to utter degradation.* It's as if the form of the book itself makes us sit still and listen during some of the most difficult shares at a meeting.

348 **to lay responsibility for themselves**...Wallace, *Infinite Jest*, 863.

348 **It's a rough crowd**...Wallace qtd. in D. T. Max, *Every Love Story Is a Ghost Story* (New York: Viking, 2012), 139.

348 **They listened because, in the last analysis**...Wallace, "An Ex-Resident's Story," http://www.granadahouse.org/people/letters_from_our_alum.html.

349 **literary opportunity**...Max, *Every Love Story Is a Ghost Story*, 140.

349 **"Heard in Meetings"**...David Foster Wallace, handwritten note, David Foster Wallace Papers, University of Texas at Austin.

349 **single-entendre writing, writing that meant what it said**...Max, *Every Love Story Is a Ghost Story*, 158.

349 **Recovery shifted Wallace's whole notion of what writing could do, what purpose it might serve**...For an astute discussion of the relationship between Wallace's creativity and his life in recovery, see also critic Elaine Blair, "A New Brilliant Start," *New York Review of Books*, December 6, 2012.

349 **An ironist in a Boston AA meeting is a witch in church**...Wallace, *Infinite Jest*, 369.

353 **I don't want to sound melodramatic here**...Qtd. in "Note on the Texts," *Collected Stories*, ed. William Stull and Maureen Carroll (New York: Library of America, 2009), 993. Perhaps it was the aversion to melodrama that came across so forcefully in Lish's edits that made Carver self-conscious about becoming too "melodramatic" in his resistance to them.

353 **I'm serious, [they're] intimately hooked up**...Qtd. in "Note on the Texts," 995.

353 **bleakness**..."Note on the Texts," 991. As Stull and Carroll note of Lish's edits, "As [Lish] later said, what struck him in Carver's writing was 'a peculiar bleakness.' To foreground that bleakness, he cut the stories radically, reducing plot, character development, and figurative language to a minimum."

353 **he also pushed back against what he understood as the lurking threat of sentimentality**...In "The Carver Chronicles," the first journalistic account of Lish's substantial editorial role in shaping Carver's early work, D. T. Max made use of Carver's archives at the Lilly Library, Indiana University. This article made the extent of the editorial changes public before the original versions were reprinted in full in the 2009 *Collected Stories*. Max describes Lish pushing back against "creeping sentimentality." "The Carver Chronicles," *New York Times Magazine*, August 9, 1998.

354 **I remember Ray's bafflement at one particular suggestion**...Tess Gallagher, "Interview," in *Collected Stories*, ed. William Stull and Maureen Carroll (New York: Library of America, 2009).

354 **called his students to cancel class because he was too sick to teach**... Details about Carver's teaching near the end of his drinking from Carol Sklenicka, *Raymond Carver: A Writer's Life* (New York: Scribner, 2009), 256 and 259.

354 **When he came back to Iowa City to give a reading before his first book came out**...Ibid. The workshop director had to get on stage and tell him to stop, saying maybe he could come back again and read when he was sober. Certain dreams were coming true for Carver, but he was barely around to appreciate them. His body had shown up, but the rest of him couldn't—and his body wouldn't last much longer anyway. Ibid.

354 **If you want the truth, I'm prouder of that**...Raymond Carver, interview by Mona Simpson and Lewis Buzbee, "The Art of Fiction No. 76," *Paris Review* 88 (Summer 1983).

355 **no one else could ever love me in that way, that much**...Carver, "Where Is Everyone?" *Collected Stories*, 765.

355 **Booze takes a lot of time and effort if you're going to do a good job with it**...Carver, "Gazebo," *Collected Stories*, 237.

355 **When Carver first saw Lish's versions, not just whittled but spiritually rearranged, he couldn't stomach the thought of their publication...** "My very sanity is on the line here," he wrote to Lish. "All this is complicatedly, and maybe not so complicatedly, tied up with my feelings of worth and self-esteem since I quit drinking." Carver to Gordon Lish, qtd. in "Note on the Texts," *Collected Stories*, 993–94.

355 **unkindness and condescension of some of these stories**...Michael Wood, "Stories Full of Edges and Silences," *New York Times Book Review*, April 26, 1981.

356 **I don't want to lose track, lose touch with the little human connections**...Carver to Gordon Lish, qtd. in Sklenicka, *Raymond Carver: A Writer's Life*, 362.

356 **It's not clear why Carver allowed his stories to be published with the edits**...The notes in the Library of America edition of Carver's *Collected Stories* narrate the fraught editorial process that resulted in the published version of *What We Talk About When We Talk About Love*, including the letters Carver wrote to Lish, but the decisive phone call isn't transcribed. When Lish described the process decades later in a *Paris Review* interview with critic Christian Lorentzen, he put it like this: "For all those years, Carver could not have been more enthusiastic, nor more complicit — or complacent." Though Carver's letters suggest more friction in the process, Lish certainly believes he deserves the credit for the amount of attention Carver's work has received: "Had I not revised Carver, would he be paid the attention given him? Baloney!" ("The Art of Editing, No. 2," *Paris Review*, Winter 2015).

356 **"It is about Scotty. It has to do with Scotty, yes"**...Carver, "The Bath." *Collected Stories*, 251. The story describes its characters communicating in minimal ways, with "the barest information, nothing that was not necessary."

356 **warm cinnamon rolls just out of the oven, the icing still runny...They listened to him**...Carver, "A Small, Good Thing," *Collected Stories*, 830.

357 **stab[bing] at the eye with a length of blue silk thread**...Carver, "After the Denim," *Collected Stories*, 272.

357 **He and the hippie were in the same boat...[he felt] something stir inside him again, but it was not anger this time**...Carver, "If It Please You," *Collected Stories*, 860, 863.

357 **This time he was able to include the girl and the hippie in his prayers**...Ibid., 863. This closing prayer is expansive in its reach, evoking not only "all of them" but also the end of James Joyce's "The Dead": *snow falling faintly through the universe and faintly falling, like the descent of their last end, upon all the living and the dead.* Joyce's story is also about a man coming to terms with his marriage, and with the ways in which his marriage is haunted by mortality — not only his wife's impending mortality, and his own, but also the death of her first love, Michael, and the presence of his abiding ghost.

358 *If you have a resentment you want to be free of…* "Freedom From Bondage," *Alcoholics Anonymous*, 552.

358 **the wet eyes of the sentimentalist betray his aversion to experience…his arid heart…** James Baldwin, "Everybody's Protest Novel," *Notes of a Native Son* (Boston: Beacon Press, 1955), 14.

358 **Gordon, God's truth, and I may as well say it out now…** Carver to Gordon Lish, qtd. in "Note on the Texts," 984.

360 **You gone risk vulnerability and discomfort and hug my ass…** Wallace, *Infinite Jest*, 506.

360 **fucking up in sobriety…** Ibid., 444.

361 **He uses his pinkie finger to mime the world's smallest viola…** Ibid., 835. The wraith is the ghost of James Incandenza, the filmmaker whose cartridge animates the entire novel, and whose suicide casts a long shadow over it.

361 **No one single instant of it was unendurable…** Ibid., 860.

361 **Gately wanted to tell Tiny Ewell that he could totally fucking I.D.…** Ibid., 815–16.

361 **Gately becomes a huge mute confessional booth…** Gately is described in this capacity in ibid., 831.

361 **the sort of professional background where he's used to trying to impress…** Ibid., 367.

361 **at a lavish Commitment podium, like at an AA convention…** Ibid., 858.

362 **readers who look to novels and novelists for instruction on how to lead their lives…** Christian Lorentzen, "The Rewriting of David Foster Wallace," *Vulture*, June 30, 2015.

362 **sometimes human beings have to just sit in one place and, like, *hurt*…** Wallace, *Infinite Jest*, 203.

362 **Too simple?…Or just that simple?…** Wallace, marginalia written in his copy of Alice Miller's *The Drama of the Gifted Child*, qtd. in Maria Bustillo's "Inside David Foster Wallace's Private Self-Help Library," *The Awl*, April 5, 2011.

363 **DR. BOB** *(Inching his chair closer):* **If I don't drink, I'm a monster…** Samuel Shem and Janet Surrey, *Bill W and Dr. Bob* (New York: Samuel French Inc., 1987). Play first staged at New Repertory Theater, Newton, Massachusetts. David Foster Wallace Papers, University of Texas at Austin.

364 **Hello, my name is Gabor, and I am a compulsive classical music shopper…** Gabor Maté, *In the Realm of Hungry Ghosts: Close Encounters with Addiction* (Toronto: Knopf Canada, 2008), 110.

364 **Describing the thousands of dollars he has compulsively spent on classical music…** In addition to Maté's account of his classical music addiction (*In the Realm of Hungry Ghosts*), see also his interview with Jeff Kaliss, "Losing Yourself in the Music: Confessions of a Classical Music Shopper," *San Francisco Classical Voice*, January 29, 2013.

364 **the frantic self-soothing of overeaters or shopaholics…** Maté, *In the Realm of Hungry Ghosts*, 2. See also the interview on Maté's website, http://drgabormate.com/topic/addiction/.

364 **Addiction attribution…** Eve Kosofsky Sedgwick, "Epidemics of the Will," *Tendencies* (Durham, NC: Duke University Press, 1993), 132.

365 **When the American Psychiatric Association released the fifth edition of its Diagnostic and Statistical Manual of Mental Disorders...** "Substance-Related and Addictive Disorders," in American Psychiatric Association, *Diagnostic and Statistical Manual of Mental Disorders (DSM-5)* (Washington: American Psychiatric Association, 2013).

365 **many scientists were afraid that its broadened criteria...** For example, see the public statement about the *DSM-5* by Thomas Inse that was released by the National Institute of Mental Health, http://www.nimh.nih.gov/about/director/2013/trans forming-diagnosis.shtml. See also: Christopher Lane, "The NIMH Withdraws Support for DSM-5," *Psychology Today*, https://www.psychologytoday.com/blog/ side-effects/201305/the-nimh-withdraws-support-dsm-5; commentary on the *DSM-5* from Stuart Gitlow, president of the ASAM (American Society for Addiction Medicine), http://www.drugfree.org/news-service/commentary-dsm-5-new -addiction-terminology-same-disease/; Gary Greenberg's *The Book of Woe: The Making of the DSM-5 and the Unmaking of Psychiatry* (New York: Blue Rider Press, 2013); and the interview with Greenberg, "The Real Problems with Psychiatry," *The Atlantic*, May, 2, 2013, http://www.theatlantic.com/health/archive/2013/05/the -real-problems-with-psychiatry/275371/.

365 **It is not till many fixes pass that your desire is need... It was what I'd been born for, waiting for all my life...** George Cain, *Blueschild Baby* (New York: McGraw Hill, 1970), 199.

371 **We tell ourselves stories in order to live...** Joan Didion, "The White Album," *The White Album* (New York: Simon and Schuster, 1979).

375 **But one of the Seneca counselors, Madeline, said that Shirley needed to put her sobriety before everything else—kids, marriage, career...** After the first time she spoke to Shirley on the phone, Madeline told Shirley to call her whenever she felt like taking a drink. If they could talk for ten minutes, Madeline promised, they could outlast the urge. Once, when Shirley called, Madeline said, "You know, Nixon's not such a bad egg," knowing it would get Shirley talking—and it worked, spurring Shirley into a half-hour rant. That got them past the ten-minute mark and then some.

375 **When Shirley showed up at Seneca, in 1973, she was its 269th guest...** This material about Shirley's stay at Seneca drawn from interviews with the author, as well as her pseudonymous *Baltimore Sun* piece: Barbara Lenmark, "An Alcoholic Housewife: What Happened to Her in 28 Days," *Baltimore Sun*, November 18, 1973.

378 **It was absolutely honest, syllable for syllable...** Charles Jackson to Warren Ambrose, March 1, 1954, Charles Jackson Papers, Dartmouth College.

378 **I keep dreaming of what a good and happy marriage...** Rhoda Jackson to Frederick Jackson, 1951, Charles Jackson Papers, Dartmouth College.

378 **early AA newsletters listed loner meetings...** *The Group Secretary's Handbook and Directory* (New York: The Alcoholic Foundation, 1953). Center of Alcohol Studies, Rutgers University.

379 **We always say it's not a successful tour...** Annah Perch qtd. in Lisa W. Foderaro, "Alcoholics Anonymous Founder's House Is a Self-Help Landmark," *New York Times*, July 6, 2007.

379 **no time did I ever find a place**...Marginal notes, "The Rolling Stone," *Alcoholics Anonymous* original manuscript. Stepping Stones Foundation Archives.

383 **flatten[ed] him out...for the mindless**...Jackson, "The Sleeping Brain," qtd. in Blake Bailey, *Farther and Wilder: The Lost Weekends and Literary Dreams of Charles Jackson* (New York: Vintage, 2013), 349.

383 **apathy, spiritlessness, blank sobriety, and a vegetable health**...Jackson qtd. in ibid., 348.

383 **Should I say the hell with it and return to my former indulgence**...Ibid., 360.

386 **that he must tell an unqualified success story or not speak**...C. H. Aharan, "Problems in Cooperation between AA and Other Treatment Programs," speech delivered at the 35th Anniversary International Convention, Miami Beach, 1970, 9. Center of Alcohol Studies Archives, Rutgers University.

XIII. RECKONING

393 **"The Hunter in the Forest"**...All the quotations from "The Hunter in the Forest" are from a handwritten version of the story at the end of Berryman's "Recovery" notebook. John Berryman Papers, University of Minnesota.

398 **choke a bit on the rock mythology**...Steve Kandell, "Amy Winehouse: Rock Myth, Hard Reality," *Spin*, July 25, 2011. Kandell has also been part of this mythology, of course, which was part of what he was acknowledging—he'd written a cover story about Winehouse for *Spin* in 2007, at the height of her fame.

398 **If you think dope is for kicks and for thrills**...Holiday, *Lady Sings the Blues*, with William Dufty (New York: Doubleday, 1956), 212–3.

398 **This is so boring without drugs**...*Amy* (dir. Asif Kapadia, 2015).

399 **She had the complete gift**...Tony Bennett, qtd. in ibid.

400 **around collapsible tables looking very much like people stuck in a swamp**...Denis Johnson, "Beverly Home," *Jesus' Son* (New York: Picador, 2009), 126.

401 **All these weirdos, and me getting a little better every day right in the midst of them**...Ibid., 133.

402 **I had sobered up just in time to have a nervous breakdown**...Johnson, "Beverly Home," unpublished draft, Denis Johnson Papers, University of Texas at Austin.

402 **Johnson first tried to dry out in 1978 in his parents' home in Tucson**...Jesse McKinley, "A Prodigal Son Turned Novelist Turns Playwright," *New York Times*, June 16, 2002.

402 **I was addicted to everything...Now I just drink a lot of coffee**...Johnson qtd. in David Amsden, "Denis Johnson's Second Stage," *New York Magazine*, June 17, 2002.

402 **concerned about getting sober...typical of people who feel artistic**...Ibid.

402 **Approval was something I craved more than drugs or alcohol**...Johnson, "Beverly Home," unpublished draft, Denis Johnson Papers, Ransom Center, University of Texas at Austin.

402 **I want to thank you for your unfailing support and friendship**...Unknown author to Denis Johnson, 1996, Denis Johnson Papers, Ransom Center, University of Texas at Austin.

404 **We are the chain gang, the only female chain gang**...See Hari, *Chasing the Scream* (New York: Bloomsbury, 2015), 104.

404 **If I had to design a system that was intended to keep people addicted**...Maté qtd. in ibid., 166.

405 **dealing with addiction by chaining, by humiliating**...Goulão qtd. in ibid., 237.

405 **Tent City was the brainchild of one of his protégés, Joe Arpaio**...Tent City finally announced its closure in April 2017, and the process of closing the facility was due to be completed by the end of that year. See Fernanda Santos, "Outdoor Jail, a Vestige of Joe Arpaio's Tenure, Is Closing," *New York Times*, April 4, 2017.

405 **You got a good guy there**...Arpaio qtd. in Hari, *Chasing the Scream*, 105.

405 **These people are in the same category as lepers**...Anonymous Los Angeles Police Department officer, qtd. in Harry Anslinger and William Tompkins, *The Traffic in Narcotics* (New York: Funk and Wagnalls, 1953), 272.

405 **In 2009, at a prison twenty-two miles west of Tent City, one prisoner—Number 109416—was literally cooked alive in a cage in the middle of the desert**...For Marcia Powell's death, see Hari's *Chasing the Scream*; also Stephen Lemons, "Marcia Powell's Death Unavenged: County Attorney Passes on Prosecuting Prison Staff," *Phoenix New Times*, September 1, 2010, in which Donna Hamm (from an advocacy group called Middle Ground Prison Reform) notes that Powell's eyes "were as dry as parchment."

405 **Before she died in a holding cell, Prisoner 109416 lived as Marcia Powell**...See Hari's *Chasing the Scream*, 103–15, for his full account of Marcia Powell, who was kept at a facility near Tent City in Arizona. Marcia Powell was serving time for solicitation of prostitution, but the criminalization of her drug problem was part of the shaping condition of her life—both in taking her to sex work, deepening her addiction, making it harder for her to find another life. At nearby Tent City, thousands of other addicts were serving time for drug offenses in similar conditions.

407 **When I finally visited the Narcotic Farm in 2014—eight decades after it opened**...In 1998, the facility had been officially converted to a federal medical center for federal prisoners who needed medical or mental health care.

407 *Programmable:* **the troubling descendant of an older faith in the ways an institution could "rearrange" someone**...As one newspaper had called the original Narco Farm treatment: "a skillful rearrangement of the intangibles that go to make up human existence." "Destiny of Man 'Traded in' at Kentucky Laboratory," *Chicago Daily News*, August 23, 1938.

412 **like trying to make a bed while you're still in it**...Catherine Lacey qtd. in "Leslie Jamison and Catherine Lacey's E-mail Conversation about Narcissism, Emotional Writing and Memoir-Novels," *Huffington Post*, March 30, 2015.

413 **drinking in the morning—drinking on the job—These are not the marks of a social drinker**...John Berryman, typescript with handwritten additions and edits, undated (1970–71), John Berryman Papers, University of Minnesota.

413 **I have lately given up the words**...Berryman, *Recovery* (New York: Farrar, Straus and Giroux, 1973), 168–69.

413 **May I Do My Will Always**...Ibid., 156. This slip of the pen confesses everything: the difficulty of giving up the old delusions of creative grandeur as well as

willpower itself. As Lowry had it, "The will of man is unconquerable!" In meetings, I'd heard the urban legend of a bar near Hazelden that offered a free drink in exchange for your thirty-day chip, its wall decorated with them, and it wasn't hard to picture Berryman trading in his own chip, then getting another, then trading that one in, too; his novel openly confessing how cyclical the process of sobriety had become for him.

413 **I doubt if this will be an acceptable first step**...Berryman, handwritten note, John Berryman Papers, University of Minnesota.

414 **with the appearance of real interest**...Handwritten annotations on typescript unpublished manuscript of *Recovery*, John Berryman Papers, University of Minnesota.

414 **he felt — depressed...felt — nowhere**...Berryman, *Recovery*, 18, 172.

414 **His letters are very childish**...Ibid., 165.

414 *Dear Dad, I've done well in school this quarter*...Paul Berryman to John Berryman, undated, John Berryman Papers, University of Minnesota.

415 *FOR MY SON: On the eve of my 56th birthday*...John Berryman to Paul Berryman, October 24, 1970, John Berryman Papers, University of Minnesota.

416 **END OF NOVEL**...These notes about possible endings for the book are in Berryman's archives and reprinted at the end of *Recovery* itself.

416 **Just try...Happy a little, grateful prayers**...Berryman, handwritten notes in notebook labeled "Recovery," John Berryman Papers, University of Minnesota.

416 **If I don't make it this time, I'll just relax and drink myself to death**...Berryman, *Recovery*, 55.

416 **It's *enough!* I can't BEAR ANY MORE**...Berryman, handwritten note, week of May 20, 1971, qtd. in John Haffenden, *The Life of John Berryman* (London: Methuen & Co., 1984), 397.

416 **He'd relapsed just days before jumping...after eleven months of sobriety**...For more information on Berryman's last bout of sobriety, and his suicide, see Haffenden as well as Paul Mariani's *Dream Song: The Life of John Berryman* (London: William Morrow & Co., 1990).

416 **I can't bear much more of my hideous life**...Jean Rhys to Peggy Kirkaldy, March 21, 1941, *Jean Rhys Letters, 1931–1966*, ed. Francis Wyndham and Diana Melly (London: Andre Deutsch, 1984).

417 **another I who is everybody**...Rhys qtd. in Carole Angier, *Jean Rhys: Life and Work* (New York: Little, Brown, 1991), 375. The dream of narrative as a vehicle for self-escape hounded Rhys for years — the possibility that writing might offer not just an occasion for empathy but something more like self-transcendence. In a fragment called "The Forlorn Hope," she describes an ecstatic experience on a bench overlooking the Mediterranean: For a few hours, she felt "merged with other human beings" and got "the feeling that 'I,' 'you,' 'he,' 'she,' 'they' are all the same — technical distinctions not real ones." She believed literature could sustain this sense of merging more powerfully than daily experience. "Books can do this," she wrote. "They can abolish one's individuality, just as they can abolish time or place." Rhys, handwritten fragment, "The Forlorn Hope," July 3 (most likely 1925), during a period of time when she was living in a hotel at Theoule. Jean Rhys Archive, University of Tulsa.

417 **Jean could not listen!**...Vaz Dias, "It's Easy to Disappear," 4. Jean Rhys Archive, University of Tulsa. Full quote: "Jean could not listen! How does she manage this complete identification with characters when she gives the impression that she is somewhere else utterly remote, when you are talking to her. She does not seem to connect."

417 **I've dreamt several times that I was going to have a baby then I woke**...Jean Rhys to Diana Athill, March 9, 1966, Jean Rhys Archive, University of Tulsa.

417 **I'll come armed with a bottle!**...Diana Athill to Jean Rhys, March 23, 1966, Jean Rhys Archive, University of Tulsa.

418 **Don't drink any more**...Rhys, *Wide Sargasso Sea*, in *The Complete Novels* (New York: W. W. Norton, 1985), 548.

418 **It grants some diluted version of the relief her nurse's obeah once offered**... Ibid., 554.

418 **I knew him as a young man. He was gentle, generous, brave**...Ibid., 160.

419 **I am not used to characters taking the bit between their teeth and rushing away**...Jean Rhys to Eliot Bliss, July 5, 1959, Jean Rhys Archive, University of Tulsa.

419 **When Rochester tells Antoinette that he was forced as a young man to keep his emotions hidden**...Rhys, *Wide Sargasso Sea*, in *The Complete Novels*, 539. This awareness of other people as victims is foreshadowed early in *Wide Sargasso Sea*, when one of Antoinette's black servants—a girl named Tia, whom Antoinette had always imagined as oblivious to pain ("sharp stones did not hurt her bare feet, I never saw her cry")—throws a stone at Antoinette's face. Instead of retreating into default posture of righteous woundedness, Antoinette feels a strong sense of identification. "We stared at each other, blood on my face, tears on hers. It was as if I saw myself. Like in a looking-glass." It's a blinkered comparison—Antoinette conflating her suffering with the plight of an indentured servant whose family has only recently been emancipated from slavery—but it's also a moment when Antoinette understands that other people suffer too, and that almost every victimizer is also a victim. The agent of destruction is a girl inhabiting a wounded body of her own (41). At the close of the novel, just before burning down Thornfield Hall, Antoinette dreams of looking over the edge of a jungle pool and seeing not her own face but the reflection of Tia: the girl with the jagged stone, both wounded and wounding, the one who made her own pain legible, and somehow transferrable, by hurting someone else. It is directly after she wakes from that dream that Antoinette picks up a candle, determined to make her own pain legible by way of grand destruction (171).

419 **mad lady, who was as cunning as a witch**...Charlotte Brontë, *Jane Eyre* (1847; repr., New York: W. W. Norton, 2016), 455.

419 **Now at last I know why I was brought here**...Rhys, *Wide Sargasso Sea*, in *The Complete Novels*, 171.

419 **She told a friend that ghost stories and whiskey were the only things that brought her comfort**...Rhys to Robert Herbert Ronson, December 10, 1968, Jean Rhys Archive, University of Tulsa.

420 **Her monthly booze bill sometimes rivaled all her other household expenses combined**...A number of Rhys's liquor store receipts and monthly budgets can be found in her archives at the University of Tulsa.

420 **Avoid argumentative subjects like politics...12:00. Drink. Only when she asks for it and in a small wine glass...I stay with her then until 7-o-clock...**Diana Melly, handwritten notes, unpublished, undated, 1977. Jean Rhys Archive, University of Tulsa.

421 **All of writing is a huge lake...Give me another drink, will you, honey?**...David Plante, "Jean Rhys: A Remembrance," *Paris Review* 76 (Fall 1979).

425 **It's not so much to *play*...**James Baldwin, "Sonny's Blues," *Going to Meet the Man* (New York: Dial Press, 1965).

425 **I don't want you to think it had anything to do with me being a musician...**Ibid.

XIV. HOMECOMING

435 **I've had two different lives...**Raymond Carver interview with Mona Simpson and Lewis Buzbee, *Paris Review* (Summer 1983). Carver's comment was an allusion to L. P. Hartley's novel *The Go-Between*.

435 **Eventually we realized that hard work and dreams were not enough...**Carver, "Fires," *Collected Stories*, ed. William Stull and Maureen Carroll (New York: Library of America, 2009), 740.

435 **chaotic...without much light showing through...**Carver, "Fires." *Collected Stories*, 739.

435 **It sounds like a cigar, but it's my first electric typewriter...**This Carver quote, and the story of his new electric typewriter, are from Carol Sklenicka's *Raymond Carver: A Writer's Life* (New York: Scribner, 2009), 349.

435 **I was trying to learn my craft as a writer...**Carver, "Author's Note to 'Where I'm Calling From,'" *Collected Stories*, 747.

436 **I replaced my vision of Drunk Carver, delirious and darkness-facing at the Foxhead, with Sober Carver...**It's true that "Sober Carver" wasn't always sober. Carver smoked weed during the last decade of his sobriety, and did coke occasionally, and though—in my own life—I wouldn't consider that "full sobriety," I'm also not in the business of judging what felt like sobriety to him. Certain parts of Carver's sobriety felt muddled or messy, as he acknowledged in "Where I'm Calling From": But there was another part. This was the part of Carver that spent much of that last decade smoking weed; that did coke with McInerney in a Manhattan apartment the same night John Lennon was shot; that went to an ER in Washington for cocaine a few years later; that started eating pot brownies once he'd gotten his first lung tumor removed but whose cancer killed him anyway—all those years of smoking, like Bill Wilson: both men killed by that *other* addiction after reckoning with the first. See Carol Sklenicka's *Raymond Carver: A Writer's Life* (New York: Scribner, 2009), 364 and 400, for the incidents with cocaine and other substances during sobriety. See also this interview with Jay McInerney in the *Paris Review*: http://www.theparisreview.org/interviews/6477/the-art-of-fiction-no-231-jay-mcinerney.

436 **He lived on Fiddle Faddle...he wanted to return to Zurich as the "Tobler Chocolate Chair in Short Fiction"...**These details about Carver's sobriety, his sweet tooth, and his attempts to navigate the logistics of sober living are taken from Sklenicka's *Raymond Carver: A Writer's Life*, 318, 485, 324, 384, 386.

436 *It took me at least six months—more—after I stopped drinking*...Raymond Carver to Mr. Hallstrom, September 17, 1986, qtd. in *Carver Country: The World of Raymond Carver*, photographs by Bob Adelman (New York: Charles Scribner's Sons, 1990), 105–7.

436 **in a cabin they shared together during that first sober summer**...Information on Carver's early writing in that cabin, and his twentieth wedding anniversary celebration, from Sklenicka, *Raymond Carver: A Writer's Life*, 312–13.

437 **"Bad Ray" from the alcoholic past sent dispatches**...See ibid., 327.

437 **Each day without drinking had a glow and a fervor**...Gallagher qtd. in ibid., 350.

437 **I'm not into catch and release**...Carver qtd. in ibid., 416.

437 **considered writers "luminous madmen who drank too much and drove too fast"**...Jay McInerney, "Raymond Carver: A Still, Small Voice," *New York Times*, August 6, 1989.

437 **Ray respects his characters**...Rich Kelly, Interview with Tess Gallagher, https://loa-shared.s3.amazonaws.com/static/pdf/LOA_interview_Gallagher _Stull_Carroll_on_Carver.pdf.

437 **There but for the grace of God go I**...Carver qtd. in Sklenicka, *Raymond Carver: A Writer's Life*, 383.

438 **Part of me wanted help. But there was another part**...Carver, "Where I'm Calling From," *Collected Stories*, 460.

438 **Keep talking, J.P....Don't stop now, J.P....I would have listened if he'd been going on about how one day he'd decided to start pitching horseshoes**...Ibid., 454, 456, 456, 456.

438 **I have a thing / for this cold swift water**...Carver, "Where Water Comes Together with Other Water," *All of Us: The Collected Poems* (New York: Knopf, 1998), 64.

438 **as clear as glass and as sustaining as oxygen**...Tess Gallagher, "Interview," *Collected Stories*.

438 **It pleases me, loving rivers**...Carver, "Where Water Comes Together with Other Water," 64.

438 **The writer Olivia Laing finds a "boiled down, idiosyncratic version" of the Third Step in this moment**...See Olivia Laing's *The Trip to Echo Spring: On Writers and Drinking* (New York: Picador, 2014), 278–79.

439 **bond of mutuality**...Gallagher, "Introduction," *All of Us: The Collected Poems* (New York: Knopf, 1998), xxvii–xxviii.

439 **smoke all the cigarettes I want...[eat] jam and fat bacon**...Carver, "The Party," *All of Us*, 103.

439 **My boat is being made to order**...Carver, "My Boat," *All of Us*, 82.

439 **He nods and grips his shovel**...Carver, "Yesterday, Snow," *All of Us*, 131–32.

440 **That life is simply gone now**...Raymond Carver interview with Mona Simpson and Lewis Buzbee, *Paris Review* (Summer 1983).

440 **He'd known for a long time / they would die in separate lives**...Carver, "The Offending Eel," *All of Us*, 272.

440 **What you've really done / and to someone else**...Carver, "Alcohol," *All of Us*, 10.

444 *I traveled across the country to find myself at your grave...I come here from Japan to tell you the truth...*These notes in the notebook quoted from Jeff Baker's "Northwest Writers at Work: Tess Gallagher in Raymond Carver Country," *The Oregonian*, September 19, 2009.

444 *Spending is an escape just like alcohol. We are all trying to fill that empty hole...*Qtd. in Laing, *The Trip to Echo Spring*, 296.

445 **Billy Burroughs Jr....died of cirrhosis at the age of thirty-three, after even a liver transplant couldn't keep him from drinking...**Three years after his son's death in 1981, William Burroughs Sr. wrote an afterword to Billy Burroughs Jr.'s pair of novels, *Speed* and *Kentucky Ham*. It's a note full of quiet grief, implicit guilt, and an uneasy sense of resignation: an awareness of their bond alongside an awareness of what it lacked. Burroughs Sr. recounts the time his son was supposed to come join him in London but was arrested for writing a fake prescription; so Burroughs Sr. went to visit in Florida instead, leaving his opium behind because he was afraid of Customs, and spending that whole month in the grip of withdrawal from a habit "not so small" as he'd thought. Father and son lived parallel lives, not simply in their dependence but in the kinds of difficulty their dependence yielded. But these parallels didn't offer the solace of resonance so much as the compounding of burdens: the burdens of distance, obstruction, and removal. In his afterword, Burroughs Sr. remembers "the time [Billy Jr.] called me long distance from a hospital in Florida after a car accident. I could hear him, but he couldn't hear me. I kept saying, 'Where are you, Billy? Where are you?'—strained and off-key, the right thing said at the wrong time, the wrong thing said at the right time, and all too often, the wrongest thing said and done at the wrongest possible time....I remember listening to him playing his guitar after I had gone to bed in the next room, and again, a feeling of deep sadness."

This is no vision of recovery through understanding; no vision of salvation through reciprocal identification; it's just empathy without purchase or effect. Whether the procedure is personal or not, the plea remains the same: *Please don't fail me.* The music of private suffering is audible but perpetually distant. William Burroughs Sr., "The Trees Showed the Shape of the Wind," in *Speed and Kentucky Ham*, ed. William Burroughs Jr. (1973; repr., Woodstock, NY: Overlook Press, 1984).

445 **pretty and hard, like a beautician in a Carver story...**William Booth, "Walking the Edge," *Washington Post*, September 16, 2007.

AUTHOR'S NOTE

449 **Buprenorphine, for example, works as a partial agonist, binding to opiate receptors in a way that blocks other opiates from binding...**Lucas Mann, "Trying to Get Right," *Guernica*, April 15, 2016.

451 **Abstinence is just not a model you can force on everybody...**Gabor Maté qtd. in Sarah Resnick, "H," *n + 1* 24 (Winter 2016).

452 **If we see people as people, then we'll treat people as people. Period...**Johnny Perez, panel discussion, Vera Institute of Justice, *Chicago Ideas*, February 23, 2017, https://www.vera.org/research/chicago-ideas-it-doesnt-have-to-be-this-way.

BIBLIOGRAPHY

Aharan, C. H. "Problems in Cooperation between AA and Other Treatment Programs." Speech delivered at the 35th Anniversary International Convention, Miami Beach, 1970. Center of Alcohol Studies Archives, Rutgers University, New Brunswick, New Jersey.

Alcoholics Anonymous. "A.A.: A Uniquely American Phenomenon." *Fortune*, February 1951. Center for Alcohol Studies Archives, Rutgers University, New Brunswick, New Jersey.

———. *Alcoholics Anonymous: The Story of How Many Thousands of Men and Women Have Recovered from Alcoholism.* By Bill Wilson, Ed Parkhurst, Sam Shoemaker et al. New York: Alcoholics Anonymous World Services Inc., 1939.

———. *The Book That Started It All: The Original Working Manuscript of Alcoholics Anonymous.* Center City, MN: Hazelden, 2010.

———. *'Pass It On': The Story of Bill Wilson and How the AA Message Reached the World.* New York: Alcoholics Anonymous World Service Inc., 1984.

———. "Pattern Script for Radio and Television." General Service Headquarters of AA, 1957. Center for Alcohol Studies Archives, Rutgers University, New Brunswick, New Jersey.

Alexander, Anna, and Mark Roberts, ed. *High Culture: Reflections on Addiction and Modernity.* Albany: SUNY Press, 2003.

Alexander, Bruce, B. L. Beyerstein, P. F. Hadaway, and R. B. Coambs. "Effect of Early and Later Colony Housing on Oral Ingestion of Morphine in Rats." *Pharmacology Biochemistry and Behavior* 15, no. 4 (1981): 571–76.

Alexander, Jack. "Alcoholics Anonymous: Freed Slaves of Drink, Now They Free Others." *Saturday Evening Post,* March 1, 1941.

Alexander, Michelle, *The New Jim Crow: Mass Incarceration in the Age of Colorblindness.* New York: The New Press, 2010.

Alvarez, A. "Down & Out in Paris & London." *New York Review of Books,* October 10, 1991.

Amsden, David. "Denis Johnson's Second Stage." *New York Magazine,* June 17, 2002.

Angier, Carole. *Jean Rhys: Life and Work.* New York: Little, Brown, 1991.

Bibliography

Anonymous. "An Ex-Resident's Story." Granada House, http://www.granadahouse.org/people/letters_from_our_alum.html.

Anslinger, Harry, and William Tompkins. *The Traffic in Narcotics*. New York: Funk and Wagnalls, 1953.

Aubry, Timothy. *Reading As Therapy: What Contemporary Fiction Does for Middle-Class Americans*. Iowa City: University of Iowa Press, 2011.

Augustine. *Confessions*. Oxford: Oxford University Press, 2009.

Azimi, Negar. "The Madness of Queen Jane." Newyorker.com, June 12, 2014.

Bailey, Blake. *Cheever: A Life*. New York: Knopf, 2009.

———. *Farther and Wilder: The Lost Weekends and Literary Dreams of Charles Jackson*. New York: Vintage, 2013.

———. *A Tragic Honesty: The Life and Work of Richard Yates*. New York: Picador, 2003.

Baldwin, James. "Everybody's Protest Novel." *Notes of a Native Son*. Boston: Beacon Press, 1955.

———. "Sonny's Blues." *Going to Meet the Man*. New York: Dial Press, 1965.

Bateson, Gregory. "The Cybernetics of 'Self': A Theory of Alcoholism." *Psychiatry* 34 (1971): 1–18.

Bellow, Saul. "Foreword." *Recovery*, by John Berryman. New York: Farrar, Straus and Giroux, 1973.

———. "Foreword." Typewritten draft. John Berryman Papers, University of Minnesota, Minneapolis.

Berlant, Lauren. *Cruel Optimism*. Durham, NC: Duke University Press, 2011.

Berryman, John. *The Dream Songs*. New York: Farrar, Straus and Giroux, 1969.

———. "Fourth Step Inventory Guide." Minneapolis, MN, n.d. John Berryman Papers, Upper Midwest Literary Archives, University of Minnesota, Minneapolis.

———. *Love & Fame*. New York: Farrar, Straus, and Giroux, 1970.

———. *Recovery*. New York: Farrar, Straus and Giroux, 1973.

Bishop, Elizabeth. "A Drunkard." *Georgia Review*, Winter 1992.

———. *One Art: Letters*. Edited by Robert Giroux. New York: Farrar, Straus and Giroux, 1995.

———. "The Prodigal." *Elizabeth Bishop: Poems, Prose, and Letters*. Edited by Robert Giroux and Lloyd Schwartz. New York: Library of America, 2008.

Blackburn, Julia. *With Billie: A New Look at the Unforgettable Lady Day*. New York: Pantheon, 2005.

Blair, Elaine. "A New Brilliant Start." *New York Review of Books*, December 6, 2012.

Brontë, Charlotte. *Jane Eyre*. 1847. New York: W. W. Norton, 2016.

Brooks, Peter. *Reading for the Plot: Design and Intention in Narrative*. Cambridge, MA: Harvard University Press, 1992.

Broxmeyer, Jennifer. "Prisoners of Their Own War: Can Policymakers Look Beyond the 'War on Drugs' to Drug Treatment Courts?" *Yale Law Journal* 118 (2008–2009).

Burns, Stacy Lee, and Mark Peyrot. "Tough Love: Nurturing and Coercing Responsibility and Recovery in California Drug Courts." *Social Problems* 50, no. 3 (August 2003): 416–38.

Burroughs, William. *Deposition: Testimony Concerning a Sickness* (1960). Reprinted in *Naked Lunch*. New York: Grove Press, 1962.

Bibliography

————.*Junkie: Confessions of an Unredeemed Drug Addict*. New York: Ace Books, 1953.

————. "The Trees Showed the Shape of the Wind." *Speed and Kentucky Ham*. By William Burroughs Jr., 1973. Woodstock, NY: Overlook Press, 1984.

————. *The Yage Letters*. Unpublished manuscript. William Burroughs Papers, Columbia University, New York.

Burroughs Jr., William. *Kentucky Ham*. New York: E. P. Dutton, 1973.

Bustillos, Maria. "Inside David Foster Wallace's Private Self-Help Library." *The Awl*, April 5, 2011.

Cain, George. *Blueschild Baby*. New York: McGraw Hill, 1970.

Campbell, Nancy, J.P. Olsen, and Luke Walden. *The Narcotic Farm*. New York: Abrams, 2010.

Cantwell, Mary. "Conversation with Jean Rhys, 'the Best Living English Novelist.'" *Mademoiselle*, October 1974.

Carver, Raymond. *All of Us: The Collected Poems*. New York: Knopf, 1998.

————. "The Art of Fiction No. 76." Interview by Mona Simpson and Lewis Buzbee. *Paris Review* 88, Summer 1983.

————. *Carver Country: The World of Raymond Carver*. Photographs by Bob Adelman. New York: Charles Scribner's Sons, 1990.

————. *Collected Stories*. Edited by William Stull and Maureen Carroll. New York: Library of America, 2009.

Casey, Karen. *My Story to Yours: A Guided Memoir for Writing Your Recovery Journey*. Center City, MN: Hazelden, 2011.

Casey, Robert. "Destiny of Man 'Traded in' at Kentucky Laboratory." *Chicago Daily News*, August 23, 1938. RG 511, National Archives, College Park, MD.

Chasnoff, Ira. 1993. "Missing Pieces of the Puzzle." *Neurotoxicology and Teratology* 15:287–88.

Cheever, Susan. *My Name Is Bill: Bill Wilson—His Life and the Creation of Alcoholics Anonymous*. New York: Washington Square Press, 2005.

Coates, Ta-Nehisi. *Between the World and Me*. New York: Spiegel & Grau, 2015.

Cohen, Joshua. "New Books." *Harper's Magazine*, September 2012.

"Collaborative Studies on Genetics of Alcoholism (COGA) Study." NIAAA, https://www.niaaa.nih.gov/research/major-initiatives/collaborative-studies-genetics-alcoholism-coga-study.

Cooper, Clarence, Jr. *The Farm*. New York: Crown Publishers, 1967.

Cornell, Ervin. Letter to the US Bureau of Narcotics, June 26, 1939. RG 511, National Archives, College Park, MD.

Crowley, John. *The White Logic: Alcoholism and Gender in American Modernist Fiction*. Amherst: University of Massachusetts Press, 1994.

Cushing, Richard. "The Battle Against Self." Speech, August 30, 1945. Repr. Works Publishing. Center of Alcohol Studies Archives, Rutgers University, New Brunswick, New Jersey, undated.

Davies, Hunter. "Rip van Rhys." *Sunday Times*, November 6, 1966.

Day, Douglas. *Malcolm Lowry: A Biography*. Oxford: Oxford University Press, 1984.

Dean, Michelle. "Drunk Confessions: Women and the Clichés of the Literary Drunkard." *The New Republic*, September 8, 2015.

Bibliography

De Quincey, Thomas. "Confessions of an English Opium-Eater." *London Magazine*, 1821.

Derrida, Jacques. "The Rhetoric of Drugs: An Interview." *Differences* 5 (1993).

Didion, Joan. *The White Album*. New York: Simon & Schuster, 1979.

Duras, Marguerite. *Practicalities*. London: William Collins Sons, 1990.

Erickson, Carlton. *The Science of Addiction: From Neurobiology to Treatment*. New York: W. W. Norton, 2007.

Farrar, John. "A Preface to the Reader—Sixteen Years After." *The Lost Weekend*. New York: Farrar, Rinehart, and Young, 1960.

Fitzgerald, F. Scott. *Tender Is the Night*. New York: Charles Scribner's Sons, 1934.

Franzen, Jonathan. "Farther Away." *The New Yorker*, April 18, 2011.

Frey, James. *A Million Little Pieces*. New York: Random House, 2003.

———. "Note to the Reader." *New York Times*, February 1, 2006.

Fulford, K. W. M., Martin Davies, Richard Gipps, George Graham, John Sadler, Giovanni Stanghellini, and Tim Thornton, eds. *The Oxford Handbook of Philosophy and Psychiatry*. Oxford: Oxford University Press, 2013.

Gayle Jr., Addison. "Blueschild Baby." *New York Times*, January 17, 1971.

Gilmore, Leigh. "Boom/Lash: Fact-Checking, Suicide, and the Lifespan of a Genre." *Auto/Biography Studies* 29, no. 2. (2014): 211–24.

Ginsberg, Allen. "Introduction." *Junkie*. By William Burroughs. 1953. New York: Penguin, 1977.

Grimes, William. "George Cain, Writer of 'Blueschild Baby,' Dies at 66." *New York Times*, October 29, 2010.

Haffenden, John. *The Life of John Berryman*. London: Methuen & Co., 1982.

Hampl, Patricia. "F. Scott Fitzgerald's Essays from the Edge." *The American Scholar*, Spring 2012.

Hanlon, Kevin, dir. *Bill W.* Documentary film, Page 124 Productions, 2012.

Hardwick, Elizabeth. "Billie Holiday." *New York Review of Books*, March 4, 1976.

Hari, Johann. *Chasing the Scream*. New York: Bloomsbury, 2015.

Harris, Oliver. *William Burroughs and the Secret of Fascination*. Carbondale: Southern Illinois University Press, 2003.

Hart, Carl. *High Price: A Neuroscientist's Journey of Self-Discovery That Challenges Everything You Know about Drugs and Society*. New York: Harper, 2013.

Helbrant, Maurice. *Narcotic Agent*. New York: Ace Books, 1953.

Helmer, John, and Thomas Vietorisz. *Drug Use, the Labor Market and Class Conflict*. Washington, DC: Drug Abuse Council, 1974.

Hemingway, Ernest. *The Sun Also Rises*. New York: Charles Scribner's Son, 1926.

Hentoff, Nat. *A Doctor Among the Addicts: The Story of Marie Nyswander*. New York: Rand McNally, 1968.

Holiday, Billie. *Lady Sings the Blues*. Cowritten with William Dufty. New York: Doubleday, 1956.

Holland, Mary. "'The Art's Heart's Purpose': Braving the Narcissistic Loop of *Infinite Jest*." *Critique* 47, no. 3 (Spring 2006).

Howard, Jane. "Whisky and Ink, Whisky and Ink." *Life Magazine*, July 21, 1967.

Hughes, Helen MacGill, ed. *The Fantastic Lodge: The Autobiography of a Girl Drug Addict*. Boston: Houghton Mifflin, 1961.

Bibliography

Humphries, Drew. *Crack Mothers: Pregnancy, Drugs, and the Media.* Columbus: Ohio State University Press, 1999.

Hyde, Lewis. "Alcohol and Poetry: John Berryman and the Booze Talking." *The American Poetry Review,* October 1975. Repr. Dallas: The Dallas Institute, 1986.

———. "Berryman Revisited." In *Recovering Berryman.* Edited by Richard Kelly and Alan Lathrop. Ann Arbor: University of Michigan Press, 1993.

Jackson, Charles. *Earthly Creatures.* New York: Farrar, Straus, and Young, 1953.

———. *Farther, Wilder.* Unpublished manuscript. Charles Jackson Papers, Rauner Library, Dartmouth College, Hanover, New Hampshire.

———. *The Lost Weekend.* New York: Farrar and Rinehart, 1944.

———. Speech. Alcoholics Anonymous, Cleveland, OH, 1959.

———. "We Were Led to Hope for More." Review of *Selected Letters of Malcolm Lowry. New York Times,* December 12, 1965.

Jamison, Leslie. *The Gin Closet.* New York: Free Press, 2010.

———. "The Relapse." *The L Magazine,* July 2010.

Jefferson, Margo. *Negroland.* New York: Pantheon, 2015.

Johnson, Denis. *Jesus' Son.* New York: Picador, 1992.

———. *Shoppers Carried by Escalators into the Flames.* New York: Harper Perennial, 2002.

———. *The Throne of the Third Heaven of the Nations Millennium General Assembly: Poems Collected and New.* New York: Harper Perennial, 1995.

Kalstone, David. "The Record of a Struggle with Prose and Life." *New York Times,* May 27, 1973.

Kandell, Steve. "Amy Winehouse: Rock Myth, Hard Reality." *Spin,* July 25, 2011.

———. "Lady Sings the Blues: Avoiding Rehab with Amy Winehouse." *Spin,* July 2007.

Kazin, Alfred. Review of Burroughs' *A Book of the Dead. New York Times,* December 12, 1971, 4. William Burroughs Papers, Columbia University, New York.

Kermode, Frank. *The Sense of an Ending: Studies in the Theory of Fiction.* Oxford: Oxford University Press, 1967.

King, Stephen. *Doctor Sleep.* New York: Gallery Books, 2013.

———. *On Writing: A Memoir of the Craft.* New York: Scribner, 2000.

———. *The Shining.* New York: Doubleday, 1977.

Knapp, Caroline. *Drinking: A Love Story.* New York: The Dial Press, 1996.

Koob, G. F., and M. Le Moal (1997). Drug abuse: Hedonic homeostatic dysregulation. *Science* 278, 52–58.

Laing, Olivia. *The Trip to Echo Spring: On Writers and Drinking.* New York: Picador, 2014.

Lamar, Jacob. "The House Is On Fire." *Time,* August 4, 1986.

Lattin, Don. *Distilled Spirits: Getting High, Then Sober, with a Famous Writer, a Forgotten Philosopher, and a Hopeless Drunk.* Berkeley: University of California Press, 2012.

Lewis, Sinclair. Blurb. Undated. Charles Jackson Papers, Rauner Library, Dartmouth College, Hanover, New Hampshire.

Lewis-Kraus, Gideon. "Viewer Discretion." *Bookforum* (Fall 2012).

Lish, Gordon. Interview with Christian Lorentzen. "The Art of Editing, No. 2." *Paris Review* 215 (Winter 2015).

London, Jack. *John Barleycorn.* New York: The Century Company, 1913.

Lorentzen, Christian. "The Rewriting of David Foster Wallace," *Vulture,* June 30, 2015.

Bibliography

Lowell, Robert. "For John Berryman." *New York Review of Books*, April 6, 1972.

——. *New Selected Poems*. Edited by Katie Peterson. New York: Farrar, Straus and Giroux, 2017.

——. "The Poetry of John Berryman." *The New York Review of Books*, May 28, 1964.

Lowry, Malcolm. *Dark as the Grave Wherein My Friend Is Laid*. London: Jonathan Cape, 1969.

——. *Under the Volcano*. New York: Reynal and Hitchcock, 1947.

Malabou, Catherine. "The Phoenix, the Spider, and the Salamander." *Changing Difference*. Trans. Carolyn Shread. Cambridge: Polity Press, 2011.

Mann, Lucas. *Lord Fear*. New York: Pantheon, 2015.

——. "Trying to Get Right." *Guernica*, April 15, 2016.

Mariani, Paul. *Dream Song: The Life of John Berryman*. London: William Morrow & Co., 1990.

"Matching Alcoholism Treatments to Client Heterogeneity: Project MATCH Posttreatment Drinking Outcome." *Journal of Studies on Alcohol and Drugs* 58, no. 1 (January 1997): 7–29.

Maté, Gabor. *In the Realm of Hungry Ghosts: Close Encounters with Addiction*. Toronto: Knopf Canada, 2008.

Mauer, Marc, and Ryan S. King. *The Sentencing Project, a 25-Year Quagmire: The War on Drugs and Its Impact on American Society* 2 (2007).

Max, D. T. "The Carver Chronicles." *New York Times Magazine*, August 9, 1998.

——. "Day of the Dead." *The New Yorker*, December 17, 2007.

——. "D. F. W.'s Favorite Grammarian." Newyorker.com, December 11, 2013.

——. *Every Love Story Is a Ghost Story*. New York: Viking, 2012.

McCaffery, Larry. "A Conversation with David Foster Wallace." *The Review of Contemporary Fiction*. 13, no. 2 (Summer 1993).

McGurl, Mark. "The Institution of Nothing: David Foster Wallace in the Program." *Boundary 2* 41, no. 3 (2014).

McInerney, Jay. "Raymond Carver: A Still, Small Voice." *New York Times*, August 6, 1989.

Miethe, Terance D., Hong Lu, and Erin Reese, "Reintegrative Shaming and Recidivism Risks in Drug Court: Explanations for Some Unexpected Findings." *Crime and Delinquency* 46 (2000): 522, 536–37.

Millier, Brett. "The Prodigal: Elizabeth Bishop and Alcohol." *Contemporary Literature* 39, no. 1 (Spring 1998): 54–76.

Morgan, John P., and Lynn Zimmer. "The Social Pharmacology of Smokeable Cocaine: Not All It's Cracked Up to Be." In *Crack in America: Demon Drugs and Social Justice*, edited by Craig Reinarman, Craig and Harry Levine. Berkeley: University of California Press, 1997.

Moses, Milton. Letter to US Narcotics Bureau. May 8, 1938. National Archives, College Park, MD.

Nixon, Richard. "Special Message to the Congress on Drug Abuse Prevention and Control." Speech delivered June 17, 1971.

O'Hara, Frank. *The Collected Poems of Frank O'Hara*. Edited by Donald Allen. Berkeley: University of California Press, 1995.

O'Hara, John. *Appointment at Samara*. New York: Harcourt, 1934.

Peabody, Richard. *The Common Sense of Drinking*. Boston: Little, Brown & Co., 1931.

Bibliography

Peretz, Evgenia. "James Frey's Morning After." *Vanity Fair*, April 28, 2008.

Pfaff, David. *Locked In: The True Causes of Mass Incarceration, and How to Achieve Real Reform*. New York: Basic Books, 2017.

Pizzichini, Lillian. *The Blue Hour: A Life of Jean Rhys*. New York: W. W. Norton & Company, 2009.

"Playboy panel: the drug revolution. The pleasures, penalties and hazards of chemicals with kicks are debated by nine authorities." Panelists: Harry Anslinger, William Burroughs, Ram Dass, Leslie Fiedler, etc. *Playboy* 17, no. 2 (February 1970).

Provine, Doris Marie. *Unequal Under Law: Race in the War on Drugs*. Chicago: University of Chicago Press, 2007.

Reeves, Jimmie L., and Richard Campbell, *Cracked Coverage: Television News, the Anti-Cocaine Crusade, and the Reagan Legacy*. Durham, NC: Duke University Press, 1994.

Reinarman, Craig, and Harry Levine, ed. *Crack in America: Demon Drugs and Social Justice*. Berkeley: University of California Press, 1997.

———. "Crack in the Rear-View Mirror: Deconstructing Drug War Mythology." *Social Justice* 31, nos. 1–2 (2004).

Resnick, Sarah. "H." *n +1* 24 (Winter 2016).

Rhys, Jean. *The Complete Novels*. New York: W. W. Norton, 1985.

———. *Jean Rhys Letters, 1931–1966*. Edited by Francis Wyndham and Diana Melly. London: Andre Deutsch, 1984.

———. *Smile Please: An Unfinished Autobiography*. New York: Harper & Row, 1979.

———. "The Trial of Jean Rhys." Jean Rhys Archive, University of Tulsa.

———. *Wide Sargasso Sea*. New York: Norton, 1992.

Rich, Motoko. "James Frey and His Publisher Settle Suit Over Lies." *New York Times*, September 7, 2006.

Ronell, Avital. *Crack Wars: Literature Addiction Mania*. Lincoln: University of Nebraska Press, 1992.

Schenkar, Joan. *The Talented Miss Highsmith: The Secret Life and Serious Art of Patricia Highsmith*. New York: St. Martin's Press, 2009.

Sedgwick, Eve Kosofsky. "Epidemics of the Will." *Tendencies*. Durham, NC: Duke University Press, 1993.

Sheff, David. *Beautiful Boy*. New York: Houghton Mifflin Harcourt, 2008.

Shem, Samuel, and Janet Surrey. *Bill W and Dr. Bob*. New York: Samuel French Inc., 1987.

The Shining. Directed by Stanley Kubrick. Screenplay by Stanley Kubrick and Diane Johnson, 1980.

Sklenicka, Carol. *Raymond Carver: A Writer's Life*. New York: Scribner, 2009.

Sloman, Larry "Ratso." *Reefer Madness*. New York: St. Martin's Press, 1998.

Socar, Chester. Telegraph to "Bureau of Narcotics." September 6, 1941. National Archives, College Park, MD.

Sontag, Susan. *Illness as Metaphor*. New York: Picador, 2001. First published 1978 by Farrar, Straus and Giroux.

———. *Regarding the Pain of Others*. New York: Picador, 2003.

Stewart, Kathleen. *Ordinary Affects*. Durham, NC: Duke University Press, 2007.

Stewart, Sherry H., Dubravka Gavric, and Pamela Collins, "Women, Girls, and Alcohol." *Women and Addiction: A Comprehensive Handbook*. New York: The Guilford Press, 2009.

Stitt, Peter. "Interview with John Berryman, The Art of Poetry No. 16." *Paris Review* 53 (Winter 1972).

———. "John Berryman: Poetry and Personality." *Ann Arbor Review*, November 1973.

Stringer, Lee. *Grand Central Winter*. New York: Seven Stories Press, 1998.

Szalavitz, Maia. *Unbroken Brain: A Revolutionary New Way of Understanding Addiction*. New York: St. Martin's Press, 2016.

Szwed, John. *Billie Holiday: The Musician and the Myth*. New York: Viking, 2015.

Thompson, John. "Last Testament." *New York Review of Books*, August 9, 1973.

Wallace, David Foster. Commencement Address. Kenyon College, 2005. Repr. *This Is Water: Some Thoughts, Delivered on a Significant Occasion, About Living a Compassionate Life*. New York: Little, Brown, 2009.

———. *Consider the Lobster*. New York: Little, Brown, 2005.

———. *Infinite Jest*. New York: Little, Brown, 1996.

———. *A Supposedly Fun Thing I'll Never Do Again: Essays and Arguments*. New York: Little, Brown, 1997.

West, Rebecca. "The Pursuit of Misery in some of the New Novels." *The Daily Telegraph*, January 30, 1931.

White, Edmund. "In Love with Duras." *New York Review of Books*, June 26, 2008.

White, William. *Slaying the Dragon: The History of Addiction Treatment and Recovery in America*. Bloomington, IL: Chestnut Health Systems, 1998.

Wieseltier, Leon. *Kaddish*. New York: Vintage, 2000.

Wilson, Bill. "Alcoholics Anonymous." *New England Journal of Medicine*, September 14, 1950.

———. "Bill's Story." Original typescript. Stepping Stones Archives, Katonah, New York.

———. *Bill W.: My First Forty Years*. Center City, MN: Hazelden, 2000.

———. Speech, AA Conference, Prince George Hotel, Halifax, Nova Scotia, April 27, 1958. Stepping Stones Archives, Katonah, New York.

———. Speech, March 24, 1948, San Diego, California. Stepping Stones Archives, Katonah, New York.

Wilson, Bill, and Ed Dowling. *The Soul of Sponsorship: The Friendship of Fr. Ed Dowling and Bill Wilson in Letters*. Center City, MN: Hazelden, 1995.

Wood, Michael. "The Passionate Egoist." *New York Review of Books*, April 17, 2008.

Wylie, Philip. "Review of *The Lost Weekend*." *New York Times Book Review*, January 30, 1944. Charles Jackson Papers, Rauner Library, Dartmouth College, Hanover, New Hampshire.

Yagoda, Ben. *Memoir: A History*. New York: Riverhead, 2009.

Zieger, Susan. *Inventing the Addict: Drugs, Race, and Sexuality in Nineteenth-Century British and American Literature*. Amherst: University of Massachusetts Press, 2008.

INDEX

Index

ABOUT THE AUTHOR

Leslie Jamison is the author of the essay collection *The Empathy Exams*, a *New York Times* bestseller, and the novel *The Gin Closet*, a finalist for the Los Angeles Times Book Prize. She is a contributing writer for the *New York Times Magazine*, and her work has appeared in publications including *The Atlantic*, *Harper's Magazine*, the *New York Times Book Review*, the *Oxford American*, and the *Virginia Quarterly Review*. She directs the graduate nonfiction program at Columbia University and lives in Brooklyn with her husband, the novelist Charles Bock, and their two daughters.

ALSO BY LESLIE JAMISON

NONFICTION

The Empathy Exams: Essays

FICTION

The Gin Closet